# Local Theology
## for the Global Church

## Principles for an Evangelical Approach to Contextualization

# Local Theology
## for the Global Church

## Principles for an Evangelical Approach to Contextualization

Edited by:

Matthew Cook

Rob Haskell

Ruth Julian

Natee Tanchanpongs

**WILLIAM CAREY**
LIBRARY

Local Theology for the Global Church: Principles for an Evangelical Approach to Contextualization

Published by
William Carey Library
1605 E. Elizabeth Street
Pasadena, California 91104
www.missionbooks.org

William Carey Library is a ministry of the
U.S. Center for World Mission
Pasadena, California
www.uscwm.org

Printed in the United States of America
15 14 13 12 11 10    6 5 4 3 2 SFP

Library of Congress Cataloging-in-Publication Data

Local theology for the global church : principles for an evangelical approach to contextualization / edited by Matthew Cook [... et al.].
p. cm.

ISBN 978-0-87808-111-0

1. Missions--Theory. 2. Christianity and culture. 3. Evangelicalism. I. Cook, Matthew.

BV2063.L45 2010

230--dc22

2010021964

# Contents

# Foreword

This book began as a discussion during the World Evangelical Alliance Theological Commission in 2006. Thanks to the encouragement of Rolfe Hille, then Chairman of the Commission, the discussion resulted in the creation of the "Contextual Theology working group" of the Theological Commission, which brought together theologians, biblical scholars, missiologists, and cultural anthropologists representing eleven nations—through either their cultural background or place of ministry—to consider different aspects of the problem of "universal revelation and socially located theology." Most of the authors who ultimately contributed to this volume met in August 2008 at Oxford, England. The majority of the expenses for this conference were underwritten by Nyack College/Alliance Theological Seminary. Wycliffe Hall of Oxford University graciously hosted the gathering. We thank especially David Parker, Former Executive Director of the WEA Theological Commission, for his encouragement and help to make possible both the conference and the resulting book. Also, our thanks belong to William Carey Library for bringing this work to print. Finally, in addition to the scholars represented in this volume, we are also grateful to Jesudason Baskar Jeyaraj, Rose Dowsett, and Mark Young who joined us for the Oxford conference to richly contribute their expertise.

The later two experts came as representatives of the World Evangelical Alliance - Mission Commission, which is working on a volume intended to be companion and complement to this one. Their volume, to be completed shortly, will provide discussion of topics related to those in this book, but will punctuate them with even more contextualization case studies. These two volumes are not intended to be the definitive word on contextualization, but contributions to the dialogue in order to help the evangelical community take further steps toward biblical and contextually appropriate obedience to Christ.

This book clearly is not about doing theology in general nor even determining controls on that theology. Rather, we are concerned to offer guidelines which rest within two limiting adjectives: The first adjective is "evangelical". We are not concerned with how everyone does theology. Nor are we concerned to justify our position with respect to non-evangelicals. Our commitments are markedly and unapologetically evangelical.[1] Our concern is that other evangelicals recognize the implications of their commitments in doing contextual theology.

The second adjective is "contextual": the processes, the means, the limits, and the criteria necessary for Christian leaders from diverse cultures to construct local evangelical theologies.

---

1    The official statement from the World Evangelical Alliance on "What we mean by 'evangelical,'" is publicly available: http://www.worldevangelicals.org/aboutwea/evangelical.htm, consulted 2 November, 2009.

Our desire is to see local theologies which remain evangelical but which richly contribute to the global evangelical community.

The goal of the study unit, and this book which has resulted, has been to state clearly an evangelical position on issues that impact contextual theology and to offer guidance toward contextual evangelical life that avoids syncretism. The clear hope of these authors is that the Church of Jesus Christ will benefit and God, himself, will be glorified through this work.

*Matthew Cook*
*Chargé de cours en Théologie*
*La Faculté de Théologie Évangélique de l'Alliance Chrétienne (FATEAC)*
*Abidjan, Côte d'Ivoire*
*Convener of the WEA-TC Contextual Theology Working Group*

# Introduction:

# Aims and Themes of the Project

## *Rob Haskell*

*Rob Haskell grew up in Argentina as the son of missionaries and is currently the director of Senderis, a ministry for pastoral training and leadership development in Latin America. He has written a forthcoming book on hermeneutics for the Latin American context which will be available at the end of 2009 (Editorial CLIE) and is currently participating in various projects to develop resources for the Spanish speaking church. He lives in the US with his wife Cathy and children Autumn (10) and Aidan (7). Education: BTh in NT Greek (Prairie Bible College), MCS in NT (Regent College), ThM in NT (Regent College, in process).*

## Some Serious Complications

The gospel addresses itself to the whole of the human being, the whole of society and the whole of creation. This means that every aspect of any culture or society will be related to the gospel in some way. Because of this, contextualization must be comprehensive,[1] not merely a rubric under which to discuss the best way to preach the gospel in cross-cultural situations. Contextualization must be a holistic integration of the gospel message into the warp and woof of particular cultures in which Christians live.

Though most evangelicals would probably agree that contextualization ought to be comprehensive, its sweeping agenda is easier to announce than to implement. The moment we set out to practice it in different cultures we are faced with some serious complications. First, when we use words like "comprehensive" it sounds a lot like we are talking about a particular Christian culture (usually "Western") imposing its worldview on another and going so far as to insist that this worldview be incorporated in every area of the recipient culture. Is this gospel proclamation or religious imperialism? How do we tell the difference? Second, insights from cultural anthropology and sociology suggest that each culture imposes its categories on human consciousness and that real communication across cultural boundaries is therefore not really

---

1   To borrow A. Scott Moreau's apt phrase ("Contextualization That Is Comprehensive," Missiology: An International Review 34, no. 3 [July 2006]: 325).

possible. This complication feeds back into the gospel preacher for it suggests that his own proclamation is not the transcendent message he thought it was, but just an accident of his own cultural location.

### First Question: Is Cultural Location Fatal?

In the following pages these complications are addressed under two broad subject areas. The first concerns the question of whether cultural location really does radically determine our thinking and behavior patterns. Failure to answer this question would be problematic for evangelical Christianity, for we affirm that the revelation of God in Scripture is a universal revelation that speaks to all peoples, cultures and times. A strong view of the affects of culture on understanding would imply that the gospel never left First Century Judaism and that what Christians have called the gospel for centuries has been nothing more than syncretism. The answer that we see in the following pages recognizes the validity of much that is affirmed about cultural location but it also qualifies the impact of this reality by insisting that in spite of the fact that our ideas and behavior patterns are tied to a particular time and place, we can still communicate across cultures. Cultural location is important but not wholly determinative.

But this answer breeds a new question: are we defending biblical authority by leaving some room for objectivity, or are we giving away too much? Some would argue that any concession to cultural location is a denial of biblical truth. Should not the Bible be literally true and unchanging regardless of culture? In the following pages we trace a path that lies between these two extremes of cultural subjectivism and theological literalism. Our answer to the latter is that contextualization is practiced in the very pages of Scripture and is therefore wholly appropriate.

### Second Question: How Might We Create a Contextual Theology?

Once we decide that cross cultural communication is possible and that contextualization is appropriate we must determine how we ought to conceive the task of creating local theology. This is the second theme that runs through these pages. Do we simply translate tried and true theological notions from one culture to another or do we encourage each culture to do its own theologizing based on its own questions and priorities? And if the latter, what ought to be the center of that system of thinking? What ought to be its categories? How much freedom do we have in this task? The answers given in this area are that the basis for contextualization ought to be the biblical text as it is read in a particular culture, not a pre-packaged theological system, that dialogue between different cultures is crucial, and that contextual theologies are both healthy and biblical.

In what follows I will summarize each of the chapters of the book and also show how each one speaks to our major themes.

## Flemming: Paul the Contextualizer

Although most evangelicals agree that in order to understand Scripture we must understand the context in which it was written, they do not always realize the implication: this means that even in Scripture itself the truth about God has been contextualized. Flemming shows us how Paul contextualized his Christology to a particular situation.

The book of Colossians was written to combat a false doctrine in the church of Colossae. This doctrine seems to have been a mixture of Christian teaching and local religious philosophy that presented itself as a supplement to the gospel. We can tell from Paul's discussion that it prescribed certain taboos, ascetic practices, visions, worship of angels, and the veneration of "powers".

Paul's response to the Colossian philosophy is to insist on the cosmic supremacy of Christ and his work, and as such it is an unambiguous rejection of syncretism. And yet, this cosmic supremacy is announced in categories that are appropriate to the Colossian context. Flemming notes that in this epistle, Paul's terminology is unique. Terms like justification and righteousness, which figure so prominently in his explanation of the work of Christ in Romans and Galatians, do not even appear in Colossians. Rather, "many of the metaphors for Christ's death in Colossians come directly out of the day-to-day world of his readers."[2] He describes Christ's defeat of "the powers," and identifies Him as the mystery of God. Appealing to the cultural awareness of the pax romana (which was achieved by victory in military contest), Paul presents Christ as making peace. He also uses the image of a Roman triumphal procession to paint the picture of Christ's triumph over the powers that the Colossians appear to have venerated. In short, the Christology that Paul develops in Colossians is highly dependent on both contextual cultural imagery and on the categories and terminology of the Colossian false doctrine. It is a contextualized Christology. And yet, it is interesting that in systematic theology the categories Paul uses in Colossians are often taken to be contextless truth statements.

But Paul's response to the Colossian teaching is not merely doctrinal or notional. He is quick to show how the supremacy of Christ plays into the moral conventions of the cultural context. For example, it has been noted that Paul's lists of virtues and codes of conduct for household members were standard features of Roman society. But Paul has not used them merely to reiterate Roman common sense. He has imbued them with Christological significance and he has changed their content to accord with a Christ inspired ethic of self-sacrifice that contrasts to the meaningless practices that flow from "hollow philosophy" (veneration of angels, etc.).

Flemming highlights four dimensions of Paul's contextualization based on his analysis of Colossians. These provide an apt infrastructure for our own thinking about contextualization. First, Paul affirms culture by using its content and categories to develop the Christian response to the Colossian philosophy. But second, he also relativizes culture, for just as he has a healthy view of creation, he is also a preacher of the new creation which generates a new and transcending standard. Third, since the world is also a realm of darkness that is controlled by enslaving powers, the gospel confronts culture and there is a sense in which the gospel is countercultural in every situation. Finally, Paul's contextualization transforms culture. Paul does not invent new terminology and social institutions, but as we have seen he redefines them and imbues them with Christological significance.

---

2    Dean Flemming's chapter, "Paul the Contextualizer," in this volume, 9.

If we look at the global issues of contextualization, then, Paul in Colossians points in the direction of a flexible theology that can reshape culture. It also engages individuals on the level of their worldview. The alternative of imposing a one-size fits all theology on every culture carries the seeds of further syncretism, for if the entire world view of a target culture is not engaged there will be pressure to find supplements to Christ in order to address perceived gaps, just as it appears to have been the case in Colossae. Another way of saying this is that syncretism results from the failure to apply the lordship of Christ to all of life.

## Dembele: What Shall We Name God?

When the gospel is brought in to a new culture that has no concept of the biblical God, it is often important to refer to God in the local language. The choice of terminology is not always easy, for outsiders do not necessarily understand the connotations of the local language. Youssouf Dembele takes up the important question of whether Allah, the Muslim name for God, may be used by Christians to refer to the biblical God. Dembele's study is also important because, like Flemming's, it highlights the presence of contextualization in the Bible itself.

In the Old Testament, one of the most common names for God is El, who was originally a deity in the Ugaritic pantheon. He is a creator and a father who is benign and merciful. These qualities fit well with the biblical idea of God. But El also has two wives and two sons (Dawn and Dusk) and it is clear that the biblical usage of El has only kept characteristics that are amenable to the Abrahamic/Mosaic revelation of God. In the New Testament we have a similar phenomenon. Already the Septuagint had rendered both El and Yahweh by the Greek term Theos. The New Testament authors follow suit and use that term, which has a wide range of meanings, to reference the God and father of Jesus Christ.

Based on these observations, Dembele concludes that it is appropriate in principle to use the name of the creator-god of a particular culture to refer to the biblical God. But he adds that there must be a significant number of shared traits between the biblical revelation of God and the local name for God. Especially, the local name must include the notion of a universal creator, which is essential to the biblical idea of God.

The next question is whether the specific term "Allah" may be used for the biblical God. Dembele notes that Allah shares many characteristics with the biblical God (sovereignty, omnipotence, omniscience, omnipresence, holiness), and also has a historical connection to biblical revelation because of the way in which Arab and Jewish history has been intertwined throughout the centuries. Before the rise of Islam, Arabic Christians used Allah to refer to the biblical, Trinitarian God of the Christian faith. Further, the Quran itself states that Allah is the God of Abraham, Ishmael, Isaac and other biblical figures. Finally, he notes that the practice of using Allah to reference God appears to be a very effective tool for the communication of the gospel, as experience among Muslims suggests.

Dembele's article is also important because it helps us, in the same way as Flemming's, to see that contextualization is thoroughly biblical. The scriptures do not use notionally pure nomenclature to refer to God, but describe him with terms that are borrowed from the local context, thereby both explaining him in familiar categories while at the same time redefining those categories.

## Blomberg: We Contextualize More Than We Realize

We are defending contextualization against two critics. The first is the person who thinks that cultural relativism has nullified the task of contextualization. The answer to her will be (in later articles) to acknowledge some of her points and to then argue that in spite of them, contextualization is still a viable activity. The second audience is the conservative evangelical who is concerned that contextualization compromises the absoluteness of biblical truth, because it opens the door to non-literal interpretation of the Bible and perhaps also implies that doctrine is not really truth, but just another opinion.

Blomberg addresses his paper to this second audience. If the biblical text is inerrant, does it not follow that we ought to strictly limit the ways in which the concepts, rituals and practices of that text are incorporated into other cultures? In many evangelical contexts any change away from the literal meaning of Scripture is seen as a change for the worse (and admittedly this is often true!). But Blomberg argues that respect for the biblical text need not lead to a rejection of contextualization or even to a very narrow practice of contextualization. Not only does Scripture itself exhibit a broad approach to contextualization, but evangelical Christians who hold the biblical text in high esteem have shown themselves to be quite open to creative communication of the gospel.

According to Blomberg, the tendency in some circles to prefer a literal translation of the Bible because it is more accurate is misguided. Rather, a good balance between formal equivalence and dynamic-equivalence generally communicates well both the meaning and impact of the original text. This observation provides us with a sort of pattern for contextualization, highlighting the notion that mere literalism is not necessarily good communication. It is also illustrated in the pages of the New Testament, where we find both literal and free renditions of quotations from the Old Testament.

Blomberg points to instances of contextualization that have been welcomed by evangelicals. Don Richardson's Peace Child is one example. Here, the gospel gains a foothold in an indigenous culture because of the local custom of giving a child to guarantee peace among warring tribes. Another widely accepted contextualization of the atonement is the sacrifice of Aslan for the treacherous Edmund in C.S. Lewis' Chronicles of Narnia. Neither of these are complete or precise analogies, but they make good points about the atonement (the vicarious representation of the peace child, and the fact that God himself is the sacrifice in Lewis). The very generosity accorded the analogies strengthens Bloomberg's case, for it is clear that evangelicals do not demand exact precision from their "redemptive analogies."

Other practices of contextualization among evangelicals range from the controversial to the very controversial: concepts in science fiction help us imagine biblical ideas, the question of whether Muslim converts ought to use the term "Son of God" when referring to Jesus, the use of offensive language in gospel communication, and whether God should be referred to as feminine, among others. Blomberg's motivation in highlighting these is not to convince us that particular contextualizations are good or bad so much as to highlight the need to recapture the meaning and significance of the gospel in our context.

## Julian: Ground Level Contextualization

Julian introduces us to two concepts from cultural anthropology that speak to the task of contextualization. Worldview refers to the assumptions about reality which are shared by a culture. These assumptions are foundational to the individual's thinking and are rarely questioned. Another more specific term for this phenomenon is preunderstanding.

There is a sense in which our preunderstanding will lead us to certain conclusions when we approach the Bible. We will ask certain questions and prefer certain biblical passages based on our sense of the importance of particular issues. For example, Julian points to the example of a student at her school in Congo who did not think the command to evangelize applied to pygmies, since she did not think of them as human beings. How, then, can we hope to understand the biblical message if we are so determined by our preunderstanding? To answer this, Julian appeals to the idea of the hermeneutical spiral. Here, interaction between our preunderstanding and Scripture leads to ever increasing adjustment of our notions to biblical thinking. Even if one may initially come to Scripture with ideas that lead to forced interpretations, the interpretive process still has an impact on those ideas. The process is a spiral because the circular interplay between Scripture and preunderstanding leads to increasing clarification.

A lack of appreciation for the fact that Christians are embedded in culture has sometimes led to an emphasis on contextualizing high religion, which deals with larger thematic ideas, at the expense of folk religion, which deals with the more intimate issues of life—daily practices and concerns. And yet, in many cultures life is centered on the realities of folk religion (note Julian's illustration of the floating island). Thus, an appreciation of preunderstanding and worldview helps us see the need for contextualization that addresses small scale practices and beliefs (contextualization that is comprehensive). Contextualization should speak not only to beliefs about the nature of the universe or justification by faith, but also practical concerns like protection from evil spirits in the middle of the night, or crop failure and drought. Sometimes, in fact, these practical concerns have greater impact on worldview than the ideas of high religion, and issues related to folk religion are frequently the motivating factors for syncretism.

## Cook: Contextual But Still Objective?

The word "objective" has recently become important in evangelical discussion precisely because of claims that cultural location makes objectivity unattainable. Matt Cook notes that the tendency in evangelical circles has been to recognize that culture can influence our theology and to respond by stressing the need to overcome those cultural influences to arrive at a place of objectivity. Cook shows us that this not the appropriate strategy because the influences of culture are not so easily dismissed.

The idea that we can be objective is often criticized by the notion of "social location," which is a way of describing the intimate connection between what we think and where we live. Cook outlines four ways of understanding the impact of social location on theological objectivity:

Social location means that: (a) objective truth is stated using the vocabulary and concepts of a particular context; (b) theology is created for a particular location; (c) theological constructions are unique to a particular context and are not necessarily true in other situations; (d) theological constructions made in a particular context cannot be understood elsewhere or be criticized by outsiders.

The crux of Cook's argument is the transition from (c) to (d). Cook is willing to go as far as (c) and admit that not all theology is applicable in all situations. Various examples illustrate this: "Jesus is my healer" may be appropriate in one culture, but in a culture with shamans it may sound heretical. Cook's point is not that there are different truths for different locations, but that we are so enmeshed in our locations that faithful theology must be profoundly situated. If it were not, it could not address the specific features of the location. This does not, however, mean that we must take the leap to (d) and agree that our theology is wholly located and that there is therefore no communication between social locations (this position is known as in-commensurability). To take this step would be a denial of the universality of the gospel. Cook points out that there is overlap in our different languages and because of this we can communicate between social locations. The very fact that we know there is a communication problem shows that we can communicate. It also shows that we must work hard at communication.

Thus, while every social location has its own deeply seated ways of thinking and communicating and therefore of doing theology, we still can communicate both across cultures and across the gap of history to dialogue and correct each other in light of the biblical text. v

## van den Toren: Can We See the Naked Theological Truth?

It has been common for evangelicals to posit a body of truth that exists outside of culture which can be translated into specific contexts. This truth is extracted from the biblical text, formulated in the abstract and then available for application to different situations. Although this seems like an intuitive method, Van den Toren argues that it is not, and that although the supra-cultural core of the gospel surely exists, we can never explain that core without using the categories and language of a specific culture.

We are again confronted with the problem of truth versus subjectivism, for it would seem to follow that if we do not have direct access to a supra-cultural formulation of Christian faith, we will have no firm basis on which to proclaim a message that applies to all cultures. One of Van den Toren's answers to this conundrum is to point out that it is very much a problem that comes from Western thinking, especially from the philosophy known as foundationalism. In this thinking, the quality of one's knowledge depends entirely on the veracity of the key notions that uphold that knowledge, just as a building depends on its foundation for structural stability. But Van den Toren notes that foundationalism does not accurately represent our thought process, which is more analogous to reading a book than to building a structure. We do not start thinking from nothing and then build up to something. We enter into a context already thinking and we adjust our thinking in dialogue with that context. With this in mind, it is not so crucial to have a supra-cultural "foundation" from which to build our theology. Rather, we enter into a dynamic relationship with the gospel in our context.

Another important concept for Van den Toren is the canon of Scripture as a witness or testimony to the revelation of God in Jesus Christ. This canon, he says, is authoritative for all subsequent generations because it bears witness to the supra-cultural core of the gospel. And yet, even here the expression of that truth is embedded in the human language and culture of the first century; not only the incarnation of the Son of God, but also the testimony to that incarnation were all culturally understood and formulated. This testimony (Scripture) is not a supra-cultural exception that is different from all our other knowledge. The Bible was crafted in culture and is understood in culture. However, the biblical testimony is fully adequate for understanding the gospel message.

## Tanchanpongs: Developing a Palate for Authentic Theology

One important area of contextualization theory will always be the border between adaptation of theology to a particular culture and excessive mixing with the ideas of that culture. The later occurs when the gospel is so adjusted to a culture that it loses its distinctiveness, even while at the same time retaining some of its original form. This has usually been labeled, negatively, as syncretism.

To help us explore the issues, Tanchanpongs uses two metaphors. The first comes from cuisine and it helps us see two inadequacies in some evangelical approaches to evaluating syncretism. The identification of good contextualization is something like the evaluation of authentic regional food. How does one conclude that a certain dish is "authentic"? Of course, by tasting it. Further, it is generally assumed that a person who has lived in a particular area will be qualified by his or her experience to adjudicate in such matters. However, although it is possible to come to agreement among culinary judges about the authenticity of a particular dish, the process of adjudication is not a clear, rational process. There is no one dish which one can point to and say "this is the essence of Thai food," for example, and then compare all dishes to that essential dish. Neither is it a matter of simply analyzing the nature and quantity of ingredients. Determining authentic regional food is a matter of drawing on experience and memory and is ultimately an intuitive and physical activity.

The first problem the cuisine metaphor helps us see is that evangelicals tend to judge matters of contextualization on the basis of a canon within the canon, which is analogous to treating a particular ethnic dish as the most authentic to the exclusion of other dishes. But, as Harvey Conn has pointed out, syncretism can be construed as allowing only a part of Scripture to speak, which is what happens in the canon within the canon approach. Rather, the whole of Scripture must be allowed to speak to the cultural situation, just as there is a large repertoire of flavors which are part of any regional cuisine. The second problem with evangelical assessments of contextualization is that they have tended to judge syncretism structurally by noting how two systems mix and then judging whether particular parts of those systems may or may not be appropriately integrated. But Tanchanpongs argues, in keeping with the culinary metaphor, that meaning is found not so much in the ingredients of theology as in the outcome.

But the cuisine metaphor only goes so far. It helps us to see problems in certain approaches but it does not help us construct appropriate principles to guard against syncretism. To address this, Tanchanpongs appeals to a cruising metaphor, or the "context-to-text" approach. Under this category we find two helpful criteria. First, if a church is identical to the society in which it exists, this is a sign of syncretism. Theologically, if the words and concepts of Christian theology are identical to those of the housing culture, there is also a problem with syncretism. Second, contextualization of the theology of one community into another community without a proper scriptural direction or anchor is also a form of syncretism. Contextualization must begin in an interpretive context and move towards fuller biblical grounding.

## Segura-Guzmán: The Practice of Theology

We move now away from defining the limits and shape of evangelical contextualization to the positive construction of theology in the environment of evangelical contextualization. Segura affirms that good theology is practical theology. Theology is not merely an intellectual exercise, but something which is produced from the interaction of the biblical text and the human context in which the text is read. Segura sets out to describe a model for doing good theology based on two different sets of criteria, each highlighting the interaction between theology and the context of the individual Christian.

The first set of criteria for evaluating good theology is taken from Clemens Sedmak and it is based on the premise that theology can be judged by its fruits. The criteria begin with sustainability, which refers to the fact that mission must be sustained by the kingdom narrative. The purpose of the kingdom text is to shape and change. This has been lost in the modern, intellectual approach to exegesis which places emphasis on the historical character of the text to the neglect of personal placement in the biblical narrative. Appropriateness means good theology must be formed in response to a particular situation. This means that a good theologian will be a good listener. Empowerment describes the way in which good theology is a community exercise (not just something the theologian does), and therefore the theologian, beyond being a teacher, is also a facilitator of community reflection and a guide to praxis. Challenge refers to the way in which good theology will bring about change in a situation. It will produce practice which is both ethical and communal.

The second model that Segura uses to construct his theological method is the Ignatian pedagogical process, developed by Ignatius of Loyola for use in spiritual formation. Here there is a core of three elements: experience, reflection and action. These are surrounded by context and evaluation. For the professional theologian (analogous to the spiritual leader in the Ignatian model), context means interaction with the world of the student—the social and cultural context of the learner—in order to address the student's inner and outer reality. Experience highlights the need for the student to fully engage in learning with mind, heart, hand and also with emotions. Emotions are especially important because they create pressure to change and develop. Reflection is the evaluation of the experience and it includes interpretation and judgment of the experience. Action entails assuming a "personal posture in light of the truth that has been discovered" (p. 145) and making an ethical decision which becomes concrete through implementation. Finally, evaluation is the closing bracket to context in which the entire process is analyzed in order to ensure that the actions have produced an outcome that is consistent with the whole.

As can be seen, the two models work together, for as the process of spiritual formation proceeds it also fulfills the criteria for good theology. The process is circular because once one has arrived at evaluation/challenge, the context has changed and it is necessary to do a fresh analysis.

## Siu: Theologizing Locally

We have already argued for the propriety of localizing theology. How exactly do we go about doing this? What are the goals and priorities? Paul Siu presents us with a model for crafting a theology to a particular cultural subset.

In South-East Asia, the negative aspects of globalism have led to an increasing awareness of social ills such as urban and environmental problems, loss of values and increasing social inequalities. Theologically, the challenge is increasingly the fact that the theological resources of the Western church are inadequate for this situation due to their concern with abstraction rather than concrete human situations. Additionally, this Western approach to theology is pervasive. It is often noted by third world theologians that the West seems to think it has "a monopoly on God, the gospel, and the way of constructing theology." (157) Meanwhile, there is a common call among third world theologians for a theology that is more localized and more grounded in human experience.

For a proper theological response to this situation, Siu recommends a balance between global and local issues. This means an ongoing dialogue with Christian communities that leads to consensus. He also commends center-set thinking, where objects within a set are judged by their relation to each other rather than by their relation to the border of the set as is done in bounded-set thinking. The bounded-set is a feature of the Western thinking that has tended to give exaggerated significant to the doctrinal periphery rather than the center. But for intercultural theological dialogue between Christians to be successful, the flexibility of the centered-set is crucial.

Based on these priorities, Siu now proceeds to develop a theology specifically for the East Asian situation. First, he points out the significant features of East Asian theological context: current theological work has tended to be issue oriented and focus on prolegomena to the neglect of the historical doctrines of the church. Second, East Asian society venerates the ancient religious texts of its religions and even the Bible. This is an advantage to Christian theologians because it is intuitively understood that theological authority resides in the text of Scripture. Third, the Asian notion of truth includes more than Western factuality. Truth also promotes harmony, it is also that which is correspondent to human reality and there is a deeply humanistic ethic in Asia which Siu sees as a preparation for the gospel. Finally, suffering is seen not so much as something to overcome as a means to experience communion with the divine. A theology for South-East Asia, argues Siu, must engage these features from a grounding in the biblical text and also in dialogue with other theological traditions.

## Moreau: Evangelical Models of Contextualization

As we continue to think about the task of contextualization, it is clear that there are many possible approaches. Moreau reviews some of the most significant analytical tools and models that have been used in recent years to guide contextualization along lines that are faithful both to Scripture and to culture. Though others have done this type of work more generally, Moreau is interested in surveying only the evangelical approaches.

Moreau first lists seven terms that have been used by evangelicals to describe contextualization to help us get an idea of the kinds of models of contextualized ministry that evangelicals have used. Adaptation seeks to translate the traditional themes of theology into particular cultures. The focus of indigenization has been to encourage development of local churches that are self-maintained and also more recently self-theologizing. In the translation model, a core universal truth is translated into each different culture. Critical contextualization emphasizes the interaction between Bible and culture and the need to arrive at a culturally appropriate response. The counter-cultural approach sees the gospel challenging culture and in that process opening up new views to God. Translatability is a way of describing the fact that the gospel can be translated into an infinite number of cultures and situations. Finally, praxis focuses contextualization on justice and political issues.

The core of the article outlines four categories of models, each of which recommends a trajectory for contextualization: linear, two-way, cyclical and non-focused. Moreau provides an evaluation of each category, but he is primarily interested in cataloguing them, not in commending one approach over another. The linear models work from specific situations which arise (an issue in culture, an interpretation, etc.) and they recommend a specific procedure to follow in order to arrive at an appropriate in-culture outcome. Positively, these models are simple to implement and their progress is easy to track. However, Moreau points out that they can lack flexibility and in practice have tended to rely too much on outside experts. Dialogical models see contextualization as a dialogue between three poles: culture, Bible and the contextualizer, with the Bible as the normative pole. These models have the advantage of promoting wider participation in the contextualization process, but because of this they are also more likely to produce conflicts and splits. Cyclical models emphasize the ongoing nature of the contextualization process and rely on insights from the hermeneutical circle/spiral. The models envision a narrowing spiral that increasingly intertwines scriptural understanding and cultural experience and also emphasize action and social analysis. The strength of cyclical models is that they give proper due to the ongoing nature of the task of contextualization and they also lead to awareness of social justice issues. But their complexity can be confusing to the practitioner. Additionally, it is not always easy to discern whether one's process of contextualization is "spiraling in" or "out." Organic models are less process oriented and more interested in building orientations. More emphasis is laid on "principles of map reading rather than charting out directions from one point to the next" (197). They can use metaphors such as navigating a river or growing in wisdom. These models are helpful because of their flexibility, non-mechanical approach, and approximation of real-life. But this very flexibility also leads to possible aberrations and makes them difficult to use.

Moreau's catalogue of models is intended as a resource to help further our thinking about how we approach contextualization by better understanding what others have done.

# Harrison: Bridging Theory and Training

Harrison offers several practical suggestions to helps us bridge our discussion of contextualization in this book with its concrete application in the educational setting. These are geared primarily to building awareness of contextualization in the academic environment where Christian leaders are being prepared.

First, we must clarify the task of contextualization. It is not merely to contextualize another culture's theology, but to embody the biblical message in a particular situation. Contextualization should also be mentioned in mission statements and other defining documents as an explicit goal so that it is part of organizational thinking. Three important suggestions are related to recruiting leaders. First, an effort ought to be made to recruit leaders who are gifted and qualified for leadership in the Christian community so that the contextualized training they receive actually has an impact on the church. Second, efforts should be made to train leaders in their own context. Sending students away to the city to study in a foreign environment can sometimes limit the value of the education. Finally, academic deans should be aware of the ratio of foreign professors to local professors. In order for the content of the teaching to be relevant, the instructor must understand the situation.

The theological educator must also be aware that he or she is teaching two different target groups. The first is the student in the classroom and the second is the people in the student's future field of ministry. Contextualization of theology must include consideration of possible ministerial contexts so that students study with expectation of contextualizing the material they are learning and are also aware of important cultural features. Often contextualization is seen as referring to culture in the broadest sense, but Harrison points out that our theological education should be as specific as possible and interact with all the dimension of a cultural context, like the geographical setting, the historical context, political issues, and others.

A serious effort should be made to contextualize the curriculum. Harrison offers two suggestions. First, interaction with other Christian traditions is important because it helps students realize that there have been many other interpretative contexts and applications of the biblical message. This helps them understand that theology is not a once for all statement of truth, but an attempt to think biblically in a particular location. Second, the topics covered in theological education should be crafted to the situation. For example, an urban college may deal with a certain set of topics that is not necessarily relevant to a village context. Aside from the content, the educational strategies should be reproducible for the student. Will the leader have laptops and data projectors in his future ministry? If not, these technologies should not be the principle educational strategy in the leader's education. It is also important to look at the "hidden curriculum" or the subtle messages that are embedded in the learning situation. For example, a college where foreign faculty is favored, where most of the books in the library are in a foreign language and where lectures are difficult to understand because of strong accents will tend to send the message that the local culture is not important. Indeed, it will not be equipped to interface with the local culture. In keeping with this, then, contextualization implies a significant effort to create materials in local languages that address local issues.

# Contextualization in Word and Deed

## Theology in Mission

Jürgen Moltmann made the point that, contrary to the picture that form critics paint, the New Testament was not written by archivists, but by missionaries.[3] We might add that it was not written by professional theologians either. I do not say this to criticize the theological discipline as a whole (for after all, here I am theologizing). But I do think it is notable that theology has often lost its connection to mission.

A good example of the way in which theology has missed mission is the theological reading of the epistle to the Romans, Paul's great treatise on faith. This epistle is a favorite book for systematic theologians partly, no doubt, because of the crucial role it played in the formulation of Protestant doctrine.[4] Shedd's description of the book as "a complete statement of religious truth"[5] seems to underlie the treatment many other theologians have given this epistle. However, it often goes unnoticed that Romans is a missional book. First, Paul, himself a missionary, was helping his readers understand the logic of his mission to the Gentiles. Since that mission is ancient history to us, there is an unfortunate tendency to see in Romans the explanations of why "we" (Gentiles) can be saved and miss the fact that, for Paul, the issues of the letter were urgently connected to the expansion of the church. The second missional aspect of Romans is that Paul is writing in order to gain support for his current project—a mission trip to Spain (Rom. 15:24).[6] Romans is a book written from and for mission.

Unfortunately, the discipline of theology has often defined its purpose as the organization and defense of biblical truth without reference to context. The implications of this "theology from nowhere" branch out into two separate problems. The first is the notion that in doing theology we may achieve truth about God and the universe that is not conditioned by human limitations. The second problem is that because of the first emphasis, the practice of theology can at times receive a lesser emphasis than the definition of theology. Both of these tendencies are mentioned in our articles and they correspond to the two major areas of focus. Epistemologically, it was necessary to clarify that the task of theology is not the construction of an objective system of thought which shall apply to all peoples everywhere, but the development of bibli-

---

3    Jürgen Moltmann, *Theology of Hope* (New York: Harper and Row, 1965), 188.

4    Witness the influential commentaries on Romans written by theologians: Hodge, Barth, Nygren. See *Reading Romans through the Centuries* (Grand Rapids: Brazos, 2005) for a historical survey. Granting that the distinction between theologian and biblical scholar is somewhat recent, it is still striking that the chapters are dedicated primarily to what famous theologians said about the epistle: Augustine, Luther, Calvin, Hodge, etc..

5    Quoted in Leon Morris, The Epistle to the Romans (Grand Rapids, MI: Eerdmans, 1988), 8. For a useful catalogue of the reasons that have been suggested for the writing of the letter see 7-18.

6    Paul's various statements about the purpose of the letter (1:8-15 to visit, 1:16-17 as a theme statement, and 15:24 to apprize readers of his plans) have often been taken as a problem to be solved, but it seems to me that they work well together. See James D. G. Dunn, *Word Biblical Commentary: Romans 1-8*, Word Biblical Commentary, vol. 38A (Dallas, TX: Word, 2002), liv-lviii for discussion. But also, as Dunn points out, Paul may have had any number of reasons for writing the letter. Nothing limits them.

cal thinking in a particular situation. In the area of practice it was necessary to emphasize that theology is meant to underpin practice, in contrast to a merely notional view of the task.

## Objective and Subjective

Though I doubt many theologians would pretend that their own theologies are "absolute truth," there is no doubt about a broadly shared assumption in evangelicalism that Christians have access to truth that exists outside the flow of human thought and culture. So, for example, Blomberg addresses an interlocutor who, based on a high view of Scripture, is concerned about guarding the literalness of the Bible against different cultural appropriations. This position betrays the premise that the Bible just says true things that should not be interpreted, for that would lower their truth status. Ruth Julian also notes that there is resistance among evangelicals to thinking about knowledge in the categories of cultural anthropology because of the implied loss of objectivity.

However, as Cook points out, unconditioned objectivity is not available to human beings. One problem with assuming that it is, highlighted by Siu, is the imposition of a "one size fits all" doctrine on every culture without paying sufficient attention to the differences between cultures. A related problem, noted by Tanchanpongs, is that of then attempting to contextualize that "objective theology" in a new situation rather than allowing a culture to take its own journey towards Scripture. Flemming and Julian both noted, also, that the one size fits all approach, since it leaves perceived gaps and does not address the whole situation, will create pressure towards syncretism in order to fill those gaps which appear to lie outside the purview of the biblical message. Van den Toren reminds us that, in fact, the only way theology can speak to the whole situation (the only way it can be comprehensive) is for it to be contextualized theology.

The insistence on one "objective theology" for all peoples and all times comes from the failure to see the implications of contextualization. Once we have accepted that each culture conceives of theology in its own categories, we have also accepted by implication the contextual nature of all theology, even the theology of the culture that has initiated the contextualization process by sending missionaries and preaching the gospel. Thus, we are faced with the irony that "theology from nowhere" is actually more often than not theology from "the North"—tied up very strongly with the intellectual, theological and philosophical traditions of Western thinking. This is not to say that theological traditions of the Western or Eastern churches ought to be devalued because they are mere products of time and culture. Siu reminds us that they are important and should not be ignored. But the history of doctrine shows ample evidence that every generation and every culture renders Christian thought into its own categories. It would be strange to ignore that testimony and pretend that a particular time and place has arrived at an objective theology.

Must we despair? Are we left with mere "subjective theology"? Does the affirmation that unconditioned objectivity is impossible mean that we must abandon the prophetic confidence that Scripture demands from gospel emissaries? Do we have any basis on which to argue that Christianity is true? The answer our authors give us, as already noted, is that a qualified recognition of the limits of human understanding is a healthy thing, and that those limits are not sufficient for us to give up on truth claims. We must be wary of either-or thinking. The recognition that we do not have access to absolute truth does not mean that we can no longer appeal to reason, construct reasonable arguments or adjudicate between factual claims. It only means the rejection of the notion that we humans can have God-like knowledge. Most Christians would readily admit this anyway. The reason this acknowledgement of limitation is healthy is that it serves as a reminder that the foundation for Christian thought is Scripture—not a philosophical method that leads inexorably to right theology; not a particular systematic theology; not a set of key doctrines. It also opens the much needed space for cross-tradition and cross-cultural dialogue among equals. Because all Christians everywhere are struggling to understand Scripture, we are all talking about the same thing and can all learn from each other and care for each other.

## Theory and Practice

The second critique of objective theology or theology conceived solely as the construction of philosophical abstractions is that it divorces truth from action. Because it lays emphasis on the production of true statements, it carries the implication that ideas are of first importance and that the application of ideas to concrete experience is an optional, if commendable, step. But Flemming notes that Paul's interest in correcting the Colossian philosophy that was leading believers astray was tied directly to practice. The wrong way of thinking led to a futile kind of lifestyle, but new life flows from a proper understanding of the work of Christ. This practical premise runs through most of the presentations.

The theme of practice or praxis is taken up most explicitly by Segura. It is important to see that he does not argue that once we have done our merely notional theologizing we must then take an additional step, called application, which lies outside the limits of the theological discipline. Segura includes practice in his theological method. He defines good theology by the fruit it produces. The Ignatian pedagogical model he uses is suffused with practice: it begins with the lived context—theological notions are to be experienced by the whole person and they are to result in concrete moral actions—and finally the entire process is evaluated to ensure that the result of the action has been consistent with the whole. In this model, one cannot pry apart ideas and practice. They are mutually embedded and closely intertwined.

The problem with a merely notional view of theology is that it assumes a false distinction between ideas and practice, as if one could begin theological reflection in a "practiceless" state. Just as all thinking takes place in a cultural context, it also takes place in a praxis context, and all practices have ideas embedded in them. This is why liberation theologian Gustavo Gutierrez famously defined theology as critical reflection on practice based on Scripture. Theological reflection begins in the midst of practice. It is perhaps in the light of Gutierrez' definition that we can appreciate the foundationalist influences at work in Western theology where, as Van den Toren notes, knowledge is seen as a structure built on firm foundations. That kind of metaphor allows us to think about theology as an independent exercise whose success depends on nothing more that its explicitly stated foundations. But life, thought and Christian practice are much more complex than the foundationalist model. Ideas, practices and the biblical text all intermingle in the process of discipleship. A similar point is made by the hermeneutical spiral that Julian describes, where a feedback process between worldview and Bible leads to increasing understanding, and the context-to-text movement of Tanchanpongs' paper. As Julian says, one of the risks of focusing exclusively on high theological concepts is that everyday practices which are laden with theological meaning fall beneath the contextual radar and this opens the door to syncretism: combining the high concepts of Christian theology with the "low" practices of local religions. When we ignore the application of theology we are not doing nothing, as is usually thought. When we ignore application we are still practicing, but we are doing so uncritically and, very likely, heretically. We are probably behaving in ways that are superficially Christian but typical to our cultural context.

## Conclusion

I want to return to Siu's claim that theologians from the two-thirds world are more aware of the importance of practice. He notes Vanhoozer's statement that "Third World theologians share a conviction that Western theology was largely unaware of and uninterested in context."[7] René Padilla has argued that the call for a more earthly Christology has been a common theme among Two Thirds world theologians.[8] He compares theologies of Jon Sobrino (Latin America), Chao Sen Song (Asia) and Albert Noland (Africa) and concludes that Two Thirds World theology: (1) by emphasizing the humanity of Christ challenges us to awareness of the gospel's social implications; (2) by seeing Jesus' death as the result of his life challenges us to suffer for the sake of righteousness; (3) by stressing his historical life challenges us to commit to the transformation of the world.[9] Samuel Escobar affirms that the theological contribution of Latin American theology to the global church is its Christology. In contrast to the Catholic Christ inherited from Spain, who lives outside the problems of the world, Protestant theologians emphasized his humanity and therefore his interest in daily life, social justice and political transformation.[10]

We have, then, significant voices from different quarters pointing the way forward for us. We hope that the following articles will encourage evangelical theologizing that is faithful to Scripture and also faithful to location, that engages in cordial dialogue among equals from different cultures, and that results in the contextual practice of righteousness.

---

7    Kevin J. Vanhoozer, "One Rule to Rule Them All?" in *Globalizing Theology: Belief and Practice in an Era of World Christianity*, ed. Craig Ott and Harold A. Netland (Grand Rapids, MI: Baker Academic, 2006), 95.

8    René Padilla, "Christology and Mission in the Two Thirds World" in Vinay Samuel and Chris Sugden, Sharing Jesus in the Two Thirds World (Grand Rapids, MI: Eerdmans, 1984): 12-32.

9    Padilla, "Christology and Mission," 27-28.

10    See Samuel Escobar "The Search for Missiological Christology in Latin America," in William A, Dyrness, *Emerging Voices in Global Christian Theology* (Grand Rapids, MI: Zondervan, 1994): 199-228. These contrasting Christologies were first noted by Protestant Scottish missionary to Peru John Mackay in *The Other Spanish Christ* (London: Student Christian Movement Press, 1932).

# 1

# Paul the Contextualizer

## Dean Flemming

**Dean Flemming** *is a Lecturer in New Testament and Intercultural Communication, European Nazarene College. In addition to writing various articles for professional and popular journals and multi-author works, Dean is the author of Contextualization in the New Testament: Patterns for Theology and Mission (InterVarsity Press, 2005), which received a 2006 Christianity Today book award. He has been a missionary with the Church of the Nazarene since 1987. He has also served as a local church pastor in Japan and the US and was ordained in 1982. Education: BA (Mid-America Nazarene University), MDiv (Nazarene Theological Seminary), PhD in New Testament Exegesis (University of Aberdeen, Scotland).*

## Introduction

Evangelicals are still not quite sure about what to do with contextualization. We want a theology that speaks to our life setting. But we are concerned that trying to make our theology fit the context might end up compromising biblical truth. As a result, sincere Christians in a variety of global settings feel caught between the need to express the faith in culturally relevant ways and the fear of giving away too much of the gospel in the process.

This is not just theory. In practice, authentic contextualization is never easy to do well. When it comes to engaging our cultures with the gospel, some go too far; others don't go far enough. Nearly two decades ago, Dean S. Gilliland wisely observed that contextualization is

> "a delicate enterprise if ever there was one…. the evangelist and mission strategist stand on a razor's edge, aware that to fall off on either side has terrible consequences. Fall to the right and you end in obscurantism, so attached to your conventional ways of practicing and teaching the faith that you veil its truth and power from those who are trying to see it through very different eyes. Slip to the left and you tumble into syncretism, so vulnerable to the impact of paganism in its multiplicity of forms that

you compromise the uniqueness of Christ and concoct 'another gospel which is not a gospel.'"[1]

Are there biblical resources that can help us carve out theologies and practices with local fit on the one hand, while avoiding the slippery slope of syncretism on the other? I believe there are. The biblical writers not only offer us normative theological and moral content; they also model a *process* for doing theology in authentic, context-sensitive ways. The New Testament is teeming with "case studies" in contextualization. Some of these come in the form of narratives of how the good news is targeted to different audiences of unbelievers. Paul's missionary preaching in Acts—to Jews at the synagogue in Pisidian Antioch (Acts 13:13-52), to some rustic pagan Gentiles at Lystra (Acts 14:18-20), and to a group of educated pagans in Athens—offers some compelling examples of evangelistic contextualization.

Or we could turn to the Gospel accounts of Jesus' own ministry. When Jesus speaks the good news of God's liberating kingdom, he draws on local resources from his cultural world. Jesus uses the earthy images of rural life in first-century Palestine—farming and fishing, weeds and wineskins, salt and soil. He tailors his theology to specific people and occasions. He speaks differently to the crowds than to the Pharisees, differently to a rich would-be disciple (Mt. 19:16-22) than to a paralytic on his bed (Mt. 9:2-8), differently to Nicodemus (Jn. 3) than to the woman of Samaria (Jn. 4). This is simply an extension of the *incarnation* principle. Becoming flesh, Jesus "exegeted" the Father to us (Jn. 1:18); he embraced our human context in all of its scandalous particularity, as one "born of a woman, born under the law" (Gal. 4:4). As one has put it, "The eternal Word of God only ever speaks with a local accent."[2] At the same time, although Jesus was at home in Palestinian Jewish culture, he prophetically challenged that culture's religious and social norms; he sought to transform them from within.

In addition to these stories of contextualization, the New Testament writings themselves model the theological task. Each of the four Gospels, we could say, contextualizes the story of Jesus for a different target audience. Paul writes letters that become a word on target for diverse mission communities. The Revelation of John offers Asian Christians a countercultural perspective on a world that is dominated by the oppressive engines of Roman power and idolatry. Using compelling images, John calls his readers to a radically transformed vision of their world.[3] Each of the New Testament writers sings the gospel story in a different key.

Obviously, we cannot imitate the way that Luke or Paul or John did theology in a direct "photocopy" fashion. Our contexts and cultures are different. But we can learn from their examples of doing theology in context. In this essay, rather than looking at the broad sweep of biblical precedents for the task of contextualization, I will focus on one instructive "case study." Paul's letter to the Colossians[4] is perhaps the classic New Testament instance of contextualizing

---

1    Dean S. Gilliland, ed., *The Word Among Us: Contextualizing Theology for Today* (Dallas, TX: Word, 1989), vii.

2    Glen Marshall, cited in "Incarnational Missiology," *Organic Church,* accessed 7 December 2007; available from <http://www.anabaptist.co.uk/ocarchive/archives/2004/09/15/incarnational-missiology>; Internet.

3    For a fuller treatment of the examples I have mentioned, see my *Contextualization in the New Testament: Patterns for Theology and Mission* (Downers Grove, IL./Leicester: InterVarsity Press/Apollos, 2005).

4    The question of who wrote Colossians is by no means settled. The problem is complex, and it involves issues such as style of writing, vocabulary, theology, the use of secretaries, the role of pseudonymity, and the

the gospel over against the problem of *syncretism*—the blending of incompatible beliefs and practices.[5] I have chosen this particular case study for two reasons. First, it gives us a positive model for doing context-sensitive theology. Second, Colossians, I believe, can help us in the important task of recognizing the difference between genuine contextualization and the kind of "relevance" that goes too far.[6]

## The Gospel and Syncretism: the Colossian Context

Colossians is written to a church of mainly Gentile Christians from a pagan background (1:21, 27; 2:13). These young believers were living in a part of Asia (present day Turkey) where syncretism and religious pluralism were stitched into the very fabric of life. Paul has received word—probably from the church's founder Epaphras (Col. 4:12-13)—that a rival "philosophy" (2:8) has bubbled up in the Lycus Valley. This teaching threatens to kidnap the Colossians (2:8) by offering them what Paul believes is a toxic substitute for the gospel of Christ. Paul's theological reflection in the letter in part responds to this lurking danger.

What was the nature of this false teaching? It is hard to be precise. Paul assumes that his readers know perfectly well what he is referring to. As a result, he does not go into as much detail about it as we might like.[7] Various scholars have suggested a background in some early form of Gnosticism, or Judaism, or Greek philosophy.[8] It seems best, however, to understand the Colossian "philosophy" as a syncretistic stew, which combined a number of different religious ideas and practices. This also fits with what we know about the local context. Clinton E. Arnold has shown that popular religion in first-century Asia Minor was syncretistic to the core. In particular, it was characterized by a belief in various spirit and astral powers that were seen as a threat to everyday life.[9] In addition, ancient people felt victimized by impersonal Fate, which was thought to control their lives like an unpredictable storm.[10]

It is likely, then, that the Colossian "philosophy" tried to supplement the gospel of Christ with various ways of helping people cope in a world that was dominated by forces beyond their control. These "add-ons" probably included observing taboos (2:21), subduing the body with

---

relationship of Colossians to Ephesians and to Philemon. Although many scholars opt for a post-Pauline writer, I find no compelling reason to overturn the traditional Pauline authorship of the letter; see, e.g., the arguments of Peter T. O'Brien, *Colossians, Philemon*, WBC (Waco, TX.: Word Books, 1982), xli-xlix. Ultimately, however, the matter cannot be proven one way or the other, and the observations in this paper about contextualization in Colossians are largely relevant in either case.

5    For more nuanced definitions of syncretism and its relationship to contextualization, see the essays in Gailyn Van Rheenen, ed., *Contextualization and Syncretism: Navigating Cultural Currents* (Pasadena, CA: William Carey, 2006).

6    Due to space constraints, I cannot lay out the full exegetical underpinnings for the conclusions I draw from Colossians. For a more detailed presentation, see Flemming, *Contextualization*, 214-33. The following discussion is adapted from this previous study.

7    Any explanation of the "philosophy" must therefore be tentative. In any case, recognizing how Paul does situation-specific theology in Colossians does not depend on any single view of the Colossian error.

8    For a comprehensive discussion of the options, see R. Mcl. Wilson, *A Critical and Exegetical Commentary on Colossians and Philemon* (London/New York: T & T Clark, 2005), 35-78.

9    See Clinton E. Arnold, *The Colossian Syncretism The Interface between Christianity and Folk Belief at Colossae* (Grand Rapids, MI.: Baker, 1996), 234-44.

10    For references, see Charles H. Talbert, *Ephesians and Colossians* (Grand Rapids, MI: Baker, 2007), 18-19.

ascetic practices (2:23), offering worship to angels (2:18) and experiencing visions (2:18). The rival teachers also apparently borrowed elements from Judaism, such as rules about eating and drinking and calendar observances (2:16), as further ammunition for dealing with the powers.[11] What is more, in Colossians we encounter frequent and at times rather polemical references to "wisdom," "knowledge," "understanding," "mystery," and "fullness" (see 2:2-3, 23). This suggests that the philosophy may have promised a deeper understanding and experience of God than the Colossians already had.

Above all, Paul is convinced that the teaching devalued the role of Christ. Perhaps it reduced Christ to one among many supernatural powers.[12] In any case, from the perspective of the philosophy, what God had done in Christ was not enough to provide security in a world of unseen powers; one needed the help of additional practices, mystical experiences, and celestial beings.[13]

In sum, this counter message probably represents a blending of the Christian gospel with elements of the worldviews, beliefs, and practices that flourished in the local culture. Such a religious cocktail may well have appealed to young converts—Christians who may have been struggling to make a full break from their old ways of thinking and living (see 2:20).

What is Paul's response? The situation calls for a fresh articulation of the gospel into categories and language that speak to the issues the Colossians were facing. As a result, Paul launches a two-pronged strategy for de-fanging the "philosophy." Negatively, he unmasks the syncretistic teaching as "empty deception" and warns the Colossians not to be hijacked by it (2:8). Paul's direct attack on the philosophy is concentrated in 2:8-23. There he apparently seizes a number of catchwords from his opponents (e.g., "insisting on self-abasement," "the worship of angels" [2:18]; "Do not handle, Do not taste, Do not touch" [2:21]) in order to show his audience how utterly incompatible such practices are with the gospel they received (2:6-7).

But Paul is not content simply to criticize. His main response is to positively reflect on the meaning and implications of the gospel he and the Colossians share. This theological response does not simply address his readers' *thinking*; it also calls them to a new way of living (3:1-4:6). Writing out of a missionary-pastor's heart, he seeks transformation in their worldviews, beliefs, attitudes, and behaviors. Paul's reflections on Christ and the gospel thus become a word on target for the Colossians in the midst of challenging circumstances. In the process, several key themes emerge.

---

11    The presence of a sizable Jewish population in Phrygia during this period makes it hardly surprising that the syncretistic teaching incorporated elements from Judaism.

12    Wilson, *Colossians and Philemon*, 235.

13    For descriptions of the Colossian "philosophy" along these general lines, see Arnold, *Colossian Syncretism*, 228-44; Andrew T. Lincoln, "The Letter to the Colossians," in *The New Interpreter's Bible*, ed. L. E. Keck (Nashville, TN: Abingdon, 2000), 11:560-68. For a stimulating but not fully successful attempt to read Colossians primarily against the background of the power structures of the Roman Empire, see B. J. Walsh and S. C. Keesmaat, *Colossians Remixed: Subverting the Empire* (Downers Grove, IL.: InterVarsity Press, 2004).

# A Cosmic Christ

In light of the threatening philosophy, Paul does some of his most creative and profound reflection on the person of Christ. John Barclay asserts that the theology of Colossians is "at every point Christological. . . . Christ is the center of all reality that integrates and energizes the letter."[14] This radical Christological focus is wholly appropriate, given the setting to which Paul is writing. Apparently, the rival teachers did not deny Christ and his saving work as such. Rather, they seem to have downgraded his status; they questioned his ability to fully deliver people from the unseen powers. The net result was a small-scale savior who was part of the cosmos, not its sovereign Lord.

In contrast, Paul proclaims that Christ is supreme over all things. The Christology of Colossians reveals the cosmic dimension of Christ's role in creation and reconciliation in a way not seen in the earlier writings of Paul. If letters such as Galatians and Romans focus on God's salvation in Christ in relation to Israel and the Law, Colossians spotlights Christ's relationship to creation, the world, and the powers.[15] In Colossians, Christ is the lead actor who plays his part on a cosmic stage.

The Christology of Colossians is articulated above all in the magnificent Christ hymn of 1:15-20.[16] Echoing the Wisdom traditions of the Old Testament and Hellenistic Judaism, this poetic rhapsody is the theological centerpiece of the letter. The hymn sings praise to Christ as unrivaled Lord of both creation (1:15-18a) and redemption (1:18b-20). The claims are comprehensive. Paul's repeated use of the word "all" underlines the sweeping scope of God's action in Christ: "*all things* have been created through him and for him" (1:16); "in him *all things* hold together" (1:17); and through him God has reconciled "*all things*" (1:20). Indeed, "*all*" of God's fullness dwells in him (1:19).

A key feature of the poem is its assurance that Christ is sovereign over the powers that are active in the universe. He is the head of every created thing, including "things invisible"—here named as "thrones or dominions or rulers or powers" (1:16-17). In this context, it seems that Paul primarily has hostile, not friendly powers in his sight.[17] Given the overblown status his readers apparently gave the unseen powers, the hymn's creation emphasis is right on target.

---

14    John M. G. Barclay. *Colossians and Philemon* (Sheffield: Sheffield Academic Press, 1997), 77.

15    Marianne Meye Thompson, *Colossians and Philemon* (Grand Rapids, MI: Eerdmans, 2005), 148.

16    On the Christology of Col. 1:15-20, see Gordon D. Fee, *Pauline Christology: An Exegetical-Theological Study* (Peabody, MA.: Hendrickson, 2007), 298-313.

17    O'Brien, *Colossians, Philemon*, 46. There has been sharp debate over the role of the "powers" in Colossians and Paul's thought in general. Some scholars, particularly in the West, want to depersonalize the powers, identifying them with human structures and institutions—social, political, intellectual, etc. See especially the influential work of Walter Wink, who tries to combine a structural understanding of the powers with a recognition that there is a "spiritual" dimension to all earthly institutions and systems (e.g., *Naming the Powers: The Language of Power in the New Testament* [Philadelphia: Fortress, 1984], 5). Similarly, Walsh and Keesmaat argue that in Colossians Paul's "power" language refers primarily to Caesar and the power structures of the Roman Empire (*Colossians Remixed*, 91-93). It is true that for Paul, the "powers" can operate at a variety of levels, including individual, cosmic, social and political (for the latter, see 1 Cor. 2:8). But both the historical context and exegesis of the relevant passages lead me to conclude that in Colossians Paul in the first place is talking about cosmic powers. See further, Clinton E. Arnold, *Ephesians: Power and Magic, The Concept of Power in Ephesians in Light of Its Historical Setting* (Grand Rapids, MI.: Baker, 1989), 44-51, 129-34.

"Paul deflates the power of the powers by insisting they are a part of the order that was created and is now sustained through Christ and are thereby subject to his sovereign rule."[18] The powers are "no match for their maker."[19]

What's more, God has *reconciled* all things through the death of Christ (1:20). This reconciliation embraces not just the church (1:18), but also the dominions of darkness. In the latter case, however, "making peace" takes the form of *pacifying* the powers by subjecting them to Christ's rule. Such an idea would no doubt have rung bells with the Colossian Gentiles. They lived in a climate that was saturated with the Roman Empire's notions of peace.[20] In the Roman world, global peace, the *pax romana*, was secured by conquest—the subduing of all of Rome's enemies. Thus, in the recital of his acts, we hear emperor Augustus say, "The provinces of the Gauls, the Spains, and German . . . I *reduced to a state of peace*."[21] At the same time, the message of Colossians stands in shocking contrast to the claims of Rome. Christ's way of pacifying his enemies is not with the mighty machines of imperial glory. Instead, it comes by means of a lowly and shameful crucifixion—"through the blood of his cross" (1:20).

Here we see Christ reconciling the whole of fallen creation, in anticipation of his end-time victory. Reconciliation in Colossians therefore has a different thrust than in either Romans 5:10-11 or 2 Corinthians 5:18-20, where God's people are mainly in view. The hymn's vision of God's all-encompassing reconciliation in Christ sounds a note of encouragement for people who feel threatened by the powers of darkness. As Peter T. O'Brien insists, the subjugated powers "cannot finally harm the person who is in Christ, and their ultimate overthrow in the future is assured."[22]

Later in chapter 2, Paul describes Christ's victory over the powers with three striking metaphors taken from the Greco-Roman world (2:15). In the cross of Christ, God "disarmed" the powers of darkness, stripping them of their power; he "made a public example of them," exposing them as weak and worthless; and he *triumphed* over them. This final image recalls the familiar Roman triumphal procession, in which a victorious general would parade his conquered enemies behind him for all to see. These audacious images flip all usual expectations within the Roman world on their head. According to ordinary ways of seeing things, it was *Christ*, not the powers, who was stripped, publicly humiliated, and defeated when he was nailed to a cross. Far from conquering his enemies, it appeared that Jesus was the helpless victim of the powers. N. T. Wright captures this reversal of expectations well: "The cross was not the defeat of *Christ* at the hands of the *powers*: it was the defeat of the powers at the hands—yes, the bleeding hands—of Christ."[23] Christ's cosmic triumph liberates all of creation, including humans, from domination by the enslaving powers.

---

18     Flemming, *Contextualization*, 220-21.
19     Talbert, *Ephesians and Colossians*, 191.
20     Ibid., 196.
21     *Res gestae divi Augusti* 13; cited in Talbert, *Ephesians and Colossians*, 196 (emphasis by Talbert).
22     O'Brien, *Colossians, Philemon*, 56.
23     N. T. Wright, *Following Jesus: Biblical Reflections on Discipleship* (Grand Rapids, MI.: Eerdmans, 1994), 19.

Paul also accents the supremacy of Christ by identifying him with the "mystery" (*mystērion*) of God (1:26-27; 2:2; 4:3). This is a mystery that is no longer mysterious; God has revealed it publicly in the person of Christ and the gospel preaching about him. Although Paul's understanding of the term "mystery" is rooted in the Old Testament and Judaism, the term was also linked to the Greek mystery religions of the day. Arnold observes that some of the Gentile converts in Colossae may have had a background in the mysteries that were related to local deities.[24] Even so, Paul does not boycott such "dangerous" language. He risks taking over a term that carries religious and cultural baggage within the Greco-Roman world in order to speak a compelling word to his hearers. God's mystery is not reserved for a privileged few, those with access to special experiences or secret wisdom. The Colossians have received *the* mystery of God's great purpose for the world: "Christ in you, the hope of glory" (1:27). For Paul's audience, this is good news indeed.

## A Sufficient Salvation

The Colossian "philosophy" also failed to grasp the character of the salvation Christ was able to bring. From the perspective of the rival teaching, what God did in Christ was deficient. It needed assistance, in the form of ascetic and ritual practices, legal rules, mystical experiences, and so forth. Paul's response to this "Christ plus something else" way of thinking is plain: Christ is not only supreme; he is also *sufficient* to save people completely. Nothing else is needed.

Consequently, Colossians focuses on the fullness of redemption that believers experience in Christ. As with Romans, Colossians insists that Christians participate in the story of Christ's death and resurrection. But there is a difference. In Romans we hear that Christians have died with Christ and *will be* raised with him in the future (Rom. 6:7-8; 8:11). But Colossians makes the bold claim that they have *already* been raised with Christ to a new heavenly life (Col. 2:12-13; 3:1). Paul, it appears, has weighted the tension between the "already" and the "not yet" of salvation firmly on the side of Christians' present experience of God's transforming power and grace. This is not because Colossians has forsaken a future hope (see 1:5, 22, 27, 28; 3:4, 24). Rather, Paul's special emphasis on the "now" of salvation comes as a targeted word for his readers. "By participating with Christ in his resurrection they share in the fullness of resurrection life, in particular his deliverance from the tyranny of the unseen powers."[25]

Paul brings out the present reality of salvation in Christ in a variety of ways. Some of these speak directly to the concerns raised by the rival philosophy. In a remarkable passage, found in a polemical context (2:9-10), Paul affirms that all of the *fullness* of deity dwells bodily in Christ. But the apostle then applies this reality to the church: "and *you* have come to *fullness* in him." Has Paul co-opted the term "fullness" (*plērōma*) from the Colossian situation and given it a new, Christ-centered meaning? We cannot be sure. In any case, the Colossians could not miss the point. Because God's fullness dwells in Christ, they need no other mediators, powers, or practices. Nothing is lacking in their relationship to God.[26] Moreover, partaking in Christ's

---

24   Arnold, *Colossian Syncretism*, 272; cf. Thompson, *Colossians and Philemon*, 42.
25   Flemming, *Contextualization*, 224.
26   Lincoln, "Letter to the Colossians," 623.

fullness means that they also share in his "headship" over the principalities and powers (2:10b; cf. 1:18; 2:19).

At the climax of his prayer for the Colossians in chapter 1, Paul assures them that they have already been rescued from the dominion of darkness and transferred into the kingdom where Christ reigns (1:13). Here Old Testament language describing Israel's deliverance from bondage ('rescue' 1:13; "redemption" 1:14) is reapplied. It now speaks of God's ability to liberate the church from the enslaving powers of sin and darkness through Christ.

Later Paul reminds his readers that they have "died to the elemental spirits of the universe" (*stoicheia tou kosmou*; 2:20; cf. 2:8). The term *stoicheia* could simply refer to "the basic principles or tenets that represent the world's point of view."[27] More likely, however, it stands for the astral and cosmic powers that were thought to exert their sinister control over peoples' daily lives.[28] Whereas elsewhere Paul speaks of Christians having died with Christ to the powers of sin and the law (e.g., Rom. 6-7), here participation in the death of Christ specifically brings liberation "from" (not "to") the hostile powers (Col. 2:20).

A further benefit of salvation in Christ is access to the wisdom (1:9, 28; 2:3; 3:16; 4:5) and knowledge (1:6, 9-10, 27; 2:2-3; 3:10) of God. Probably in response to the philosophy's claims to wisdom (2:23), Paul assures his audience that Christ is the embodiment of wisdom.[29] Paul seems to say, "You cannot tap into divine wisdom through ascetic acts and visionary experiences. The riches of God's wisdom and knowledge are yours only by being united with Christ" (2:2-3).

## A Sacred Story

All of Paul's targeted theological reflection in Colossians is anchored in a sacred narrative—a "master story" of what God has done in Christ. The gospel narrative in Colossians is a sweeping story. It "begins with God's creation of the world and aims at its final re-creation."[30] Christ's death and resurrection are the focus of this story. It is primarily through those events that God accomplishes his reconciling purposes for humanity and the universe. The Colossians are invited to embrace this gospel narrative as a controlling story, one that excludes all other competing stories.[31]

Both the death and the resurrection of Christ are central to Paul's theological argument in Colossians. But how he interprets those events is molded for the setting. Paul uses a kaleidoscope of images to unpack the meaning of Christ's death in Colossians, some of which we have already mentioned. These include: redemption of those in slavery (1:14); forgiveness of sins (1:14; 2:13); reconciliation of enemies and of the whole world (1:20-22); making peace through the cross (1:20); liberation from the powers (1:13; 2:15); transfer into a new realm

---

27    Thompson, *Colossians and Philemon*, 53.
28    See Arnold, *Colossian Syncretism*, 154-94; Lincoln, "Letter to the Colossians," 565-67.
29    Lincoln, "Letter to the Colossians," 575-76.
30    Thompson, *Colossians and Philemon*, 130.
31    Walter T. Wilson, *The Hope of Glory: Education and Exhortation in the Epistle to the Colossians* (Leiden: Brill, 1997), 191, 261.

(1:13); an inward spiritual circumcision (2:11); participation in Jesus' death (2:12-13; 3:3); granting of new life (2:12-13; 3:3-4); and canceling of a debt (2:14).

This army of images not only shows the breadth of Paul's understanding of the cross; it also testifies to how he tailors his interpretation of Christ's death to the needs at hand. It is worth noting that the language of righteousness and justification that looms so large in letters like Galatians and Romans does not even make a cameo appearance in Colossians. Does this imply that such concepts are no longer important to Paul? Not at all. Rather, it seems that he calls on other ways of expressing the gospel that speak more directly to his present concerns.

This ought to caution us about lifting up any single way of articulating God's gracious work in Christ—whether "justification by faith," "being born again," "substitutionary atonement" or "getting saved"—to a dominant role. Paul helps us recognize both the richness of the language available to us and the diversity of circumstances that language must address. In addition, many of the metaphors for Christ's death in Colossians come directly out of the day-to-day world of his readers. They communicate the meaning of Christ's death in language and pictures that connect with Paul's Gentile audience.

Christ's *resurrection*, if anything, plays an even greater role in Paul's expression of the gospel in Colossians. As we have seen, here Paul puts more emphasis on the meaning of God's raising Christ for his readers' present life than he does on the promise of resurrection life in the future. Focusing on this part of the story is surely appropriate, since the Colossians need a current assurance of Christ's power to overcome the powers. At the same time, Jesus' resurrection has implications for the whole cosmos. As Marianne Meye Thompson puts it, "What God did for Christ in raising him from the dead to new life, God will do for all the world."[32] Paul, then, wants to help the Colossians' see their own place in the grand drama of God's salvation. They are a church living in Christ's resurrection power and victory in anticipation of his renewal of the whole of creation.[33] God's great purpose to restore all things is presently being worked out in story of the church.

## A Transformed Life

The story of Christ's death and resurrection also has profound implications for Christian discipleship and the moral formation of the community. Christology and ethics are married in Colossians. Nowhere is this clearer than in 3:1-4. Here Paul gives his readers a Christological basis for his instructions on living as a transformed community in 3:5- 4:6. They are called to a new moral vision, determined by their experience of dying with Christ and their union with the risen and exalted Lord (3:1, 3).[34] As people who share in the death and resurrection of Christ, they must put to death the old way of living that is inconsistent with their new Christ-oriented life (3:5). This involves a completely new way of imagining the world. They are to seek "the things that are above," where the exalted Christ is, not the norms and values that operate on earth (3:1-2). This new life is a response to the lordship of the risen Christ. As they received Jesus as Lord, they must "walk in him" (2:6).

---

32  Thompson, *Colossians and Philemon*, 113.
33  Ibid., 137.
34  Flemming, *Contextualization*, 227.

Paul's ethical instructions in chapter 3 would have struck some familiar notes for his audience. We see the influence of a number of standard conventions found in the moral teaching of the Greco-Roman world. These include:

- Traditional motifs, like the language of "taking off" and "putting on" (3:9b-10) lists of vices and virtues (3:5-17)
- Codes of conduct for members of the household (3:18--4:1).

In each case, however, Paul reworks these cultural conventions and gives them a Christological basis and motivation. For example, the virtues named in 3:12-17 are attitudes that reflect the cruciform love of Christ: compassion, kindness, humility, meekness, patience, and forgiveness (3:12-14). Paul goes on to ground the community's common life in the ruling peace and indwelling word of Christ (3:15-16). This all builds to a climax in 3:17, where the church is urged to gratefully do "everything" under the lordship of Jesus.

At the same time, Paul's moral teaching, like his theological reflection, is sensitive to the needs of the audience. Paul's response to the philosophy has in its crosshairs a counterfeit form of holiness, which featured human "do's and don'ts," ascetic practices, and ecstatic experiences. Paul considers such practices to be utterly useless for restraining sinfulness (2:23). At stake in Colossians is not only bad theology, but also a bogus idea of what constitutes holy living. I agree with Robert W. Wall that 3:1-4:6 is "the moral flip side of [Paul's] theological argument against the 'hollow and deceptive philosophy.'"[35] The household codes, for instance, seem to offer an alternative to asceticism and exclusive knowledge by engaging the everyday institutions of the Greco-Roman world in a transforming way. This is not to say that Paul's moral instruction in Colossians is limited to a specific response to the errant teaching. But Colossians surely offers a radical contrast to the kind of external forms of piety the syncretism promotes.

Specifically, Paul sees the praxis of the false teachers as an extension of their wrongheaded Christology. The Colossians do not need the "shadow" of ritual observances enforced by the philosophy. They already have the "real thing" that belongs to Christ alone (2:16-17). Here Paul does not condemn religious ritual as such. Rather, these practices, seemingly motivated out of a regard for the cosmic powers (2:20), become irrelevant in light of God's heart-transforming grace in Christ. Paul sees the Christian lifestyle as part of a renewed creation, where Christ is "all and in all" (3:11).

Such a radical Christological basis for moral teaching might help to explain one of the puzzles of the letter—why the Spirit plays a relatively minor part when Paul talks about salvation and the Christian life.[36] As Thompson observes, in Colossians, Christian "spirituality" "is a matter of living according to the dominion of Jesus rather than the dominion of darkness."[37] Eduard Lohse surely is right that the ethical teaching in Colossians "is stamped with the leitmotif that

---

35    Robert W. Wall, *Colossians and Philemon* (Downers Grove, IL.: InterVarsity Press, 1993), 129.

36    There is only one explicit reference to the Spirit in the Colossians (1:8). This stands in striking contrast to, e.g., Romans, 1 & 2 Corinthians, Galatians and Ephesians.

37    Thompson, *Colossians and Philemon*, 153.

runs throughout the letter from beginning to end: Christ is Lord over everything—over powers and principalities, but also over the Christian's daily life."[38]

# The Gospel and Culture

The engagement between the gospel and culture is basic to contextualization. Does Colossians shed any light on this question? Obviously, Paul never directly addresses the modern idea of culture, so we need to tread carefully here. Nevertheless, when Paul speaks to a Christian community of the first-century Roman world such as that in Colossae, what he says has clear implications for the gospel's interaction with the dominant Greco-Roman culture. That relationship is complex and multi-layered. I see at least four dimensions to the gospel's intersection with the cultural world of Paul's audience:[39]

## Affirming Culture

Paul does not reject Greco-Roman culture as a whole or preach against it. The apostle was no dualist. Rather, he has a robust theology of creation, which affirms that all things were created through and for Christ (1:17). Paul assumes that the Triune God is present and active in the created order, which includes human cultures. Although the pagan world is severely sinful, it has the capacity to be reconciled and remade by the God who made it in the first place. It is the arena of God's gracious activity. Consequently, Paul can affirm and identify with aspects of pagan culture and use them to bring the story of Christ to the pagan world.

Paul can therefore draw upon a notion such as "reconciliation," which comes out of a secular Greco-Roman context.[40] People in Paul's day used this language to talk about restoring peace between enemies and exchanging friendship for hostility. But in Paul's hands, this secular image becomes a prime way to picture God's reconciling activity in the death of Christ (1:20-22). Likewise, although Paul grounds his theological reflection in Jesus' death and resurrection, he conscripts familiar images from the worlds of commerce (e.g., certificate of indebtedness 2:14), agriculture ("bearing fruit," "growing" 1:6, 10) or politics (Roman triumph 2:15) to explain these events. In this way, the gospel speaks a fresh word that resonates with his readers.

Furthermore, Paul taps into the culture's literary and rhetorical conventions. He adopts and adapts both the standard form for ancient letters and conventional persuasive strategies in order to address Gentile readers in a credible and convincing way.[41] For instance, Aristotle identified three forms of persuasion that were necessary for effective communication, all of which feature in Colossians.[42]

---

38     Eduard Lohse, *Colossians and Philemon*, trans. W. R. Poehlmann and R. J. Karris (Philadelphia: Fortress, 1971), 178.

39     For a fuller discussion of this issue, see Flemming, *Contextualization*, 125-51.

40     See S. E. Porter, "Peace, Reconciliation," in *Dictionary of Paul and His Letters*, ed. G. Hawthorne, R. P. Martin and D. G. Reid (Downers Grove, IL.: InterVarsity Press, 1993), 695.

41     For one attempt to analyze Colossians as a primarily "deliberative" speech (calling for a future change in belief and behavior) according to the structure of ancient rhetoric, see Lincoln, "Letter to the Colossians," 557-60. As always, however, we must be careful not to force Paul into rhetorical pigeonholes. Paul regularly adapts the conventions discussed in the ancient rhetorical handbooks for his own purposes.

42     See Aristotle, *Rhetoric* 1.2.

First, Paul argues from his own character and credibility (*ethos*). This happens when he appeals to his relationship with his coworker Epaphras as the link that binds him to the church (1:7-8; 4:12-13), or when he speaks of his special role as one commissioned by God to impart the mystery of the gospel to them (1:27-28).

Second, an argument from *pathos* appeals to the listeners' emotions. Paul elicits *pathos* by recalling his sufferings on the church's behalf (1:24) and his imprisonment for the sake of the gospel (4:3, 18).

Third, Paul fashions his arguments to be logically persuasive (*logos*). We see evidence of this throughout the letter, such as when Paul confronts the deceptive philosophy in 2:6-23.

Paul, then, does not stigmatize Gentile culture. It is not something from which Christians should escape to some holy island. Rather, Paul seems to recognize the breath of God's Spirit in human culture, and the apostle becomes a catalyst, consciously or otherwise, for the gospel's enculturation in it. He can therefore draw from a whole variety of cultural materials—from language, religion, politics, ethics, philosophy, rhetoric, literature, social institutions, or community life—as connecting points for the gospel.

## Relativizing Culture

A second stream flows out of the gospel's engagement with culture in Colossians: former cultural distinctions are relativized in light of God's new creation. Paul is convinced that God has done something radically new in Christ. The old order of relationships among human beings has come to an abrupt end. Jesus' reconciliation of "all things" (1:20) means the dismantling of all barriers to community, whether national, cultural, or social. Paul's readers must envision a world that is stunning in its difference from the default setting of the culture. In the renewed creation, categories that promote Jewish distinctiveness and superiority—"Greek and Jew, circumcised and uncircumcised"—collapse in a heap. Likewise, in the new humanity "there is no longer . . . barbarian, Scythian" (3:11). Such terms were used by Gentiles to sneer at the culturally inferior status of non-Greeks. In short, "every culture becomes provisional in light of the cross."[43]

What is more, a person's *social* position—whether a slave or free—is relativized in view of one's primary relationship to Christ (3:11). Slave owners, along with slaves, serve the same Master in heaven (4:1). Even if legal codes in the Roman Empire determined that slaves belong to their human masters, in the redeemed community both slaves and master are equally enslaved to the Lord Christ.[44]

Does this mean that the gospel simply deletes all cultural differences? Do Christians blend into a bland sameness? That is not Paul's point. The gospel *relativizes* cultural and social distinctions; it doesn't remove them. Paul does not ask Jews to stop being Jews. Nor should Greeks surrender their Greek identity. Paul can affirm cultural particularity (see 1 Cor. 7:17-20; 9:20; 10:32), but at the same time reject cultural and soteriological privilege. This has profound

---

43   Flemming, *Contextualization*, 136.
44   Thompson, *Colossians and Philemon*, 96.

implications for contextualizing the gospel. Because no cultural expression can claim to be ultimate, the gospel is free to become meaningful in a rich diversity of circumstances and cultures. At the same time, the gospel cannot be heard apart from a cultural home. God addresses Jews as Jews, Greeks as Greeks, Thais as Thais, postmoderns as postmoderns. Our contextualization of the gospel must be culture-specific, but never culture-bound.

## Confronting Culture

There is a third dimension of Paul's attitude toward what we think of as culture. Not only is the world in which culture operates God's creation and the scene of God's gracious activity; it is also the arena of darkness and sin. The cosmos is presently enemy-occupied territory. It is subject to the powers of darkness (1:13) and the elemental spirits of the world (2:8, 20). Human beings have wrongly given over their allegiance to these enslaving powers. The earmark of the human situation is alienation and hostility (1:21). The Gentiles are caught up in "evil deeds" (1:21), disobedience (3:6), and idolatry (3:5), acting against how the Creator intended for people to live. This sober analysis of fallen humanity not only describes individual sinners; it also applies to human societies and cultures in a collective way. Cultures, along with their worldviews, structures, and social behaviors, are far from simply being neutral channels for the gospel. They are pervaded with the cancer of sin.

As a result, when the gospel engages pagan culture, it speaks a "no" as well as a "yes." The gospel cannot be good news without prophetically challenging the sinful elements in human cultures. In Colossians, the gospel confronts aspects of the culture that clash with the creative and redemptive purposes of God: it judges the syncretistic worldview that gives too high a place to the powers. It excludes sinful patterns of behaving that might have seemed quite normal in pagan society (see 3:5-7). It subverts the cultural myth of the *pax romana* that proclaimed universal peace at the blood-price of military oppression (1:20).

Colossians illustrates what is true in a wider sense: the gospel is in important ways *counter-cultural* to every culture. We must be willing to courageously critique what is sinful in every culture, especially our own.

## Transforming Culture

When the gospel intersects culture, judgment is not the last word. Paul's optimism of grace opens the possibility for cultures to be transformed from within. Even as sin has affected cultures in a negative way, so God's new creation in Christ has the potential to influence culture, with its values and practices.[45] Ultimately, this will mean the total renewal of the whole world (1:20). In the mean time, however, God's reconciling purposes focus on the church, as both a transformed community and an agent of transformation.

One way of engaging culture in order to reshape it is by reinterpreting its language. Paul is not afraid to "convert" language that was part of pagan belief systems. In Colossians, he apparently seizes terms from the religious culture of the day ("mystery," "wisdom," "power," "gospel") and injects them with Christ-oriented meaning. Granted, most of these ideas had impressive Old

---

45    William A. Dyrness, *How Does America Hear the Gospel?* (Grand Rapids, MI.: Eerdmans, 1996), 8.

Testament and Jewish credentials. But for Paul's readers they would likely have triggered associations with pagan ideas and practices. This reminds us that to a large extent Christians do not invent their own special language. They use language from their cultural and religious worlds in fresh and transforming ways.[46]

The gospel also has transforming implications for the values and conventions that influence behavior in Greco-Roman culture. Paul's instruction for members of the household in 3:18-4:1 is a prime example. This kind of moral teaching would have sounded quite familiar to Paul's Gentile hearers.[47] Indeed, it promotes an ethic that shares much in common with contemporary standards of behavior. Does this "household code," then, simply endorse the patriarchal norms of the dominant culture?[48]

Such a conclusion misses an important factor. Not only is there considerable overlap between the Colossian code and conventional behavior. There is also a deep internal difference.[49] Three features bring this out. The first is the context of these instructions within the letter. The verses leading up to this section describe the Christ-like character and relationships of those who are being renewed in the image of the Creator (3:5-17). That renewal means that in Christ no group has an inherently superior status over against another (3:10); that love and humility will govern all interpersonal relations in the community (3:12-14).[50] In particular, 3:18-4:1 illustrates what it means to "do everything in the name of the Lord Jesus" (3:17). If "Christ is all and in all" (3:11), then every family relationship, every social or cultural reality, becomes an expression of life under Christ's lordship.

Second, whereas instructions from Aristotle and others protected the interests of the household power brokers—husbands, fathers, slave owners—Paul's list stands apart in its mutuality. Wives, children, and even slaves are addressed and treated as morally responsible persons.[51]

Third, when Paul injects the phrase "in the Lord" into his admonitions to wives and children (3:18, 20), or when he tells slaves that working for human masters is actually service to their heavenly Lord (3:23), he is not simply slapping a thin coat of Christian paint on a pagan structure. Rather, Paul gives these ordinary household relationships a new orientation and motivation. Thompson rightly insists that "[i]t is simply impossible to live on the model of Jesus Christ within the structures of society and to leave the relationships within them fundamentally unchanged."[52]

---

46    Miroslav Volf, "When Gospel and Culture Intersect: Notes on the Nature of Christian Difference," in *Pentecostalism in Context: Essays in Honor of William W. Menzies*, ed. William M. and Robert Menzies (Sheffield: Sheffield University Press, 1997), 228, 232.

47    See James D. G. Dunn, *The Epistles to the Colossians and to Philemon* (Grand Rapids, MI.: Eerdmans, 1996), 243-44 for references to various ancient parallels to the New Testament household codes. Dunn cautions, however, that there is no standard form of "household rules" in the ancient world.

48    See, e.g., A. J. M. Wedderburn, "The Theology of Colossians," in A. T. Lincoln and A. J. M. Wedderburn, *The Theology of the Later Pauline Letters* (Cambridge: Cambridge University Press, 1993), 56-57.

49    See the helpful discussion in Ben Witherington III, *The Letters to Philemon, the Colossians, and the Ephesians: A Socio-Rhetorical Commentary on the Captivity Epistles* (Grand Rapids, MI: Eerdmans, 2007), 183-87.

50    Thompson, *Colossians and Philemon*, 89.

51    See O'Brien, *Colossians, Philemon*, 218.

52    Thompson, *Colossians and Philemon*, 94.

But if the gospel has transforming implications for the culture, why doesn't Paul challenge the power structures of the Greco-Roman world more directly? We should note that Paul does not grant divine approval to the institution of slavery or mandate contemporary ways of ordering the family or state. In a sense, he plays with the cards he is dealt as a citizen of the Roman Empire.[53] As a minority and marginalized community within a dominant culture, the church did not have a platform from which to quickly restructure the whole society. Instead, Paul's approach is one of transforming engagement from within. Christians are to live out their calling within their circumstances, even as they display a visible, internal difference. Over time the gospel leaven would do its renewing work.

Contextualization today, as well, must have a transforming purpose. It is not enough simply to "relate" to the culture in which we find ourselves. We must engage that culture in its multiple dimensions—worldview, language, symbols, rituals, beliefs, politics, social behaviors, moral values—with a view to reshaping them from within. This mainly happens as communities of believers authentically live out the gospel in the worlds they share with unbelievers. But here is our challenge. On the one hand, our message and conduct need to be enough a part of the culture that they do not come across as being irrelevant. On the other hand, we must maintain enough distance from the culture that, by the Spirit's enabling, we are in a position to shape, and at times, even subvert it.[54] We stand, as it were, with one foot inside our own culture—enabling the gospel to make sense to people where they are—and one foot outside, embodying a cross-shaped alternative to what is "normal" in our world.[55]

## Paul's Method of Contextualization . . . and Ours

The letter to the Colossians carries importance well beyond its length for our understanding of precedents for contextualization in the New Testament. It gives us a fascinating glimpse into how the gospel encounters challenging new circumstances and the reality of syncretism. Let me conclude with some summary observations about Paul's way of doing theology in Colossians and how that might inform the global church today.

I have argued that Paul responds to the Colossian context with *both* fidelity and innovation. This means, first, that "the word of truth, the gospel" (1:5) cannot surrender to syncretism or blend in with a religiously plural context. Paul is more than happy to become "all things to all people" in nonessential matters (1 Cor. 9:19-23). But he draws bold boundaries when it comes to the unique supremacy of Christ, his sole sufficiency to reconcile human beings and all of creation, or his lordship over all of life. Such core concerns are off the negotiating table.

Likewise, *our* efforts at contextualization must reflect a clear vision of the normative gospel. Otherwise, our theology is in danger of drifting from its anchor. For many so-called contextual theologies that have emerged in recent years, this has been a particular risk. In the theological dance between the constant gospel and changing circumstances, the gospel must take the lead.

---

53    See Ibid., 92.

54    See Robert Wuthnow, *Communities of Discourse: Ideology and Social Structure in the Reformation, the Enlightenment, and European Socialism* (Cambridge, MA.: Harvard University Press, 1989), 3-5.

55    See Miroslav Volf, *Exclusion and Embrace: A Theological Exploration of Identity, Otherness, and Reconciliation* (Nashville, TN: Abingdon, 1996), 49.

Whenever the voice of the interpreter or the context drowns out the voice of Christ revealed in Scripture, that reading moves out of bounds. Furthermore, in a time when postmodern thinking shudders at the very thought of an overarching metanarrative, we have no other course but to ground our theological reflection in the one saving story of what God has done for us in Christ.

Second, at the same time, Paul's theologizing in Colossians shows remarkable flexibility and sensitivity to the context. Colossians does not articulate the Christian message with the same language, images, or arguments as we find, say, in Romans or 1 Thessalonians. Instead, Paul enables the abiding story of God's loving intervention in Christ to come to fresh expression for new circumstances. For instance, it seems that the challenges in Colossae served as a catalyst for Paul to reflect more deeply on the implications of Christ's lordship and redemption for the whole of creation than he had done previously.

We have also seen that Paul uses language that is shared by the local religious and philosophical culture (e.g., "mystery"). He takes over images from the day-to-day world of his audience (e.g., the Roman triumphal procession). And he enlists familiar ethical conventions such as instructions to the household, all in the service of the gospel. At the same time, he does not hesitate to draw upon traditional biblical language (e.g., forgiveness 1:14; 2:13: 3:13, redemption 1:14; circumcision 2:11-13) and recontextualize it for Gentile Christians.

As Paul sensitively engaged his world in all of its specificity, so we must engage ours. This does not mean that we can ignore the differences between the apostle's situation and our own. As Scripture, Paul's ways of formulating the message have a level of authority that ours do not. They remain foundational for us. Nevertheless, we cannot be content to slavishly imitate Paul's terminology or to limit ourselves to images and thought forms that were meaningful to people in the first-century Greco-Roman world.

 If we would learn from Paul, we will look for ways of telling and living the gospel, under the guidance of the Spirit, that make sense to people where they are. We will utilize our own stories and cultural resources, while remaining rooted in the witness of Scripture. For example, Croatian theologian Miroslav Volf reflects on his experience of the bitter ethnic conflict in the Balkan peninsula with the powerful images of *exclusion* and *embrace*.[56] These metaphors enable a fresh engagement between God's word and a splintered world. They point to the healing embrace of the crucified Christ, which in turn enables us to enfold others in our arms. Such contextualized readings, arising from our particular locations, can in turn help the wider global church come to a richer grasp of God's good news in Christ.

Third, underlying Paul's contextual theology in Colossians is a sacred narrative of what the Triune God has done in creation and in Christ, and what God *will* do to bring about a new creation and the consummation of Jesus' reconciling mission. The church today, as well, must locate its theological compass in this grand narrative told in Scripture. Perhaps focusing on the biblical narrative is the most direct path toward finding unity and coherence in the midst of our theological diversity. We may talk about and embody our commitment to Christ in many different ways. This defining story, however, continually draws us back to our shared under-

---

56    Volf, *Exclusion and Embrace.*

standing of and participation in the gospel. If Scripture gives us a true metanarrative, a story of all stories, then it is bigger than any contextual expression of it. Or, as Kevin Vanhoozer imagines it, our local theologies are like "regional performances" of the one biblical *theodrama* of God's missional purpose for the world in Christ.[57]

Fourth, Paul's contextualization of the gospel reshaped the theological imaginations of his hearers. When Paul co-opts the "power" language of the religious culture or the image of the Roman triumph, it is not merely to identify with his audience; rather, he gives them an alternative way of seeing the world. Even the crucifixion itself, in Paul's world a symbol of Roman cruelty and unspeakable shame, becomes the instrument of God's reconciling peace for the whole creation (1:20). Paul's example encourages us to mine the resources that are available to us—from Scripture, tradition, and the wider culture—in order to prophetically re-imagine our world.

Fifth, Paul's contextualization of the gospel in Colossians is not simply a matter of offering a better "theology." Even as the syncretistic threat had to do with more than just wrong *beliefs*, so the implications of the gospel that Colossians conveys are comprehensive. The gospel, as Paul sees it, will engage his readers' worldviews and fears, their behaviors and values, their ritual practices and religious experiences, their social relationships and political perspectives—in short, it will change all of life.

Today, as well, we must practice holistic contextualization.[58] The goal is to lead God's people to reflect Christ with their hearts, heads, and hands. Our theological reflection may score high marks for doctrinal precision. Or it may excel in relevance. But if it does not help to shape God's people in their shared life of discipleship and their participation in God's mission in the world, it is only a parody of authentic contextualization.

Sixth, Paul had no single strategy for responding to pagan culture. We saw that he could affirm aspects of Greco-Roman culture and use them as points of contact for the gospel. Other dimensions of the culture needed to be relativized in light of new creation realities. Still others could only be rejected and replaced. Ultimately, the goal of the gospel's engaging Greco-Roman culture was its transformation from within.

In practice, these four attitudes—affirming, relativizing, confronting, transforming—often overlap. Contextualization in our complex cultures today may take any of these forms. It will probably touch all of them. Our great challenge is to discern, through the Spirit's leading, when to identify with the culture and when to undermine it; when to connect and when to confront; how to let the gospel to speak a transforming word to the culture, yet not impose a foreign culture upon it.

Seventh, the sublime Christ hymn of Colossians 1:15-20 reminds us that theology cannot be divorced from *doxology*. Paul communicates his most powerful response to the Colossian threat in the language of poetry, worship, and praise. As Richard Bauckham comments regarding the

---

57    Kevin J. Vanhoozer, "'One Rule to Rule Them All?' Theological Method in an Era of World Christianity," in *Globalizing Theology: Belief and Practice in an Era of World Christianity*, ed. Craig Ott and Harold A. Netland (Grand Rapids, MI.: Baker, 2006), 108-26.

58    On holistic contextualization, see A. Scott Moreau, "Contextualization That Is Comprehensive," *Missiology* 34, no. 3 (July 2006): 325-35.

book of Revelation, "the truth of God is known in genuine worship of God."[59] Paul uses doxology to give his readers an alternate vision of the way things are, in which Christ is supreme and the powers are exposed as weaklings. When God's people worship, they announce that all other powers and the idols of the dominant culture are dethroned. It is out of our worship of God, then, that our theological perspective must flow. Without this experience of celebration and worship, our theology might be contextual, but it may be far too flimsy to challenge the sinful powers of our world.

Finally, Colossians offers an instructive model for the church in its engagement with syncretism today. We do not have to look far to find analogies to the Colossian problem in many global contexts—places where established religions, animistic folk beliefs, and Christianity regularly share the same quarters. I recall an occasion when a grandmother in the Philippines, a professing Christian, was asked why she kept a spirit house behind her home to ward off evil spirits. Her reply: "I just want to make sure that all the bases are covered."

But the desire to "cover all the bases" is no stranger to the church in the West, as well. The growing influences of postmodern tolerance and religious pluralism have given birth to a greater openness to "mix and match" theologies—self-described born again Christians who also believe in reincarnation, for example. And syncretism hides under other masks, such as the "gospel" of consumerism and prosperity.

In reality, the lines between contextualization and syncretism are seldom easy to draw. The Spirit must help us learn to recognize when the gospel cannot be bent without breaking. Paul's penetrating challenge to any attempt to supplement the gospel stands in bold contrast to a contemporary spirit of flabby religious and moral tolerance. At the same time, Paul's approach to the Colossian syncretism reveals an artist's sensitivity, not a commander's heavy hand. He refuses to impose a pre-packaged, one-size-fits-all theology and praxis as a guard against syncretism, as sometimes happens today.

We can learn from this. Some well-meaning Christians are afraid that any attempt at contextualization will automatically water down the "pure" gospel and syncretize the message. Because some have altered the truth of the gospel in the name of relevance, they distrust the whole enterprise. But could it be that *refusing* to contextualize the gospel poses an even *greater* risk of syncretism?

Consider the situation today—not unlike that of Colossians—when the gospel meets worldviews that are burdened with the fear of unseen powers thought to control practical realities such as crops, health, and family relations. In many cases, the Christian message that has been imported to these contexts from the West has failed to address such issues. As a result, people can easily assume that Jesus is powerless to overcome the forces that influence their daily lives.[60] Like the Colossian syncretists, converts may look for supplements—shamans, amulets, rituals,

---

59    Richard Bauckham, *The Theology of the Book of Revelation* (Cambridge: Cambridge University Press, 1993), 162.

60    Hwa Yung, for example, asserts that a contextualized theology in Asia that does not address the issue of the spirit world risks being evangelistically impotent and pastorally irrelevant. Hwa Yung, *Mangoes or Bananas? The Quest for an Authentic Asian Christian Theology* (Oxford: Regnum Books International, 1997), 72-75.

or occult practices—to protect them from the hostile spirits. Ironically, a gospel that neglects such worldview issues may unwittingly end up promoting syncretism instead of preventing it.

In the end, however, the targeted gospel in Colossians does not focus on the threats to Christ's supremacy. Instead, Paul concentrates on lifting up Christ, in comparison to whom all human and cosmic powers wither. If we learn anything from Colossians, it is that our attempts at contextualization must be Christ-centered and Christ-exalting from beginning to end. Such a positive rearticulation of the gospel, whatever the century, leaves no legitimate reason to syncretize the faith.

## Discussion Questions

1. Can you think of other contextualization "case studies" in the Bible, besides those mentioned in this chapter?

2. The Colossian syncretism tried to "supplement" the gospel of Christ in order to make it more attractive and effective. In what ways do Christians sometimes try to provide "add-ons" to the gospel in your context today?

3. In Colossians, Paul drew on familiar metaphors from his world in order to portray the theological meaning of Christ's saving work on the cross. Are there images from your cultural and social world that might help people today to better understand Christ's saving work?

4. The chapter mentions four aspects of the gospel's engagement with culture: affirming, relativizing, confronting, and transforming. Which of these do you think is most needed in your ministry setting, and why?

5. Reflect on the statement: "In reality, the lines between contextualization and syncretism are seldom easy to draw." Can you think of specific examples in which this might be true in your setting?

# 2

# What Shall We Name God?

## *Youssouf Dembele*

*Youssouf Dembele has been a Bible translation consultant with the United Bible Societies since 2001. He is based in Bamako, Mali, his native country. He started a new church in December 2002 that currently counts 170–200 attendees. Since 2003, he has been the chairman of the National Council of the Evangelical Protestant Church of Mali, the second largest Church denomination, with 160 pastors and national missionaries. In his spare time, he teaches Systematic Theology at La Faculté de Théologie et de Missiologie Evangéliques au Sahel (FATMES) in Bamako. He is interested in the translation of the Bible into African languages and teaching theology in national languages. Education: Engineering (Cuba and Mali), ThM (Faculté Libre de Théologie Évangélique), PhD in Biblical and Systematic Theology (Trinity International University), Studies in Linguistics at GIAL (Dallas, USA). He also contributed to the African Commentary of the Bible.*

## Introduction

A name is not a mere label; it says something about the real personality of its bearer. This is true about the God of the Bible. The Bible stresses the importance of God's name.  The pious call on the name or call upon the name of the Lord in Gen. 4:26; 12:8; 13:4; 21:33. We read that Moses was not content to tell the Israelites: "The God of your fathers has sent me to you;" he wanted to specifically answer the Israelites when they asked, "What is his name?" (Ex.3:13). God's answer to Moses validated his question: "Say to the Israelites, 'The Lord, the God of your fathers—the God of Abraham, the God of Isaac and the God of Jacob—has sent me to you.' This is my name forever, the name by which I am to be remembered from generation to generation" (Ex. 3:15). Later, God explained his purpose in raising up Pharaoh: that "my name might be proclaimed in all the earth" (Ex. 9:16). The commandments also emphasize the importance of God's name—the third commandment forbids misusing the name of the

Lord: "You shall not misuse the name of the Lord your God, for the Lord will not hold anyone guiltless who misuses his name" (Ex. 20:7). And positively, the Bible tells us that, "Everyone who calls on the name of the Lord will be saved" (Joel 2:32; Acts 2:21; Rom. 10:13). Since the name of God is so important, how do we name God in languages other than the original language of revelation?

The Bible asserts that in the beginning, "the whole world had one language (*šāphāh 'ehad*) and a common speech (*dhᵉbhārîm 'ahādhîm*)' (Gen. 11:1). Sin entered the world through Adam and Eve and thwarted God's plan. God responded by confusing the languages of the people (Gen. 11: 6-9). This response was both a divine act of judgment against and a divine measure of grace in favor of the human race. Humankind moved from monolingualism to multilingualism and, as a result, the one Creator came to be called by diverse names.

Sin afflicted humankind with "madness, blindness and confusion of mind" (Deut. 28:28). A shroud enfolded all peoples, and a sheet covered all nations (Is. 25:7). Human beings became godless and wicked. "Although they knew God, they neither glorified him as God nor gave thanks to him, but their thinking became futile and their foolish hearts were darkened. Although they claimed to be wise, they became fools and exchanged the glory of the immortal God for images made to look like mortal man and birds and animals and reptiles" (Rom. 1:18-23). Consequently, false creator-gods proliferated among the cultures of the world.

In this context of multilingualism and polytheism, the Lord wants the good news of salvation to be proclaimed to all nations: "And this gospel of the kingdom will be preached in the whole world as a testimony to all nations, and then the end will come" (Mt. 24:14). The fulfillment of this commission requires translation as its major condition of possibility. An important aspect of the translation of the gospel is the translation of divine names. How do we name the God of Abraham in the target culture? Do we maintain and transliterate the Hebrew names, *YHWH*, *'Ēl*, and *'Ēlōhîm*, at the risk of presenting the God of the Bible as a foreign God with whom the target culture cannot relate? Do we coin new names for God? Or do we adopt names that are already used for the divinities in the target culture? How legitimate is it to use the "creator-god" of these cultures to explain the God of Abraham, Isaac, and Jacob? What about the other connotations of this "creator-god"? Peripherally connected is the difficult question: Do Christians and Muslims worship the same God? How legitimate is it to use "Allah" to explain the God of Abraham, Isaac, and Jacob in the Muslim context?

This work aims at answering these questions and at proposing a methodology that can serve as a guideline to using the name of the "creator-god" of another culture to explain the God of Abraham, Isaac, and Jacob. It posits that Scripture itself offers models of contextualization to follow while taking into account the specificities of each local context. The first step, therefore, is to explore the legitimacy of using the "creator-god" of other cultures to explain the God of Abraham, Isaac, and Jacob. The next is to explore the legitimacy of specifically using the name "Allah" to explain the God of the Bible. Finally, a methodology is offered to guide the use of another culture's creator-god name to render the God of Abraham, Isaac, and Jacob.

# The Legitimacy of Using the "Creator-God" of Non-Biblical Cultures to Explain the God of Abraham, Isaac, and Jacob

Lamin Sanneh, professor of Missions and World Christianity at Yale University, notes that translation is "the characteristic mode of Christian expansion through history" and an important principle in Christian mission.[1] This important principle applies to the naming of God in other cultures. We must define the criteria that serve as touchstones to the legitimacy of such a use. We posit that it will be legitimate to use the creator-god of non-biblical cultures to explain the God of Abraham, Isaac, and Jacob if we have examples of that practice in the Bible itself, if that creator-god enjoys some theological neutrality or shares enough commonalties with the God of Abraham, and if we can demonstrate biblically that God clearly approves such a move.

## The Practices of the Bible

What do we find in the Bible about names we use for God? Foundationally, the Bible strongly asserts the unity of God (Deut. 6:4; Isa. 45:22; 1 Cor. 8:4). The apostle Paul confesses: "For even if there are so-called gods, whether in heaven or on earth (as indeed there are many 'gods' and many 'lords'), yet for us there is but one God, the Father, from whom all things came and for whom we live; and there is but one Lord, Jesus Christ, through whom all things came and through whom we live" (1 Cor. 8:5-6). To the unique Creator, the Tanakh assigns several Hebrew names: *'Ēl, 'Ēlōhîm, YHWH*, borrowed from other cultures. The Tanakh became the Septuagint (LXX) through translation from Hebrew to Greek without ceasing to be Holy Scripture. The New Testament, written in Greek, quotes either the Tanakh or the LXX, and how the New Testament writers use this translation gives us a model to follow.

### The Hebrew Bible

One of the major creator-gods of the period of the patriarchs is *'Ēl*, a deity of the Ugaritic pantheon. To Frank Cross, Hancock Professor of Hebrew and Other Oriental Languages, Emeritus, at Harvard University, *'Ēl* is father and creator.[2] He is creator of earth. He is eternal, ageless, the ancient one. His decree is wise and his wisdom eternal. He is king father of years. *'Ēl* is merciful, benign, kind, and compassionate. He has two wives and two sons, Dawn and Dusk. He is the primordial procreator and patriarch, the primordial father of gods and men. He hunts and feasts. *'Ēl* behaves as a divine warrior. He is *'Ēl* the Warrior (*'Ēl Gibbōr*). He is a mighty man of war. "'The particular wars of El are to establish his headship in the family of the gods. His wars are against his father Shamēm, Heaven, in behalf of his wronged mother' Arts, Earth."[3]

In the Tanakh, the same word *'Ēl* came to be used for the name of the God of Abraham, Isaac, and Jacob. YHWH, whose name Abraham calls upon, is *'Ēl 'ōlām* (the Eternal God; Gen.

---

1    Lamin Sanneh, "Domesticating the Transcendent. The African Transformation of Christianity: Comparative Reflections of Ethnicity and Religious Mobilization in Africa," A. Brenner and J W. van Henten, ed. *Bible Translation on the Threshold of the Twenty-First Century, Authority, Reception, Culture and Religion* (Sheffield, UK: Sheffield Academic Press, 2002), 71- 85.

2    Frank M Cross, "*'Ēl,*" in *Theological Dictionary of the Old Testament*, ed. J. Botterweck and H. Ringgren, trans. J. T. Willis, vol. I, revised edition (Grand Rapids, MI: Eerdmans, 1974),  242-261.

3    Ibid., 251.

21:33). Jacob set up an altar in the city of Shechem in Canaan and called it *El Elohe Israel* (Gen. 33:20). In this context, *'Ēl* appears as a quasi proper name and the phrase "*Elohe Israel*" seems to be used adversatively to oppose *El Elohe Israel* to *El Elohe Canaan*. God himself declared to Jacob: "I am the God (*'Ēl*) of Bethel" (Gen. 31:13). At Beersheba, Jacob offered sacrifices to the God (*'Ēlōhîm*) of his father Isaac. God answered Jacob and declined anew his own identity: "I am God (*'Ēl*), the God (*'Ēlōhîm*) of your father" (Gen. 46:2-3). *'Ēl* is combined with other names to form new appellatives: *'Ēl 'Ēlōhê hārûchôth* (God, God of the spirits; Num. 16:22); *'Ēl 'Ēlōhîm YHWH* (God, God the Lord; Josh. 22:22; Ps. 50:1).

The Bible recognizes the existence of things that some people call gods: *'Ēl* or *'Ēlōhîm* (Exod. 34:14; Ps. 2, 46, 48:7, 76; Jer. 25:15-38). Yet it asserts that God is one and Yahweh is the only God (Gen. 17:1; Deut. 6:4; Isa. 45:22; Zech. 14:9). Yahweh authoritatively declares: "I am God (*'Ēl*), and there is no other" (Isa. 45:22). Thus, we can assert that other beings are called "god" only by usurpation. The wide overlap in attributes, epithets, and names of the God of Abraham, Isaac, and Jacob with *'Ēl* explain the use of the latter as an appropriate equivalent of the former. However, the striking differences between the understanding of *'Ēl* in the surrounding cultures of Israel and the biblical concept of God, shows that in the Bible, *'Ēl* has been pruned of its negative connotations. The use of the creator-god of other cultures to render the God of the Bible is, therefore, legitimate when this creator-god shares enough commonalities with the God of the Bible and when it is possible to rid it of its dross without making it meaningless.

### The Septuagint

The Septuagint is the first translation of the Hebrew Tanakh into popular Greek, made before the Christian era. It was the Scripture of the early church. How does the Septuagint render the divine names of the Hebrew Bible? It does so in different ways. The translators of the Septuagint use *theos* to render any of the Hebrew names of the God of Abraham, Isaac, and Jacob. Lord God (*YHWH 'Ēlōhîm*) is rendered as *theos* (Gen. 2:4, 5) or as *Kurios ho theos* (Lord God).

What are the characteristic traits, that is, the distinguishing qualities of *theos* in ancient literature? How do they differ from the traits of *theos* in the Bible? The Greeks apply *theos* not only to a plurality of personal divine beings, but also to human beings, impersonal objects, and even to abstract concepts.[4] In using *theos* to explain the God of the Bible, the translators of the Septuagint apply to this name the traits of the God of the Bible. Their goal was not to change the concept of God in the Bible, but to transmit the biblical concept of God to Greek speaking audiences, using the name for God they already knew. The sacred writers of the New Testament quote the Greek translation of the Tanakh. This endorsement of the Greek version authorizes us to imitate the way the Septuagint rendered the divine names.

### The New Testament

The New Testament reports that at Pentecost, the disciples "were filled with the Holy Spirit and began to speak in other tongues as the Spirit enabled them. . . A crowd came together in bewilderment, because each one heard them speaking in his own language." All the people

---

4    P. W. van der Horst, "God (II)," in *Dictionary of Deities and Demons in the Bible*, second ed., edited by K. van der Toorn, B. Becking, and P. W. van der Horst (Leiden: Brill, 1999), 365.

gathered there could hear the wonders of God in their own language (Acts 2: 2-6, 11). It is fair to infer from this text that the people heard at the same time the name of God in their own language. This event attests that "Babel was not to be God's final and fateful verdict on the human race."[5] It points to God's approval for translation of the good news of salvation and thereby of his name in other languages.

The practices of the writers of the New Testament corroborate this conviction. The use of Old Testament Scripture within the New show how the sacred authors deal with the divine names. Matthew 1:23 quotes Isaiah 7:14, and translates the name "*Immanuël*" as "God (*Theos*) with us." *Theos* appears as the equivalent of *'Ēl*. In Matthew 4:4, "*pî YHWH*" (the mouth of the Lord; Deut. 8:3) is rendered by "*stomatos theou*" (the mouth of God) so that "Theos" is used as the equivalent of "YHWH." One notices with surprise that *YHWH*, the only proper name of the God of Abraham, is neither borrowed, transcribed, nor transliterated in the New Testament. It is simply rendered with Kurios, as evidenced in the quotation of Joel 3:5 ("And everyone who calls on the name of the Lord (*YHWH*) will be saved") in Acts 2:21 and Rom. 10:13 ("And everyone who calls on the name of the Lord (*Kurios*) will be saved"). The inspired authors of the New Testament did not use Hebrew names to explain the God of Abraham to their reader. They rather used the names that were already known in the Greek world: *Theos* and *Kurios*.

In spite of the change of name from one language to the other, the New Testament makes it clear that God is the same through the two testaments. Thus, Jesus quotes Exod. 3:6 "I am the God of Abraham, the God of Isaac, and the God of Jacob" to buttress his case that there will be a resurrection of the dead (Matt. 22:32). The first and greatest commandment in both testaments remains: "Love the Lord your God with all your heart and with all your soul and with all your mind" (Deut. 6:5; Matt. 22:37). It is the "God of Abraham, Isaac and Jacob, the God of our fathers" who displayed his power in the healing of the crippled beggar to glorify his servant Jesus (Acts 3:13). The authors of the New Testament clearly posit that the God (*Theos*) they are worshipping is the Creator of all things when they pray: "'Sovereign Lord (*Despotēs*),' they said, 'you made the heaven and the earth and the sea, and everything in them. You spoke by the Holy Spirit through the mouth of your servant, our father David'" (Acts 4:24-25a).

In Athens, the apostle Paul shows another way to use the God of the target culture to explain the God of Abraham. The Athenians worshipped many gods to whom they could assign attributes, functions, relations, and some kinds of adoration. To be sure that no god was left out, they dedicated an altar to the "unknown God," that is, the God for whom they do not know the attributes, functions, and relations. Paul started his proclamation of the good news by declaring that the "unknown God" (*'Agnōstō Theō*; Acts 17:23) of the Athenians is the very God he proclaims to them. This *'Agnostos Theos* is the God who made the world and everything in it. He is the Lord of heaven and earth and does not live in temples built by hands (Acts 17:24). The "unknown God" (*'agnōstos Theos*) of the Athenians was theologically neutral enough to be invested with all the traits of the God of Abraham, Isaac, and Jacob. When there are many

---

5    Glen G. Scorgie, "Introduction and Overview," in *The Challenge of Bible Translation: Communicating God's Word to the World*, edited by Glen G. Scorgie, Mark L. Strauss, Steven M. Voth (Grand Rapids, MI: Zondervan, 2003), 21.

creator-gods in a culture, the most theologically neutral should be preferred as a means of explaining the God of the Bible.

These practices of the New Testament legitimize the use of the creator-god of the target culture to explain the God of Abraham, Isaac, and Jacob.

## Other Creator-Gods and the God of Abraham, Isaac, and Jacob

The name of the creator-god that is being used for translation of the God of Abraham, Isaac, and Jacob should share essential characteristic traits.

### The God of Abraham, Isaac, and Jacob is a Creator-God

The Tanakh strongly asserts in its opening that "the heavens and the earth, the sea, and all that is in them" are the products of a creative act (Gen. 1:1; Ex. 20:11). The creator is named "God" (*'Ělōhîm*, Gen. 1:1) or YHWH (Ex. 20:11). Adam and Eve knew God as their Creator and as the sole Creator of the universe (Gen. 1-3; 2:18-24). The Tanakh uses four main verbs to depict his creatorship: to create (*bārāh*), to make (*'āśāh*), to fashion (*yātsar*), and to found (*kûn*). These four verbs are gathered in one single verse in Isaiah 45:18: "For this is what the Lord (*YHWH*) says—he who created (*bārāh*) the heavens, he is God; he who fashioned (*yātsar*) and made (*'āśāh*) the earth, he founded (*kûn*) it; he did not create (*bārāh*) it to be empty, but formed (*bārāh*) it to be inhabited—he says: "I am the Lord, and there is no other" (NIV 1984). The same verse serves to establish that the words "Lord" (*YHWH*) and "God" are used to refer to the same referent, the one who created the heavens, formed, made, and established the earth.

The Lord (*YHWH*) reveals himself to the prophet Isaiah as Creator: "I am the Lord, who has made all things, who alone stretched out the heavens, who spread out the earth by myself" (Isa. 44:24b). Along the same lines, the prophet Jeremiah declares: "He who is the Portion of Jacob is not like these, for he is the Maker of all things, including Israel, the tribe of his inheritance—the Lord Almighty is his name" (Jer. 10:16; 51:19). Melchizedek blesses Abram by *'Ēl 'Elyōn*, Creator (*qōneh*) of heaven and earth (Gen.14:19). Abram identifies *'Ēl 'Elyōn* with YHWH: "I have raised my hand to the Lord (*YHWH*), God Most High (*'Ēl 'Elyōn*), Creator (*qōneh*) of heaven and earth" (Gen. 14:22). The creatorship of Yahweh "provides the means by which faith in Yahweh could be linked as a fulfillment of the promise to the Fathers who did not yet know God by this name (Ex. 6:2f.)."[6] In Israel's hymns, God is praised as creator of the world (Ps. 8; 136; 148) and of his people (Ps. 100).[7] Some texts establish a link between God's fatherhood and creatorship (Deut. 32:6; Mal. 2:10).

The authors of the New Testament take for granted the Old Testament's understanding of God as Creator and Father. They recognize: "For from him and through him and to him are all things" (Rom. 11:36; Heb. 2:10). They understand that "our Lord (Kurios) and God (Theos) is he who "created all things" (Eph. 3:9; Rev. 4:11). The Creator of all things is "Lord of heaven and earth" (Matt. 11:25). Because the God of the Bible is the Creator of "all things" and the

---

6    Brevard Childs, *Biblical Theology of the Old and New Testaments*, (Minneapolis, MN: Fortress Press, 1993), 110.

7    Ibid., 113.

"Lord of heaven and earth," he can commit "all things" to the Son (Luke 10:22; John 13:3). The apostle Paul confesses: "yet for us there is but one God, the Father, from whom all things came and for whom we live" (1 Cor. 8:6). He moves on to incorporate Jesus in the creative activity of God.[8] Jesus is understood as the Word (*logos*) who was in the beginning with God (*Theos*), who was God (*Theos*). "Through him all things were made; without him nothing was made that has been made. In him was life, and that life was the light of men" (John 1:1-2). Similarly, Paul strongly asserts: "For by him all things were created: things in heaven and on earth, visible and invisible, whether thrones or powers or rulers or authorities; all things were created by him and for him. He is before all things, and in him all things hold together" (Col. 1:16-17).

The God of Abraham was the Creator. The commonality of functions serves as the basis for using the creator-god of other cultures to explain him. Yet fatherhood is a constitutive trait[9] of the God of Abraham, Isaac, and Jacob; therefore, it will be inadequate to use a creator-goddess to explain him.

### The Unique Creator-God Revealed Himself to All Cultures

The God of Abraham revealed himself to all cultures. This self-revelation began with Adam and Eve. A careful reading of Genesis 2-3 convinces that Adam and Eve did not know God only through his creation, but through his self-communication to them. God spoke with them and cared for them. They could hear and understand God's communication to them. Their sons, Cain and Able were subsequently taught to serve only the true God. Cain brought some of the "fruits of the soil as an offering to the Lord and Abel, fat portions from some of the firstborn of his flock" (Gen. 4:3-4). From this family, God made every nation in order that they would seek him, as the apostle Paul writes: "The God who made the world and everything in it is the Lord of heaven and earth and does not live in temples built by hands. And he is not served by human hands, as if he needed anything, because he himself gives all men life and breath and everything else. From one man he made every nation of men, that they should inhabit the whole earth; and he determined the times set for them and the exact places where they should live. God did this so that men would seek him and perhaps reach out for him and find him, though he is not far from each one of us" (Acts 17:24-27).

"What may be known about God is plain" to the people of other cultures because God has made it plain to them (Rom. 1:19). They are without excuse, for since the creation of the world God's invisible qualities—his eternal power and divine nature—have been clearly seen, being understood from what has been made (Rom. 1:20). Yet, though God revealed himself to all cultures, their understanding of him has been distorted. Paul continues: "For although they knew God, they neither glorified him as God nor gave thanks to him, but their thinking became futile and their foolish hearts were darkened. Although they claimed to be wise, they became fools and exchanged the glory of the immortal God for images made to look like mortal man and birds and animals and reptiles" (Rom. 1:21-23).

---

8    Ibid,, 391.
9    Fatherhood is an attribute of the being of God. See chapter 3 by Blomberg in this volume.

The God of Abraham, Isaac, and Jacob is the unique Creator-God who revealed himself to each culture. Consequently, many cultures of the world make room for the existence of a creator-god who created everything. It is fair to say that the creator-god of these cultures has no other referent but the God of the Bible. Comparative studies of the creator-god or creator-gods and the God of the Bible have revealed both striking commonalities and shocking differences. In some cultures, the unique-creator, whose name varies through time and space, created everything, that is, not only all that exists in heaven and on earth, but also heaven and earth. Nothing comes to being without the Creator. The Creator is of matchless goodness through his creating. In many cultures, the creator-god is so distorted that he is barely recognizable. "In Egypt, the role of Creator of everything is attributed to several gods."[10] In most cultures, a direct and intimate relationship between human beings and the creator-god is lacking, making the mediatorship of Jesus Christ indispensable.

## Legitimacy from Practical Efficiency

Christ did not send his followers to translate the Bible, but to evangelize all nations of the world. Yet, the missionaries understood that the reception of the message was contingent upon a clear hearing and understanding. Evangelism and Christian nurturing were the main causes of the missionaries' active promotion of Bible translation into vernacular languages. An important aspect of this task was finding the appropriate way of naming the God of Abraham, Isaac, and Jacob in the vernacular language so that the native people could hear God speaking to them and respond to him in their own language and culture and to express this response in their way of life, ritual and celebration, in their spiritual and theological reflection.

In some rare cases, the choice of the local name for God has tended to hinder evangelism and the people's response to the Good News. The people have wondered how the missionary could learn from them the true name for God and then turn around to teach them again about God. Elsewhere, some intellectuals are very convinced that the Creator-God of their cultures and the God of the Bible are the same. They wonder why they should resort to the mediatorship of the Nazarean if the God who reveals himself in their cultures is the Universal, Unique, True God, Creator of heaven and earth, Owner of life, of death and of the universe.[11]

Part of the reason for this dilemma is that for many cultures, this single originator is less an ever-present religious reality than a remote reality. Amadou Hampte Bâ, Malian scholar, confirms that in the majority of cases, the Supreme Being is considered too far away from men for them to worship him directly. Between the Creator and man, there exist intermediary agents, which govern the happiness and misfortune of men. To these agents the people address ritual words, more incantations than prayers, and propitiatory offerings intended to appease them when they fly into a rage.[12]

---

10    M. C. A. Korpel, "Creator of All," in *Dictionary of Deities and Demons in the Bible,* second edition, edited by K. van der Toorn, B. Becking and P. W. van der Horst (Leiden: Brill, 1999): 208.

11    Mudimbe quoted in Kalamba, *Révélation du Créateur.* [In http://www.webzinemaker.com/admi/m7/page.php3?num_web=11006&rubr=4&id=59553.]

12    Amadou Hampate Bâ, *Aspects of African Civilization,* 1972. In [http://pender.ee.upenn.edu/~rabii/toes/BaAspectsCh1.html].

In general, however, the use of the creator-god already known has been a facilitating factor for evangelism and church planting. The Western Bible translators did not coin new words for God in English, French, German or Spanish. They used the names *God*, *Dieu*, *Gott*, and *Dios* that were already available in the language. Similarly, the missionaries who came to Africa used the names of the God who was and is already known by African peoples—such as Ama, Mungu, Mulungu, Katonda, Ngai, Olodumare, Asis, Ruwa, Ruhanga, Jok, Modimo, Unkulunkulu and thousands more. These were not empty names. Independently of the question whether these names were those of the One and the same God, the Creator of the world, the Father of our Lord Jesus Christ, they were invested with new meanings drawn from the Bible so that today, nobody questions the legitimacy of their being used to explain the God of Abraham, Isaac, and Jacob. Through this translation effort, Christianity ceased to be a foreign religion in order to become a native experience. "Jesus of Nazareth was a man accredited by God (*Theos*) to you by miracles, wonders and signs, which God (*Theos*) did among you through him, as you yourselves know" (Acts 2:22). Similarly, we may see God's sanction for the use of the creator-god of other cultures to explain the God of Abraham, Isaac, and Jacob in the success of evangelism and church planting, the transformation of the believers' lives, and in the answering of their many prayers.

## The Legitimacy of Using Allah to Explain the God of Abraham, Isaac, and Jacob

How is it legitimate to use "Allah" to explain the God of Abraham, Isaac, and Jacob? Do Christians and Muslims worship the same God? The second question came to the fore in late 2003 following a remark of President Bush that he believed Muslims and Christians "worship the same God." The remark sparked criticism from some Christians, who thought Bush was being politically correct, but theologically inaccurate. Ted and Winnie Brock asked several scholars to consider the question. Here we focus on the legitimacy of using "Allah" to explain the God of the Bible, but in doing so, we will contribute to the answer of the second question.

The use of Allah to explain the God of Abraham is a particular instance of the use of a culture's creator-god. The legitimacy of rendering the God of Abraham with Allah can be buttressed on several accounts: philological, historical, theological, missiological, and practical.[13]

### Philological and Historical Legitimacy

Allah is not a Muslim God. Islam did not coin the word "Allah." "Allah" is a Semitic word parallel to the Hebrew "*'Ēl*," referring to the highest god, creator of all that is. Hebrew and Arabic are cognate languages (same Semitic origin, with Aramaic between Hebrew and Arabic), with many words in common, not to mention wide cultural overlap. The Arabic "Allah" comes from the same root as the biblical "God" (*'Ēlōhîm*, *'Ēl*, *'Ēlōah*) invoked by the Hebrew prophets.

---

13    It is necessary to distinguish between legitimacy and appropriateness. The legitimacy of using Allah implies that it is acceptable to use Allah for the God of the Bible in contexts influenced by the Arabic langue on philological, historical, theological, missiological, and practical grounds. Yet, in practice, it may not be appropriate to do so in some contexts on other grounds.

Like *'Ělōhîm* and *'Ēl*, "Allah" can be used to refer to the one creator of the universe or to other objects of worship (Qur'an 26:29: an *ilah* (a god); Qur'an 16:51: *ilâhaîn* (two gods).

Historically, we have identified our "object of worship" as the God of Abraham. No Christian contests that Christians and Jews worship the same God, the God of Abraham, Isaac, and Jacob. Since Arabs and Jews share the same ancestor Abraham, it is important to ask: Did Abraham and Ishmael worship the same God? Did Ishmael and his younger brother Isaac worship the same God? A scrutiny of the Scriptures allows an affirmative answer to these questions. The angel of the Lord the God of Abraham gave Ishmael's name. The final "*'ēl*" in the name of "Ishmael" signifies the God of Abraham, and it is the "*'Ēl* of Abraham" who heard Hagar and saw her misery (Gen. 16:11). The name "Ishmael" is used among the Israelites (2 Kings 25:23; 1 Chron. 9:44; 2 Chron. 9:11). The God of Abraham heard Hagar and promised to bless Ishmael, to make him fruitful, and to greatly increase his numbers (Gen. 17:20; 21:13). Abraham and his son Ishmael were both circumcised on the same day to fulfill the command of the God of Abraham (Gen. 17:26). The third son of Ishmael is named Adbeel which means: "chastened of God" (Gen. 25:13). This is clear evidence of Ishmael's faith in "*'Ēl*," the God of Abraham and Hagar.

We conclude that, historically, Arabs and Jews shared the same ancestor, the same language, and the same God. The evolution of the same language led to a multiplicity of names for the same referent. "Allah" is the only Arabic word for this unique referent. From his status of "The Only God," Allah fell into that of "the highest god" among other gods of the pre-Islamic shrine at Mecca. Thus, the Qur'an mentions Arabian monotheists by the name of *hanif*, and Muhammad claims them as precursors of Islam. When Muhammad finally marched triumphantly into Mecca, he cleansed the pagan shrine of all other deities and dedicated it solely to the One True God, Allah. But before Muhammad, Arab Christians had been using "Allah" to explain the God of the Bible, and they continue to do so today. Christianity and Islam both made use of a word for God that was already available in Arab culture and religion. "Allah" is not different from the creator-god of another culture as to its ability to explain the God of Abraham.

## Allah in the Qur'an and the Claims from Muslims

Who is Allah in the Qur'an? What do Muslims claim concerning the relationship between Allah and the God of Abraham? Muslims confess that there is only one God and that there is no other God but Allah. "And your *Ilâh* (God) is One *Ilâh* (God - Allâh), *Lâ ilâha illa Huwa* (there is none who has the right to be worshipped but He), the Most Beneficent, the Most Merciful" (Qur'an 2:163; 7:59-85). This Muslim confession follows and imitates older confessions that are in the Bible: "Hear, O Israel: The Lord our God, the Lord is one" (Deut 6:4). "Now this is eternal life: that they may know you, the only true God, and Jesus Christ, whom you have sent" (John 17:3). Or "yet for us there is but one God, the Father, from whom all things came and for whom we live" (1 Cor 8:6). Christians and Muslims claim to worship the one God.

The attributes of the God the Muslims invoke show great similarities with the attributes of the God of the Bible. Both Christians and Muslims view God as absolutely sovereign, omnipotent, omniscient, omnipresent, holy, just, and righteous. Both Islam and Christianity believe in the one God who is the Creator of everything in the universe. The Qur'an, in many passages, gives witness to the Supreme God, creator of the heavens and the earth, the God of Adam, Abraham, Ishmael, Isaac, Jacob, David, and other biblical figures as well. It affirms that Allah is One (Qur'an 112:1). Allah is Creator of the heavens and the earth. He is transcendent above his creation. He is All-Hearer and All-See-er (Qur'an 42:11). The Qur'an expresses Allah's immanence by saying that he is nearer to a man than his jugular vein (Qur'an 50:16). Allah has the ability to do anything (Qur'an 2:106). He is enemy of those who deny the truth (Qur'an 2:98). Good and evil are from Him (Qur'an 4:78). He grants life and death (Qur'an 44:8, 53:44). He has no son (Qur'an 43:81, 72:3). He is everywhere (Qur'an 2:115). He is All-knowing (Qur'an 2:115). He is the First and the Last, the Most High and the Most Near. And He is the All-Knower of everything (Qur'an 57:3). He loves those who behave equitably (Qur'an 49:9).

The Qur'an and Muslims claim that Jews, Christians, and Muslims share the one and the same God. When the Qur'an speaks of God, it means the One Creator-God of the Bible, the God of Abraham, Ishmael, Isaac and Jacob. According to the Qur'an when death approached Ya'qûb (Jacob) he said unto his sons: "'What will you worship after me?' They said, 'We shall worship your *Ilâh* (God - Allâh), the *Ilâh* (God) of your fathers, Ibrâhim (Abraham), Ismâ'il (Ishmael), Ishâque (Isaac), One *Ilâh* (God), and to Him we submit (in Islâm)'" (Qur'an 2:133). The Qur'an continues: "Say (O Muslims), 'We believe in Allâh and that which has been sent down to us and that which has been sent down to Ibrâhim (Abraham), Ismâ'il (Ishmael), Ishâque (Isaac), Ya'qûb (Jacob), and to *Al-Asbât* [the twelve sons of Ya'qûb (Jacob)], and that which has been given to Mûsa (Moses) and 'Iesa (Jesus), and that which has been given to the Prophets from their Lord. We make no distinction between any of them, and to Him we have submitted (in Islâm)'" (Qur'an 2:136). This last verse proves convincingly that Allah has the same referent as YHWH and *'Ĕlōhîm*. Muhammad claimed that his Lord has guided him to a Straight Path, a right religion, the religion of Ibrâhim (Abraham), *Hanifa* (Qur'an 6:161/162). To the Jews and Christians the Qur'an says, "We believe in the revelation that has come down to us and that which came down to you; our God and your God are One, and it is to Him that we bow" (Qur'an 29:46).

Miles notes that "Muslims battled those who worshipped false gods, beginning with the Arab polytheists of Mecca and Medina, but they officially tolerated Jews and Christians because they understood the latter to be worshiping the one true God, the God or, in Arabic, Allah."[14] Levenson is certainly right to argue that since monotheism means that there is only one God, no monotheist can ever accuse anyone of worshiping another god, only of improperly identifying the one God that both seek to serve. The charge that the two other traditions have seriously misidentified the God of Abraham is not necessarily the same as the claim that they worship another god.[15] Along these lines, Woodberry wants to distinguish between the Being to whom we refer and what we understand about the character and actions of that Being in the two

---

14    Jack Miles, *God: A Biography,* quoted in Steven Waldman, "Do Muslims and Christians Worship the Same God?", posted Dec. 17, 2003 on http://slate.msn.com/id/2092762/.

15    Jon D. Levenson, "Do Christians and Muslims Worship the Same God? Part One," in *The Christian Century,* (April 20, 2004): 32-33 [http://www.religion-online.org/showarticle.asp?title=3052].

faiths.[16] He concludes: "As monotheists we both refer to the One and only Creator-God, but what we understand about the character and actions of God are significantly different."

In spite of deep differences, the similarities between the Muslim understanding of Allah and the Christian understanding of the God of Abraham legitimize the use of Allah to explain the God of Abraham. The content of the term Allah stands in need of some corrections and enrichment on the basis of a sound interpretation of the Bible.

### Missiological and Practical Legitimacy

From the assertion that Allah is the God of Abraham, some scholars conclude that both religions are correct and, therefore, Christians should not try to convert Muslims, and that the mediatorship of Christ is unnecessary to access to God. These conclusions are in sharp contradiction with several biblical declarations: "Now this is eternal life: that they may know you, the only true God, and Jesus Christ, whom you have sent" (John 17:3). "Jesus answered, 'I am the way and the truth and the life. No one comes to the Father except through me'" (John 14:6). "For there is one God and one mediator between God and men, the man Christ Jesus" (1 Tim. 2:5).

Starting with "Allah", Christians communicate the Good News of salvation through Jesus Christ (Isa al-Massih) to the Muslims in the hope that many of them may be saved. This is neither waste of time nor rude. The question is not whether Christians and Muslims are talking about or worshipping the same God, but rather redefining who is the God they all claim to worship and how do they enter into a saving relationship with him. Arabic translations of the Bible use "Allah" for the Greek "*ho Theos*," meaning that Arab Christians read their Bible with Allah, address their prayers to Allah, and receive answers to their prayers from Allah. The use of Allah to render the God of Abraham serves as a bridge to facilitate communication and mutual understanding between Christians and Muslims and the growth of the church among Muslims is the best argument in favor of this method.

Using Allah to explain the God of Abraham does not require a total equivalence between the two concepts. Though the Qur'an flatly rejects the notion of the Triune God, and even rejects that God has a Son (Sura 4:157, 171; 112:2-3), this assertion took place long after prior Arab Christians confessed Allah as the Triune God. The rejection by some Christians of the notion of a Triune God does not require changing the name "God." Likewise, the Muslim rejection of some constitutive traits of Allah does not negate using this translation. It is the missiological task of the church to bring truth to the name used.

## Methodology

If we assert the legitimacy of using the creator-god of other cultures to explain the God of Abraham, we also recognize that no creator-god, including Allah, is a perfect match of *YHWH*. We need to deal with the limitations and connotations inherent to the use of the creator-god of those cultures. How do we exploit the advantages of using the creator-god of other cultures

---

16    Dudley J. Woodberry, "Do Christians and Muslims Worship the Same God? Part Three," *The Christian Century*, (May 18, 2004): 36-37.

to explain the God of the Bible and at the same time avoid its biblically negative connotations? We propose to develop a methodology which can be used as a guide explaining and translating the name of the God of the Bible.[17]

## Study of the Concept of Creator-God in the Target Culture

The first step is a thorough study of the concept of the creator-god in that culture. This study aims at understanding the nature, names, attributes, functions, and relations of the target culture's creator-god within its worldview. The differing functions of the term may create a hindrance to the reader's understanding, and we need to be sure that the creator-god of the target culture ultimately fits properly in the biblical worldview. Thomas notes the role of language in the self-understanding of religious communities and their relationships with one another as a particularly critical issue.[18] The study also should ensures that the use of the creator-god of the target culture to explain the God of the Bible will not be objected to by the followers of the traditional religion as a usurpation of their distinctive name or by Christians as being syncretistic and/or a threat to their identity. The study enables one to draw out the similarities and dissimilarities between the culture's deity and the biblical concept of God. An important aspect of the process is the determination of the social and symbolic significance of the creator-god to both Christians and non-Christians in the target culture. This will avoid using a name that is considered the exclusive term of a specific group.

## Basic Translation Principles

A major issue in explaining and rendering God in another language is avoiding both accommodation and foreignization. In the former case, the God of the Bible appears as one of the gods of the local pantheon, meaning there would be no need to become Christian since the people of the culture are already following that god. In the latter, he is a totally foreign God with whom the people have nothing to do. We should maintain four basic principles:

1. The creator-god of the target culture must be culturally relevant and recognized by the whole Christian community as a legitimate equivalent of the God of the Bible and thus be a basis for the unity of the church;

2. The use of the creator-god must be acceptable to both Christians and non-Christians, serving as a bridge for understanding, dialogue and witness between Christians and non-Christians of the target community.

3. The concept of the creator-god of the target culture should be theologically adequate to communicate the biblical concept of God. It must share essential similarities with the God of the Bible so that it is possible to prune it of its negative or anti-biblical connotations and to enrich it with new biblical content to become the full equivalent of the biblical concept of God.

---

17    I will follow here the model of Kenneth Thomas, "The Use of Arabic Terminology in Biblical Translation," in *The Bible Translator: Technical Papers*, Vol. 40, No. 1 (January 1989): 101-108.

18    Ibid., 101-108.

4. The use of the creator-God of the target culture should prove to be missiologically and liturgically efficient (practical efficiency).

These principles serve to determine the appropriateness of the use of a particular creator-god to explain the God of the Bible.

## The Use of Allah for Elohim in the Bamanan Bible

In the translation of the Bible in Bamanankan (the major language of Mali), there was no question about the legitimacy of using Allah to explain the God of the Bible. Allah has been so integrated in the Bamanan culture that most of the people ignore it is a foreign word. A close look at the use of the word in the Bamanan Bible reveals theological differences with the use by Muslims. If the Bamanan Bible is reluctant to use Allah for the other gods and prefers the descriptive term "batofɛn" (object of worship), it makes Allah a Triune God. The Father is Allah, the Son is Allah, and the Holy Spirit is Allah. And yet, there are not three Allahs, but one and the same Allah. Allah has been invested with all the attributes of the God of Abraham so that he is the Allah of Abraham, Isaac, and Jacob. In using the four basic principles mentioned above, we realize the appropriateness of "Allah" to render the God of the Bible in this instance.

1. "Allah" is culturally relevant and recognized by the whole Christian community as a legitimate equivalent of the God of the Bible. It serves as a basis for the unity of the church in Mali.

2. The use of "Allah" as an equivalent of the God of the Bible is accepted by both Christians and non-Christians. The name serves, thereby, as a bridge for understanding, dialogue, and witness between Christians and non-Christians.

3. The concept of "Allah" is theologically adequate to communicate the biblical concept of God. It shares essential similarities with the concept of God in the Bible so that it has been possible to prune it of its negative and anti-biblical connotations and to enrich it with new biblical content so that it becomes a full equivalent of the Triune God of the God in Christian understanding.

4. The use of "Allah" has proved to be missiologically and liturgically efficient. Many Bamanan people of Mali have been saved through faith in "Allah." The whole Bible is available only in Bamanankan in Mali. It uses "Allah" to render God. The reading of this version of the Bible and the preaching from it have transformed the lives of many people. Many prayers in the name of "Allah" have been answered.

## Conclusion

The name of God is of paramount importance in the Scripture. People are saved by invoking the name of the Lord. It is, therefore, crucial to properly name God in another religio-cultural milieu. The conviction that the God of Abraham, Isaac, and Jacob is the only God, the Creator of all things, that this unique God revealed himself to all cultures, set the possibility of explaining him in all cultures.

The legitimacy of using Allah and the creator-god of other non-biblical cultures to explain the God of Abraham, Isaac, and Jacob can be established on several accounts: first, the translatability of the biblical message that legitimizes the translation of the name of God; second, God's self-communication to all cultures so that most of them make room for a creator-god; third, the practical efficiency of the use of the creator-god of the target culture. The use of the creator-god of the target culture should be done keeping in mind this question: What are the theological, missiological, and liturgical implications of this name? The use of the creator-god's name provides the reader a term that is already familiar to him. It is a great means toward bridging linguistic, cultural, and religious differences. A proper nurturing of the new believers will result in the gradual Christianizing of the creator-god's name which was used to explain the God of the Bible. The traditional concept of the creator-god will lose the negative or anti-biblical connotations and associations inherent to it in its original religious and socio-cultural context to communicate a sound understanding of the God of the Bible.

## Discussion Questions

1. What could be the advantages and disadvantages of transliterating the Hebrew names of the God of Abraham, Isaac, and Jacob in other cultures?

2. What are the advantages and disadvantages of using the creator-god of other cultures to render the God of Abraham?

3. Are some creator-gods more appropriate to explain the God of Abraham than others?

4. Are there theological and practical risks in using Allah to render the God of the Bible?

5. Explain the evangelistic and missiological advantages of using Allah to translate the God of Abraham in an area where Islam is predominant.

6. What are the advantages and disadvantages of coining new names to explain the God of Abraham?

# 3

## We Contextualize More Than We Realize

### Craig Blomberg

*Craig L. Blomberg is Distinguished Professor of New Testament at Denver Seminary. He is the author of twelve books and has co-authored or co-edited five more, along with dozens of journal articles and chapters in multi-author works. His books include three on the historical reliability and interpretation of the gospels (one specializing in John), two on interpreting and preaching the parables, three commentaries (on Matthew, 1 Corinthians and James), textbooks on Jesus and the Gospels and on Acts through Revelation, and two books on material possessions in the Bible. Academic training: BA (Augustana College), MA (Trinity Evangelical Divinity School), PhD (University of Aberdeen, Scotland).*

"How many Swedes does it take to change a light bulb?" the joker inquires. "Change?" comes back the query. Evangelicals contextualizing the gospel could sound even more oxymoronic than Swedes changing (and I speak as one of half-Swedish ancestry)! But "evangelical" has become so popular and broad a label in some contexts that the topic is indeed worth exploring. The purpose of this collection of papers has been defined as examining appropriate parameters of contextualization for evangelicals. The unstated premises behind this mandate appear to be that even some evangelicals have transgressed the boundaries of appropriate contextualization and that a reflection on the methodology that derives from a commitment to an inspired Scripture should provide some safeguards against the resulting syncretism.[1]

These concerns are not unfounded. Many who have embraced universalism began life as evangelicals.[2] Some who espouse pluralism still want to maintain their evangelical identity at some

---

1    In this volume, see esp. Natee Tanchanpongs, "Developing a Palate for Authentic Theology."

2    John Hick remains a classic example. On his universalism, see Charles M. Cameron, "John Hick's Religious World," *Evangel* 15.1 (1997): 22-27. In the Spanish-speaking world, the same is true of many liberation theologians.

level.[3] A generation ago, evangelicals were distinguished largely by their conviction that Scripture was true, interpreted according to legitimate hermeneutics, in *everything* that it taught, at the very least in all matters of faith and practice, of theology and ethics.[4] Today, some would identify themselves as evangelical while denying central tenets of historic Christian theology (such as Christ's penal, substitutionary atonement) or of basic moral teachings (such as the goodness of sex only in monogamous, heterosexual marriage).

Two broad approaches may be discerned among those who take these tacks. On the one hand, a minority of such individuals would actually define themselves as inerrantists, but argue that we have misinterpreted the key Scriptures on the topics in question, attempting to reinterpret them in ways consistent with their broader paradigms. But they still accept the authority of the biblical text once interpreted along the lines they have adopted.[5] On the other hand, the majority would operate, either implicitly or explicitly, by means of a canon within the canon. One accepts, for example, the major tenets of the historic, orthodox creeds but opts for simply a moral or classic view of the atonement rather than a penal one as well.[6] Or one approves of the bulk of biblical ethics but just rejects the universal biblical condemnation of fornication, adultery and/or homosexual practices.[7] Such a person may well fall into David Bebbington's widely adopted definition of an evangelical as someone with a generally high view of Scripture, a conversion experience, a concern for evangelism and other actions in the world expressing one's faith, and a cruciform lifestyle.[8] But they stop short of treating the *entirety* of the Bible as fully truthful and authoritative, even in certain matters of doctrine or behavior.

The natural assumption, therefore, would be that a distinctively evangelical contribution to contextualizing the gospel in the contemporary landscape would draw narrower boundaries than most as to how much a given doctrine or moral principle, a narrative or a ritual, a private experience or a corporate practice could change from the biblical contexts and cultures to other ones. In many cases, that assumption would be absolutely correct.[9] Evangelicals may agree that it is appropriate to celebrate the Eucharist at times with leavened rather than unleavened

---

3    For a thorough survey of the contemporary landscape, see Veli-Matti Kärkkäinen, *An Introduction to the Theology of Religions: Biblical, Historical and Contemporary Perspectives* (Downers Grove, IL: IVP, 2003).

4    Recall, e.g., Jack Rogers and Donald McKim, *The Authority and Interpretation of the Bible: An Historical Approach* (New York: Harper & Row, 1979); and John D. Woodbridge, *Biblical Authority: A Critique of the Rogers/McKim Proposal* (Grand Rapids, MI: Zondervan, 1982), despite their disagreement on whether or not complete inerrancy formed the historic Christian position.

5    In the theological realm, one thinks, e.g., of John Sanders in his writings on open theism (esp., *The God Who Risks: A Theology of Divine Providence* [Downers Grove, IL: IVP, rev. 2007]); in the ethical realm, of Thomas Hanks in his writings on homosexuality (esp., *The Subversive Gospel: A New Testament Commentary on Liberation* [Cleveland, OH: Pilgrim, 2000]).

6    For details and for a convincing rebuttal, see Howard Marshall, *Aspects of the Atonement* (Waynesboro, GA: Paternoster, 2007), who responds to Brian McLaren and Steve Chalke, among others.

7    This view is labeled that of "conscientious dissent" by both the Anglican Bishops' Statement on Human Sexuality (1991) and the St. Andrew's Day Statement (1995) dealing with homosexuality. See Timothy Bradshaw, ed., *The Way Forward: Christian Voices on Homosexuality and the Church* (Grand Rapids, MI: Eerdmans, rev. 2003), 9, 216-18.

8    David W. Bebbington, *Evangelicalism in Modern Britain: A History from the 1730s to the 1980s* (London: Unwin Hyman, 1989), 2-3.

9    Cf., e.g., the parameters for permissible contextualization laid down throughout the conservative evangelical work by David J. Hesselgrave and Edward Rommen, *Contextualization: Meanings, Methods, and Models*

bread or with non-alcoholic "fruit of the vine" rather than real wine, but decide that pizza and Pepsi move too far afield.[10] We may acknowledge that it is highly appropriate for Jewish Christians to continue to follow as many of the ritual or ceremonial laws of the Hebrew Scriptures as remain meaningful to them personally or which enable them to build bridges to their unsaved Jewish friends and relatives. But we should insist that imposing all of the ritual/ceremonial (or even civil) laws of the Mosaic covenant on Jewish believers or maintaining that Jesus is the Messiah only for Gentiles wreaks havoc with far too many central texts of the Bible to be tenable.[11] Numerous evangelical studies have indeed warned against the dangers of syncretism, and various principles have been suggested both for ensuring good contextualization and for avoiding its abuse.[12]

I have no concern that the other contributors to this set of studies have cast their nets too broadly. What I would like to focus on for the rest of this article, therefore, is the opposite phenomenon: the danger of fishing in too limited an area.[13] More specifically, I would like to explore the phenomenon of instances in which a commitment to interpreting, communicating and applying the inspired and entirely trustworthy word of God with the greatest possible precision and accuracy *demands* changing the way we translate, conceptualize and proclaim key facets of the gospel lest people seriously misunderstand its meaning.[14] Because this is the more counterintuitive concern of the two, I want to ensure that it is not overlooked. Dean Flemming has begun this volume by demonstrating in detail how the distinctives of a New Testament epistle like Colossians can largely be explained because Paul was contextualizing his message for a congregation infiltrated by a unique, hybrid and home-grown heresy, even to the extent of reusing and redefining key theological terms employed by that false teaching.[15] Flem-

---

(Grand Rapids: Baker, 1989). Then contrast the ecumenical or conciliar collection and analysis of John Parratt, ed., *An Introduction to Third World Theologies* (Cambridge: Cambridge University Press, 2004).

10 As happened in a church I once attended, when the youth pastor unilaterally decided to celebrate Communion with his youth group using these elements and was censured by the church leaders afterwards. More difficult to assess are those contextualizations that represent considerable advance theological reflection, often appealing to local "staples" equivalent to bread and wine in ancient Israel, e.g., the use of maize cakes and water in certain poorer African independent churches. For a thoughtful analysis that stops short of critique, see Phillip Tovey, *Inculturation of Christian Worship: Exploring the Eucharist* (Burlington, VT: Ashgate, 2004), 79-106.

11 See, e.g., Daniel C. Juster, *Jewish Roots: Foundations of Biblical Theology* (Shippensburg, PA: Destiny Image, 1995). *Contra*, e.g., Mark Kinzer, *Postmissionary Messianic Judaism: Redefining Christian Engagement with the Jewish People* (Grand Rapids, MI: Brazos, 2005).

12 See esp. Gailyn Van Rheenen, ed., *Contextualization and Syncretism: Navigating Cultural Currents* (Pasadena, CA: William Carey Library, 2006). Cf. Gary Corwin, "A Second Look: Telling the Difference," *Evangelical Missions Quarterly* 40 (2004): 282-83; Rick Brown, "Contextualization without Syncretism," *International Journal of Frontier Missions* 23 (2006): 127-33.

13 Concerns echoed already in the Latin-American evangelical world by C. René Padilla, *Misión integral: Ensayos sobre el Reino y la iglesia* (Grand Rapids, MI and Buenos Aires: Nueva creación, 1986), 80-105; and Samuel Escobar, *De la mission a la teología* (Buenos Aires: Ediciones Kairós, 1998), 7-42.

14 Cf. Dean E. Flemming, "The Third Horizon: A Wesleyan Contribution to the Contextualization Debate," *Wesleyan Theological Journal* 30 (Fall 1995): 145: "On occasion the discussion has focused on an inerrantist view of Scripture as the hedge against relativism and syncretism. In their valid critique of a situational approach to hermeneutics and theology, evangelicals at times have stressed the absoluteness of revelation and the objectivity of Biblical truth to the point that the praxilogical dimension of Scripture is lost. What is not always recognized is that this rationalistic and 'objective' hermeneutical perspective may itself be a form of contextualization."

15 *Idem*, "Paul the Contextualizer," chapter 1 of this volume.

ming's full-length monograph has already shown how similar phenomena recur throughout the New Testament.[16] Every successful cross-cultural communication of the gospel that has led to a truly indigenous church with significant social impact throughout church history has involved contextualization, whether implemented consciously or not.[17] What might be some examples of settings in which some of our greatest creativity needs to be exercised today for the sake of God's kingdom purposes?[18]

## Analogies in the Discipline of Bible Translation

I enter this discussion from the perspective of a New Testament scholar. I have thoroughly enjoyed the reading and research I have done in the field of missiology in preparation for this essay. It is scarcely the first time I have wrestled with these issues, because my previous work has often thrust me into interdisciplinary studies, including missiological ones.[19] I have been blessed with the chance to travel and minister in twenty-seven countries, and I am married to a missiologist and former local church missions director. Still, this is scarcely my primary area of expertise. I have, however, directly participated in several Bible translation projects[20] and begin by offering a few analogies from this discipline.

The misguided conviction that more literal (or better put, formally equivalent) translations are always, or at least usually, better than less literal (dynamically equivalent) ones remains too widespread, even among well-trained scholars who should know better. The original Living Bible Paraphrased was too free in places and, as author Ken Taylor admitted from the outset, based primarily on reworking the American Standard Version because he did not have the facility to work directly from the Hebrew, Aramaic and Greek. Hence, his son Mark initiated the project that has now produced the widely used and appreciated New Living Translation, a bona fide dynamically equivalent translation from the original languages.[21] On the other

---

16    *Idem, Contextualization in the New Testament: Patterns for Theology and Mission* (Downers Grove and Leicester: IVP, 2005).

17    For samplings, see Timothy C. Tennent, *Theology in the Context of World Christianity* (Grand Rapids, MI: Zondervan, 2007), 2-6. For a full taxonomy of evangelical approaches, see A. Scott Moreau, "Evangelical Models of Contextualization," in this volume, chapter 10. For a more wide-ranging taxonomy complete with suggestive criteria for evaluation of models, see esp. Ignacio C. Conte, "La contextualización en el quehacer teológico," *Estudios eclesiásticos* 81 (2006): 145-76. For a more evangelical Latin-American case study with corrective critique, cf. ¿*Una iglesia posmoderna? En busca de un modelo de iglesia y misión en la era posmoderna* (Buenos Aires: Ediciones Kairos, 2001).

18    For an outstanding philosophical grounding of this task from a contemporary conservative Spanish Catholic perspective, see Juan L. Lorda, "La evangelización de la cultura en el contexto español," *Scripta Theologica* 33 (2001): 137-51. For initial methodological proposals by a Latin American evangelical, see Edgar A, Perdomo, "Algunas tensiones metodológicas en la teología evangélica latinoamericana de principios del siglo XXI," *Kairós* 34-35 (2004): 65-88, 55-80.

19    See esp. my "The Implications of Globalization for Biblical Understanding," in *The Globalization of Theological Education*, ed. Robert A. Evans, Alice F. Evans, and David Roozen (Maryknoll, NY: Orbis, 1993), 213-28, 240-45; "The Globalization of Biblical Interpretation—A Test Case: John 3-4," *Bulletin of Biblical Research 5* (1995): 1-15; and "The Globalization of Biblical Hermeneutics," *Journal of the Evangelical Theological Society 38* (1995): 581-93.

20    As a consultant for the ESV and HCSB, as a translator for the NLT, and as a member of the (T)NIV's ongoing Committee on Bible Translation.

21    See also Bruce M. Metzger, *The Bible in Translation: Ancient and English Versions* (Grand Rapids, MI: Baker, 2001), 179-82.

hand, Leland Ryken's campaign in support of the English Standard Version, a Bible which ironically is neither distinctively English (as opposed to American) nor yet standard, misses the central point of most contemporary Bible translation efforts, and especially the New International Version, namely, that a good balance between formally and dynamically equivalent renderings is most likely in most circumstances to communicate both the original meaning and the original impact of the inspired text.[22] His concern for a version with more elegant diction akin to the King James Version, even if put in twenty-first century American English, overestimates the stylistic quality of the biblical writers.[23] One needs only to compare the Hellenistic Greek of the New Testament, for example, with the Attic Greek of the classic poets and playwrights to appreciate the vast difference between the two. Even the Elizabethan English of 1611 used in the KJV was quite close to the ordinary language of the day that even the working class used.[24] Much of its "elegance" emerged only over the centuries as its language became increasingly archaic!

A second example lands us squarely in the controversy that continues unnecessarily to swirl around Today's New International Version. Notwithstanding the fact that somewhere upwards of two-thirds of all the changes from the NIV moved the TNIV more in the direction of a formally equivalent translation,[25] a small group of highly vocal opponents complains that it is illegitimate to use plurals for singulars or second person forms for third person ones in order to avoid exclusive language in English translations of generic masculine forms for human beings in the original languages.[26] Ironically, the New Testament itself contains examples of both of these practices, both in contexts of "quoting" the Old Testament (e.g., Luke 2:23) and in settings where it "ungrammatically" switches forms, without a change of referent, in a single paragraph (e.g., Jas. 1:5-6). Thus, the TNIV's critics impugn the very practices of the inspired Scripture writers whose authority they are so concerned to uphold![27]

The New Testament offers similar precedent for a more radical change in the recounting of an inspired text when, for example, one Gospel writer contemporizes material found in an earlier Gospel for his new audience. Mark's account of the healing of the paralytic in Capernaum describes how the men who were carrying the paralyzed man on a mat "made an opening in the roof above Jesus by digging (*exoruxantes*) through it and then lowered the mat the man was lying on" (Mark 2:4). Luke's version, on the other hand, states that they "went up on

---

22    Leland Ryken, *The Word of God in English: Criteria for Excellence in Bible Translation* (Wheaton, IL: Crossway, 2002). Ryken astonishingly lumps versions as disparate as the NIV and *The Message* together under the category of "dynamic equivalence" (47-64, 191).

23    *Ibid.*, 157-72.

24    Jack P. Lewis, *The English Bible from KJV to NIV: A History and Evaluation* (Grand Rapids, MI: Baker, 1991), 43. A largely parallel debate afflicts much of the Spanish-speaking world as countless conservative Christians still lobby for the use of the RV (Reina Valera), largely due to familiarity and to its traditional sound (including all the second-person-plural "vosotros" verb forms used still today in Spain but not in normal Latin American vernacular), rather than the more accurate and understandable modern translations such as the NVI (Nueva Versión Internacional).

25    See my "*Today's New International Version*: The Untold Story of a Good Translation," *Bible Translator* 56 (2005): 187-211.

26    See esp. Vern S. Poythress and Wayne A. Grudem, *The Gender-Neutral Bible Controversy: Muting the Masculinity of God's Word* (Nashville, TN: Broadman & Holman, 2000), esp. 111-232.

27    Blomberg, "*Today's New International Version*," 205-8.

the roof and lowered him on his mat through the tiles (*dia tōn keramōn*)" (Luke 5:19). For the most part, village homes in Galilee did not have tile roofs, nor does one dig through tiles. But elsewhere in the ancient Mediterranean world, tile roofs were common, so that Luke has most likely contextualized the description for it to be more understandable among his Gentile churches.[28]

Similarly, in Mark's parable of the mustard seed, the sower sows his seed on the "ground" (or in the "earth"—Mark 4:31). Jews were forbidden to cultivate mustard seeds in gardens; for them this was a seed for their farms. Hence, Matthew, the most Jewish of the four Gospels, has the sower scatter his seed in a "field" (*agros* Matt. 13:31).[29] But Luke explicitly locates the sowing in a garden (*kēpos* Luke 13:19), precisely where Gentiles elsewhere in the Mediterranean basin would have cultivated their mustard plants. There may be a formal contradiction, but there is no material one. Luke changes the wording precisely so that his audience is not distracted from Jesus' lessons by puzzling over an apparently improbable practice but receives his teaching with the same impact as the original audience—recognizing in an everyday, ordinary situation an analogy about the nature of the kingdom of God.[30]

Examples could be multiplied, but hopefully the point is clear. Of course there are many times when the New Testament (or the Septuagint) translates the Old Testament in a highly formally equivalent fashion or when one Gospel reproduces the wording of another verbatim. Thus, we have biblical precedent for translations as literal as the New American Standard and for paraphrases as free as *The Message*. But, except for versions that go beyond even standard paraphrase to entirely contemporize portions of Scripture for a particular subculture (e.g., the Cotton Patch Version that employed imagery and language from the American South during the civil rights movement of the 1960s, so that Jesus was born in Gainesville, Georgia, and lynched in Atlanta by the state governor and his religious henchmen),[31] it is usually recognized that Bible translators do not have the same freedom to contextualize as do Bible expositors.[32] When it comes, however, to *explaining* the concepts of Scripture to people in cultures considerably different from the biblical ones, we must work extra hard at using language and imagery that will reproduce the originally intended meaning of the Bible, along with its original intended effects.[33] If the Bible itself, in translating and reproducing earlier sources, can legitimately

---

28    Cf. Craig A. Evans, *Luke* (Peabody, MA: Hendrickson, 1990), 91-92.

29    Thus also matching Matthew's unparalleled v. 24. See Pierre Bonnard, *L'Évangile selon Saint Matthieu* (Neuchâtel: Delachaux & Niestlé, 1963), 201.

30    Or else the lines of development went from the purity of planting the seed in the field to the impurity of planting it in the garden, to stress Jesus' overthrowing the laws of ritual purity. For both options, see Bernard B. Scott, *Hear Then the Parable: A Commentary on the Parables of Jesus* (Minneapolis, MN: Fortress, 1989), 376.

31    Cited by Gordon D. Fee and Mark L. Strauss, *How to Choose a Translation for All Its Worth* (Grand Rapids, MI: Zondervan, 2007), 33.

32    John Beekman and John Callow, *Translating the Word of God* (Grand Rapids, MI: Zondervan, 1974]) remain an excellent resource, esp. pp. 137-50 on translating metaphor and simile and pp. 345-51 on further considerations related to idiomatic translations. Cf. also D. A. Carson, "The Limits of Dynamic Equivalence in Bible Translation," *Evangelical Review of Theology* 9 (1985): 200-13.

33    Cf. Lamin Sanneh, *Translating the Message: The Missionary Impact on Culture* (Maryknoll, NY: Orbis, 1989), 199: "it is hard to exaggerate the importance of 'recipiency' in determining what is or what is not a successful translation" (here meaning translation of the gospel message not of the words of the Bible *per se*). Charles Kraft, in the preface to the 25th anniversary edition of his *Christianity in Culture: A Study in Biblical Theologizing in Cross Cultural Perspective* (Maryknoll, NY: Orbis, rev. 2005), xxv, observes that those who have successfully

turn thatched rooftops into tiled ones and fields into gardens, then presumably preaching and teaching can initiate even greater transformations for the sake of clarity and not putting unnecessary obstacles in the path of a proper reception of the message (cf. esp. 1 Cor. 9:19-23).[34] Or as Darrell Whiteman more memorably phrases it, contextualization "helps us offend people for the right reasons, not the wrong ones."[35]

# Comparatively Non-Controversial Examples

## Peace Child

Don Richardson's broadly acclaimed *Peace Child* tells the story of the Sawi people of Dutch New Guinea. This was a tribe of headhunters, whose heroes were individuals who displayed the most praiseworthy form of treachery—"fattening" enemies with friendship only to turn on them. As Richardson shared the gospel with them, he discovered them applauding Judas as the hero! How could he disabuse them of this notion? Then he discovered another custom of the area. When a warring tribe wanted to make peace with its neighbors, a chief could offer a "peace child"—one of his own biological offspring—to his counterpart in the other tribe. If the offer was reciprocated, the two tribes were bound to peace with each other and bound to protect and nurture the children who had been exchanged. To betray a peace child was the worst form of evil. At last Richardson understood how to contextualize the story of Jesus' death for the sins of humanity. God made Jesus a peace child, even knowing in advance how humanity would betray him, in order to make peace with human beings a viable option. And he extended this reconciling offer to all the tribes of the world rather than just to one. In a comparatively short time, a significant number of Sawi people came to Christian faith.[36]

Richardson proceeded to refer to customs like these, which provided bridges for sharing the gospel in cultures otherwise quite foreign to it, as "redemptive analogies." In later writing, he raised the question of whether the presence of such analogies in numerous world cultures might not provide an answer to the question about the unevangelized. Perhaps God had left traces of his original revelation of himself to humankind throughout the world in ways that could prove redemptive even when the Christian message had not explicitly reached a given location or people group.[37] Debating the viability of such a conclusion lies outside the scope

---

adopted his approach to contextualization regularly cite his emphasis on and principles for "receptor-oriented communication"

34    Daniel J. Rode ("La adaptación de San Pablo y San Pedro," in *Misión y contextualización: Llevar el mensaje bíblico a un mundo multicultural*, ed. Gerald A. Klingbeil [Libertador San Martín, Entre Ríos, Argentina: Editorial Universidad Adventista del Plata, 2005], 209) declares, "Adaptation [his preferred synonym for contextualization] is more than an evangelistic strategy; it is a Christian lifestyle that must be followed if one wants to be faithful to Christ." Again, "whatever other egoistic objective such as wanting to gain popularity for oneself or pretense in front of church leadership for fear of losing prestige is condemned as hypocrisy that puts missions at risk" (translation mine).

35    I.e., only for the inherent scandal of the cruciform gospel (1 Cor. 1:18-2:5). See Darrell L. Whiteman, "The Function of Appropriate Contextualization in Mission," in *Appropriate Christianity*, ed. Charles H. Kraft (Pasadena, CA: William Carey Library, 2005), 64.

36    For the full story, see Don Richardson, *Peace Child* (Glendale, CA: Regal Books, 1974).

37    See esp. his *Eternity in Their Hearts* (Ventura, CA: Regal Books, 1981).

of this study,[38] because our concern is for Christians contextualizing the gospel in places where they *do* get to share it.

Rather, the point is that few, if any, evangelicals have found Richardson's original contextualization anything other than a providential gift and stellar example of how to re-create the meaning and effect of those in the first century who first heard of Judas' betrayal of Jesus and of Jesus' death and resurrection. Nor is it particularly significant that not all of the details of the analogy correspond to the details of Christ's atonement. Would-be Christians do not offer their children to God in the same way that he offered his son to us. Peace with God required the *death* of his Son, whereas in the New Guinea practice, the children were to remain alive. But, as a basic illustration of vicarious, substitutionary, representative, penal atonement, the analogy works. Indeed, for the point of this study, this form of contextualization seemed *mandatory* if missionaries were to reach the Sawi with the true import and impact of Jesus' crucifixion.

## Aslan and the White Witch

A second example comes from a context much closer to home for many of us. For modern (and now postmodern) cultures who find blood sacrifice an outdated and even repugnant concept, C. S. Lewis' magnificent opening volume to the *Chronicles of Narnia* contextualizes the crucifixion brilliantly. At the end of *The Lion, the Witch, and the Wardrobe*, Edmund, who has betrayed his siblings and friends to the white witch, discovers that in so doing he has forfeited his life to her. Thus, "in a legal or at least law-like fashion, she now has rights concerning him."[39] The witch declares that Aslan knows "the Deep Magic" well enough that only the exchange of another creature's lifeblood for his can liberate Edmund. So Aslan allows himself to be tied with ropes to a large stone table to be executed. Just prior to his death, the witch mocks the lion: "And now, who has won? Fool, did you think that by all this you would save the human traitor? Now I will kill you instead of him as our pact was and so the Deep Magic will be appeased. But when you are dead what will prevent me from killing him as well?" She concludes triumphantly, "Understand that you have given me Narnia forever, you have lost your own life and you have not saved his. In that knowledge, despair and die"![40] But what the witch does not realize is what Aslan explains after he miraculously returns to life. "There is a magic deeper still which she did not know. . . .when a willing victim who had committed no treachery was killed in a traitor's stead, the Table would crack and Death itself would start working backwards. . . ."[41] And so the witch is defeated in a final battle involving Aslan, the children and many of the animals of Narnia.

Again, the analogy is not perfect. But as an illustration of the evil designs of Satan, of his creatureliness and of limited knowledge despite his great power, the witch's role works well. The deep magic corresponds to the need for a blood ransom in order to liberate humans from their treachery or sin. The deeper magic explains how the sinless Jesus could be resurrected

---

38   But see esp. Bruce A. Demarest and Richard J. Harpel, "Don Richardson's 'Redemptive Analogies' and the Biblical Idea of Revelation," *Bibliotheca Sacra* 146 (1989): 330-40.

39   Charles Taliaferro, "A Narnian Theory of the Atonement," *Scottish Journal of Theology* 41 (1988): 76.

40   C. S. Lewis, *The Lion, the Witch and the Wardrobe* (New York: Macmillan, 1961), 125-26.

41   *Ibid.*, 132-33.

and triumph over the devil after voluntarily going to the cross. What Narnia lacks, if Aslan is a Christ-figure, is a separate, personal God-figure, although the deeper magic corresponds in part to the idea of just and merciful principles transcending Aslan himself. But in light of modern complaints about the concept of penal, substitutionary atonement, this lacuna is not terribly crucial. What clearly shines through in Lewis' novel is the idea that it is God *himself* in Christ who is paying the price for the sins of the world. The atonement is scarcely the "divine child abuse" that many critics and even a few evangelicals have imagined it to be (see n. 6 above). Here Aslan's behavior illustrates God's *self*-sacrifice even better than the "peace child," who was clearly separate from his father. It may increasingly be the case that, without the kind of contextualization that Lewis has provided, the heart of the historic Christian doctrine of the atonement may be at best unintelligible and at worst anathematized.[42]

## Science Fiction and Eschatology

A final, relatively non-controversial example of contextualizing key doctrines involves eschatology. Even a half-century ago, few Christians had their faith shaken by Yuri Gagarin, the Soviet Union's first cosmonaut, declaring from space that he saw no God and no heaven! Whatever the cosmology of the ancients, it was intuitively obvious to most moderns that biblical teaching about heaven (or hell) did not require them to be places to which one could travel simply by aiming a spaceship in the right direction (or digging toward the center of the earth in the proper locale). These were otherworldly dimensions of existence that were described in Scripture using culturally appropriate descriptors for perfect bliss or horrible agony.[43] The key non-metaphorical core of heavenly existence is that it is a place in which believers will exist consciously forever with Christ and the company of the redeemed from all time, so that "God's dwelling place is now among the people, and he will dwell with them. They will be his people, and God himself will be with them and be their God. He will wipe every tear from their eyes. There will be no more death or mourning or crying or pain, for the order of things has passed away (Rev. 21:3-4).[44] Hell, on the other hand, may be best non-metaphorically depicted in 2 Thessalonians 1:8-9. Jesus "will punish those who do not know God and do not obey the gospel of our Lord Jesus. They will be punished with everlasting destruction and shut out from the presence of the Lord and from the glory of his might." Of course, more familiar

---

42    Gregory A. Boyd ("Christus Victor Response," in *The Nature of the Atonement: Four Views*, ed. James Beilby and Paul R. Eddy [Downers Grove, IL: IVP, 2006], 100-5) argues that Lewis' story illustrates the classic view of the atonement (Christ conquering the devil) combined with the "substitutionary" piece of penal atonement but that the story does not illustrate a penalty being paid to *God* but to Satan (the witch). But that penalty is then cancelled out and overcome by Christ's final victory. But no "deeper magic" would have been needed in the story if the "deep magic" was not very real, powerful and unalterable. Otherwise, Aslan could have just devoured the witch at once and set the children free. That it was God, not Satan, who needed to be propitiated *is* missing from the story, at least explicitly, though the fact that Aslan is described as good but not safe, even for the children, reminds us that we do have to fear God's potential wrath over our sin and deal with it as well as the devil's ploys.

43    This position is well articulated in William V. Crockett, "The Metaphorical View," in *Four Views on Hell* (Grand Rapids, MI: Zondervan, 1992), 43-76.

44    Cf. Robert H. Mounce, *The Book of Revelation* (Grand Rapids, MI: Eerdmans, rev. 1997), 383-84: "Eternal blessedness is couched in negation because the new and glorious order is more easily pictured in terms of what it replaces than by an attempt to describe what is largely inconceivable in our present state."

and graphic are the various biblical portraits of hell as eternal fire or outer darkness.[45] But if either of these is interpreted literally, it precludes a literal interpretation of the other.[46] So both portraits are much more likely to be metaphorical.

Modern science fiction, wittingly or unwittingly, has offered us new and helpful ways to contextualize biblical eschatology. Although Gene Rodenberry certainly intended to raise metaphysical and spiritual questions in his series of Star Trek television shows and movies, he had no intention of promoting Christianity.[47] Still, the image of people stepping into a "transporter room," "dematerializing," and "rematerializing" in a new location offers an intelligible (if not yet actualizable!) image for how multiple universes might exist simultaneously and people who no longer live in one might be reconstituted bodily in another. Is the classic Christian belief in the resurrection of the body any more fanciful, even if modern science teaches us that our bodies exchange a full slate of molecules a number of times over throughout our lives? The God who first created us can re-create us with just the right amount of continuity and discontinuity between our original bodies and our resurrected ones for all his promises about the eternal state to be fulfilled.[48]

Or, returning to C. S. Lewis, consider his marvelous little science-fiction novel, *The Great Divorce*. How can an infinite hell be the appropriate punishment for a finite amount of sin during a person's life? Of several important replies, a key one is that probably those who consistently reject Christ in this life would have no desire ever to leave hell for heaven, even if the next life were to give them a chance. Much of Lewis' novel develops this thought in vivid, narrative form.[49] While one cannot turn to an explicit set of passages in Scripture that teach precisely this point, it is at the least suggestive that at the end of the millennium (however one fits it into one's apocalyptic calendar), when people are given one last chance to align themselves with Satan and fall prey to his deceptions, the number who do so "are like the sand on the seashore" (Rev. 20:8). Even after Satan has been bound for a thousand years, after everyone on the planet has experienced Jesus Christ reigning on earth and providing unparalleled blessings for humanity and the world, when given a choice many choose to rebel and reject everything good. Given the considerable similarity between the millennium (Rev. 20) and the new heavens and earth (Rev. 21-22), it is not too hard to imagine the same pattern recurring in the eternal state, were the opportunity offered.[50] But without the kinds of contemporization

---

45    Charles Masson (*Les deux Épitres de Saint Paul aux Thessaloniciens* [Neuchâtel: Delachaux & Niestlé, 1957], 88) rightly observes that "this evoking of judgment contrasts by its sobriety and spirituality with the descriptions of Jewish apocalyptic."

46    George E. Ladd, *A Theology of the New Testament*, rev. Donald A. Hagner (Grand Rapids, MI: Eerdmans, 1993), 196.

47    Indeed, he consistently challenged the conventional answers of organized religion and promoted a very pluralistic approach to religious questions. See Jennifer E. Porter and Darcee L. McLaren, eds., *Star Trek and Sacred Ground: Explorations of Star Trek, Religion, and American Culture* (Albany, NY: SUNY Press, 1999).

48    The dilemmas are well probed in Dale C. Allison, Jr., *Resurrecting Jesus: The Earliest Christian Tradition and Its Interpreters* (New York: T & T Clark, 2005), 221-28. The helpfulness of the transporter-room analogy from Star Trek was discussed at the SBL annual meeting in San Diego, Nov. 2007, in a panel discussion responding to Allison's work and by Allison himself.

49    C. S. Lewis, *The Great Divorce* (New York: Macmillan, 1946).

50    Cf. Grant R. Osborne, *Revelation* (Grand Rapids, MI: Baker, 2002), 716: "After a thousand years of experiencing Christ, the unbelieving nations throw themselves after Satan the first chance they get. The message is

and contextualization offered by writers like Rodenberry (unintentionally) and Lewis (intentionally), some people today might simply be unable to imagine how they could accept the biblical teachings.[51]

# Somewhat More Controversial Examples

The examples thus far have hopefully reminded us that contextualization occurs any time we communicate the gospel in any fashion other than just quoting excerpts of Scripture verbatim. It is scarcely something unique to contemporary cross-cultural contexts.[52]  Indeed, as Kenneth Bailey and others have reminded us, more traditional, pre- or semi-literate, largely oral cultures in the Two-Thirds World today may in many instances have to cross less of a cultural gap from the biblical worlds to theirs in making sense of numerous texts and themes of Scripture than do many Westerners.[53]  Where similar dynamics of honor and shame, concentric circles of kinship loyalties, ritual purity and impurity or patronage and reciprocity exist, it is often easier for those who encounter biblical narratives and instructions to understand them in the ways their authors originally intended.[54]  So it should cause no surprise that some of the most urgent needs for contextualization come right within our modern and postmodern worlds.

The "comparatively non-controversial examples" I discussed in the previous section fall into that category for evangelicals in large part because they enable or have enabled non-Christians or liberal Christians to understand and embrace a central orthodox tenet of the faith more readily.  But sometimes conservative Christians are the ones who have had blinders on to certain facets of biblical truth, so that contextualizing the gospel enables them to see more clearly what they have been missing.  But if they are not prepared to broaden their own understanding and formulations, perhaps acknowledging that they have been promoting their own de facto "canon within the canon,"[55] they will tend to resist the contextualization under the guise that it distorts the gospel.

## *C5 Evangelism and Ecclesiology*[56]

Even more controversial is the quickly growing practice in evangelizing Muslims (and, increasingly, Buddhists and Hindus) of so contextualizing the gospel that individuals choosing to follow Jesus are not asked to leave the religious cultures in which they have been living nor even, at times, the houses of worship they have been frequenting.  Instead, they remain among their

---

that in a billion years, a trillion years, they would do the same!"

51    It is, of course, important to distinguish positive or neutral illustrative uses of science fiction from those in which an anti-Christian world view is inherent.  For the latter, see James A. Herrick, *Scientific Mythologies: How Science and Science Fiction Forge New Religious Beliefs* (Downers Grove, IL: IVP, 2008).

52    Flemming, "The Third Horizon," 143.

53    See his consistent appeal to traditional Arab, Lebanese and Palestinian village practices and teachings in the twentieth-century Middle East throughout Kenneth E. Bailey, *Poet and Peasant* and *Through Peasant Eyes*, 2 vols. bound in 1 (Grand Rapids, MI: Eerdmans, 1983).

54    For an excellent discussion of the key, distinctive, sociological issues of which to be aware, see David A. deSilva, *Honor, Patronage, Kinship and Purity: Unlocking New Testament Culture* (Downers Grove, IL: IVP, 2000).

55    Cf. David W. Kling, *The Bible in History: How the Texts Have Shaped the Times* (Oxford: OUP, 2004).

56    For the significance of this nomenclature, see John Travis, "The C1 to C6 Spectrum," *Evangelical Missions Quarterly* 34 (1998): 407-8.

people so as to witness to Christ from within the movements of which they have been a part. Thus, Muslim-background followers of Jesus may continue to attend the mosque but reinterpret the meaning of their prayers and confessions of faith in fashions consistent with Christian theology. Yet because of the seemingly unalterable associations in Islamic culture of the term "Christian" with "Western," "sexually immoral," and "imperialistic," such followers may never apply that adjective to themselves. They may meet in small groups for fellowship and instruction in biblical truths, but they may never make a clean social or organizational break from the religious institutions of their past.[57]

The issue of coming out of the mosque (or temple) is a complex one. What the various rituals in these non-Christian houses of worship mean to a given individual vary widely. Paul's teaching in 1 Corinthians 8-10 remains particularly *a propos* here. Followers of Jesus trying to determine if a given practice is permissible must ask if in the process they can avoid the worship of false gods,[58] as Paul insists that behind these practices is the demonic (10:14-22). Does remaining in a house of foreign worship indeed result in opportunities to share the gospel with a positive impact that eludes people elsewhere? Or does it merely lead onlookers to believe that one is still no different from other unconverted members of that religion/culture or, worse still, that one has converted from Christianity to Islam, Buddhism or Hinduism?[59]

Nevertheless, at least in theory, if one can avoid syncretistic theology or ritual oneself, such contextualized outreach should prove possible. In view of the logical corollary of the uniquely divine origin of Scripture that the Bible alone is the Christians' flawless and authoritative norm, nothing in Scripture specifies where a fellowship of believers must congregate or prescribes more than the most rudimentary structures or organizational forms for such a congregation.[60] On the other hand, the biblical call for the church to display unity despite cross-cultural diversity, especially for the sake of evangelism (see esp. Eph. 3:10, John 17:20-23),[61] suggests that at best, such fairly secret fellowships within hostile contexts should be viewed as temporary stopgaps until more public, heterogeneous congregations can emerge.[62] But before we criticize C5 Muslim-background believers and their counterparts among other world religions too severely for not taking this next step, we would do well to ask ourselves how many

---

57   Cf. Joshua Massey, "Misunderstanding C5: His Ways Are Not Our Orthodoxy," *Evangelical Missions Quarterly* 40 (2004): 296-304; Phil Parshall, "Lifting the *Fatwa*," *ibid.*, 288-93; and Kevin Higgins, "Identity, Integrity, and Insider Movements," *International Journal of Frontier Missions* 23 (2006): 117-23.

58   Or at least avoid what Jean Héring (*La première Épître de Saint Paul aux Corinthiens* [Neuchâtel: Delachaux & Niestlé, rev. 1959], 86) calls "a dangerous communication . . .established with the forces of evil" (translation mine).

59   Cf. Phil Parshall, "Danger: New Directions in Contextualization," *Evangelical Missions Quarterly* 34 (1998): 404-10.

60   *Contra* the development of the monarchical episcopacy in the second century. Cf. esp. Arthur G. Patzia, *The Emergence of the Church: Context, Growth, Leadership and Worship* (Downers Grove: IVP, 2001).

61   Cf. esp. Bruce W. Fong, "Addressing the Issue of Racial Reconciliation according to the Principles of Eph 2:11-22," *Journal of the Evangelical Theological Society* 38 (1995): 565-80. James Bartley (*Juan* [El Paso: Editorial Mundo Hispano, 2005], 355) labels "the unity of the body of believers" as "the most convincing proof for a skeptical world that Jesus really came as the one sent by / from God to redeem the world, the awaited Messiah, the eternal God incarnate" (translation mine).

62   Timothy Tennent, "Followers of Jesus (Isa) in Islamic Mosques: A Closer Examination of C-5 'High Spectrum' Contextualization," *International Journal of Frontier Missions* 23 (2006) 101-23.

of our congregations have actively sought to attract socially, ethnically and culturally diverse people into our fellowships even when we risk so much less when we do so.

## Offensive Language and Perlocutionary Effects

Reflecting on how speakers of Arabic recoil at the sound and thought of "son of God," because in Arabic it refers to a literal biological offspring of Allah,[63] raises the question of the affective dimension of ministry once again and in an acute fashion. As speech-act theory has taught us, language has locutionary, illocutionary, and perlocutionary dimensions.[64] A commitment to a high view of Scripture should make us that much more concerned that we approximate as closely as possible all of these dimensions of communicative activity. Contextualizing the gospel comprehensively requires that we consider such elements as the shock value of various original parts of Scripture. Bailey describes how, at one stage in his career even after twenty years of ministry in the Middle East, he still had not dared to contextualize the parable of the Good Samaritan, in which the hated enemy becomes the hero, with a good Jew helping a severely wounded Arab or a "noble Turk" helping an Armenian. Teaching in Lebanon at the time, he feared for his own safety if he did so.[65] Yet Jesus' teaching spawned multiple, aborted attacks on his life before the final, successful plot that led to the crucifixion. Can American evangelicals in 2008 tolerate the thought of Jesus narrating how an al-Qaeda leader rescued a wounded G.I. in Iraq? Or a black feminist atheist homosexual Democrat coming to the aid of President George W. Bush?[66]

What about the horror and significance of the crucifixion itself? Scum of the Earth Church in Denver, in which my wife and I actively participate, is a niche church that reaches out particularly to the artistic subculture of urban Denver, the homeless, and twenty-somethings who have been alienated from more traditional churches.[67] A majority of the congregants have significantly dysfunctional and even abusive upbringings, sometimes even by faithful churchgoing parents. These young people can spot hypocrisy a mile away. Yet they long for authentic, positive, long-term Christian relationships, especially with older mentors. A preaching team carefully vets each sermon for theological orthodoxy but also for relevance to the target audience. One of the young associate pastors, Jesse Heilman, preached a Lenten sermon one year (2007) on the crucifixion, which was a paradigm of accurate and effective contextualization for its audience, entitled "The Perfect Suck." Heilman must have used "suck" in its various noun and verb forms at least two dozen times in his message. It was clear from audience twitters that even those who used this term regularly in their vocabulary (and who assured me that it is

---

63    See chapter 2 of this volume by Youssouf Dembele, "What Shall We Name God?"

64    John R. Searle, *Speech Acts: An Essay in the Philosophy of Language* (Cambridge: Cambridge University Press, 1969). Kevin Vanhoozer (*Is There a Meaning in This Text? The Bible, the Reader and the Morality of Literary Knowledge* [Grand Rapids: Zondervan, 1998]) effectively mediates this theory to Christian theological hermeneutics, particularly by noting the parallels between Father, Son, and Holy Spirit and author, text, and reader, respectively.

65    Bailey, *Through Peasant Eyes*, 48.

66    Cf. my attempts to contemporize various parts of various parables throughout *Preaching the Parables: From Responsible Interpretation to Powerful Proclamation* (Grand Rapids, MI: Baker, 2004).

67    The church's vision is phrased as reaching "the right brained and the left out." For a sympathetic description, see Susie Oh, "Church Welcomes 'the Scum of the Earth'," posted 11/02/07 at http://www.baptiststandard.com/postnuke/index.php?medule=htmlpages&func=display&pid=7045.

not nearly as offensive a term in their subculture as it was in mine at their age) found it anomalous for it to become so central a focus of a Christian sermon. Yet they came away profoundly in touch with the meaning of the cross.[68]

Without having taken a single note to which I can refer back, I can still reproduce the heart of the Heilman's message. Christ's death sucked because it was cruel and agonizing. It sucked because he in no way deserved it. It was the *perfect* suck, in the sense of "a complete injustice," because he was the sinless Son of God. But it was also the perfect suck, in the sense of that which flawlessly accomplished its objective—to atone for the sins of the world. And it was the perfect *suck*, because Christ suffered what we deserved to suffer. Only as fully human could he adequately substitute and represent us. Only as fully God could he offer an eternal sacrifice. The multiple, clever plays on words make it easy to reconstruct the core scriptural teachings on the atonement, while the shock of the contextualization etches it well in one's memory. Crucifixions were likewise considered so shocking and horrifying that in Roman circles one did not speak about the practice in polite company.[69] Can contemporary exposition that does not adequately re-create that shock effect be said to have fully communicated God's perfect and flawless word?[70]

## Extremely Difficult Examples

In this category I am not thinking of contextualizations that may cause great flack or even attack. We have seen some examples of these already. Rather, by "extremely difficult examples," I mean those where I find it almost impossible to make a decision among competing options.

### God as Mother

Almost entirely off limits for American evangelical discussion is the motherhood of God. No doubt a lot of this attitude at the moment stems from the rampant *mis*representation of evangelical egalitarians and inclusive-language Bible translations like the TNIV as promoting feminine terms for deity, even though they do not do so.[71] Another barrier involves the frequent connection in liberal Christian circles between inclusive language for the Godhead and other, more clearly unbiblical doctrines or practices, including Gaia (or mother earth) worship, promotion of homosexual lifestyles as healthy, and so on. But what if we recognize that this issue need not be a stepping stone to anything else and evaluate it simply on its own merits?

---

68    For a more truly controversial service, but with similar issues involved, see Skye Jethani, "Expletive Undeleted: Dropping the F-bomb in Church," posted 11/8/05 at http://blog.christianitytoday/outofur/archives/2005/11/expletive_undel_1.html.

69    For full details of the historical and theological significance, see Martin Hengel, *Crucifixion in the Ancient World and the Folly of the Message of the Cross* (Philadelphia, PA: Fortress, 1977).

70    For a partially equivalent approach from an explicitly Hispanic liberationist perspective toward the urban poor in the Americas that takes the next step after contextualizing Jesus' suffering to redemptive social action, see Harold J. Recinos, "El barrio: contexto teológico de una nueva iglesia," *Cuadernos de teología* 23 (2005): 123-37.

71    A flurry of studies appeared in the early-to-mid 1990s, but scarcely any have appeared since. The first inclusive-language revision of the NIV, published only in the U.K. , appeared in 1997. One important exception to this recent moratorium is Mark Strauss, *Distorting Scripture? The Challenge of Bible Translation and Gender Accuracy* (Downers Grove, IL: IVP, 1998), 60-73, but even this limits itself to what is acceptable in translating the Bible rather than dealing with what is acceptable practice for Christians speaking about God in other contexts.

On the one hand, the Bible never calls God mother, not even just descriptively. It uses maternal metaphors for God but stops with that. Prescriptively, Jesus teaches his disciples to pray, "Our Father in heaven. . ." (Matt. 6:9). Certain character traits central to Scripture's portrait of God that are more often associated with fathers than mothers, at least in a sizable majority of the world's cultures (leader, authority, judge), would be jettisoned if God were called *only* Mother. Of course, a balance of references to God as both Mother and Father would solve the last of these problems.

On the other hand, what do we say to the person whose father in this life so abused them that they can scarcely begin to associate any positive thoughts with the term, even when used metaphorically? We are reminded of the controversy over the translation of "Son of God," discussed above. No command of Scripture ever forbids us to call God mother. Perhaps it would simply have been too radical a concept in the biblical cultures for it to have been employed, whereas today more and more parts of the world may be ready for it? Or perhaps because the ancient Near and Middle East, apart from Judaism and Christianity, was almost entirely polytheistic in nature, references to God as both Father and Mother could too easily have suggested a god and goddess, as in the pagan nations surrounding Israel, and lead down a slippery slope to polytheism.

At the same time, polytheism is increasingly returning to the center of the religious stage, especially in the postmodern North and West, while it remains common in most parts of the non-Islamic East and South. So, even if there is no explicit biblical prohibition against calling God Mother, perhaps the wisdom of the ancients in avoiding the label still makes sense for many of the same reasons. And if it is hard for those sorely abused by earthly fathers to think of God as Father today, how much harder must it have been in the context of the Roman *patria potestas* for children of heavy-handed patriarchs to look lovingly on God with paternal appellations? And yet we get no hint of addressing God as mother in the Jewish and Christian segments of the ancient Mediterranean world.[72]

Just when I thought I had the issue settled along the standard evangelical line of acknowledging maternal imagery for and dimensions to a God who ultimately transcends all gender, while not feeling free to actually call God Mother, I encountered the sizable segment of New Zealand evangelicalism that feels quite free to do so. Empowering women has become an even more central feature of the recent decades of Kiwi culture than it has in most of the rest of the English-speaking world. Neo-orthodoxy and neo-liberalism have barely ever taken root in this society. That which goes by the name of Christianity either identifies itself as evangelical or is so liberal as to barely believe in a personal, knowable God at all, and the latter is scarcely a force to be reckoned with in size. Historically, Christianity has never been the force in New

---

72    For an outstanding presentation of both sides of the debate in all their complexities, acknowledging a certain impasse, see Richard S. Briggs, "Gender and God-talk: Can We Call God 'Mother'?" *Themelios* 29.2 (2004): 15-25. It is not surprising that this was published in the U.K., since the debate over inclusive-language translations has, in general, not been as acerbic there. For the diversity of perspectives on the nature of God that impinges on this debate both within evangelicalism and within Christianity more broadly, see, respectively, Aída B. Spencer and William D. Spencer, eds., *The Global God: Multicultural Evangelical Views of God* (Grand Rapids, MI: Baker, 1998); and Veli-Matti Kärkkäinen, *The Doctrine of God: A Global Introduction* (Grand Rapids, MI: Baker, 2004). These treatments also include explicit discussion of feminist perspectives both within and outside of evangelical circles.

Zealand that it still is in the United States and that it once was in most of the former British Commonwealth (save perhaps Australia). So there are few slippery slopes, just a big chasm between the two branches of the faith, and evangelicals feel they can ill afford to further alienate the majority of their lost kin except where the very saving core of the gospel is at stake.[73] Perhaps in this setting a more encompassing evangelical feminism is appropriate. Perhaps such contextualization is even necessary. But I confess I remain only "almost persuaded." I will hardly make it an issue over which to divide from other Christians. I have a wonderful mother, so that is not the issue. But I cannot envision myself addressing God as Mother at any time in the foreseeable future.

## God in Mongolian

An intriguing dilemma presented itself to me this past fall. A long-time American missionary to Mongolia and close friend of one of my retired colleagues was in town and wanted to meet with me. He is stymied by what he perceives as a seeming impasse and damaging rift among the fledgling Christian community in that country over the two major translations of the Bible in Mongolian. One uses a non-indigenous term for God, *Yertuntsiin Ezen* ("Lord of heaven") which makes Christianity appear foreign and the Christian God separate from anything Mongolians have previously known. The other uses the common, indigenous term, *Burhan*, but ninety percent of the time in Mongolian conversation, this missionary estimated, the word means Buddha. Documentation sent to and produced by Gailyn van Rheenen confirms the basic contours of the debate and the depths of the division involved.[74] Both of the major options manage the task of contextualization for the sake of clear understanding and a desirable response only very partially and each introduces significant problems.

While immediately recognizing the complexity of the issue, I almost instinctively wanted to find a way to make the indigenous term work. What about the other ten percent of the uses of *Burhan*? Why not just support regular teaching on the meaning of this name for God *in a Christian context*? Didn't the Bible take over terms like the Hebrew *'El* and its many offshoots or the Greek *theos* and re-contextualize with Jewish and Christian meanings? Didn't these terms often refer to pagan gods and goddesses—indeed to entire pantheons of them?[75] Kwame Bediako presents a somewhat parallel scenario in Africa for using an indigenous name for God on the basis of John's uses of *logos* for Jesus.[76] But yes, there are also reasonably clear examples of monotheism or at least henotheism in the cultures surrounding biblical Israel, and more

---

73   For excellent anthologies on New Zealand evangelicalism and Christianity, respectively, see John Stenhouse, Brett Knowles and Anthony Wood, ed., *The Future of Christianity: Historical, Sociological, Political and Theological Perspectives from New Zealand* (Adelaide: ATF Press, 2004); and Susan E. Emilsen and William W. Emilsen, eds., *Mapping the Landscape: Essays in Australian and New Zealand Christianity* (New York: Peter Lang, 2000).

74   Gailyn Van Rheenen, "Case Study: Translating God in Mongolia," 2007, accessed at http://missiology. org/mmr/PDF%20Files/mmr40.pdf on 1/20/08.

75   See, e.g., Terence E. Fretheim, "אל," in *New International Dictionary of Old Testament Theology and Exegesis*, ed. Willem A. van Gemeren, vol. 1 (Grand Rapids: Zondervan, 1997), 400; and J. Schneider, C. Brown, and J. Stafford Wright, "θεοϛ," in *New International Dictionary of New Testament Theology*, ed. C. Brown, vol. 2 (Grand Rapids, MI: Zondervan, 1976), 66-67.

76   Kwame Bediako, "The Doctrine of Christ and the Significance of Vernacular Terminology," *International Bulletin of Missionary Research* 22 (1998): 110-11.

remotely, in the African contexts Bediako cites. In none of these instances do the indigenous names for God potentially mislead as consistently as with *Burhan* in Mongolian.

Maybe Christians in Mongolia must therefore come to acknowledge that their faith *does* have foreign roots but stress that these roots are not Western but Middle Eastern. Maybe in time the foreign sounding term *Yertuntsiin Ezen* will become more commonplace and seem less like something imposed from outside. But what of those who die without coming to Christ in the meanwhile? Could they have been won via better contextualization? Students of evangelistic forays into Korea, Japan and the many parts of China at various stages in Christian history seem to have demonstrated that Far Eastern cultures react dramatically better to the gospel when indigenous terms for God are used.[77] But varying social, political and economic factors complicate the analysis.[78] And clearly, no matter how indigenous a term, if its meaning is inherently (or almost inherently) syncretistic, it is hard to imagine a successful campaign of adequate redefinition so as to salvage it for communicating authentic Christian truth. Without additional resources being readily accessible, I must, to my frustration, remain undecided. Even with such resources, I could not guarantee being able to come to a decision with which I was entirely pleased. Our finite and fallen existence, not to mention the complexity of reality more generally,[79] guarantees that this will occur more than we would probably like. We need to be prepared for godly, educated, Bible-believing Christians to arrive at periodic impasses on issues like these and we need to support one another in good faith rather than attacking or scolding each other even if we arrive at different answers for our personal lives and ministries.

## Conclusion

The sheer number and diverse nature of the examples to which I have appealed may strike some readers as biting off more than anyone should even try to chew. But I have chosen to range as widely as I have for several reasons. First, if readers disagree with my positions on one or two of my topics, perhaps others will commend themselves more. Second, if we are going to make any valid generalizations we must have as many examples as possible from which to generalize. Third, the majority of the many studies on contextualization that I have read remain almost entirely at the theoretical level or, if they introduce sample applications, they focus on only a very few. Finally, I hope that a broad cross-section of case studies will suggest an equally broad array of additional issues and illustrations on which proper contextualization can be further tested. I have no doubt that those more familiar with the field than I am may well be able to come up with even better examples for the kinds of issues I have sought to illustrate.

My goal in this study has, in fact, been a modest one. Many readers might first imagine that a uniquely evangelical approach to contextualizing the gospel would be the most cautious and conservative of all in suggesting significant departures from biblical terms and imagery, either

---

77    Ralph R. Covell, *Confucius, the Buddha, and Christ: A History of the Gospel in Chinese* (Maryknoll, NY: Orbis, 1986), 87-90; Bong Rin Ro, "Communicating the Biblical Concept of God to Koreans," in *The Global God*, ed. Spencer and Spencer, 222-23.

78    Kyo Seong Ahn, "Christian Mission and Mongolian Identity: The Religious, Cultural, and Political Context," *Studies in World Christianity* 9 (2003): 103-24.

79    On which, see, e.g., Marcelo Trejo, "El quehacer teológico en el nuevo contexto paradigmático de la complejidad," *Cuadernos de teología* 23 (2005): 153-62.

in translation or in exposition. In many instances such readers would have been right. But sometimes inherent caution proves counterproductive. Of what value is the preservation of traditional and/or biblical language (or concepts or imagery), if people remain lost in their sins?[80] I am the spiritual product of a fairly radical contextualizing of the gospel for teenagers, having come to faith in Jesus through the ministry of Campus Life/Youth for Christ to my high school at the beginning of the 1970s, as club leaders sought to attract non-Christian students by staging crazy games for icebreakers, facilitating discussion on the key issues the youth culture of that volatile period in American history wanted to discuss, and showing how Jesus could uniquely meet the true needs behind the quests for happiness through promiscuity, drugs, peace movements, the military, all in the context of welcoming peer relationships.[81] I still vividly recall one of our more provocative but effective slogans: "Get high on the big J." We saw an encouraging number of our friends come to Christ through carefully thought through contextualized presentations of the gospel and many of them remain active Christians, even in professional ministry, to this day. Interestingly, a number of our high school friends who attended very conservative, fundamentalist churches were discouraged or downright forbidden to participate in our club activities because we were not a local church and usually because something in our games or our teaching didn't quite fit their narrow doctrinal and lifestyle statements. But when we asked when the last time was that high schoolers from outside those congregations had come to faith through the ministries of those churches, no one could remember it having happened!

So I have amassed an array of illustrations which I hope demonstrate this essay's thesis. While there are plenty of places in which to guard against excessive contextualization, when the very most central doctrinal and ethical teachings of the gospel are compromised, it is easy for evangelicals to forget that often the changes in modern and postmodern Western cultures and, to a lesser extent even in more traditional cultures, require quite different language and imagery *if the original meaning and significance of the gospel is to be recaptured in a distinctively different context today.*[82] Or as John Davis phrases it, the Bible

> is quite likely more concerned with eliciting functionally equivalent responses of obedience than with achieving exact arithmetical precision of reporting. Evangelicals are prepared to admit quite readily the use of approximations by the writers of Scripture. If this recognition could be generalized to apply to other variations on the basis of a theory of approximate coherence and approximate correspondence—'coherence and correspondence within providentially permitted tolerances of variation'—then perhaps

---

80    Cf. George Reyes, "De la interpretación a la contextualización del género narrative bíblico," in *Teología evangélica para el context latinoamericano*, ed. Oscar Campos (Buenos Aires, Ediciones Kairós, 2004), 104: "No one who understands that contextualization is nothing other than the force for making both the world and the message of the narrative text [of Scripture] pedagogically and pastorally relevant has the capacity to remain quiet in a context like the current one. . ." (translation mine).

81    Particular thanks are due to our three successive (Rock Island High School, IL) club staff: Hugh Rohr, Tom Dudenhofer and Dick Kemple, in the 1970-71, 1971-72 and 1972-73 school years respectively.

82    See the exemplary model and outlines of his larger systematic theology for China in Paul Siu, "Theologizing Locally," in this volume, 143-166. Contrast the prodigious new *Teologia sistemática* in Portuguese by Franklin Ferriera and Alan Myatt (São Paolo: Vida Nova, 2007), which claims to be contextualizing but differs from older English-language works only by adding a few doctrinal comparisons and contrasts with various world religions.

some of the tensions in the contemporary discussions of biblical authority could be overcome.[83]

A greater awareness of when a faithful *hearing* of the word is better facilitated by greater creativity and contextualization in sharing the gospel would doubtless also result. We also need to do a better job at ranking our confidence levels about different kinds of contextualizations and helping others to do the same. Just as abuses of the principle do not imply there are *no* proper uses, illustrations about which we can be enthusiastic do not mean there are not plenty of other about which we ought to be more cautious. But, again, unless so central a tenet of the faith is affected so that those who adopt a given contextualization will be lost for all eternity by adopting it, if there is good reason to think some will be genuinely brought into a saving relationship with Jesus by a certain contextualization, we should allow it to be tried. We must agree to disagree in love, supporting rather than separating from one another, even when we ourselves may choose not to adopt a certain proposal.

## Discussion Questions

1. How do you react to the overall thesis of this essay—that one may have to change the presentation of a key teaching of Scripture in order to preserve its meaning and impact for modern audiences? Why do you react the way you do and how legitimate do you think that reaction is?

2. Are certain examples more persuasive than others? If so, which ones and why? If not, why not?

3. What additional examples can you think of that might be particularly important and relevant to your culture?

4. What pitfalls should we be aware of in this kind of contextualization? In other words, what criteria can we use to make sure we change what needs to be and not what shouldn't be?

5. Does your particular Christian community focus more on preserving traditions for the sake of those already believers or on creative change for the sake of winning unbelievers? Are both of these goals equally important in church life or should one take precedence over another? Explain your rationale.

---

83    John J. Davis, "Contextualization and the Nature of Theology," in *The Necessity of Systematic Theology*, ed. John J. Davis (Grand Rapids, MI: Baker, 1980), 184-85.

# 4

## Ground Level Contextualization

### Ruth Julian

*Ruth Julian has been a missionary with The Christian and Missionary Alliance in the Republic of Congo for eight years. She is a professor at the Alliance Bible Institute of Congo and is also a visiting professor at several seminaries and Bible schools in both the Republic of Congo (Brazzaville) and the Democratic Republic of Congo (Kinshasa), teaching in the areas of mission and contextualization. Along with her teaching responsibilities, she also enjoys being involved in one to one and small group discipleship. Ruth is married and has four children. Education: BA (University of Illinois), MDiv (Alliance Theological Seminary), PhD (Asbury Theological Seminary).*

It's early in the morning as I walk beside and look out over one of the largest rivers in the world. The fishermen are rowing their dugout canoes back to shore after spending hours standing, throwing their nets out, and pulling them in. As the sun reflects off the water, the *Kongo ya sika* float lazily down the river toward the cataracts of the Congo River. What are these *Kongo ya sika*? They are the "new Congo," islands of grass and weeds that have pulled away from the shore and enter the current that flows to the ocean. Although the surface of these "islands" may seem large, what one can see at the surface is dwarfed by the reality of the root mass that is hidden from view, the unseen part that holds the "island" together.

As we look at contextualization, I would like to take this image of *Kongo ya sika* as a picture of culture, with the concealed root mass being an illustration of worldview. In our approach to Scripture and the theological process as a whole, we come as people embedded in culture with a worldview that has been shaped by this culture. In this paper, we will investigate the interplay between worldview and the task of contextualizing theology. An important question in this exploration is: "Does worldview have a place in the task of contextualizing theology?" A related question is: "How is folk theology, which lies at the level of worldview, implicated in the task of contextualizing theology?" Before discussing the influence of worldview on the task of con-textualizing theology, we must first understand the term "contextualization."

## What Is Contextualization?

Although the term was first introduced by Shoki Coe in 1972 at the World Council of Churches consultation, the practice of contextualization has been around for a long time.[1] Many definitions of this term have been drafted since Coe's first use of it.[2] As used in this paper, contextualization is the process of making the gospel relevant to people in such a way to be able to speak to their hearts. Not only this, but through the process of contextualizing theology, the gospel should also challenge Christians when their daily walk is not following the path of biblical teaching. Andrew Walls calls this the tension between the "indigenizing" principle and the "pilgrim" principle, that is, the tension between making the gospel at home in a culture and the fact that the gospel message always brings challenges to cultural practices that are in conflict with the Word of God.[3]

The problem for many evangelicals is not with the *concept* of contextualization necessarily. We have come to see the importance of contextualization in our multi-cultural world. A problem does arise when we consider the *process* of contextualization. Where culturally does this process start? What preunderstandings do we bring consciously and subconsciously to the table when we begin the task of contextualizing theology? What keeps this process from deteriorating into syncretism? One main area of concern in this task of contextualizing theology is the role worldview.

## What Is Worldview?

Worldview is a term that has, in some ways, become devoid of meaning because it has been used in ways that are either too limiting (e.g., the "Christian worldview") or too powerful (e.g., the driving force behind why a people group acts in a certain way).[4] When the term is used like this, it cannot speak to the fact that throughout the world today, because of the impact of modernity and globalization, many of us live in fractured and eclectic societies which are practically impossible to describe as having a monolithic worldview. Given this reality, I still find the term "worldview" useful because, even in a fractured society, cultural foundations exist that hold a society together. Some people in a given society may see the world differently than others in the same society, but there will be areas of overlap in their general worldview. World-

---

1    Shoki Coe introduced this term at a World Council of Churches consultation. See Ray Wheeler. "The Legacy of Shoki Coe," *International Bulletin of Missionary Research*. 26, no. 2 (April 2002): 77-80.

2    See Bruce Nicholls, *Contextualization: A Theology of Gospel and Culture* (Downers Grove, IL: InterVarsity Press, 1979); Stephen Bevans, *Models of Contextual Theology* (Maryknoll, NY: Orbis Books, 2002); Robert   Schreiter, *Constructing Local Theologies* (Maryknoll, NY: Orbis Books, 1985) for examples. See also Krikor Haleblian, "The Problem of Contextualization," *Missiology: An International Review* 6, no 1 (January 1983): 95-111.

3    Andrew F. Walls, *The Missionary Movement in Christian History; Studies in the Transmission of Faith* (Maryknoll: Orbis Books, 2006), 7-8.

4    Kathryn Turner, for example, contends that modern cultural anthropology, with its understanding of worldview and whole cultures, is not useful. Kathryn Turner, *Theories of Culture: A New Agenda for Theology* (Minneapolis, MN: Augsburg Fortress, 1997). See also Brian M. Howell, "Globalization, Ethnicity, and Cultural Authenticity: Implications for Theological Education," *Christian Scholar's Review* 36, no. 1 (Fall 2006).

view, as used in this paper, includes categories of reality, assumptions and preunderstandings about reality, values in society, and emotions allowed or not allowed in society. All of these can and do inform how we approach Scripture.

Worldview itself is a part of culture. Because culture is so tied with context, and therefore with contextualization, it is necessary to devote some time to its discussion. For this, I will rely on anthropological insights from Louis Luzbetak and Ngindu Mushete, who both describe culture as having three levels.[5] The foundational level of culture, the deepest level, is the worldview and has to do with the mentality or psychology of a group. Worldview is where one finds "the underlying premises, emotionally charged attitudes, basic goals and drives, starting-points in reasoning, reacting, and motivating."[6]

Ideas held at this foundational level lay the ground rules for life and are rarely questioned or thought about. These premises are held at such a deep level that people do not usually even know that they exist; they are simply an aspect of reality. Mushete gives the examples of concepts about God, the world, life, death, and the afterlife existing at this level.[7]

Moving up through the levels of culture, one comes to the structural level where one finds the ideas that give reasons and purposes for what will ultimately be acted out at the surface level of culture. This structural level is the functional, rational level. The unquestioned, hidden presuppositions of the foundational level give rise to the thoughts, ideas, beliefs, and rationales of the structural level, and the two levels are fairly strongly connected. In this structural level of culture Mushete places the cultural systems (e.g., medical, family, judiciary, education).

The surface level of culture, the observable part, grows out of the structural level. Although the visible forms of the surface level are attached to the reasons developed in the structural level, the attachment is not as strong as that between the structural and foundational level. This means that the visible forms on this surface level can change relatively easily compared to the structural and foundational levels of culture. The surface level is where Mushete puts the culturally superficial things (e.g., clothes, means of exchange, means of communication).

Culture begins at the foundational, worldview level, moves up through the structural level, finally reaching into the observable surface level. The relationship between the three levels is important. One could easily assume that if there is change at the surface level, there is change at the more foundational level. This is not necessarily true.

---

5    Louis Luzbetak, *The Church and Cultures* (Maryknoll: Orbis Books, 1988): 223. Ngindu Mushete, "Modernity in Africa," *Trends in Mission: Toward the 3rd Millennium,* eds. William Jenkinson and Helene O'Sullivan (Maryknoll, NY: Orbis Books, 1991): 144. See also Paul Hiebert, *Transforming Worldviews* (Grand Rapids, MI: Baker Academic, 2008).

6    Luzbetak, 78.

7    Ngindu Mushete, 144.

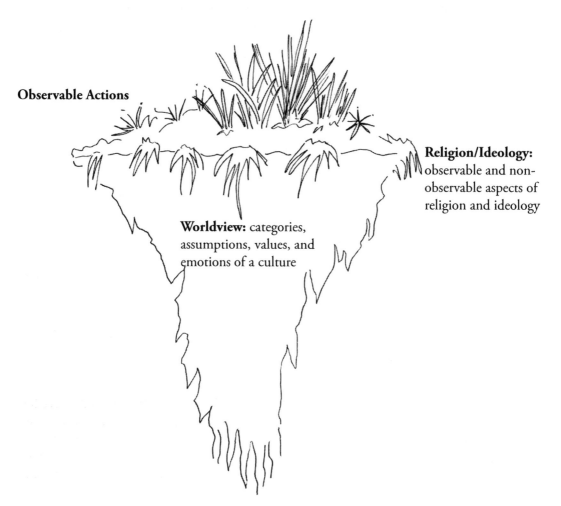

**Observable Actions**

**Religion/Ideology:** observable and non-observable aspects of religion and ideology

**Worldview:** categories, assumptions, values, and emotions of a culture

Figure 1. Worldview illustration

To illustrate this explanation of culture, I will use the phenomenon mentioned earlier of float-ing islands on the Congo River. If we take this image as an illustration of culture, it can help us understand that the major part of culture is the part that is invisible to physical observa-tion. The observable part of the floating island is only one aspect of culture.[8] Less observable is religion and ideology, which are just above and below the surface of the water. Religious preunderstandings, such as evangelical preunderstandings, exist mainly at this second level. The main component of this floating island is found well under the surface of the water. The sum of reality is taken in and filtered through categories that make sense for the culture in question. These are the categories through which the world is viewed and understood. Here dwells the culture's assumptions about the world, the values that are important to the people of the culture, as well as the emotions that are either affirmed or not accepted in society. This

---

8    Justin Kimpalu, a Congolese investigator of Congolese culture, shared this idea using a floating island to describe culture with me during a language learning lesson.

is also where cultural preunderstandings exist. If contextualization remains at the surface level of a people's culture and does not penetrate and take into account the worldview, true contextualization has not taken place. Change and transformation to follow God will only take place at the actions and religion/ideology levels of culture. These changes will still be informed and driven by the original worldview. Unless the major unseen aspect of culture (i.e., worldview) is addressed and allowed into the theological process, contextualization will remain at the surface of culture only. Contextualization must take into account the whole of the island (what is seen and what is not seen) if it is to do the dual task of listening to and bringing biblical critique to the worldview.

## Worldview and Preunderstanding and Their Influence on Hermeneutics

The concept of preunderstanding played an important role in the recent past as theologians have sought for an "objective" theology. "Preunderstanding," simply taken apart, means the understanding that comes before. For theologians, it is more than this. Nebeker defines it as:

> the personally acquired prior knowledge that, consciously or unconsciously, informs and influences one's interpretation of Scripture. Working in conjunction with our settled convictions, preunderstanding is the ever expanding conceptual or ideational grid through which we process the phenomena of life and through which we interpret Scripture.[9]

One can divide the above definition into two main parts. The first has to do with the doctrinal preunderstandings gained through religious education and can be placed at the structural level of culture. The second part of the definition has to do with cultural preunderstanding. This cultural aspect of preunderstanding is part of worldview assumptions and categories. These inform and drive the doctrinal preunderstandings. Together, these inform our worldview which we bring to the task of contextualizing theology. Bruce Nicholls, one of the early missiologists who wrestled with the term "contextualization," draws a distinction between preunderstandings about the authority of the Bible and preunderstandings about one's culture.[10] As Nicholls points out, evangelicals approach Scripture with a preunderstanding that the Bible is the Word of God for all generations. This preunderstanding is not the target of this paper. Instead, we are looking at cultural preunderstandings and those tied to the life experiences that Christians bring to the task of contextualizing theology.

The concept of preunderstanding arose out of the work of modern philosophers and theologians (e.g., Schleiermacher, Heidegger, Bultmann, Gadamer). Richard Palmer, in explaining Schleiermacher's hermeneutic, finds that Schleiermacher saw the inescapability of having preunderstanding before true interaction between the text and the interpreter could take place, stating:

---

9    Gary Nebeker, "'Who Packed Your Bags?': Factors That Influence Our Preunderstandings," ed. Greg Herrick, 2002. Online http://www.bible.org/assets/worddocs/herrick_preunderstanding.zip. Accessed February 6, 2008.

10    Bruce J. Nicholls, *Contextualization: A Theology of Gospel and Culture* (Downers Grove, IL: InterVarsity Press, 1979), 39.

Is it not vain to speak of love to one who has not known love, or the joys of learning to those who reject it? One must already have, in some measure, a knowledge of the matter being discussed. This may be termed the minimal preknowledge necessary for understanding, without which one cannot leap into the hermeneutical circle.[11]

Thiselton, also investigating Schleiermacher's hermeneutic, states that "Schleiermacher saw that what is to be understood must, in a sense, be already known."[12] Moving on to Heidegger, we see that in his probing the interaction between being, understanding and interpretation, he also indicates that understanding must already be present for interpretation to take place. He states: "To say that 'circumspection discovers' means that the 'world' which has already been understood comes to be interpreted."[13] Palmer explains:

> For Heidegger, understanding is the power to grasp one's own possibilities for being, within the context of the lifeworld in which one exists....it is the structure in being which makes possible the actual exercise of understanding on an empirical level. Understanding is the basis for *all* interpretation; it is co-original with one's existing and is present in every act of interpretation.[14]

Bultman's similar idea of existential being and understanding is seen in his statement:

> Hence it is evident that each interpretation is guided by a certain interest, by a certain *putting of the question*: What is my interest in interpreting the documents? Which question directs me to approach the text? It is evident that the questioning arises from a particular interest in the matter referred to, and therefore that a particular understanding of the matter is presupposed. I like to call this *a preunderstanding*.[15]

According to Bultman, our preunderstanding provides us the impetus to approach the text in the first place. Without preunderstanding we would not come to the text, would not pose questions of the text, and would not seek to understand the text. The hypothesis of each of these philosophers and theologians is that we cannot approach the work of interpreting Scripture without bringing along our preunderstandings. Charles Taber, an anthropologist, posits the same idea when he states: "theology, in its questions, its methods, and its language, is extremely dependent on conceptual resources that belong to the *human culture* of the theologians."[16] These conceptual resources are at the worldview level.

---

11    Richard E. Palmer, *Hermeneutics: Interpretation Theory in Schleiermacher, Dilthey, Heidegger, and Gadamer* (Evanston, IL: Northwestern University Press, 1969): 87-88.

12    Anthony C. Thiselton, *The Two Horizons: New Testament Hermeneutics and Philosophical Description with Special Reference to Heidegger, Bultmann, Gadamer, and Wittgenstein* (Grand Rapids, MI: William B. Eerdmans Publishing Company, 1980), 103.

13    Martin Heidegger, *Being and Time,* John Macquarrie and Edward Robinson, transl. (New York: Harper and Brothers, 1962), 189.

14    Palmer, *Hermeneutics*, 131 (emphasis in original).

15    Rudolf D. Bultmann, *History and Eschatology* (Edinburgh: The University Press, 1957), 113 (emphasis in original).

16    Charles Taber, "Is There More Than One Way to Do Theology?" *Gospel in Context*. 1, no. 1 (January 1978):4 (emphasis added).

We see, then, that preunderstanding, which is a part of worldview, is not something that Christians, evangelical or not, can simply shed as they approach Scripture. They may be able to identify some preunderstandings, perhaps even many, but others are so embedded in their worldview that they are beyond awareness.

Since we do bring preunderstandings to the interpretation table, we need to look at what effect these might have on the development of theology. Theologian D. A. Carson discusses potential consequences of preunderstanding on hermeneutics. One consequence is an inability to listen to and be changed by Scripture. This comes from what Carson calls "immutable non-negotiables" which form a barrier that keeps the gospel from challenging one's preunderstanding.[17] Instead of moving into a better understanding of God and his heart for the world, people's immutable non-negotiables push them to reinterpret the Scripture in such a way that it fits with their non-negotiables. Because of this consequence, evangelicals react most negatively to this meaning of preunderstanding. This is understandable. If Scripture is not able to speak into our lives, we move into a position above Scripture and move out of the arena of evangelicalism. One example of an immutable non-negotiable would be the idea from modernity that what cannot be examined scientifically does not exist. Many missionaries who came to Central Africa ignored the reality of sorcery in the culture because of their "immutable non-negotiables" that stemmed from their modern education.[18]

A second consequence, that of change, derives from what Carson labels "functional non-negotiables." These are preunderstandings that, after interaction and further insights from Scripture, can be changed and reformulated to be brought into accordance with Scripture.[19] These functional non-negotiables are more pliable than the immutable non-negotiables and can be transformed though interactions with God's Word. An example of a functional non-negotiable is a group's preunderstanding that people of another ethnic group are not actually people, but somehow sub-human. Christians from this group will not be able to hear the Scripture's message to take the gospel to every people group, including the one that they consider to be sub-human. This happened to a young woman who was attending our Bible school in Brazzaville. She considered the pygmies, who lived in a village near her village, to be sub-human. Even though she read in Scripture about preaching the gospel to every nation and making disciples of every nation, she could not see that this included pygmies. This functional non-negotiable was changed through the power of the Holy Spirit when her preunderstanding was challenged by a sermon on missions. She finally saw that the pygmies were people just like her and needed to hear the message of the gospel. She then spent the next summer vacation traveling to their village to bring the gospel to them. A change in her worldview affected her theology, which in turn influenced her actions.

---

17    D. A. Carson, "A Sketch of the Factors Determining Current Hermeneutical Debate in Cross-Cultural Contexts." *Biblical Interpretation and the Church: The Problem of Contextualization,* ed. D. A. Carson. (Nashville, TN: Tomas Nelson Publishers, 1984), 13.

18    Even immutable non-negotiables can be changed if one is open to the Holy Spirit.

19    D. A. Carson, 12.

## Value of Worldview in the Task of Contextualization?

A necessary step in this investigation into the influence of worldview on the development of an evangelical contextual theology is to pose the following questions: Are preunderstandings something that we should value as evangelicals? Should we not simply avoid preunderstandings and strive for an objective theology?[20] These are valid questions that need to be answered, especially given the fear that some evangelicals have of preunderstanding leading to a twisting or misinterpretation of Scripture.

Behind these questions is the belief that it is possible to avoid or set aside our preunderstandings in our effort to develop an objective theology, that is, a theology that is culture-free. This would require one of two assumptions. Either theologians simply assume that they do not have preunderstandings or that they can identify their preunderstandings and lay them aside as they interact with the text.

The problem with the first assumption is that everyone has preunderstandings. These derive from our worldview and influence deeply our ideas of how the world works and our place in it. No one comes to the Bible with a *tabula rasa*. We all come with our preunderstandings to the task of interpretation of the Bible as a text. As theologian William Tolar states: "No one comes to biblical interpretation without his or her own contemporary cultural preunderstandings. No reader is totally objective and free of presuppositions which profoundly influence one's interpretation."[21]

This brings us to the second assumption. Is it possible to identify one's preunderstandings and then lay them aside or control them so that they do not affect interpretation? Because preunderstandings are tied to our worldview, it is difficult, if not impossible, to identify them all. This is especially true if we are attempting to do so without interaction with others who have different worldview assumptions and preunderstandings.

I will illustrate this from something I learned through ethnographic interviews in Brazzaville, Congo. In an attempt to understand the Bakongo worldview, I was asking people questions dealing with their view of reality, human nature, and community among other categories. When I devised my questionnaire, I did not realize that the Bakongo have family chiefs. It was only upon doing several interviews that I became aware of the phenomenon. I then began to ask the interviewees about this reality and the role of a family chief. All of them spoke of having a family chief. Many even seemed surprised that I would ask if their family had a family chief. When I explained that in my culture we do not have family chiefs like they do, the interviewees were amazed that a family could exist without a family chief. Their preunderstanding is that everyone has a family chief.

Apart from my interaction with Bakongo, I was unaware of the reality of a family chief. Without interaction with me, a person from outside of their culture, the Bakongo were unaware

---

20    See Matt Cook's article, "Contextual but Still Objective?" for a more in-depth discussion of objective theology, chapter 5 of this volume.

21    William Tolar, "The Grammatical-Historical Method," *Biblical Hermeneutics: A Comprehensive Introduction to Interpreting Scripture*, eds. Bruce Corley, Steve W. Lemke and Grant I. Lovejoy (Nashville, TN: Broadman and Holman Publishers, 2002), 21.

that families exist in the world without a family chief. This shows that on our own we are unable to identify all of our preunderstandings. If we cannot recognize all of our preunderstandings, we will not be able to lay them all aside when we approach the task of interpretation and the development of theology.

Whether or not we like to think that theology is rooted in culture, more and more evidence points to the fact of culture's influence on theology. Although we can attempt to downplay its importance, this only leads to a naïve assumption about the objectivity of our theology. Christian cultures other than our own will be able to discern the cultural elements in our seemingly objective theology and might reject the theology because of these cultural elements. On the other hand, they might believe that these cultural elements are necessary for proper Christian behavior. For example, Christians may believe that only bread and wine (or grape juice) can be used for communion, even though neither of these elements are native to their culture.

Instead of seeking an "objective theology," Christians can intentionally bring the elements from their cultural setting to Scripture in order to enable them to discover where God is already working in their culture and join God there. Vincent Donovan illustrated this well in his story of how the Masai came to Scripture with their culture, learned from Scripture, and allowed Scripture to affirm and also correct their culture.[22] As I teach an introduction to missiology class in Brazzaville, Congo, I can feel the excitement of the students as we discuss culture and Scripture. They begin to see, as we bring elements of their culture to Scripture, that they can take part in many of the rituals and other aspects of their culture that had been looked down upon or ignored by the mission established church. They begin to understand that God is not against culture, but instead can use it in order to speak to the hearts of the people of that culture. God is already at work in their culture. These same students learn much from looking at some of the evils in their culture and society and brainstorming about whether or not these aspects of culture can be transformed or whether they need to be rejected outright. This gives them a taste of what can be done through contextualization. Their task of contextualizing theology as cultural insiders is only just beginning.

As the story from Congo illustrates, not only can considering culture point out the ways that God is already working in that culture, it can also show aspects of culture that are not in line with Scripture. Christians working together can bring the evils in society under the scrutiny of Scripture and begin developing a theology that enables and encourages the church to address these issues. This may not be an easy task because "evil" is a broad term, encompassing both individual and social ills. Christians may also fall into the trap of only addressing the evils that are in line with their preunderstandings. For example, a group might deal with issues of personal sins and yet ignore sins and injustices in society.

God has set us in culture. We cannot escape this fact. Our culture gives us a worldview which guides us as we live in this world. Coming to Scripture with our worldview enables us to hear God from within our culture. This brings into play Walls' "indigenizing principle" and the "pilgrim principle," mentioned earlier.[23] The indigenizing principle allows the gospel to affirm

---

22    Vincent J. Donovan, *Christianity Rediscovered* (Maryknoll, NY: Orbis Books, 2003).
23    Walls, 7-8.

us in that place and environment where God has placed us from birth. The pilgrim principle is when the gospel calls for the transformation of our lives and culture.[24] With these two principles in play, we are not forced to step out of our culture or deny our experiences. Instead, we approach Scripture with our preunderstandings about the world and with our cultural setting intact. God, through his translatable revealed Word, is then able to speak to us where we are and transform us as we allow him to do so. It is because we can bring our worldview to the task of interpreting the Bible that evangelical Christians can speak to their own culture. It is through learning other people's cultures and worldviews with their preunderstandings that evangelical Christians can in turn, through mission, make a way for the gospel to speak to people of other cultures. This is the thrust of contextualization. If one strips away all preunderstandings and ignores worldview, even if that were possible, the resulting theology would remain at a superficial level instead of reaching the people of that culture at a heart level.

## Using Worldview in the Task of Contextualizing Theology

Traditionally, evangelicals have assumed that by using the proper hermeneutical principles, one could come to the text objectively and develop an objective theology. As we became aware of the fact that no one approaches Scripture without preunderstandings, the effort was then placed on identifying these preunderstandings and doing our best to lay them aside. This, however, sets up a false sense of "objectivity" because, as illustrated above, we are not always able to identify our preunderstandings. Even if we were able to identify our preunderstandings, it would not necessarily be for the best. All of these preunderstandings, those of which we are aware and those of which we are not, form a starting place for the work of the hermeneutical spiral. The hermeneutical spiral describes the dialogical interaction between the interpreter and the text.[25] In its incipient form, philosophers and theologians understood this spiral to be a circle, viewing the interaction between the interpreter and the text as cyclical, moving from interpreter to text and back again in an effort to find a fusion between the horizon (or worldview) of the text and the horizon of the interpreter.[26]

Theologians began to see that this flat circular interaction was incomplete because it did not take into account the fact that the interpreter's context, experience, and preunderstanding both influence the interaction with the text and are influenced by the text. Viewing the task as a hermeneutical spiral moves from a starting point of preunderstanding to Scripture and back again in an ever growing spiral that evolves more and more as interaction is made between us as interpreters, our preunderstandings, our worldview as a whole, our context, and Scripture. We must allow Scripture to change us, transform us, and call us to repentance where need be. This hermeneutical spiral can be seen as part of the process of sanctification. We come to Scripture as we are and through the leading of the Holy Spirit and interaction with Scripture, we move toward being more and more conformed to the image of Jesus Christ.

---

24    Walls, 8. See also Daniel R. Shaw, "Contextualizing the Power and the Glory." *International Journal of Frontier Mission.* 12, no. 3 (July 1995): 156.

25    Grant R. Osborn, The Hermeneutical Spiral: A comprehensive Introduction to Biblical Interpretation (Downers Grove, IL: InterVarsity Press, 1991).

26    Hans-Georg Gadamer, *Truth and Method*, 2nd rev. ed., transl and rev. Joel Weinsheimer and Donald G. Marshall (New York: Crossroad, 1989).

Some may critique this process as being too optimistic. How can we be sure that the movement in the hermeneutical spiral will actually be developmental and positive? This is a valid question. While there is no guarantee that the interaction between the person or group and the Scripture will bring positive results, there are guardrails that can help in this process. One is humility. If we remain humble throughout this process, we will be more open to critique and the question of where the hermeneutical spiral is taking us. A second guardrail is to remain sensitive to the Holy Spirit. The Holy Spirit is the great teacher. We, as evangelicals, must be able to trust him not only to teach us, but also to teach those of other cultures. Third, we need to study other theologies, both historical and those developed throughout the world today. As evangelicals engage in this process of interpreting Scripture through the spiral hermeneutical process, we must do so with these guardrails in place if we desire to move in a positive development in our hermeneutic.

As we take the concept of a hermeneutical spiral and place it in the arena of world Christianity, we will see that this hermeneutical spiral, if begun by majority world theologians, will not necessarily bring these theologians to the same place where Westerners are theologically. In fact, this spiral may bring them to very different places theologically, and yet remain in the evangelical perspective. We should celebrate this phenomenon that accentuates cultural diversity.

In order to illustrate this idea, I will discuss two examples of preunderstanding stemming from worldview, one from Congo and one from North America, and show how preunderstanding has affected the understanding of the gospel and who Christ is. The first example comes from people in l'Eglise de l'Alliance Chrétienne et Missionnaire du Congo in Brazzaville, Congo. The worldview of a large sector of this people comes from the Bakongo people group. Upon study of this people's worldview, I found that the Bakongo have a strong sense of need for a protector. Traditionally, this protection has come though the family chief who is able to protect the members of the family both in the day, and spiritually speaking, at night. This ability to protect spiritually is what is most important for the Bakongo. They know that they need protection from sorcerers and rely on the family chief to provide this. When Bakongo become Christians, this part of their worldview comes with them. They live in a reality that is fraught with spiritual powers. They know that they still need protection from these powers. Therefore, along with Jesus being their Savior, he also becomes their protector. This protection is not viewed as physical protection, as may be understood by North American Christians who pray for protection during a trip, but a spiritual protection from sorcerers who may attempt to "eat their souls" and thereby kill them.

If we move to North America, where one of the basic assumptions, even as evangelicals, is that we have an inalienable right to pursue happiness in this life, one can easily find in churches people who look to Jesus as the one who can lead people to have a safe and good life. Most North American Christians do not look to Jesus as their protector from sorcerers, rather as their giver of blessing.

Here we see that Christians from different contexts have approached Scripture with different preunderstandings and have, at least potentially, begun the hermeneutical spiral. With their preunderstanding, Congolese Christians will tend to begin with Scriptures that uphold their preunderstanding of God as the protector of his people. One example is Balaam, who is not able to pronounce a curse upon the people of Israel. As the Congolese move along the spiral, their theological understanding of God needs to expand and become more complete. On the other hand, North American Christians, even those who are evangelicals, may begin their hermeneutical spiral with passages of Scripture that give reassurance for their lifestyles (e.g., passages that speak to the idea of blessing, especially material blessing). They too need to continue to move along the hermeneutical spiral to have a more complete understanding of what their lives are to be like as Christ's followers.

While evangelical theologians may not react to a slightly nuanced version of traditional evangelical contextual theology that theologians in another context develop, there may be a fear that, without some kind of criteria, following the hermeneutical spiral will take evangelical contextual theologies to non-evangelical positions. This is where we, in faith in the Holy Spirit who leads and teaches Christians in all contexts, must lay aside our distrust of preunderstandings, especially of those of another culture, and trust that Christians from other cultures will develop contextual theologies that will speak to their people and call them to repentance and transformation. The hermeneutical spiral, when Scripture is placed as the foundational and authoritative element, and when the guardrails laid out above are in place, can bring critique to the theologian's preunderstanding as well as to the worldview of the interpretive community. Although worldview can give an essential starting point for the hermeneutical spiral, it must not dictate the development of the theology. Scripture remains the foundational element in the hermeneutical spiral. However, since people are unaware of parts of their worldview, they may not know when their preunderstandings are actually dictating the process of the hermeneutical spiral instead of Scripture. This is where interaction from other traditions and cultures can be helpful. Others can often see blind spots in a theology where those from inside the culture, because of their sub-conscious preunderstandings, cannot. This requires a measure of humility on the part of those developing the theology, because it is not easy to be critiqued by another, especially when there is disagreement about interpretation. This disagreement is often based on one's preunderstanding and worldview rather than Scripture. For example, in the Chinese contextual theology developed in a later article, we can see that the Chinese church does not view suffering as something to be avoided, as a North American preunderstanding would suggest, but rather is simple part of the Christian life which, although difficult, brings maturity. [27]

The fact of following a hermeneutical spiral does not imply that exegesis and analysis of the text and its context, both literary and contextually, will not happen. These disciplines are necessary for shedding light on the hermeneutical process as a whole. Nor does it imply a non-directed approach to interpretation. This hermeneutical process, especially when done by a community for the development of contextual theology, needs to have a shepherd or leader who is sensitive to the promptings of the Holy Spirit leading the process. [28] The input of cultural outsiders, particularly because of their ability to see aspects of culture to which insiders may be blinded, can also be influential in this process, although these outsiders should not be the ones directing the outcome of the process; the task of contextualizing theology must be done by cultural insiders. For too long theology has been done by cultural outsiders (e.g., missionar-

---

27    See Paul Siu's article in this volume, "Theologizing Locally," chapter 9.

28    Schreiter discusses the importance of the whole community of faith being the theologian (*Constructing Local Theologies*, 16ff).

ies, theologians from the West, etc.). Not only do cultural insiders know their own culture, and can therefore bring critique and affirmation to this culture with respect to what Scripture says, but doing the task of contextualization themselves gives them a voice.[29] Dyrness also points out that when insiders do theology for themselves, they are able to bring to light their own understandings of the concepts in Scripture (e.g., salvation, eternal life, etc.) instead of submitting these ideas to previously developed theologies.[30] Also, church history and traditional, historical theologies can and should speak into this process. Along with all this, those who are involved in developing or encouraging contextual theologies to develop should endeavor to remain humble and cautious in their task, striving always to remain sensitive to the leading of the Holy Spirit.

## Folk Theology and Contextualization

We have looked briefly at both the value and use of worldview for the task of contextualizing theology. Another idea which should be explored before bringing this discussion to a close has to do with folk religion.

### What Is Folk Religion?

Folk religion is a term used to discuss the "religious beliefs and practices of the common people."[31] In contrast to high religion, which tends to address issues such as "origin, purpose, and destiny of persons, communities, and the cosmos," folk religion tends to address the "intimate issues" of life (e.g., fertility, mystical reasons for illnesses, protection from evil forces, etc.).[32]

Folk religion exists in both small-scale and large-scale societies and is manifested differently depending on the society in which it exists.[33] In small-scale societies, folk religion deals mainly "the traditional beliefs and rights of a particular society" and is not greatly influenced by the tenets of high religion.[34] In large-scale societies, both folk religion and high religion exist together. What ties both small and large-scale societies together with regard to folk religion is that, regardless of whether there is the influence of high religion, the attraction of the claims of folk religion is there. People seek out folk religion because it purports to bring them the results for which they are seeking. For example, people in a large-scale society take part in formal religion, but what is more important to them is the reality of "making a living and dealing with the crises of their everyday existence."[35] People in a small-scale society are seeking answers to these same questions.

---

29 William A. Dyrness, *Invitation to Cross-Cultural Theology: Case Studies in Vernacular Theologies* (Grand Rapids, MI: Zondervan Publishing House, 1992), 33-34.

30 Ibid., 35-36.

31 Hiebert, Shaw, Tiénou, 75. See also Schreiter, 124-125 for a further discussion of the terms "popular religion," "common religion," and "folk religion."

32 Matthias Zahniser, *Symbol and Ceremony: Making Disciples Across Cultures* (Monrovia, CA: MARC, 1997), 47.

33 Peter W. Williams, *Popular Religion in America: Symbolic Change and the Modernization Process in Historical Perspective* (Urbana, IL: University of Illinois Press, 1989), 9-17. Hiebert, Shaw, Tiénou, 75-77.

34 Hiebert, Shaw, Tiénou, 76.

35 Ibid., 76.

## Why Is Folk Religion Important for the Task of Contextualizing Theology?

An assumption that stands behind much of the theologizing endeavor implies that theology needs to target and bring people into the understanding and acceptance of the tenets of Christianity as a high religion (e.g., God as creator, redeemer, sustainer, etc.).[36] The assumption is that as the elements of high religion increase in importance, the aspects of worldview which exist at a folk religion level will then diminish in importance. Missiologist Paul Hiebert did some ground-breaking work when he alerted the mission world to the fact that often missionaries work with a ministry framework that has an "excluded middle."[37] In his transformational article, Hiebert states that not only do theologians need to develop a theology that deals with high religion, but they also need to address and develop a theology that deals with how God is involved in both human and natural history.[38]

If we can transpose this idea of folk religion onto our question at hand, that of worldview, we can see that many of our preunderstandings exist at the folk religion level. In our understanding of the hermeneutical spiral, do we as evangelicals expect this spiral to bring all theologies around the world to the level of high religion theology?

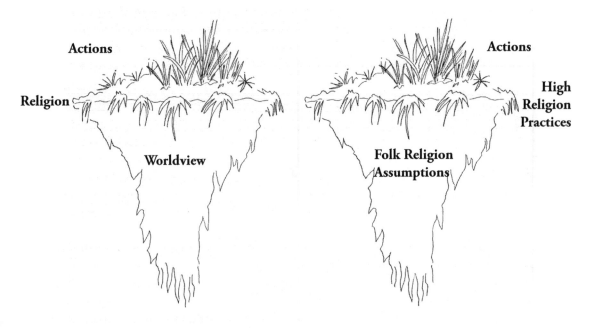

Figure 2. Comparison of Worldview Level and Folk Religion Assumption Level

I propose that not only do missionaries and Christians in a given culture need to understand and deal with folk religion in order to bring it in line with Christian "high religion" theology,

---

36    Ibid., 13; Schreiter, 122.

37    Paul G. Hiebert, "The Flaw of the Excluded Middle" *Missiology* 10, no. 1 (January 1982): 35-48.

38    Ibid., 45-46.

they need to go further and *focus* on folk religion. While the high religion aspects of Christianity should not be absent in the development of contextual theology, the elements of folk religion must be addressed and brought into this development of contextual theology. Folk religion deals with the questions and issues of people's everyday lives. With regard to the levels of culture discussed above, folk religion exists at a more foundational level than does high religion. High religion exists basically at the surface and structural levels of culture (illustrated by the oval at the water level in Figure 2), whereas folk religion, which is tied more strongly to the worldview, is found at the foundational level of worldview. Folk religion exists at the level of assumptions and preunderstandings about the world.

Theology needs to be developed at, and even target, the folk religion level if it is going to be real for people. Instead of attempting to bring people out of folk religion, those involved in contextualizing theology should strive to make sure that this process addresses concerns at the folk religion level and that the truths of Scripture are touching people through folk religion. As Schreiter states:

> Interest in popular religion is of special importance for developing local theologies. A close reading of the shape of popular religion gives us a unique perspective on the nature of religious activity and experience in concrete social contexts....To undertake the development of local theologies while rejecting or ignoring the religious patterns already present in a community suggests the very kinds of paternalism against which local theology has struggled. Hence to be able to develop an adequate local theology one must listen to the religious responses already present in the culture.[39]

The preparation for and celebration of a ceremony described to me by a pastor from Guinea Bissau will illustrate the importance of this.[40] The land was no longer being productive. The people were sick and dying. The pastor of a church in the capital city heard from the Lord that the covenant made by his ancestors with evil spirits needed to be broken and the region placed into the hands of Jesus. With the prayer support of his church coupled with forty days of fasting during daylight hours, he sent intercessors into the main village to "spy out the land." They had confrontations with people oppressed by evil spirits, reclaimed areas that were used as shrines for ritual sacrifices to the spirits, and informed the government authorities that they were going to have a three-day ceremony to break the power of the old covenant and begin a new covenant with Jesus Christ. The government officials accepted. The first day of the ceremony, the indigenous king (who was not a Christian) broke the covenant with evil spirits. The second day, the prayer warriors rebuked the spirits who had possession of the land. The third day, the people spoke to the land itself. They picked up handfuls of soil and spoke to it and blessed it, saying: "You, land that is barren, you will no longer be barren, but blessed. You will produce good crops." When I interviewed this pastor, it had only been about a month since the ceremony had taken place. I asked him what the results were; he said that it was too early to tell. This was a long-term process. As I look at this process through the lens of contextualization, however, I can already see results. The people of this region in Guinea Bissau have been affirmed in their culture and yet have also confronted aspects of their culture that are not

---

39  Schreiter, 123.
40  Personal interview November 5, 2008.

in line with Scripture. All of this has been done from the starting point of folk religion, that is, addressing the intimate, everyday needs of people.

This illustration from everyday life in Guinea Bissau illustrates the importance of focusing on, not ignoring, folk religion and beliefs. Folk religion helps us develop contextualized folk theology, that is, a theology that will speak to the common people because it deals with their needs and concerns.

## Is There a Place for Folk Theology in Contextualization?

As discussed earlier, the task of contextualization should be done by insiders. Not only do insiders understand the questions being asked by the folk religion(s) in their context, they understand the issues behind these questions. These insiders can bring their questions and issues and place them under the scrutiny of Scripture.

Heibert, Shaw, and Tiénou underscore the importance of a thorough investigation into a given folk religion and context. This investigatory step must not be circumvented because without it the theology that is developed may miss large parts of the worldview. Therefore, only after this investigation into the folk religion is done should Christians and/or missionaries begin to delve into theological investigations and the process of the hermeneutical spiral.[41] As cultural insiders bring their questions and issues to Scripture, these will be affirmed or critiqued and will, based on this judgment, bring changes to the folk religion. The process of the hermeneutical spiral has begun and must continue.

Most evangelical Christians around the world do not think of themselves as theologians. They attend church and perhaps even read and study their Bibles. Their desire is not to formulate a theology, but to live for God in the everyday world. They do, however, have a subconscious theology that they use to make sense of Scripture.[42] Theologians and missiologists tend to write for others in the academic setting, laying out principles and methods that require the developers of theology to have some kind of theological and/or missiological training. We, I am placing myself in the missiologist camp, talk about how to develop contextual theologies and yet we tend to disregard informal theologies lived out by Christians at the grassroots level.[43]

I would like to recommend that, along with developing contextual theologies that arise out of settings where those doing the theologies have had theological or missiological training, evangelicals also make a place for folk contextual theologies that arise from the average Christian or group of believers in a given context. These Christians are doing theology whether they realize it or not. They will not necessarily be developing formal theology, but as they approach Scripture, they do so with all the pressures, problems, joys, and sorrows that make up everyday life. That is to say, they approach Scripture from within their cultural setting with their set of worldview assumptions and preunderstandings. They are developing folk theology. Unfortunately, without training, a dialogical approach between Scripture and worldview does

---

41   Hiebert, Shaw, Tiénou, 369ff.

42   See Stanley J. Grenz and Roger E. Olson, *Who Needs Theology? An Invitation to the Study of God* (Downers Grove, IL: InterVarsity Press, 1996).

43   See Ibid.

not always happen. Instead, many lay-Christians use a linear approach to Bible study through which their worldview colors what is read but there is no return challenge.[44] The Bible is not given the opportunity to speak back into the reader's life and point out the areas in that life which need to be changed. When this happens, the worldview that Christians bring to Scripture dictates the interpretation instead of Scripture guiding the interpretation.

Once again, I will use an example from Congo to illustrate this. A Bible school in Brazzaville enrolls students from many church affiliations. Some of these churches have pastors who are doing theology using this linear approach. Many have not had theological training and do not know about hermeneutical principles. As they obtain training about how to read and study the Bible, several have realized that they have misunderstood passages of Scripture. What has happened is that their own preunderstandings from their worldview have controlled their interpretation without allowing Scripture to speak back into these preunderstandings.

Those of us who are in the theological or missiological arena need to encourage these lay theologians. We can promote the dialogical process of going from worldview to Scripture and back again as that is inherent in the hermeneutical spiral as part of the ordinary Christian's approach to Scripture.

## Conclusion

Throughout this investigation of worldview and its influence on the task of contextualizing theology, I have endeavored to show that we cannot approach Scripture devoid of worldview in a quest for objective theology. Instead of endeavoring to lay aside our worldview assumption and preunderstandings and ignoring our cultural setting, we have seen the importance of bringing these elements to Scripture, to both give us a starting point for our theological reflection and to have a context within which we can listen for the affirmation and critique that the Holy Spirit will bring to us out of Scripture. We have also seen the value of folk religion, recognizing that folk theology is not something that should be left behind as people pursue Christianity on the level of high religion, but instead should be a focus for contextual theology.

Theologians must keep in mind that the hermeneutical spiral, for a myriad of reasons, can be stopped along the way, causing a people's view of God and the gospel to become stilted and stagnant. Developing a theology should not be the ending point of contextualization. Contexts are constantly changing, especially in the contemporary world. Theologies should continually be brought back into the hermeneutical spiral to be honed to have both a greater relevance and a greater prophetic voice in a given culture. Along with the continuing interaction with a changing context, ideally there would also be dialogue with other theologies, both historic and contemporary, whereby theologians could critique theirs and other's theologies. Christians from different cultures can lovingly, but in truth, critique each other's theology and sharpen these theologies as iron sharpens iron. The result with be a contextual theology that speaks into the daily lives of Christians, pushing them forward in their pursuit of being Christ-like.

---

44   See Taber.

## Discussion Questions

1. What elements of our worldview inform our theology?

2. In what ways could we be more proactive in bringing our preunderstandings/worldview to the interpretive process in developing a contextual theology?

3. What areas of folk theology/religion are important for our context?

4. Do you agree that we should focus on the folk theology level instead of working to bring people into a better understanding of the high religion elements of Christianity? Why or why not?

# 5

# Contextual But Still Objective?

## Matthew Cook

*Matthew Cook is Chargé de cours en Théologie systématique at La Faculté de Théologie de l'Alliance Chrétienne in Abidjan, Côte d'Ivoire. Matt served as senior pastor for five years of a Christian and Missionary Church before moving, with his family, in 1999 to Africa to begin teaching at FATEAC. In 2006, he became involved with the Theological Commission of the WEA. From that involvement he has chaired their contextualization study group which has produced this volume. His concerns remain the localization of theology and its contribution to the global understanding of our life before God. Education: BS in Chemical Engineering (Case Western Reserve University), MDIV (Trinity Evangelical Divinity School), PhD in Systematic Theology (Trinity International University).*

"Whoever frames the problem is king." The business world understands this axiom. The ministry world understands this axiom. It is time the theological world understood this axiom as well.

The one who frames the problem is able to make distinctions between categories and use vocabulary that influences how the problem is understood. When a problem is confronted, "finance" wonders if they should allow "marketing" to frame the question or "product development" or they, themselves. The framing controls the *techniques* used to find a solution and the *nature* of that solution. Sometimes, those techniques and nature are specific to one field or another and give an advantage to one field over another.

That there are many ways to frame a problem does not mitigate against the real existence of the problem nor that most would agree on the problem. In all likelihood, everyone was feeling the need to do something about this problem, it just happens to be that each one could frame it slightly differently according to his/her understanding of the world, field specific category distinctions, or field specific vocabulary.

Contextual evangelical theology is moving in the direction of "whoever frames the problem is king." We have revelation that needs to address real life. There is an object that informs and real access to that reality. Theology must be faithful to that revelation. But "framing" is necessary; theology must be socially located—there are different ways to separate the categories, arrive at a theology, and understand that theology. Even evangelical theology, which accepts the authority of Scripture as the norm of theology, is socially located. The social locatedness of theology comes from framing the problem. Contextual evangelical theology strives for faithfulness to the Bible, framed in culturally specific way.

I will be taking the rest of the chapter to explore how it is possible and necessary that theology be both objective and socially located. To do that, definitions must be revisited and clarified, old or unhelpful components excised, and balance carefully applied. Balance is especially needed in this work to bring together two realities which have previously been viewed dichotomously.[1]

## What Is Objectivity in Theological Reflection?

Objectivity has an overly modernist definition in evangelical circles. A typical (although unfortunate) definition affirms that theological statements are "independent of the believing person and the process of knowledge."[2] That definition reaches back to philosophical correspondence ("true" statements correspond to the thing in itself), but is not identical to it.[3] "Objective theology" is already and always correct. For evangelicals, this means objective theology already corresponds to what the Bible has to say and cannot be changed or improved. While I like very much the idea that our theology matches biblical teaching, I think that this definition needs to be nuanced. First, God is too big for our theological statements;— paraphrasing Augustine, "If you understand it, it isn't God."[4] God, and his revelation found in the Bible, are more complex than any one formulation. Second, the proposition is the only literary form that makes truth statements and, therefore, fits into this type of objective theology. There are many ways in which the Bible communicates, but "objectivity" has traditionally only been about the correspondence, or "truth," of a theological proposition to reality. This cannot be done with poetry, aphorisms, or even narrative.[5] An overly propositional endeavor

---

1    Two examples are sufficient: "...objective theology, and an objective view of Scripture is not possible this side of heaven" David Phillips' blog, http://www.wdavidphillips.com/2008/07/08/experiential-theology, consulted 31 January 2009. "...there is no objective theology. Every theology is shaped by its context" from Malena Björkgen, "Liberation Theology and Feminist Theology: Similarities and Differences," http://www.koed.hu/mozaik13/malena.pdf, consulted 31 January 2009.

2    Fritjof Capra and David Steindl-Rast, with Thomas Matus, *New Paradigm Thinking in Science and in Theology* by Fritjof Capra and David Steindl-Rast, with Thomas Matus, (1992), (http://www.srds.co.uk/begin/papers/paradigms.pdf, consulted 31 January 2009.)

3    D. A. Carson uses "objective" to mean "having extra-mental reality or validity," *The Gagging of God: Christianity Confronts Pluralism* (Grand Rapids, MI: Zondervan, 1996), 120.

4    Augustine, *"Of the words of St. Matthew's Gospel, Chap. iii. 13, 'Then Jesus cometh from Galilee to the Jordan..."* *NPNF (V1-06)* by Schaff, Philip, sec.16.http://www.ccel.org/ccel/schaff/npnf106.vii.iv.html, consulted 31 January 2009.

5    Kevin Vanhoozer, "The Semantics of Biblical Literature: Truth and Scripture's Diverse Literary Forms," in *Hermeneutics, Authority, and Canon*, ed. D. A. Carson and John D. Woodbridge (Grand Rapids, MI: Zondervan, 1986), 49-104.

will severely limit the ability of Scripture to communicate, therefore obviating what should be understood, felt, and emulated. We need a bigger understanding of objectivity that goes beyond propositions. Third, the Bible, although revelatory, offers this revelation through occasional documents. Each of the books of the Bible was written for a specific purpose and a specific place and time. Careful hermeneutics with due attention to the nature of Scripture in its literary context is necessary. That attention to the occasional nature of the documents will narrow the application of any particular explanation of the text. This limits the universality of theology. Fourth, and perhaps the most important part of the definition which has always been implied but not explored, objectivity implies communication: another person or culture which receives and understands the original reality. There is a cultural component in this communication. Therefore, "objective" statements, like the biblical witness itself, are limited by both place and time. The words which so effectively communicated God to one culture (objectively) may be unhelpful in another culture.

Objective theology, instead, should focus on the object (God) and the norm of the theology (the Bible) and the effective communication that revelation.[6] An objective theology will evidence faithfulness to revelation. There needs to be correspondence between what we say and the object about which we speak, but that correspondence has to actually reach the recipient in the way it was intended in the scriptural communication. This means objective theology will not remain unchanged from one culture to another, from one time period to another. We can certainly learn from and communicate with one another, but effective communication requires that the recipient be taken into account. In so doing, humility before a large God, attention to diverse literary forms and to occasion-specific documents will lay the foundation for objective theology.

To some, this may sound like subjectivity. It is not. Subjectivity requires that our time or culture hinders or interrupts the flow of information from or faithfulness to the biblical data. It requires that the *control* over what is being communicated be given to the subject. While such subjectivity is possible, it is not a necessary result of culture's involvement in the theological process.[7]

## How We Have Tried to Attain Objectivity in Evangelical Theology

We evangelicals, especially during the modern period, have wanted to diminish the influence of our presuppositions or our culture in order to attain objective theology. The seemingly prevalent attitude among evangelicals twenty or thirty years ago could be summarized as the following: "Bultmann is right: theology without presupposition is impossible. Schleiermacher

---

6    Mark Young, Professor of Missions at Dallas Theological Seminary, recently (World Evangelical Alliance- Mission Commission, November 2008) orally gave the following criterion for contextual theology: "belief in, worship of, allegiance to the one true God as revealed in the Bible." The importance of the Bible cannot be overlooked when searching for objective theology.

7    Matthew Cook, A Contemporary Epistemology for Theological Prolegomena: Objectivity in the Task of Systematic Theology (Ph.D. Thesis, Trinity International University, 1995).

is right: we need a hermeneutical circle to make our preunderstanding interact with the text.[8] Gadamar is right: there has to be a fusion of our horizon with the horizon of the text. We cannot ignore our cultural influence when doing theology. Therefore, to do objective theology, we have to recognize our cultural influences and biases through cultural analysis and personal reflection. Then we account for them or compensate for them in order to have a theology as non-culturally biased or, even, culturally based as possible. Our goal is objective theology free from cultural influence…a theology available to all and valuable for all."[9]

There are at least three significant problems with this attitude: (1) This understanding of objective theology excludes culture by definition. Is it any wonder that evangelicals have had difficulty understanding how theology could be contextualized? We have, in the recent past, understood cultural influence to be a bad thing in our theology. The time has come to recognize that the admission of cultural influence is unavoidable and, even, valuable. That leads to the second point. (2) The second half of this historical position, charting a path for objective theology, contradicts the first half, recognizing the unavoidable "obstacle" of culture. If culture is unavoidable, as the first half agrees, then we cannot merely recognize it and compensate for it. Ruth Julian, in her chapter of this volume, makes clear that culture is always there in the way we think and act, in the way we do exegesis and theology. Even though we have owned up to the fact of culture's initial affect, we have not owned up to its formative character and, therefore, its enduring influence on how we understand the world and our theologies. (3) This position denigrates the value of culture itself. Categorizing culture as an obstacle puts it in the same category as a skateboard on the sidewalk or an island in a shipping waterway. They are regrettable and inconvenient, but ultimately unimportant.

Objective theology does not have to be something that is unchanged for all (merely translating the words but in the same format), valuable for all (at the same level of efficacy). Objective theology has to enable communication between the biblical teaching and the reader/listener. Since listeners are different, so will that objectively theology be different. Since listeners are affected by their culture, objective theology must take into account that culture. It must not seek to avoid the cultural influence.

## Complete and Universal Truth in Theology Is Not What Objective Theology Should Be

We need to clearly reject another part of the implicit definition of objective theology which has grown up over time amongst evangelicals: If our theology is faithfully representing God and his revelation, the Bible, then it ought to be universally valid. J. I. Packer presented what, to him, was the driving question of theology: "How may we best state and apply the *complete* Christian faith, topic by topic and as a whole, in the light of current interests, doubts, assumptions, per-

---

8    Or a Hermeneutical Spiral according to Osborne. Grant Osborne, *Hermeneutical Spiral* (Downers Grove, IL, IVP, 1991).

9    Even in the late 1980s, when I was doing my theological study, this position was well articulated by both students and some professors at a leading evangelical seminary in America.

plexities, questions, protests, and challenges?"[10] Is it possible to state the "complete" Christian faith? The position for which I am arguing affirms, on the one hand, accessibility to revelation and ability to communicate it effectively while, on the other hand, recognizes that the access and communication will be tied to the context and culture of the one doing the communication. Any theology is a partial truth. There are two reasons for this.

First, few theologians have the hubris to say that their theological affirmations are the only ones that can be made about a particular subject. Most theological books (including this one) are limited in length by the publisher and other practical considerations (the feared exhaustion of the reader). They are not exhaustive treatments of the subject. In discussing healing, one theology may say nothing about the continued role of Jesus while another would emphasize that aspect in its discussion of healing. As another example, one theologian addresses human freedom from the perspective of divine sovereignty while another addresses it existentially. In the face of these seemingly almost contradictory statements, it is better to recognize that neither the first nor the second have understood the entirety of the problem or the revelation. Insufficient evidence may have provoked incomplete statements. Cultural idiosyncrasies may have provoked different emphases. That does not mean these are subjective theologies (controlled by either the author or his social location). They can still be verifiably faithful to revelation (my definition of objectivity) while communicating that revelation in a manner that reaches the culture.

Second, statements on the same subject may not even make sense (at first glance) to someone from another culture. It is not just a matter of using foreign words (Jésus est mon guérisseur) but of using foreign connotations (embedded in a culture or language system). "Jesus is my healer" may be true (a faithful theological and religious representation of the biblical revelation) in my context. But this same statement would be very non-Christian, even if it were linguistically translated into the appropriate language, for certain parts of Africa where the healer is a shaman who manipulates the spirit world through magic. In no sense of the biblical revelation could we say that Jesus fits into that social and religious reality. It is heretical. What was good theology in my context may be heretical in another. To the Buddhist who is trying to get out of the cycle of eternal life and reach Nirvana, the phrase "eternal life" is not attractive and would not be a helpful way of communicating the value God offers to that person.[11]

Many theological statements have universal communicability. They can be translated linguistically, culturally, conceptually, etc., so that someone in another culture can understand the intention of the original statement. But they may not have universal validity. Even after having understood the intention in the original context, the interlocutor in the secondary context may not be willing to make the same connection between the revelation and the theological point made earlier, or she may just not see the point in bothering to make that connection. Cyprian

---

10    J. I. Packer, "Is Systematic Theology a Mirage? An Introductory Discussion," in *Doing Theology in Today's World,* eds. John D. Woodbridge and Thomas Edward McComiskey (Grand Rapids, MI: Zondervan, 1991), 23 (emphasis mine).

11    This example thanks to Ruth Julian, personal communication. See also, the very helpful chapter by Craig Blomberg in this volume. Most importantly, Natee Tanchanpongs' chapter below makes clear that using theology from other social locations can produce heretical, syncretistic results. Cf specifically his second criterion, p. 120.

of Carthage had a tremendous amount of difficulty configuring a biblical pattern to follow when faced with Christians who handed over their Bibles to the authorities under persecution yet later wanted to be re-admitted to the church. Try presenting that same problem to modern America (or other developed country which has both an abundance of Bibles and religious freedom). The validity of Cyprian's conclusion lacks because the situation of the church is significantly different.

I certainly do not find myself in the camp that affirms "my truth is not your truth." However, there are limitations to what it means to faithfully represent revelation in a context.

## Why Everything We Do Is Socially Located

Objective Theology (that which faithfully represents revelation) in one social location is not objective theology in another social location. One of this chapter's theses contains the yet-undefined phrase "social location." Saying that theology is socially located means to some that (a) It is stated according to a specific social location and, therefore, relies upon vocabulary, concepts, and worldview of that context. Every human product is constructed using language. Every language uses vocabulary, concepts, and to some extent worldview, as part of its linguistic system. (b) It was created in and for a specific location. So, the specificity makes it most useful for a particular context. If we talk about theology, the Christian is addressing a specific issue using specific language which comes from her social location. It makes sense that it would be most useful—have the greatest impact and the greatest ability to communicate—in that same location. That is not to say that it is useless or untrue elsewhere. (c) Because the theology came from a specific social location, the words, concepts, and worldview limit its truthful communication to that location. It is not necessarily true elsewhere. Now we get to contentious statements. The motivation for this statement comes from the definition of objective theology given above: it faithfully accesses the object/revelation and then communicates that to the listener. That full communication is necessary for truth (as correspondence). Since every communication requires a human language system[12] then objective theology relies on that as well. In order to evaluate ant statement, one may admit that there are overlaps in language systems. If that is the case (and I argue below that it is), then option (c) only applies in those places where there is no overlap, no translatability. If we assume that there is no overlap *at all* between language systems, we land on the next option. My understanding of "social location" incorporates all three of the preceding positions. (d) It is not understandable or able to be criticized elsewhere. I cannot support this position. However, it frequently seems to be implied when limits of theological discourse imposed by social location are discussed. One person may argue that I am so socially located (being an American) that my critique of their position (which, say, integrates African traditional religions into their understanding of the Bible) is not valuable. That person would say that I have only understood things from my perspective and I cannot understand their perspective. There is no overlap between the conceptual schemes or, therefore they imply, between the language systems.

---

12   This could be as large as the semiotic system. See, Robert Hodge and Gunther Kress, *Social Semiotics* (Ithaca, NY: Cornell: 1988).

As much as some would like to maintain this defense against criticism, this fourth position does not hold up. Donald Davidson offers an appropriate and powerful argument on the ability of one context to understand and evaluate the contextual theology of another context. Davidson says that if conceptual schemes are incommensurable, lacking a basis of comparison, then we would not even know that they exist?[13] Incommensurability entails non-translatability. Since nothing from one conceptual scheme can be translated into another—in this unacceptable position—there are no data to imply that such an alternative scheme exists at all. Since this whole discussion centers on the awareness of the subjective interpretation of other schemes, then something of them has been translated and understood. They can be somewhat translated, however imperfectly. We are confident of this because we are confident that there are points of view different from our own. But if the comprehension extends that far, then we are no longer necessarily restricted from working to understand the interaction with other cultures and concepts on an issue. This argument has not eliminated problems of translation, but rather the barrier of total intranslatability.[14] When there is no overlap in the language systems (intranslatability), people cannot communicate. However, there is overlap. Therefore, social location eliminates neither understanding, dialogue, nor an ability to criticize positions from another social location.

"Social location" is more than mere packaging: a sentence is constructed in a linguistic system. Words are not free-floating. They "land" and have meaning only with the linguistic system which is integrated into a particular social location. Different communities use the same words differently. That is part of the social location. "Someone jacked my car" may mean that an unknown person placed a mechanical jack underneath the car in order to raise it up. Perhaps that person had helped change a flat tire. In another social location, using another set of linguistic assumptions, it may mean that someone has stolen the car. It depends on the context of the statement—not only the linguistic context but the systemic, cultural context. The distinction in this example is not so great between these social locations that the translation could not be easily made. Many statements are translatable through adequate interaction between the associated cultures.

There are different underlying cultural assumptions of reality that influence each statement. For example, it is common today in North America to hear theologians discuss the fundamental interaction of all of the parts of a human: That there is a significant unity of the person in the way that she functions physically, emotionally, mentally, etc. The old discussions of dichotomism (human as body and soul/spirit) or trichotomism (human as body, spirit, and soul) have lost primacy of place. However, when discussing this topic in Africa, there is a strongly entrenched understanding in some of the West African cultures that a human is clearly two parts.[15] The functions and distinctions of the two parts are not identical to the old North American dichotomism, but there is, nonetheless, a clear concern to understand the human as

---

13    Cf. Donald Davidson, "On the Very Idea of a Conceptual Scheme," Proceedings and Addresses of the American Philosophical Association 47 (1973-1974): 5-20. For a different interpretation of Davidson, see Manuel Hernández-Iglesias, "Incommensurability without Dogmas," Dialectica 48 no. 1 (March 1994): 29.

14    One cannot deny partial intranslatablity, of course. Cf. Robert L. Politzer. "A Brief Classification of the Limits of Translatability," The Modern Language Journal 40, no. 6 (October 1956): 319-322.

15    Just within West Africa there is strong disagreement. The Baoule culture, of Cote d'Ivoire, presumes four parts. Yet African culture, in general, emphasizes a unity of the person as well as integration of all aspects of reality.

a collection of two parts. Which one is right? Which one is true? The long-standing debates even in the West indicate that the Bible teaches certain things about theological anthropology, but does not decide everything on the topic. There are certain things (like the human constitution) which will continue to be decided by our cultural understandings as long as they conform or are conformable to the biblical witness. So, finally, is the human a psychosomatic unity? He is understood so by certain North Americans. He is not understood so in certain African cultures. Good theology, faithfully (objectively) accessing revelation in an understandable manner, in one context is not always so in another.

While there is significant overlap (translatability) between linguistic systems, there remain certain statements (theological or otherwise) which are either unique to one linguistic system or, more frequently, incomprehensible to some other linguistic systems/social locations. "God fights for his people" makes little sense and has even less value to a pacifist. "Demons were speaking to me" indicated more about mental stability than theological accuracy in certain Christian groups in America fifty years ago. "God takes care of us" to a Russian entrenched in communistic atheism is simply laughable.[16] These statements have the appearance of being semantically correct—there is a subject, a verb, a compliment—but they have no sense at all in that context. The idea that God would fight (to a pacifist) or that God would care or even "be" (to an atheist) do not fit the cultural understandings of the words being used. I do not wish to imply that concepts or definitions cannot change. Rather, that every statement has a social location where it works and possible locations where it does not work. Statements (including theological statements) are constructed in and for a specific context (social location). For them to faithfully reflect the biblical revelation (be objective), they have to use the vocabulary, concepts, and background of that context for effective communication (be socially located). Once that is done, the statement is rooted in the culture. It usually can be transplanted (translated) into another culture, but that takes work, dialogue, interaction, and time.

Sometimes, translation into another social context, although possible, is just not valuable. Statements from one social location may be irrelevant. They create a mental yawn in another context. They address a non-issue in the secondary context even though they address an important topic from the bible in the primary context. The inerrancy question continues to occupy North American evangelicals, but those in Africa are rarely concerned about it at all. Abortion is a much more significant question in America than in Europe. Church discipline for church members who make sacrifices to ancestral spirits occupies far more African theologians than those in the West. The issue can certainly be understood, but those who do not deal with that question wonder why it would even be important to discuss it.

That everything we do is socially located is not true simply because we use words. We are people who live in a culture. That our thoughts and statements and theology can be partially understood by people of other cultures only urges us to recognize the power of the social location from which they spring.

---

16    And did, indeed, provoke laughter for just such a person when I spoke of God's provision to him in Paris, October 2008.

## Some Hindrances to Good Theology Which Are Not the Result of Social Location

At least three things are mixed together and make the interpretive process difficult: insufficient information, human inadequacy, and cultural influences, the last of which is the specific subject of this chapter.

The source of disagreement between theologies is "insufficient information" when the Bible just does not tell us enough about a particular topic to have a complete picture.[17]  As an example, we can understand that Jesus died on the cross to relieve all who believe on him from the penalty of their sins.  But there has been a great deal of discussion, even argument, about the causal connection between his death and our redemption.  It may be the case that no more information is available than has already been mined from the Bible (insufficient information).

The source of disagreement between theologies is "human inadequacy" when information is available from revelation which has been accidentally overlooked or not adequately incorporated.  Either of these cases leaves gaps.  To compensate for this lack of information, we fill in the gaps with our cultural linguistic connectors.  In English, we have words like "and," "but," and "or" which are called conjunctions.  They function to group parts of sentences together in a meaningful way.  Each of the three will group sentence fragments in different ways.  Likewise, cultures will group biblical information in different ways.  These are cultural judgements; "a basic mental operation in which something is identified, distinguished, or connected."[18] Certain ways will make sense in a culture and others will not.  Theologians must be careful not to make the subjective assumption that the conjunctions from one culture are part of the biblical information, however.

The breadth of the second element, human inadequacy, makes its influence difficult to categorize.[19]  Above, I said it was accidental.  However, it could include purposefully ignoring biblical or non-biblical information; confusion of genre types, functions, or rules for interpreting that genre; incorporating non-biblical—even cultural—information into a theological formulation as though it had the same authority as Scripture, etc.  In my opinion, this is the source of much theological error.  Purposeful corruption of the theological process may produce these influences, but it could also be merely distorted priorities, laziness (and other qualities not associated with the fruit of the spirit), inability or unwillingness to recognize when another genre, say, speaks to the topic at hand and ought to be incorporated into the discussion, or, most importantly for this discussion, an undue value placed on a particular cultural formation of theology. The Prosperity Gospel ("health and wealth") may have been based on the legitimate blessing of God for his people.  But the undue weight it has accumulated in certain

---

17    D. A. Carson used the analogy of a jigsaw puzzle "Unity and Diversity in the New Testament," in *Scripture and Truth*, eds. D. A. Carson and John D. Woodbridge (Grand Rapids: MI: Zondervan, 1983), 91-92.

18    Kevin Vanhoozer, "Always Performing? Playing New Scenes with Creative Fidelity: The Drama-of-Redemption Approach," in *Four Views on Moving beyond the Bible to Theology*, (Grand Rapids:, MI: Zondervan, 2009).

19    See also D. A. Carson, *Doing Theology*, 69, "...it becomes clear that spiritual, moral experience may not only shape one's systematic theology, but may largely constrain what one actually "hears' in the exegesis of Scripture."

theologies seems to be due to the incorporation of cultural judgments which have surpassed or suppressed biblical judgments.

Social location is not the same as theory laden data. Social location means that every word comes from a specific culture. In this sense, access to any communication depends on the involvement of our culture. When I use the phrase "theory laden data," I refer to the position that data are never "raw." They are never without some theoretical construction that ordered the acquisition and controlled the understanding of those data. In some circles, social located-ness results in theory laden data and precludes all discussion of validity.[20] The data have been determined and controlled by the theory to the extent that there is no expectation or assurance of correspondence between our statements and reality, between our theology and revelation. I disagree with that position: The discussion above on the fourth understanding of "social loca-tion" and its refutation by Davidson opens the dialogue between socially located positions. Data cannot be completely controlled by the theory, the theology. Our social location is not incommensurable with others'.

Unfortunately, it is frequently difficult to distinguish the reason for differences in theology: Is it insufficient information which allows different formulations and wholly legitimate divergent theologies? Is it human inadequacy which breeds syncretism or heresy in extreme cases? We need to create theology and means of verifying theology from different social locations, which will give us confidence of faithfulness to the scriptural judgments[21] no matter what culture we are using.[22]

## Forming Theology May Be Socially Located[23]

There are many activities involved in the process of doing theology. The hermeneutical spirals present the most important of them for this context,[24] as they push the hermeneutical circle (where one's preconceived ideas interact with the biblical text) to move toward a goal (the sense

---

20    The thesis of Thomas Kuhn in his *The Structure of Scientific Revolutions* (University of Chicago: 1962) offers the classic example of this position: the scientist's subjectivity makes even science a relativistic endeavor.

21    Cf. Vanhoozer, "Always Performing?" for more discussion on Scriptural judgments.

22    Cf. Natee Tanchanpongs' chapter in this volume.

23    Even though sources will not be discussed here, as they are implicitly discussed elsewhere, here is the official list of sources for doing theology in African Instituted Churches:

1. The Christian Scriptures: The guiding source remains a continuous engagement with the Christian Scriptures.
2. The Founders' Visions (i.e., the founding traditions of the church).
3. The sense of the faithful (sensus fidelium—expressed through the elders, or other members of the church, through their various representative bodies).
4. The work of the Spirit in the church (in hymns, sermons, prayers, dreams, visions, prophecies).
5. Values, epistemology, and cosmology of the African religious heritage.
6. The process of reflection in particular political and socio-economic contexts.
7. Informal and formal dialogue with those of other Christian traditions and other faiths, i.e., engagement with Christian tradition and teaching throughout history and across the world.

From the Department of Theology of the Organization of African Instituted Churches. http://www.oaic.org. content.view/16/31. Consulted 6 January 2009.

24    Grant Osborne, *The Hermeneutical Spiral: A Comprehensive Introduction to Biblical Interpretation* (Downers Grove, IL: IVP, 1991).

of the text as viewed from the context). Each person has his or her own spiral on any particular verse or paragraph. They have their own starting points, but also their own finishing points.

I had always been uncomfortable advocating anything like ethnohermeneutics, where each culture may use its own rules for determining the meaning of the text, because I thought that good hermeneutic processes were the means for objectivity. I still think that good hermeneutics produces good theology. I have come to admit, however, that the process does not guarantee the result and the process is not the criterion for affirming that good theology has resulted. Objective theology, faithfully communicating the biblical text, has to be measured. Let us take as an example the interpretation of a single passage. If the interpretation of that text is found using traditional evangelical hermeneutics (grammatical-historical method), something more radical (say, social reconstruction), or even a dream, we still evaluate the interpretation by the same means: trying to understand—in the interpreter's context—how that meaning represents the teaching, impact, and life of the text in every way.

By saying that even our methods for arriving at the sense of a text are contextual, I do not see any reason for saying that our statements are, therefore, subjective or untrue or unsupportable or unsustainable or unconnected to the textual meaning to which we wish to remain faithful. The criteria for evaluating the validity of a theology will be addressed below.

## How Contextual Evangelical Theology Should Be both Objective and Socially Located[25]

Contextual evangelical theology has been conceived in various ways. Many of these are helpful even if all have problems.

(a) Some have conceived of contextual theology as using local vocabularies to state the timeless truths of theology.[26] This position corresponds only to the first idea of social locatedness, above, that truths must only be restated in the vocabulary of a context. It is a position which troubles numerous theologians trying to do contextualization:

> Many in the Western church harbor a paternalistic attitude that their theology is "objective" and uninfluenced by Western culture. Consequently, they believe that non-Western theologians should simply accept theologies worked out in the West or that, at most, fresh non-Western theologies should be adaptations of the "objective" theology Westerners have already done.[27]

---

25    Scott Moreau has enumerated far more extensively and empirically what is happening in the world of contextual evangelical theology in a later chapter of this book. What I am trying to present here is a progression of appreciation of the context and how that applies to objectivity. Other reviews of contextual methods can be found in such classic and foundational works as the following: David J. Hesselgrave and Edward Rommen, *Contextualization: Meanings, Methods, and Models* (Grand Rapids, MI: Baker, 1989), 39-126. Steven Bevans, *Models of Contextual Theology,* rev. and expanded ed. (Maryknoll, NY: Orbis, 2006), 37-137.

26    Osborne, *Spiral,* 319. "A plenary verbal, inerrantist approach to contextualization accepts the supracultural nature of all biblical truth and thereby the unchanging nature of these scriptural principles."

27    Steve Strauss, "The Role of Context in Shaping Theology," in *Contextualization and Syncretism: Navigating Cultural Currents,* ed. Gailyn Van Rheenen (Pasadena, CA: William Carey Library, 2006), 120.

In spite of the agreement that God, a timeless being, has revealed himself and that he has done so in a changeless Scripture, we still cannot extract, formulate, and understand scriptural judgments in a timeless, cultureless manner.[28] That would be to neglect—even deny—our encultured humanity. Contextual theology must certainly strive to faithfully represent the timeless God in actual cultures, but that task is much heavier than merely using local vocabularies to translate "truths" extricated and enunciated in another context. While "objective" has been applied to this type of theology in the past, it runs the risk of distorting theology by placing that which was faithful in one context into a completely different context, one in which that same theology may quite possibly be unfaithful to the Bible.[29]

(b) Contextual theology *addresses* local issues using vocabulary, concepts, or situations which may not have been used in other contexts. It is helpful that this contextual theology starts with a local problem, which is then addressed by the norm of Scripture using local vocabularies and concepts.[30] There is neither agenda nor presentation imposed from outside the social location. We are using the second idea of social location, presented above, that socially located theology is created in and for a specific context. It is a local reading of Scripture which produces this contextual theology. Of course, the local process must progress using a hermeneutical spiral. This orientation seems, to me, to press for both objectivity and social location.

(c) Contextual theological formulations may appear contradictory (or even heretical) when compared to other cultures' formulations until the full context is understood. Now we have introduced the third understanding of social location above that affirmations from one context will not always work in another context. Some may find it difficult that a faithful reading of Scripture in one culture appears like heresy to those trying to faithfully read that same Scripture in another culture. Some may find it strange until they remember the christological and trinitarian debates of the early church. Actual heresy needed to be excluded, but a great deal of the debate (angry and violent, sometimes) between orthodox theologians resulted because of differences in cultural formulations.[31] Miscommunication occurs when language systems do not overlap. Those are the cases which need more dialogue between cultures to understand the theology of each other.

## The Value of the Community (Local and Historical) for Global Verification

Contradictory statements in the same system indicate that one of them is wrong because of the law of non-contradiction. When dealing with socially located theologies, different cultures comprise distinct, although (partially) translatable, systems. They are separate enough to allow seemingly contradictory statements… seemingly heretical theologies. Euclidian geometry is normally taught in schools. But there are other systems of geometry, which have significantly

---

28   See the chapter by Benno van den Toren in this volume.

29   Again, I refer to the second criterion used by Natee Tanchanpongs below, p. 120.

30   This idea, left intentionally vague, does not necessarily match Tillich's method of correlation, which is very existentialist. cf. John Clayton, *The Concept of Correlation: Paul Tillich and the Possibility of a Mediating Theology,* (Walter de Gruyter, 1980).

31   David F. Wells, *The Person of Christ: A Biblical and Historical Analysis of the Incarnation* (Wheaton, IL: Crossway, 1984), 86-96.

different rules.[32] If they were taught in other schools, then the two groups of students may have difficulty, at first, seeing that they are speaking about the same object.

On the other hand, cultures offer systems that are translatable enough to be able to check their theological statements against one another. It is in understanding how revelation impacts that culture and is read by Christians in that culture that the theology can be understood and compared to the rich stream of theological reflection that has flowed through the millennia and throughout the world.

This translatability opens up the possibility of reading the Bible together, across cultural lines, to determine not the (static) truth contained therein, but if a particular cultural reading is a faithful rendering of scriptural judgments in that context. By reading together, we are not seeing a universal communication of truth, but we are seeing a contextual communication of truth which is as accurate as possible. In this way, we are encouraging each other to strive for objectivity while remaining content with the limits of social location. Starting from our place in culture, this conversation allows us to approach asymptotically, as in mathematics, ever closer to the reality communicated in Scripture. Because the culture is involved, the form of that asymptotic approach will not look like it would in another culture. The truth will not look like it would in another culture. But dialogue allows us to understand and critique the faithfulness of the reading.[33]

Church history helps adjudicate between different cultures.[34] Translatability implies that we can compare theological formulations. Even if they seem, at first, antithetical (mutually hereti-

---

32    Notably with respect to Euclid's fifth postulate, the parallel postulate. "If two lines are drawn which intersect a third in such a way that the sum of the inner angles on one side is less than two right angles, then the two lines inevitably must intersect each other on that side if extended far enough. This postulate is equivalent to what is known as the parallel postulate." (http://mathworld.wolfram.com/EuclidsPostulates.html, consulted 2 November, 2009).

33    Offering criteria beyond "dialogue" would go far beyond the limits of this discussion. If I were to proceed with this discussion, it would build on the following base: (1) faithfulness to the data ("a comprehensive synthesis of all the Bible's relevant didactic content" [Packer, "Is Systematic Theology a Mirage?" 33.] as well as the data from these other sciences, sociology, psychology, philosophy, etc., that tell us about man, the world, and other relevant topics); (2) coherence and understandability ("an internal relatedness of the statements" [Carl F. H. Henry, Toward a Recovery of Christian Belief (Wheaton, IL.: Crossway, 1990), 88]); (3) an expanding opportunity for reflection ("a guiding presupposition which, when made basic to further Bible study, deepens insight into the meaning and force of particular passages and so becomes the means whereby fresh truth comes to light" [Carson, "The Role of Exegesis in Systematic Theology," 45.]); (4) comprehensiveness (there can be no relevant data ignored); (5) criticizability (there is always room for new data to change one's conclusions [cf. Kevin J. Vanhoozer's discussion of fallibilism, "Christ and Concept: Doing Theology and the 'Ministry' of Philosophy," in Doing Theology in Today's World, ed. John D. Woodbridge and Thomas Edward McComiskey (Grand Rapids, MI: Zondervan, 1991), 130-142.]); (6) logical consistency (this point is particularly contextual; the proposed theology must be consistent with the language and culture in which it is formed and in which it must be lived. That alone makes it intelligible); (7) congruence with experience and conclusions from other fields of inquiry; (8) clarity in its conclusions; (9) the possibility of bearing ethical fruit (Harold A. Netland, Dissonant Voices: Religions Pluralism and the Question of Truth [Grand Rapids, MI: Eerdmans, 1991], 193).

34    The value of the historical and believing community is discussed in both "Five guiding principles in determining biblical orthodoxy" on the Open Source Theology web site. (http://www.opensourcetheology.net/node/19, consulted 31 January 2009) and in Paul Hiebert, Anthropological Reflections on Missiological Issues (Grand Rapids: Baker Book House, 1994), 101.

cal), they can normally be compared. This is important for a historical church. Continuity within the church does not apply simply to the fact of using similar vocabulary over the millennia. There is a book, the Bible, which has served as Scripture to the church.[35] There is, also, a broad reading Scripture whose continuity can be identified even if there has been clear diversity. We are guided by the family resemblance of the readings. There is a stream of faithfulness to the same revelation. "Systematicians with comparable training but from highly diverse backgrounds can come together and check one another *against the standard of the Scripture that all sides agree is authoritative.*"[36]

## The Limitation of Culturally Diverse Applications

The proposal in this chapter limits the geographic application of what we consider as true: we cannot assume that the statements which are true in our context will be true in another context. This is the case *not* because geographic displacement controls the truth or falsity of a statement. Rather, it is the case because another culture may not have divided up its categories in the same way or may not have the linguistic precisions available in the source culture. To repeat what was a true statement without all the cultural and linguistic baggage that allowed its truth to be justified opens the possibility that it will even be a false statement in the new situation. The new culture's language will not accommodate it in the same way. The new culture's categories do not hold together in the same way or distinguish the parts of reality in the same way. The new culture's imagination is not able to conceive of it in the same way.

The affirmation of objectivity which I have put forward means that we really are stating truths. Theology expressed from different cultures addresses different aspects of reality.[37] Revelation is much larger than one culture can accommodate. Therefore, we can say that there is a limitation in geographic and historical application of truths articulated in any particular place at any particular time. Contextual evangelical theology should not be inhibited by or restricted to the theological formulations of other cultures. Make theology local. Be prepared to justify that theology according to the norm of Scripture.

---

35    Kevin J. Vanhoozer, "Christ and Concept: Doing Theology and the "Ministry" of Philosophy," in *Doing Theology* (Grand Rapids, MI: Zondervan, 1991), 108-109.

36    D. A. Carson, "The Role of Exegesis in Systematic Theology," in *Doing Theology* (Grand Rapids, MI: Zondervan, 1991), 53f, emphasis his.

37    Both the clearly evangelical *Symphonic Theology: The Validity of Multiple Perspectives in Theology* by Vern Poythress (Grand Rapids, MI: Zondervan, 1987) and the older *Truth is Symphonic: Aspects of Christian Pluralism* by Hans Urs von Balthasar, translated by Graham Harrison (San Francisco, CA: Ignatius Press, 1987; first published as *Die Wahrheit Ist Symphonisch: Aspekte des Christlichen Pluralismus*, Johannes Verlag, Einsiedeln, 1972.) are instructive in this regard. This touches on the issue of rationality and religion. The discussion can be found elsewhere: Alvin Plantinga and Nicholas Wolterstorff, eds. Faith and Rationality: Reason and Belief in God (Notre Dame, ID.: University of Notre Dame Press, 1983); Peter Isaacs, "Theology, Rationality and Contemporary Epistemology," Saint Mark's Review 102 (June 1980): 13-18; J. Wentzel van Huyssteen, The Shaping of Rationality: Toward Interdisciplinarity in Theology and Science (Grand Rapids, MI: Eerdmans, 1999); F. LeRon Shults, ed. *The Evolution of Rationality: Interdisciplinary Essays in Honor of J. Wentzel van Huyssteen* (Grand Rapids, MI: Eerdmans, 2006).

## The Expansion of Global Truth

One exciting implication of this perspective is that there is an expansion of truth. As more cultures address the plenitude of God, the enormity of his truth, and the exigencies of living *coram deo* (before God), then we will see not a greater confluence, but a greater fullness of understanding of life with God. This is the globalization of which Paul Siu speaks in this volume.[38] As I have stated above, all truth communicated in Scripture cannot be understood by one culture. It takes multiple perspectives, multiple linguistic systems to adequately access what God is trying to communicate. While each of those perspectives will offer insights to the whole world, they are predominately for that social location.

We all have cultural blind spots which do not allow us to criticize our culture nor see everything that is important. This diversity in theological perspectives of which I speak, may offer the just and timely critique needed in our own culture. Yet even if we do not immediately understand everything contained in another's objective socially located theology, we can affirm with the rest of the church that the Holy Spirit resides in them as well and they are reading the same Bible as we. We can see the faithfulness to the judgments in that text through the verification process and learn from each other.

The expansion of global truth is a wonderful gift that evangelicals can give the universal church. In our given social location we will strive for faithfulness to the Bible while submitting to the historic and universal church for critique. In this way, we can strive for an objective theology for our context. But that theology will not be identical to, nor perhaps even easily understood by, other theologies. It must be socially located, culturally embedded. In this way, we are moving toward truths from God for our cultures. Contextual evangelical theology should be both objective and socially located.

## Discussion Questions:

1. How have you understood the phrase "objective theology" in the past? How is that the same and different as that which is being presented in this chapter?

2. How have you understood the phrase "socially located theology" in the past? How is that the same and different as that which is being presented in this chapter?

3. What is one step you may take to localize the theological process, the theology produced, or the verification process?

4. What are some of the difficulties and benefits of explaining, discussing, and critiquing theologies cross-culturally? Who, in your geographic region, has a different cultural background with whom you could discuss your theological ideas?

---

38    See Paul Siu's chapter in this volume.

# 6

# Can We See the Naked Theological Truth?

## *Benno van den Toren*

*Benno van den Toren is Dean of Faculty and Tutor in Doctrine at Wycliffe College in Oxford. He is from the Netherlands. He studied theology in Utrecht, Oxford and Kampen, where he did his doctoral research on apologetics, Karl Barth, and postmodernism. After working as a pastoral assistant and with the Dutch evangelical student movement, he moved with his family to French-speaking Africa, where he taught systematic theology for eight years at the Bangui Evangelical School of Theology. During those years he published in Dutch, English, and French, mainly on the nature of Christian doctrine and ethics in a multicultural world. He is married to Berdine and they have three sons. Education: MA (Utrecht), MDiv (Utrecht), PhD (Kampen).*

## Introduction

The coming of age of the younger churches in what we—for lack of a better term—call the majority world has ushered the worldwide Christian community into one of the most exciting periods of its existence. A new dialogue is going on about what it means to follow Christ in the different cultural contexts in which the church finds itself. This dialogue between older and younger churches is sometimes exhilarating and sometimes rather uneasy—as in the case of the current tension between the northern and southern partners of the Anglican Communion—but always challenging and refreshing.

This dialogue is not new and has in some ways been prepared by the ecumenical dialogue in the churches which brought the older and culturally very different Eastern Orthodox churches within the orbit of the Western theological debate. The more recent dialogue with the younger churches is, however, different in two ways. Firstly, these younger churches are fast growers which by now vastly outnumber many of the Western mother churches that stood at their origin. Secondly, evangelicals left earlier ecumenical discussions in general to mainline churches, but do now play a much greater role in this newer worldwide dialogue. They have, after all, close relationships with the newer churches in the majority world, many of which align themselves with the worldwide evangelical movement.

There is a growing awareness that the worldwide and effectively multicultural nature of the church has major implications for theology. Theologians from the majority world and Western missionaries working with them are stressing the need for contextual theologies: theologies that address the challenges of living out the life with Christ in the particular cultural, social and religious context in which they are called to do so. They criticize more traditional Western theologians for not realizing the contextual nature of their Western theological concepts and imposing them on the rest of the world. Many theorists, both Christian and non-Christian, stress that the development of contextual theologies is not optional, but inevitable: all human reflection takes place in a specific cultural context and is profoundly influenced by this setting.

While this awareness is growing, there remains a considerable unease about these developments, particularly among more conservative theologians, both protestant/evangelical and catholic. This unease is understandable. The realization of the cultural particularity of all human convictions, including religious ones, puts some of our most cherished convictions under enormous pressure. After all, some take it to imply, that Jesus Christ is no longer the Savior and Lord of all, but only of those who belong to the cultural traditions in which this message makes sense. Others may hold to some sort of universal validity of Jesus of Nazareth, but believe that our images of Him are through and through determined by our different cultural contexts. For them it no longer makes sense to ask who the real Jesus is behind all those different images. For reasons that I will develop later, these purported consequences of the cultured nature of our entire thinking are damaging to the most central traits of the traditional Christian faith.

In this paper we will discuss one common way of addressing this tension, defended by a number of evangelical and more conservative Roman Catholic theologians alike; namely, the idea that we should be able to distinguish between a supra-cultural core of the gospel and the varied cultural clothing in which it can be expressed. This approach is suggested in the guiding question of this paper itself, which asks whether it is possible to isolate such a supra-cultural core. We will argue that our understanding of the gospel is so deeply embedded in our culture that we will not be able to come up with a once-for-all formulation of such a supra-cultural core. The main intention of the paper will, however, be positive rather than negative: we will argue that from the radically different perspectives in which Christians through history and across the world encounter the gospel, they can still have a firm grasp and trustworthy understanding of this gospel which can guide the Christian community through the ages as an authoritative rule of faith. In doing so, we will move between two contrasting sides of the issue: the question whether we can talk about a recognizable *center* which is valid for all contexts and the question whether we can define *boundaries* of Christian belief, life, and identity.

This discussion will inevitably be muddled when we do not make some precise distinctions from the very outset. We need to distinguish between, on the one hand, the supra-cultural *reality* or supra-cultural *truth* to which the gospel testifies and, on the other hand, our culturally embedded *understandings* and *formulations* of this truth. Between the two poles, we have the *trans-cultural* reality of the revelation of God in Jesus Christ. This reality is not supra-cultural, for it takes shape in a particular cultural context. Yet, it is trans-cultural in the sense that it has a universal value for every existing and possible human culture. I will argue that the gospel testifies to a supra-cultural God and to his trans-cultural self-revelation in Christ. Yet, no understanding or formulation of this reality is absolute. They change over time and across cultural boundaries. This does not preclude us, however, from having an adequate and trustworthy understanding of the gospel.

## One Supra-Cultural Core?

Let us therefore begin with a consideration of the idea that there is a universal theological core that expresses the essence of the gospel that can be formulated once for all. This core can then subsequently be contextualized, expressed in different ways in different cultural contexts. The Bible itself does not directly present us with this supra-cultural core. The Bible's message is itself contextualized in a particular cultural context or rather in a variety of contexts. The idea is that the universal core of the gospel can be distilled from this cultural expression of God's revelation. This is how it is expressed by David Wells:

> It is the task of theology, then, to discover what God has said in and through Scripture and to clothe that in a conceptuality which is native to our own age. Scripture, as its terminus a quo, needs to be de-contextualized in order to grasp its transcultural content, and needs to be re-contextualized in order that its content may be meshed up with the cognitive assumptions and social patterns of our own time.[1]

In Stephen Bevans' categorization of different understandings of contextualization, this idea fits into his "translation model" of contextualization, which he sees exemplified in theologians as varied as Byang Kato, Paul Hiebert, and John Paul II: "What is clear in the minds of people who employ the translation model is that an essential, supra-contextual message *can* be separated from a contextually bound mode of expression."[2]

A similar approach is suggested in the popular NIV Application Commentary series, which aims to "discern what is timeless in the timeless pages of the Bible" and subsequently to "take these eternal truths originally spoken in a different time and culture and apply them to the similar yet different needs of our culture."[3] I guess that this is the intuitive approach to these questions of many Western evangelical Bible readers. The approach, after all, reflects a dominant modern understanding of language which sees language at its most successful when it corresponds exactly with the reality which it describes.[4]

---

1    David F. Wells, "The Nature and Function of Theology", in: Robert K. Johnston (ed.), *The Use of the Bible in Theology: Evangelical Options* (Atlanta, GA: John Knox, 1985), 177.

2    Stephen B. Bevans, *Models of Contextual Theology*, revised and expanded edition (Maryknoll, NY: Orbis, 2002), 40.

3    "Series Introduction" in: Michael J. Wilkins, *The NIV Application Commentary: Matthew* (Grand Rapids, MI: Zondervan, 2004), 9.

4    Nancey Murphy and James Wm. McClendon, Jr, "Distinguishing Modern and Postmodern Theologies," *Modern Theology* 5 (1989): 193ff.

This quest for a supra-cultural core of the gospel that should be distinguishable from its cultural expression falls short of what is nowadays more commonly understood as "contextualization." David Bosch makes a helpful distinction between the older terms of "accommodation" and "indigenization" and the newer discourse on "contextualization," which only began in the seventies of the twentieth-century. Indigenization and accommodation, according to Bosch, presuppose that there is a universal supra-cultural core to the gospel that can be formulated once for all and that presumably is formulated in Western dogmatic handbooks. This supra-cultural center can be distinguished from a periphery, from the way it is expressed and lived out and that can vary from one cultural context to another. The idea of contextualization, however, expresses the conviction that *all* of theology and *every* theology is contextual. All theology is contextual theology and even its most central expressions reflect particular cultural understandings and every theology is contextual, including Western mainstream theology.[5]

The idea that there is a universal supra-cultural core of the gospel which can be indigenized in different cultural contexts is an important and positive step in comparison to earlier understandings of the gospel and mission that were much more Eurocentric.[6] In these earlier versions of Eurocentrism, there was a tendency to see the larger part of both the Western doctrinal understanding of the gospel and of the way it was lived out in the Western world as normative for the rest of the world. This was the approach which was dominant until the first part of the twentieth century and equated mission with the spread of Western civilization. This approach alienated young converts from their cultures of origin and threw up undue cultural barriers for the acceptance of the gospel.

This newer approach, which distinguishes between the universal kernel and culturally varied husk, does, however, not go far enough. It remains Eurocentric in that it does not recognize the profound influence of culture and language in general on our understanding of the gospel. Neither does it recognize the influence of modernity on the idea itself of being able to distil such a supra-cultural core.

Postmodern theoreticians have particularly pointed to the role of language in our perception of reality. If you would want to formulate this core of the gospel, you would need to formulate it in one language or another, be it Galilean Aramaic, Greek, Latin, English or Sango—the trade language in the Central African Republic. Both the structures of the language and the different semantic ranges of the terms employed mean that "Iesus Christus Dominus est" will not mean precisely the same thing as "Jesus Christ is Lord" or "Jesus ayeke kotagbia."[7] As Lamin San-

---

5    David J. Bosch, *Transforming Mission: Paradigm Shifts in Theology of Mission* (Maryknoll, NY: Orbis, 1991), 447ff.

6    With the term "Eurocentric,", I do not refer to a geographic region, but to cultures in different parts of the world that have been dominated by modern European culture, be it in Western Europe or Northern America. The expression "Northern Atlantic culture" is rather clumsy and would still leave out important regions where this culture is dominant, such as Australia and white South Africa.

7    An expression like "Jesus is Lord" will not even mean the same thing for all the speakers of a language. English is now spoken in so many places and used in so many different cultures that similar words and expressions have diverse connotations in different cultural and social contexts.

neh and Kwame Bediako have stressed, every time the gospel is translated in a new language it takes on a new cultural expression.[8]

For many Christian theologians, postmodern reflection on the nature of language has not been the most important factor in the discovery that there is not one supra-cultural formulation of the gospel. More important was the experience of cross-cultural contact with Christians from radically different cultures, either in other parts of the world or much closer to home—or the experience of relating to Christians of different ages whom we know through their writings. There is the amazing experience that across a wide variety of cultures we recognize the same Lord and Savior Jesus Christ. We do also discover that some of our most cherished aspects of the faith are not that important for others and are understood in entirely different ways. Some have come to Christ first of all as the one who takes away their guilt before God, while others relate to Him foremost as the Conqueror of the powers of evil.

There is a deeper theological reason why we cannot isolate a non-contextualized core of the gospel. Contextualization is not something that is only needed for elements that are more peripheral to our Christian faith and life. The *center* of the gospel itself should be contextualized. Take the central confession that Jesus is Lord and Saviour. It is hard to think about anything more central to the Christian faith. I think it is not possible to come up with some sort of a universal abstract formulation of what Jesus being Lord and Saviour means which could subsequently be applied in different contexts. First of all, Jesus being Lord and Saviour is not an abstract notion, but a concrete reality. For Jesus to be truly Lord and for Jesus to be truly Savior, we need to be able to relate his saving work and his lordship to our actual lives and the actual world in which we are living. Secondly, it is only by living out this faith in different cultural contexts that it becomes clear what this truly means. As Andrew Walls has shown, the Christian understanding of Christ has grown every time He was proclaimed in a new context.[9] Already, by contextualizing the Judaic expression of the Christian faith of the disciples in Jerusalem to the wider Hellenistic world of the first generation of non-Jewish disciples, major changes were made. "Christ" or "Messiah" became more a personal name than a title and "*kurios*" gained dominance. Dean Flemming's study on Paul's Epistle to the Colossians shows how the interaction of Christ with the culture of the Colossians lead to a much deeper understanding of the cosmic implications of the Lordship of Jesus Christ.[10]

There is a final historical consideration that brings us to question the possibility to provide a once for all formulation of the core of the gospel message, that has not so much to do with its center (the confession that Jesus is Lord and Savior), but rather with its *boundaries*. While the center of the Christian faith has been clearly grasped since the time of the apostles, its boundaries have only gradually become apparent. Much of what was implicit, yet necessary

---

8    See for example Lamin Sanneh, Translating the Message: The Missionary Impact on Culture (New York: Orbis, 1989); Kwame Bediako, Theology and Identity: The Impact of Culture Upon Christian Thought in the Second Century and Modern Africa (Oxford: Regnum Books, 1992), 432, 434; Kwame Bediako, Christianity in Africa: The Renewal of a Non-Western Religion (Maryknoll, NY: Orbis, 1995), 59ff, 109ff.

9    Andrew Walls, The Missionary Movement in Christian History (Edinburgh: T. & T. Clark, 1996), 54, passim.

10    Dean Flemming, *Contextualisation in the New Testament: Patterns for Theology and Mission* (Downers Grove, IL: IVP, 2005), 219ff.

as the background to the confession of Jesus as Lord and Savior, became only gradually clear as the gospel entered into new contexts and encountered new challenges. In its confrontation with Gnosticism in the second century A.D., it became apparent that the belief in God as the Creator of the entire universe was essential background to the confession of Jesus as Savior and Lord. In the discussion with Arianism in the fourth century, similar conclusions were drawn with regards to Jesus Christ's divinity, and in the time of the European Reformation in the sixteenth century with regards to salvation by grace alone. Though the notion of "orthodoxy" as the "right teaching" of the church is logically prior to the notion of "heresy" as "false teaching," in the course of history heresies were prior. They provided the occasion for the gradual clarification of what orthodox teaching entailed.[11]

The confessions of faith that are internationally used by worldwide evangelical organizations also reflect certain debates that were crucial at the time of the growth of the evangelical movement or at the time of the writing of these confessions, such as the confession of Christ's bodily resurrection. It is not that this truth was new, but in other contexts it could remain implicit. Yet, in the context of the evangelical debate with Western liberal theology, it became clear that this confession needed to become explicit. In the context of this debate the confession of the bodily resurrection was needed in order to defend an essential element of the faith against a distortion to which a church contextualizing the gospel to a modern Western context was prone.

This leads of course to some major questions with regards to such confessional texts that have been beacons to the international evangelical community, yet that have mostly grown in the context of Western debates. On the one hand, it needs to be asked whether other elements may need to be included that are required by the new non-Western contexts in which we are called to confess Christ today. The growth of prosperity theology may, for example, require some serious reflection about where this movement represents a form of healthy contextualization and where not. We also need to ask where this movement crosses boundaries and undermines what is essential to the Christian understanding of salvation and therefore to Christian identity.

On the other hand, we need to ask whether certain formulations in these Western evangelical affirmations of the faith were not expressed in terms that are typical of Western modernity. That would open up the possibility to formulate their "judgment" in other ways that might be equally valid or even more adequate to other contexts. It has been asked, for example, whether the evangelical stance on the inerrancy of Scripture has not been formulated too much in terms of modern scientism and the modern over-estimation of scientific language. In postmodern and non-Western contexts, other ways of formulating the authority and entire trustworthiness of Scripture may be more constructive. These formulations might retrospectively help to clarify some of the blind alleys in which the earlier inerrancy debate could end up.

---

11    See Bernard Sesboüé and Joseph Wolinksi, *Le Dieu du Salut*, Series: Histoire des Dogmes 1 (n.p. [Tournai], Desclée, 1994), 47.

## What Is at Stake?

So the stakes are high. What is at stake in the contextualizing of the gospel in its entirety is the need for Jesus' Lordship and salvation being experienced, becoming a liberating reality and being lived out in ever new cultural contexts. The stakes are equally high at the other side of the debate. If our entire understanding of the gospel is colored by our cultural context, do we not risk losing the gospel itself? Do we not end up in a situation of cultural relativism where our entire belief systems are no more than "cultural-linguistic" structures which give coherence to how we live, but that have no relationship with a reality outside these "language games"?[12]

It is possible to think of a religion as a way of organizing and giving meaning to our lives without reference to a reality beyond the stories and rituals of its adherents. Yet, a Christian cannot interpret Christianity in that way without radically altering its most central beliefs. Christians don't live from the conviction that it makes sense to live "as if" Christ is Lord and Savior. Christians draw hope and courage from the belief that Christ has actually conquered the powers of death, sin and evil. As Mark Achtemeier argues:

> If the knowledge, "That I belong, body and soul, in life and death, not to myself but to my faithful Saviour Jesus Christ", is to be capable of offering concrete assurance about the eternal destiny of ordinary believers, such knowledge must of necessity be grounded in a reality (Jesus Christ) which transcends the particularities of the believer's own body, soul and historical circumstances. [13]

It is not just the case that the Christian faith depends on some trustworthy knowledge of the reality of Jesus Christ and of what He did for us as the *center* of our faith. As we already noted, we also need an understanding of the *boundaries*, of knowing what degree of variety is allowed and where people cross borders that are essential for the Christian identity. The notion of "heresy" as false and unsound teaching is crucial for the Christian faith. This is first of all because the way we live our Christian lives is closely related to what we believe. Good teaching is "sound" teaching (1 Timothy 1:10, 6:3), because it contrasts with false teaching which is "unhealthy" teaching, for it hinders a healthy flourishing of our Christian lives (1 Timothy 6:4).[14] Even more so, our salvation depends on what God has done for us in Christ. In its discussion with heretics, the church has been conscious of fighting positions that, if true, would undermine the reality of salvation. Our Christian identity therefore depends on these crucial convictions. Charles Kraft is probably right in stating that the church has sometimes condemned positions as heretical which were merely different contextual expressions of the faith of

---

12    The "cultural-linguistic" understanding of religions originates with the postliberal theologian George A. Lindbeck, who himself is ambiguous about the extra-linguistic referent of religious beliefs (George A Lindbeck, *The Nature of Doctrine: Religion and Theology in a Postliberal Age*, Philadelphia: Westminster Press, 1984). Lindbeck's position—influenced by Ludwig Wittgenstein's theory of language, Thomas Kuhn's work on scientific revolutions and Clifford Geertz' understanding of culture—reflects a much wider postmodern approach to religion in general and Christianity in particular.

13    P. Mark Achtemeier, "The Truth of a Tradition: Critical Realism in the Thought of Alasdair MacIntyre and T.F. Torrance," *Scottish Journal of Theology* 47 (1994): 355.

14    Cf. Gordon D. Fee, *1 and 2 Timothy, Titus*, revised edition, New International Bible Commentary 13 (Peabody, Hendrickson; Carlisle, Paternoster, 1995), 46.

cultural minorities.[15] It remains true, however, that the notion of "heresy" and the guarding of the true faith is an essential aspect of the Christian faith, which depends on God's saving acts on our behalf. If certain central convictions would not be true, our entire salvation would be in jeopardy.

This is the problem with forms of contextualization in which the context plays the dominant role in the formulation of contextual theologies, such as the model which Bevans' labels the "anthropological model."[16] The main question asked in this model is whether theological formulations are relevant to the context and relate well to the cultural background of the believers. As Bevans notes, this model has too optimistic an outlook on culture and forgets about the distorting nature of sin and of the "unsound" teaching that may result from it. Christ is not allowed to be a radically critical force in the culture and the full scope of his liberating Lordship and salvation cannot play itself out.

So far, we have concluded that, on the one hand, all our understandings and formulations of the gospel are influenced by the cultures which we inhabit and the languages which we speak and through which we relate to the world around us. On the other hand, what is theologically even more important, in order for Jesus Christ to be truly Lord and Savior, in order for the gospel to be truly Good News, the gospel needs not only to be contextualized in its entirety, it also needs at the same time be grounded in a supra-cultural reality. This supra-cultural reality does not depend on our cultural expressions of it, but rather makes these cultural expressions possible.

## The Universality and Supra-Cultural Origin of This Message

These two statements—concerning that cultural embeddedness of all our understandings of the gospel and concerning its supra-cultural grounding—seem mutually exclusive to many Western evangelicals. And if one of them needs to be given up, it is indeed the right choice to hold on to the anchoring of our Christian existence in a supra-cultural reality, the universal lordship of Jesus Christ. However, recent analysis of the structure of modern Western epistemologies (theories about how we come to know) has shown that these two statements do only appear to be mutually exclusive because of a crucial characteristic of modern Western epistemology in general. These epistemologies are "foundationalist," which means that it understands human knowledge after the analogy of *a building*.[17] Proper knowledge should always start with empirical observations, rational axioms or other propositions that are self-evident or for other reasons indubitable. All other beliefs should derive their certainty or probability from this foundation on which they are built and from the solidity of the building structure—the validity of the inductive or deductive reasoning that is used. This helps us understand why modern philosophy was so preoccupied with finding a universally valid starting point for its reasoning, whether this starting point was believed to be rational, empirical or other. In a foundationalist

---

15     Kraft, Charles H., *Christianity in Culture. A Study in Dynamic Biblical Theologizing in Cross-Cultural Perspective* (Maryknoll, NY: Orbis, 1979), 8.

16     Bevans, *Models of Contextual Theology*, 54ff.

17     See for a description of "foundationalism" for example, Alvin Plantinga, *Warrant: The Current Debate* (New York/Oxford: Oxford University Press, 1993), 84-86; Kelly James Clark, *Return to Reason: A Critique of Enlightenment Evidentialism and a Defense of Reason and Belief in God* (Grand Rapids, MI: Eerdmans, 1990), 32-136.

model, the building can never be stronger than its foundation and a—historically or culturally—particular starting point can never lead to universally valid conclusions. This modern quest for an indubitable foundation for our knowledge is related to the modern understanding of language as an exact representation of reality, to which we referred above. Only if our language gives an exact representation of reality, can we have an adequate foundation for such an indubitable knowledge of reality. Language that does not "represent" reality can only be "expressive"; it can only be an expression of what lives in the human speaker himself or herself.[18]

Cultural relativism—the idea that all human beliefs are so bound up with their cultural context that they have no relationship with a supra-cultural reality—does actually share a basic conviction of this modern foundationalism which it so heavily criticizes. It equally believes that unless you start with a universally valid starting point, you cannot arrive at a universally valid conclusion. They only end up at the other end of the spectrum, for in denying such a starting point, they deny the possibility that any human belief has universally validity.

This modern foundationalism has come under heavy criticism in the later part of the twentieth century, both by Western philosophers such as Michael Polanyi and Alasdair MacIntyre and by Christian theologians such as Thomas Torrance and missiologists such as Lesslie Newbigin.[19] They noted that the proposed universal foundations of knowledge were not universal at all but did rather reflect the modern Western stance of the thinker who proposed them. More important for us, this whole modern foundationalist understanding of knowledge seems to reflect specifically Western ideas and ideals. It is simply not true that you need to place yourself in a cultural vacuum in order to arrive at universally valid knowledge. Christians have of course known this all the time, because they believed that God's self-revelation in Christ in the particular cultural context of first century Palestine holds the key to what is true of all humankind. Yet in the context of modernity, Christian theologians often felt forced to play down this particular cultural and historical origin and starting point of the Christian understanding of reality. More thorough reflection reveals, however, that the universal validity of this faith is not based on the manner in which this truth was discovered—be it on the basis of a universally equally accessible starting point or not—, but on the nature of the truth it revealed: these events revealed the universal salvific purpose of the one God, Creator of the whole universe and of all humankind.

Polanyi has shown that scientific discovery similarly takes place in a very specific context, in a tradition of reflection that makes new discoveries possible. The discoveries of Newton, Einstein, and the like all happened in specific traditions of scientific reflection and research. Yet after these discoveries were made, they were presented to the wider scientific community who could, if they were open to it, look at the same reality with new eyes and see that what these scientists had uncovered was not only true in their own laboratories but was true everywhere.

---

18    Murphy and McClendon, "Distinguishing Modern and Postmodern Theologies", 193-196.

19    E.g., Michael Polanyi, *Personal Knowledge: Towards a Postcritical Philosophy*, corrected edition (Chicago, IL: University of Chicago Press, 1962), Alasdair MacIntyre, *Whose Justice? Which Rationality?* (London: Duckworth, 1988), Thomas F. Torrance, *Theological Science* (London, etc.: Oxford University Press, 1969), Lesslie Newbigin, *The Gospel in a Pluralist Society*, (London: SPCK, 1989).

Polanyi's research in the nature of scientific discovery suggests another model for the way human beliefs are developed other than the foundationalist model of the building of a house. Coming to know reality is more like the *reading of a book*.[20] When we read a book, we all come to it with our proper cultural pre-understandings. This does, however, not mean that we are forever bound to these pre-understandings. If we read the book humbly and are willing to be challenged, our pre-understanding may be shown to be inadequate. This allows us to adjust them so that in a cycle of reading and rereading, our initially flawed understanding becomes gradually adapted to the content of the book itself. The hermeneutical cycle becomes a "hermeneutical spiral"[21] in which our understanding becomes more and more congruent with the content of the book.[22]

Christians should be careful not to align themselves too closely with their culture and we should therefore avoid using these new proposals in the philosophy of science as the decisive argument for the contextual embeddedness of all theological reflection. We should avoid saying: "Studies in the philosophy of science and hermeneutics have shown that even scientific reasoning is embedded in particular historical and cultural traditions, yet they claim to yield universally valid results. Christians can therefore equally accept that all their understanding is located in specific cultural contexts, be it the first century Palestinian context of the first disciples of Jesus or the cultural contexts of those who hear today about Jesus." If we accept the cultural embeddedness of every understanding of the gospel, it is not because Western philosophy of science allows us to, but because God has chosen to make himself known in this way. Our faith does not depend on what is culturally fashionable, but on what God has done for us. Yet, these developments in the philosophy of science can help us understand how such culturally embedded experience of the gospel can still lead us to an understanding that brings us in touch with a supra-cultural reality.

These developments in the philosophy of science and hermeneutics may also free us from the fear to let go of the idea that we need some universally valid formulation of the core of the gospel in order not to lose this universal gospel itself. Our formulations of the gospel can express a supra-cultural truth about a God who was there before we believed in him, even while we accept that all Christian cultures approach this truth from different angles. They will all approach the reality of God's self-revelation in Jesus Christ in terms of their cultural pre-understandings. But in their understanding—or "reading"—of this reality, this limited understanding may be gradually enlarged and their cultural concepts may be adapted so that they become more and more adequate to understand and express this reality.

---

20    I am not aware that Polanyi himself uses this image, but it explains well what his vision implies and can draw on the traditional Christian metaphor of creation as a book, "the book of nature," which we are called to read next to the book of Scripture and the book of history.

21    The term is from Grant R. Osborne, *The Hermeneutical Spiral: A Comprehensive Introduction to Biblical Interpretation* (Downers Grove, IL: IVP, 1991).

22    Anthony C. Thiselton, *The Two Horizons: New Testament Hermeneutics and Philosophical Description with Special Reference to Heidegger, Bultmann, Gadamer and Wittgenstein* (Exeter: Paternoster Press, 1980), 104. Cf. the use of the same type of language for the description of scientific inquiry in Thomas F. Torrance, *Reality and Scientific Theology* (Edinburgh: T & T Clark), 26f.

# Learning a New Language

So far we have argued that we can have adequate knowledge of the universal truth of the gospel, yet know it from a perspective within our cultural frameworks: all our human thinking is *embedded* in our particular cultural context, yet that it is not necessarily *imprisoned* by this context. We saw this reflected in the language we need to use to express the gospel: every time the gospel is translated in a new language, the gospel takes on new meanings. This is true, but this is not the only direction in which meaning is transferred in the process of translation. A closer look at this reverse direction of the transferal of meaning helps us to comprehend even better how our understanding of the gospel needs to be expressed in the language and images of a particular cultural-linguistic framework, but how it can still point us to a supra-cultural reality. It is, after all, not only the case that the understanding of Jesus gained new depths when He was proclaimed in a Hellenistic context as "*kurios*," the word *kurios* itself also acquired new meanings when used for Jesus. Now the notion of lordship expressed by *kurios* was used of Him who is even able to defeat the powers of death, yet was willing to empty himself as a slave unto the cross.[23] When nowadays Christ is proclaimed in Sango as "*kota gbia*," "the great chief," Christ's lordship is inevitably understood in terms of the existing notions of chieftainship. That is how it should be understood, for only in that way the gospel can speak in this context. Yet, when the understanding of Christ grows, Sango words like *kota gbia* gain new and deeper meanings.

The same happens in more technical theological discussions. In the Trinitarian discussion, the church used terms such as *homoousios*, *hupostasis* and *ousia* which had been used before in other philosophical discourse, but which took on new meanings in order to be able to describe the reality of the trinity for which hitherto existing language was simply inadequate.[24]

This is where the process of the contextualization of the gospel often does not go far enough. The gospel takes on new meanings entering into new cultures, but when these cultures are not gradually renewed through their confrontation with the gospel, there remains a tension between the new cultural expressions of the gospel and the reality of the gospel it tries to express. André Manaranche gives an example of this tension when he discusses the use of traditional African names for the Creator God such as "Imana" or "Akongo" to speak of the Father of Jesus Christ. This is a valid way of indicating that the God whom Christians proclaim is not foreign to the receiving cultures, but has always been known to a certain degree, in some places clearer than elsewhere. The risk of the use of these traditional names for God is, however, that the belief in Jesus Christ is merely added on to an existing belief in a Creator God. Jesus can, however, never simply be added to an existing belief in God, be He the God of African Traditional Religions or of Islam. Jesus gives us also a radically new perspective on God, which changes the former understanding of God to the core: from now on God is known as the God

---

23 Nils Dahl argues similarly—and more astonishingly, considering the dominantly Jewish background of the term—that instances where Paul speaks of Jesus as the Messiah his understanding of Messiah is not so much determined by understandings of this notion in his Jewish background and context, but rather by the way in which Jesus actually fulfilled his role as Messiah. As the fulfilment, Jesus from now on determines what it means to be the Messiah (Nils Dahl, "The Messiahship of Jesus in Paul," in: Nils Dahl, *Jesus the Christ, the Historical Origins of Christological Doctrine* (Minneapolis, MN: Fortress Press 1991), 15-25).

24 Thomas F. Torrance, *The Trinitarian Faith* (Edinburgh: T. & T. Clark, 2006 [1991]), 129.

of the covenant, as love, as Trinity, as the God who is not only the origin but also the goal of human existence.[25]

Just as there is a double movement when the gospel is translated in other languages, there is a double cultural movement and a double movement in terms of identity change. When the gospel enters new cultural communities, it takes on new contextual expressions. At the same time, the culture of those who become Christian in this community will change. It is not simply that there will be a "triage" between those elements of the culture that should be rejected, those that can be positively embraced and those towards which we can have a neutral attitude. If the process goes well, there should rather be a reorientation of all the elements of the former culture when they become integrated in a new life with Christ as the center. The entire culture and the whole of life are re-orientated around Christ.[26]

A similar process takes place in terms of identity. In his study *Theology and Identity*, Bediako shows that the development of contextual African Christian theologies is motivated by the quest for an *African* Christian identity. It is crucial for African Christians—as well as for European Christians and others—to be able to integrate the new faith with their African past so that they can develop an African Christian identity. Yet, Bediako constantly presupposes that the identity of the African Christian is first of all a *Christian* identity, a new identity which he or she has received in Christ.[27] Kevin Vanhoozer underlines: "Our identities as Christians are found first and foremost in Christ. Cultural location and ethnicity are important, to be sure, but ultimately they do no more than qualify our fundamental identity."[28]

## The Canon

In the above we have argued that it is possible to be in touch with the supra-cultural reality of God's self-revelation in Christ from within a particular cultural context. In a following step in our quest for a supra-cultural core of the gospel, we do need to distinguish between the unique cultural context in which the first Century Palestinian followers encountered Jesus Christ and the innumerable cultural contexts in which people encountered Him later. These contexts cannot be put on par. God entered the specific cultural context of first century Palestine when He lived among us. God did not become a human being in general. A human being is always cultured, and God did become a human being as a Palestinian Jewish man in a time when Palestine was part of the Roman Empire and in touch with the larger Hellenistic cultural sphere. Yet, in this specific cultural context, Jesus played a role with a universal function that concerned every culture before, during, and after his earthly life.

Even this Jesus we do not know directly. We only encounter Him through the witness of the first generation of apostles and their companions. Because Christ is God's supreme revelation that happened once and for all and because these texts are the only trustworthy witnesses to

---

25   André Manaranche, *Le Monothéisme chrétien* (Paris : Cerf, 1985), 57ff.
26   Cf. Walls, *The Missionary Movement*, 54.
27   Cf. Bediako, *Theology and Identity*, 7, 13, 141, 206, 304, 375.
28   Kevin J. Vanhoozer, "'One Rule to Rule them All?' Theological Method in an Era of World Christianity," in: Craig Ott & Harold A. Netland (eds.), *Globalizing Theology: Belief and Practice in an Era of World Christianity* (Leicester: Apollos (IVP), 2007), 108.

his life, these Scriptures are *canonical*: they have authority for all subsequent generations whose understanding of Jesus should always be judged in the light of the words of these first witnesses.[29]

These New Testament Scriptures witness to Jesus, yet this witness itself is colored by the cultural context of the different authors and of the readers they had in mind when they wrote. The way this canonical witness functions gives us some important insights into a more loose sense in which we can still refer to a "supra-cultural" gospel, even while recognizing that every cultural formulation of it is culturally embedded.

Firstly, the writers of the Gospels and the Epistles do not witness to themselves and their own ideas. They witness to what God is doing in Christ. It is this reality that has universal significance. This means of course that this testimony also has universal significance, but precisely as *testimony*, as pointing beyond itself.

Secondly, as it has often been pointed out, the meaning of Jesus could not be exhausted with one single canonical voice testifying to him as the *center* of their interest. The New Testament itself shows that the four Evangelists approach him from different perspectives and that the writers of the Epistles bring out different aspects of the meaning of his life, death and resurrection to bear on the different life-situations of their readers. This by itself shows that there is not a one-fits-all format of the gospel. The multiplicity of the witnesses join together to give a fuller picture than any single voice could have done. As part of the canon in which we find them now, the different books are not meant to be read as disparate testimonies. In the same canon we find Paul's credo that we are saved by faith and not by works (Ephesians 2:8ff) and James' exhortation that we are saved not by faith alone, but by works (James 2:24). It is hard to know with hindsight whether those who read these individual letters would have come to radically different understandings of the Christian faith. They did, after all, read these letters against the background of a wider understanding of the faith which we cannot precisely reconstruct. However, these letters were understood on their own, today we have been given Paul and James as part of the one canon in which their distinctive voices come together to give fuller understanding of the Christian life in which both faith and work have their place.

Thirdly, the fact that we find multiple voices in the New Testament does not mean that anything goes. While we find the voice of Matthew with his strong Jewish roots, we do not find the voice of influential Judaisers, because they rejected the gospel of grace. While the Gospel of John is included with its much more Hellenistic flavor, the voice of the proto-Gnostic Christians which were around at the same time are not included, because their convictions did undermine the basic belief of God as the Creator of all that exists. In our postmodern era, it has become popular to see the New Testament as a cacophonous collection of irreconcilable voices of which we can chose or to which we can add what we like. So we end up with a variety of religious expressions to everyone's liking and cultural pre-understandings, but with no normative core and boundaries. On the level of the actual wording, we may indeed not be able to

---

29  See for this understanding of the notion of the authority of the canon in relation to salvation history: Herman Ridderbos, "The Canon of the New Testament," in Carl F. Henry (ed.), *Revelation and the Bible: Contemporary Evangelical Thought* (Grand Rapids, MI: Baker, 1959), 192ff; John Goldingay, *Models for Scripture* (Grand Rapids/Carlisle, Eerdmans/Paternoster, 1994), 257ff.

harmonize all the individual expressions of the different writers. Yet, when the New Testament writers are read as testimonies to the one Jesus Christ – as they understand themselves—, they show a remarkable unity in their subject matter and they all realize that their commitment to this subject matter means that certain *boundaries* need to be drawn.

Fourthly, all the New Testament writers, including Luke who may be the only non-Jewish contributor to the Bible, understood Jesus in the light of God's earlier history with Israel. Since Abraham, God has been working over many generations and centuries with a people to prepare them for the coming of Jesus Christ. What God was planning to do in Christ could not have been grasped in any other culture. Among this people, God had been working through the monarchy, through the priesthood and through his prophets in order to prepare them for the coming of the Messiah who fulfilled what all these institutions were meant to be. In this people God gradually inculcated the conscience that this world was not as it should be and needed a Savior that could liberate it from sin, evil, and death. Through centuries of prophetic witness, this people came to understand that there is only one God who was radically different from his creation. In a sense, this was the ethnic group who would find it hardest to deal with the incarnation. Other peoples would have much less problems to accept the idea of a god-man. But the god-man these peoples would have recognized would have been only a far shadow of the god-man that Jesus' Jewish followers finally recognized Him to be. Only a staunchly monotheistic people could grasp the meaning of the incarnation in its depth. The history of Israel and the Old Testament plays, therefore, a unique role in our understanding of Christ. It is against this background that Jesus of Nazareth should be understood as the Son of God, as the Messiah, as the Son of Man, as the revelation of God, as the Savior, as Priest and Sacrifice. Over the ages God prepared this people to receive the Messiah.[30] Though other religious traditions may function as "preparation for the gospel" they can never function as an alternative Old Testament that could replace the first part of the Christian Scriptures.

The role of the canon in Christian theology strengthens and clarifies some of the earlier conclusions in our exploration of the sense in which we can speak of a "supra-cultural core of the gospel." It shows that the different biblical writers write from a variety of cultural perspectives and that all their witness is culturally embedded. It shows that their witness has a unity in their common center of attention; in their witness to the Creator God who exists before every culture, yet, who entered the world in Jesus Christ. In Christ, God acted in a specific cultural context, yet for the benefit of humankind as a whole. Our faith is grounded in this "supra-cultural" reality of God and "trans-cultural" reality of his self-revelation in Christ. The canon shows that there is not only a center, but that there are also boundaries and that certain voices need to be rejected because they do not do justice to the God who revealed himself in Jesus. The crucial place of the Old Testament finally shows that the person and work of Jesus as God's supreme self-revelation can only be fully understood against the background of God's history with Israel and in terms of Israel's worldview.[31] Because this canonical witness to Christ

---

30    Cf. Thomas F. Torrance, *Reality and Evangelical Theology: The Realism of Christian Theology*, with a new foreword by Kurt Anders Richardson (Downers Grove, IL: InterVarsity Press, 1999), 86ff.

31    This leads, of course, into a further question of how to distinguish between those elements of the biblical worldview that are normative (such as a linear understanding of history, the idea that creation is good and the absolute distinction between Creator and creation) and the elements of the biblical worldview that reflect current

is our only access to God's supreme revelation in Christ and gives us apostolic and Spirit led interpretations of its meaning, it remains normative for all subsequent Christian reflection of the Christ-event. It does not, however, exhaust its meaning, for it points to a reality beyond itself which has implications for every possible human culture that can only gradually become apparent.

## The Historic and Worldwide Community of Believers

Reference to canon as the supreme authority in the light of which we should live out the gospel today does not, however, solve the problem of how this canon should be interpreted. Study of Christians in the history of the church and contact with Christians from all over the world shows that Christians who agree that the Scriptures is the final authority for our Christian faith and life can still understand these Scriptures very differently. Some would, for example, understand the work of Christ primarily in terms of Christ's victory over the forces of evil, while others understand it primarily as Christ carrying the penalty for sin which we have deserved. Some call for the submission of women to their husbands and to the male leaders in the Christian community, while others have become great supporters of women's liberation motivated by the same Scriptures. Only when we enclose ourselves in our own little worlds is it possible to believe that everyone should read the Bible as our little community has always done it.

It is important to realize that the church through the ages and worldwide does not just show how differently the Scriptures can be read and understood. In doing so, it provides at the same time a resource to confirm or correct our personal readings of Scripture. Evangelical Christians in the protestant tradition can easily miss this point because of the specific debates that split the church at the time of the European Reformation in the Sixteenth century. In that time, the protestant reformers felt that their call to return to biblical teaching could not be heard by the Roman Catholic establishment.  Because the establishment argued that only the institutionalized church had the right to correctly interpret Scripture, the protestant appeal to Scripture carried no authority for them. In reaction, the Reformers rightly stressed the *sola Scriptura*, the authority of Scripture alone. The church should not reign over Scripture but submit to Scripture.

In the process, however, a number of protestant theologians in the Anabaptist tradition rejected any role for the church in the interpretation of Scripture. Every Christian should be able to read, understand and apply Scripture on his or her own. This individualistic understanding of the authority of Scripture is still influential in many evangelical circles and this is one of the reasons why evangelical Christians can come up with ever new readings of Scripture without feeling the need to check those within the wider community of the faithful.

Many of the Reformers and many current evangelicals are, however, much more balanced and realize that we cannot so easily put the tradition of the church aside.[32] Doing so would be

---

perspectives that are not normative (such as the idea that the universe consists of three layers, Exodus 20:3). This question lies beyond the scope of this paper.

32    See for a recent example Alister E. McGrath, "The Importance of Tradition for Modern Evangelicalism," in: Donald Lewis and Alister McGrath (eds.), *Doing Theology for the People of God: Studies in Honour of J.I. Packer* (Leicester, UK: Apollos, 1996), 159-173.

tantamount to denying that the Holy Spirit has been given to the church before us. We can maintain that the canon of the Scriptures has the supreme authority while profiting from the vast resources of historical Christian thinking to guide our contextual theological reflection.

The Reformers did particularly reflect on the role of the church through history. The current realization that we are not only part of a historic church community, but also of a worldwide Christian community brings a whole new specter of resources to our disposal. We can not only read of these Christians, we can meet them, dialogue with them, invite them into our efforts to live out the gospel in our particular cultural contexts.[33] They can help us to gain a clearer picture of Christ and his work, the *center* of our faith. Christians from different cultural contexts can share their faith in Christ whom they know through the Scriptures. If they honestly listen to each other, they will discover how different their understandings of Christ may be, but they are also conscious that they are not just sharing their personal opinions. They share their understanding of a reality beyond themselves: God who encounters us in Jesus Christ. Because they point to a reality beyond both their personal understandings of this reality, they may in the process discover that this supra-cultural reality demands from them to enlarge or adapt their respective understandings.[34]

My own understanding of Christ has been deepened, enlarged and corrected through my contacts with Christian brothers and sisters from different parts of the world. Looking from a distance, they are freer from the enchantment of my own western European cultural context and they can therefore help me discern the syncretism to which Christians in Europe are prone. That is how they can help us establish the *boundaries* of our Christian identity. The same is of course true for my brothers and sisters in Africa and other parts of the world. In this respect, the growth of the worldwide church and the unprecedented contact between culturally varied Christian communities, stimulated by the wider process of globalization, are immeasurable gifts to today's church. As Walls notes: "Never before, therefore, has there been so much potentiality for mutual enrichment and self-criticism, as God causes yet more light and truth to break forth from his world."[35]

## Conclusion: A Humanly Accessible Supra-Cultural Gospel Message

Reviewing our rather general explorations so far, we can draw two contrasting, yet interlinked conclusions concerning the question of whether there is a humanly accessible supra-cultural core to the gospel.

On the one hand, the nature of language, of the cultural locatedness of all our theological reflection and of the development of theological thought led us to the conclusion that it is impossible to produce a once-for-all adequate formulation of this gospel core. Such a formulation would always need to use a specific language and therefore reflect perceptions of a particular

---

33 As noted by, for example, Paul G. Hiebert, *Missiological Implications of Epistemological Shifts: Affirming Truth in a Modern/Postmodern World* (Harrisburg, PA: Trinity Press International, 1999), 102, 113.

34 Cf. Thomas F. Torrance on "Theological Persuasion," in: Thomas F. Torrance, *God and Rationality* (London e.a.: Oxford University Press, 1971), 195ff.

35 Walls, *The Missionary Movement*, 15.

culture. Important elements of the message would be tacitly implied and only in other contexts would it become apparent that they need spelling out elsewhere. An example would be the conviction the implicit biblical conviction that the Holy Spirit is fully divine, which needed spelling out in the later confrontation with fourth-century heretics who believed that the Spirit was created by God.

On the other hand, we have been able to affirm that there is a universally valid gospel which testifies to God's once-for-all self revelation in Jesus Christ for our salvation, to which the canon gives a normative testimony.[36] This self-revelation is indeed *humanly* accessible, if we take into account what it means to be human. The Christian understanding of what it means to be human contrasts with both classical Greek philosophy and modern Western philosophy, where the human mind has often been understood as participating in the divine mind or analogous to the divine mind. Accordingly, true knowledge was understood to be absolute and from a standpoint outside history and culture. According to the biblical picture, this is not what humankind is like, nor what it is meant to be. We are squarely located in the specific historical and cultural contexts in which God has placed us, yet within this context, we can have adequate—not absolute—knowledge of what God has done in Jesus Christ for our salvation. We can have *adequate* knowledge by becoming incorporated in the cultural traditions in which the Christian community continues to testify to Jesus Christ as the center, the core of the gospel message.

In confrontation with this testimony, a great variety of languages can be enriched in order to be able to express this hitherto unimaginable truth. In the encounter with this reality, culturally inherited conceptual structures can be changed to become more and more adequate to understand this reality that breaks open every natural human thought structure. In confronting our own limited understandings and confessions with the abundant riches of the worldwide church, we can be enriched in our understanding of Christ. At the same time, when we discover that others come up with different, yet similar understandings of Christ and when we discover how Christ reigns and saves elsewhere, this gives us confidence that our own limited understandings can adequately reflect the reality of Christ, the reality which is bound by none of our cultural expressions of it, but rather underlies them all.

This canonical testimony has been handed down through generations and into a dazzling variety of cultural contexts. Given that this process has been going on for nearly two thousand years and has spanned the entire globe, one would have reason to suppose that most of the potential heresies have by now been tried. In the process, many boundaries of what may be considered contextualization that is faithful to God's liberating action in Christ have been uncovered. There might be more boundaries to be discovered in the future, yet, as for the first disciples, our own Christian life does not depend on knowing all the potential boundaries. It depends on living close to the center in our particular context, living a life oriented to the canonical Christ, enlightened by Him, carried by Him, and bound by Him.

---

36    See on the role of the canon as a norm for contextual expressions of the gospel message also Vanhoozer, "'One Rule to Rule the All?'" 108-126.

## Discussion Questions

1. If you would need to formulate the core of the gospel message in a few phrases, what would it look like? To what extent do you think this formulation is colored by your own language, your own culture and the needs of your own community?

2. What can give us confidence that the understanding we have of Jesus is not just a product of our own cultural context, but gives us an adequate knowledge of the real person Jesus Christ to whom the Bible witnesses?

3. How does the phrase "Jesus is Lord" translate in your mother-tongue or in the language of another people among whom you are serving? Can you indicate how the understanding of this and other central Christian beliefs is colored by this culture as soon as it is translated?

4. Can you also give examples how words or expressions from your mother-tongue can gain new meanings when used to express the Christian faith?

5. Can you give examples of how contact with Christians from other cultural contexts (through reading or personal encounter) has deepened, enlarged or corrected your understanding of the gospel?

# 7

# Developing a Palate for Authentic Theology

## Natee Tanchanpongs

*Natee Tanchanpongs is Professor of Theology at Bangkok Bible Seminary. Natee is Thai but has lived in Singapore, St. Louis and the Chicago area. He worked as a computer network engineer for many years prior to becoming an ordained pastor under the Presbyterian Church in America, a church planter with Presbyterian Mission International and a theological educator at Bangkok Bible Seminary. His doctoral research at TEDS touches on the use of linguistics in contextual theology. Natee is also on the board of a local Christian publisher (Tyrannus Center) and has forthcoming works being published in Thai. He now resides in Bangkok with his wife (Bee) and two children (Maisie and Memo). Education: BS & MS in Electrical Engineering (Washington University in St. Louis), MDiv (Covenant Theological Seminary), PhD (Trinity Evangelical Divinity School)*

## Introduction

Heads or tails? Call it in the air! Many who have probed into the issues of religious syncretism and contextualization have concluded that syncretistic practice for one may just be contextualization for another. The questions about the not-so-clear distinctions between contextualization and syncretism involve criteria to evaluate biblical authenticity of theological products. The manner in which we construe these criteria can affect many things. In general, stringent criteria stifle the opportunity to better localize various communicative intents of Scripture; too broad may just suppress them altogether. This does not however mean that it is better to err on the side of caution, which evangelicals tend to do.[1] In fact, a narrow set of criteria could just as easily but inadvertently lead to syncretistic beliefs and practices. In addition, such criteria could also impinge on the enthusiasm of Christians to theologize contextually. Having said this, evangelicals do see the need for some criteria to help adjudicate between proper instances

---

1    In this volume, Blomberg has already shown us "the danger of fishing in too limited an area," 39.

of contextualization and those that are not. Coming up with these criteria might be a much more difficult task than some may think.

I shall begin by discussing the debate on syncretism to help show the necessity for some adjudicative criteria and to set the stage to move the conversation forward. Through the use of two metaphors, I shall then single out two particular weaknesses in the traditional evangelical approaches for assessing religious syncretism and put forward that a context-to-text approach might produce better evaluative criteria for a properly evangelical contextual theologizing.

## The Debate Concerning Religious Syncretism

The debates on religious syncretism tend to revolve around the use of the term. Some call for continuing use of this term *syncretism* as a means to evaluate the authenticity of a theological product. Most evangelical scholars agree that there is both a necessity for gospel adaptation within cultures as well as dangers of excessive mixing. With the double-edge sword of intentionally mixing Scripture and culture, some choose to distinguish the process that is proper, classifying it as contextualization or enculturation, from that which oversteps the biblical bounds, calling it syncretism. Among them, Rodrigo Tano attempts a definition saying, "Syncretism occurs when critical and basic elements of the Gospel are lost in the process of contextualization and are replaced by religious elements from the receiving culture."[2] For Byang Kato, syncretism occurs "when critical and basic elements of the Gospel are lost in the process of contextualization and are replaced by religious elements from the receiving culture."[3] Still others see syncretism as "combining elements of Christianity with folk beliefs and practices in such a way that the gospel loses its integrity and message."[4] While recognizing a neutral sense of the term syncretism as the blending of ideas, attitudes, and practices, Moreau also opts for a traditional evaluative definition[5] as "the replacement or dilution of the essential truths of the gospel through the incorporation of non-Christian elements."[6]

---

2    Rodrigo D. Tano, "Toward an Evangelical Asian Theology," *Evangelical Review of Theology* 7 (1983): 159.

3    Quoted from Harvie M. Conn, *Eternal Word and Changing Worlds: Theology, Anthropology, and Mission in Trialogue* (Grand Rapids: Zondervan, 1984), 176.

4    Paul G. Hiebert, R. Daniel Shaw, and Tite Tiénou, *Understanding Folk Religion: A Christian Response to Popular Beliefs and Practices* (Grand Rapids: Baker, 1999), 177. For similar other definitions of syncretism, see Gailyn Van Rheenen, "Syncretism and Contextualization: The Church on a Journey Defining Itself," in *Contextualization and Syncretism: Navigating Cultural Currents,* ed. Gailyn Van Rheenen (Pasadena, CA: William Carey Library, 2006), 7-13.

5    Schreiter affirms that the historical use of this term tends to be negative. Robert J. Schreiter, "Defining Syncretism: An Interim Report," *International Bulletin of Missionary Research* 17 (1993): 50. Also see Charles Stewart and Rosalind Shaw, "Introduction: Problematizing Syncretism," in *Syncretism/Anti-Syncretism: The Politics of Religious Syncretism,* ed. Charles Stewart and Rosalind Shaw (New York: Routledge, 1994), 3-6.

6    A. Scott Moreau, "Syncretism," *Evangelical Dictionary of World Missions*, 924. Similarly, Saunders asserts that a transformative process of the Christian faith, which is always embedded in concrete cultural systems, is ongoing. Yet, he rejects synergetic composites of two or more religious systems. George R. Saunders, "Introduction," in *Culture and Christianity: The Dialectics of Transformation,* ed. George R. Saunders (New York: Greenwood, 1988), 3. W.A. Visser't Hooft would go so far as to identify the underlying cause of religious syncretism with Kantian pluralism. Willem Adolph Visser 't Hooft, *No Other Name: The Choice between Syncretism and Christian Universalism* (Philadelphia: Westminster, 1963), 11.

On the opposite end, there are some who view syncretism as a natural and inescapable part of contextualization. For them, the term syncretism should be neutral and free from any evaluative force. Schreiter argues for a more positive definition as a mixing of religious and cultural elements, suggesting that syncretism is an unavoidable phenomenon that occurs when two systems come into contact with each other. As such, all expressions of the Christian faith in any cultural context are syncretistic. He suggests that the modern era of contextualization is simply bringing back old questions concerning the limits of gospel interaction with culture. According to Schreiter, substituting or abandoning the use of the term syncretism in positive or neutral senses does not solve the problem because it simply evades the complexity between theological development and cultural process.[7] He concludes by offering a new model of syncretism based on a semiotic description of culture.[8]

Between these extremes are some who desire to use the term, but choose to distinguish between the positive and negative aspects of syncretism. Walter Hollenweger views Christianity as a syncretism par excellence. For him, "The question is not: Syncretism, yes or no?, but: What kind of syncretism?"[9] Given this, he calls for a theologically responsible syncretism modeled after the New Testament. Sundermeier distinguishes between two basic forms of syncretism. On the one hand, a more neutral symbolic syncretism is inevitable and indispensable for it "describes a process rather than a condition and comes into existence in all places where primal cultures and their systems of religion are dominated by differentiated and superior societies and their systems of religion."[10] On the other hand, synthetic syncretism, which is evaluative in nature, "occurs horizontally in the encounter of equal systems of religion, be it an 'exchange' between tribal religions or an urban border-crossing world religion."[11]

Others suggest that the term syncretism is no longer helpful and opt for other terms. Peter Schineller discusses the similarities between syncretism and contextualization and concludes that the term syncretism cannot be redeemed because it has too much of a pejorative overtone. He chooses a more neutral older term, inculturation, but distinguishes between the adequate and the inadequate varieties.[12]

---

7    On this point, see Schreiter, "Defining Syncretism," 50-51.

8    Robert J. Schreiter, *Constructing Local Theologies* (Maryknoll, N.Y.: Orbis, 1985), 152. Also see A. F. Droogers, "Syncretism: The Problem of Definition, the Definition of the Problem," in *Dialogue and Syncretism: An Interdisciplinary Approach,* ed. Jerald D. Gort (Grand Rapids, MI: Eerdmans, 1989), 464.

9    Walter J. Hollenweger, "A Plea for a Theologically Responsible Syncretism," *Missionalia* 25 (1997): 7.

10    Theo Sundermeier, "Inculturation and Syncretism," *Scriptura* S10 (1992): 37-38.

11    Sundermeier, "Inculturation and Syncretism," 39. There are others who wish to use the term syncretism in two distinguishable senses. Following Hiebert's critical contextualization, Vanhoozer calls for "critical syncretism" which implies that there are "uncritical" forms of syncretism (i.e., those that do not take into account canonic and catholic principles of the theodrama). Kevin Vanhoozer, "One Rule to Rule Them All? Theological Method in an Era of World Christianity," in *Globalizing Theology: Belief and Practice in an Era of World Christianity,* ed. Craig Ott and Herold Netland (Grand Rapids, MI: Baker, 2006), 102-104. Siv Ellen Kraft notes that Carsten Colpe tries to recover the evaluative aspect of syncretism by distinguishing the state of syncretism from the process of syncretization. Siv Ellen Kraft, "'To Mix or Not to Mix': Syncretism/Anti-Syncretism in the History of Theosophy," *Numen* 49 (2002): 143.

12    Peter Schineller, "Inculturation and Syncretism: What Is the Real Issue?" *International Bulletin of Missionary Research* 16 (1992).

Correspondingly, a trendier alternative is *hybridity*. Siv Ellen Kraft, in using Bakhtin, recognizes two forms of hybridization: organic and intentional.[13] Likewise, Zehner abandons the term syncretism for a more neutral *hybridity*.[14] He selects a seemingly broad term, assuming that some inevitable interactions exist between adjacent cultural and/or religious semiotic systems. In his interviews with some Buddhist converts to evangelical Christianity, Zehner observes two forms of hybridities. Through them, he suggests, the evangelicals navigate the narrow passage between orthodoxy (with an evaluative need for anti-syncretistic stance) and universality (with a missional demand for localization). Zehner writes,

> Hybridities of extension fit locally specific material into frames that are transculturally shared, while hybridities of transition exploit cognitive and terminological overlaps that facilitate a person's movement across otherwise discrete religious boundaries. Together, these orthodox hybridities give evangelical Christianity a feel of the local while preserving converts' sense of being loyal to a transculturally shared set of teachings.[15]

The hybridities of extension involve a translation-like presenting of transcultural messages with local terminologies. The hybridities of transition are more elaborate and potentially more problematic. They explore the overlapped areas between the two systems as a way to assist in the "cognitive slippage" between them. Through the particular data gathered, Zehner clarifies the concept of the transitional hybridities within the shared realm of church and culture saying,

> [Some transitional hybridities] exhibit direct overlap between Buddhist and Christian frames of meaning for employing, at least in the transitions of conversion, symbols and meanings that could be sensible in terms of both traditions. Yet as parts of transitional processes they facilitate conversion by providing points of congruence that bridge the two traditions, making conversations simultaneously sensible in both meaning systems.[16]

Even in relation to acceptable benchmarks of evangelical orthodoxy, Zehner argues that there are invisible syncretistic mixings in both forms of hybridities. First, with regard to the ability to use local material to express discourse meaning of the first from of hybridities, Zehner observes that a particular local form has its own meaning apart from the discourse that cannot simply be discarded. Same words translated mean different things in different cultures. When local words/concepts are used, they engage the underlying "cognitive grids" born out of local experience.[17] Second, transitional hybridizing activities, which operate within the overlapped region between two cultural and/or religious systems, are necessary for the "cognitive slippage" from one to the other.[18] Within this region, similar to the intermingling of forms and meanings of extension hybridities, the inner motives and outward actions of the systems intertwine.

---

13    Kraft, "To Mix or Not to Mix," 147.

14    Edwin R. Zehner, "Orthodox Hybridities: Anti-Syncretism and Localization in the Evangelical Christianity of Thailand," *Anthropological Quarterly* 78 (2005).

15    Zehner, "Orthodox Hybridities," 585.

16    Zehner, "Orthodox Hybridities," 596.

17    Ibid.

18    Zehner indicates that these "slippages" tend to happen below the level of conscious awareness, that is, the conversion story contains *slippages* that even the convert himself/herself is unaware. See Zehner, "Orthodox Hybridities," 587-588.

More importantly, at a given instant of a transitional hybridity, it is difficult to pinpoint the direction of the slippage between these systems.[19]

The debate on the terminologies associated with the concepts of proper and improper mixing of Christianity with other cultural/religious elements brings value to our discussion on the need for some adjudicative criteria. At the end of the day, you can call it as you wish, but biblical authenticity of the Christian faith in a given context must still be evaluated somehow.

## Problems with Typical Evangelical Perceptions of Religious Syncretism: A Cuisine Metaphor

### Authenticity of Thai Cuisine

Friends in the US often asked me to recommend restaurants that serve authentic Thai food. Somehow, I have always managed to come up with a list for them. And yet, I seldom ask what my underlying criteria for deliberating the authenticity of Thai cuisine in a foreign land are. Do they involve "essential" ingredients, without the taste of which the dish would not be considered real Thai? If so, what tastes among all the tastes in the Thai cuisine would constitute its essence and why? Why would the other flavors of Thai dishes not also be considered essential? At what point does the using of non-native ingredients cause a dish to no longer be Thai? Then there is of course the fact that authentic ingredients do not guarantee authenticity or palatability of a dish. Granted that ingredients play a part, how genuine and good tasting a dish is *also* has much to do with how well the cook prepares it.

These questions and problems aside, a Thai person, who may or may not know how to cook or may or may not know anything about the ingredients of Thai cuisine, can typically and tacitly deliberate the authenticity of a dish only after tasting it. Sure, there is always some subjectivity in the process. But a simple discussion among native Thais would more often than not resolve the disagreements of the in-between cases. In the end, a Thai person can more or less tell if a dish is authentically Thai by tasting it. This tacit ability to deliberate the authenticity of an indigenous cuisine can of course be acquired by non-natives. People who have spent an extended period of time in Thailand often gain a level of competency to offer deliberative opinions. It is perhaps possible even for a two-week long tourist to attain some degree of this tacit ability. After such a visit, he or she could return home and choose a restaurant that serves authentic Thai food.

### Cuisine Metaphor, Contextualization and Religious Syncretism

A brief look of how authenticity of indigenous cuisines is evaluated highlights the problems with traditional evangelical proposals for the assessment of religious syncretism and could offer a way forward. The reality is that none of us is ethnically "canonical" by birth. However, even though we are all *non-native* tasters and cooks of canonical cuisine, we still must evaluate the canonical authenticity of our theological dishes or produce dishes that are genuinely "biblical."

---

19   Zehner, "Orthodox Hybridities," 596.

As such, we must acquire the canonical tastes and the evaluative skill.[20] Vanhoozer helps us to understand the material aspect of this acquisition with his notions of canonical-linguistics and canonical competence. In his proposal, Vanhoozer makes a cultural-linguistic turn while holding fast to the primacy of Scripture.[21] He affirms a significant but non-normative role for the interpretive context and culture in biblical hermeneutics, while letting the Bible speak and exercise its autonomy.[22] Just as a non-native Thai cuisine taster must acquire the tastes of Thai food, so also must a non-native taster of canonical cuisines. And as much as one is able to acquire those tastes, he or she increasingly gains the canonical competence and the ability to assess both the authenticity of theological products and the marks of religious syncretism.[23]

Non-native tasters, however, have at least one obstacle to overcome as deliberators of cuisine authenticity. They all begin with limited tacit experiences of the native food. This problem, of course, can be reduced by time, a spirit of exploration and increasing exposure. Through this remedial process, one must remember that native cuisines vary greatly (often times according to ethnic regions) and cannot be reduced to some subset of "essential" taste. Thus, it would be incorrect to identify food from a particular region as the essence for all Thai cuisine.

This situation resembles and highlights the first problems with traditional evangelical proposals for the assessment of religious syncretism. A traditional evangelical evaluation of religious syncretism assumes a form of a canon within the canon of Scripture as its criteria; as if it is to say that some Thai tastes are more "essentially Thai" than others. There is room to debate the use and the semantics of the term *syncretism*. That which seems undeniable, at least in the evangelical community, is the need for some evaluative standards to arbitrate between proper and improper theological products.[24] Evangelicals also agree that these criteria must somehow be anchored in the canon of Scripture. However, it is the way one conceives this connection to Scripture that produces deficiencies in existing evaluative criteria for syncretism. Particularly, the language of *essential, basic, critical elements* of the gospel betrays an underlying assumption of a canon within the canon. In the same light, Zehner astutely observes that evangelicalism is

---

20    Within this metaphor, we must never forget that we, as non-native cooks of canonical cuisine, always function under the tutelage and apprenticeship of the Master Chef, the Holy Spirit.

21    Vanhoozer values the cultural-linguistic approach in at least two areas. First, it rightly emphasizes that theology is closely linked to the Christian way of life in the church. Second, a cultural-linguistic approach takes into account the sociology of language. In the canonical-linguistic approach, the practices/judgments of the biblical canon, not those of the community (ecclesial *culture*), is normative and determinative. See Vanhoozer, *Drama*, 12-13, 16, 165-185.

22    Elsewhere, Vanhoozer makes this affirmation more explicit, as he outlines the three turns to context: a turn to social location, to social situation, and to social identity. Kevin Vanhoozer, "One Rule to Rule Them All? Theological Method in an Era of World Christianity," in *Globalizing Theology: Belief and Practice in an Era of World Christianity*, ed. Craig Ott and Herold Netland (Grand Rapids, MI: Baker, 2006), 98. Vanhoozer accepts the strengths of these turns, nevertheless qualifies his approval by trumping them with a "*canonic* and *christological* principle." Vanhoozer, "One Rule to Rule Them All?" 109.

23    For the discussion of canonical competency, see Vanhoozer, *Drama*, 129, 181.

24    Hence, Moreau is right to say that a purely neutral sense of the word is unhelpful for it loses its analytical power. Moreau, "Syncretism," 924. Stewart and Shaw try to salvage to neutral use of syncretism, yet see the need for some criteria. They define *anti-syncretism* as "antagonism to religious synthesis shown by agents concerned with the defense of religious boundaries," relating it to the notions of authenticity and purity. See Stewart and Shaw, "Introduction: Problematizing Syncretism," 6-9. Cf. Schineller, "Inculturation and Syncretism: What Is the Real Issue?" 50.

adaptable to local contexts because its anti-syncretistic stance has a comparatively sharp focal point, limited only to a few core Christian beliefs and doctrines as its criteria to adjudicate syncretism. As such, "[A] good deal of local variation can be built into the local experience and practice of evangelicalism without its developing a sense of having lost its shape."[25]

*Sola Scriptura* is an important centerpiece of evangelical theology, the belief of which affixes Scripture as the primary evaluative criteria for syncretism. Even so, there is both the need to rightly construe Scripture and the need to rightly construe the *whole* of Scripture as such. The latter premise demands that one considers the entire biblical corpus and all that Scripture is intending to communicate as essential, basic and critical. On this point, Harvie Conn rightly suggests that syncretism must be framed in terms of forbidding the *whole* Scripture to speak and not simply as a damage to or replacement of an essential core of the gospel.[26] J. Nelson Jennings recounts Conn's expansion of contextualization and syncretism in a more holistic framework of submission or rebellion within the covenantal relationship. He writes,

> [Syncretism is] the loss of universal, transcendent and normative traits of the Christian faith, due to a culture's "pull" towards autonomy. … There is a protection of the status quo against all critique, no matter what normative standards of justice and mercy might attempt to speak into the situation. Finally, what is genuinely local and flexible is reified into something allegedly universal and normative—which becomes problematic when other local situations are encountered. Syncretism in this sense becomes more particular, more multifaceted, and more ongoing in its occurrences than in the instinctive "mixing of religions" sense. Because contextualization always involves a type of particular and multifaceted "mixing" of the universal-normative and the local-flexible, it would be problematic to understand syncretism only within that type of one-time religious "mixing" or interpenetration" category—especially insofar as the Christian faith thus syncretized would be understood to enter a new situation containing a fixed and unchanging "essential core," usually understood in a conceptual, theological sense.[27]

In the end, the use of the so-called "essential, basic, and critical elements of Scripture" as evaluative criteria for syncretism may not be as helpful as imagined, for doing so wrongly truncates the primacy of Scripture, just as a whole repertoire of tastes in the Thai cuisines cannot be reduced to its subsets.

Our cuisine metaphor also draws our attention to the second problem with a traditional evangelical evaluation of syncretism, namely that it tends to assume a structuralist approach. As it has already been mentioned, right ingredients do not guarantee authenticity. At the same

---

25   Zehner, "Orthodox Hybridities," 610. Apart from having a constricted view of the canon, Zehner fails to adequately discuss the role Scripture plays in the "slippage" *from* one's cultural-linguistic framework.

26   Conn, *Eternal Word*, 176-178, 184-190, 194-195. Similarly, Carson asserts that "the corpus of non-negotiable truth embraces all of Scripture." D. A. Carson, "Church and Mission: Reflections on Contextualization and the Third Horizon," in *The Church in the Bible and the World: An International Study,* ed. D. A. Carson (Grand Rapids, MI: Baker, 1987), 248.

27   J. Nelson Jennings, "Suburban Evangelical Individualism: Syncretism or Contextualization?" in *Contextualization and Syncretism: Navigating Cultural Currents,* ed. Gailyn Van Rheenen (Pasadena, CA: William Carey Library, 2006), 172

time, dishes that summon non-traditional ingredients do not necessarily dismiss their Thainess. Granted that ingredients play a major part in any cooking process, nevertheless, how a cook prepares his or her dishes is likewise significant in bringing about their outcome and their authenticity. However, a structuralist approach largely ignores the role of human agency and focuses primarily and perhaps exclusively on the interactions between cultural-linguistic systems. The evaluative criteria of a structuralist approach center around the relation between two semiotic systems. Anthropologist F. Niyi Akinnaso exposes this problem by saying,

> Syncretism takes as its starting point the clash or interplay between two or more distinct forms of religious symbolism without explaining the dynamics of the interaction, thus excluding the importance of human agency in the creation of religious knowledge. Like the structural-functionalist model within which it was embedded, syncretism recognized change without being able to explain it.[28]

This underlying assumption is detected in an evangelical description of syncretism, which typically sees it as the mixings of two or more systems resulting in inappropriate adaptations, replacements, or corruptions of essential/basic/critical elements of a particular cultural-linguistic system by elements from another system. Such structurally derived criteria fail to account for the human agency involved and the dynamics of the broader meta-linguistic framework. A further limit of the structuralist framework is evident in Zehner's otherwise helpful proposal. Within the overlapped region of two semiotic systems lie transitional hybridities, which act as vehicles for "cognitive slippages" between the two cultural-linguistic systems. With a structuralist approach that focuses only on systems, Zehner is only able to provide static snapshots of the slippage, which in themselves do not illuminate its direction or elucidate "which culture or religious meaning system is the primary one influencing a person's understanding."[29]

Authenticity is measured not as much by the presence of some certain ingredients, but by the actual outcome of the cooking discourse itself. The public meanings of cultural elements may be helpful to know, but "meaning" is found in a complex combination of cultural-linguistic system *and* its use in a discourse. Here is where Michael Polanyi's proposal on tacit knowledge is helpful. According to Polanyi, tacit knowing involves a triadic structure made up of the subsidiaries (parts), the focal (whole), and the person. In it, the personal process of knowing always begins from the parts which one have already known by experience and moves toward the whole which one wants to know or wants to make known.[30] Through this from-to framework, Polanyi claims that all human thought contains those components which one has come to tacitly know. A person uses his/her body and everything else external to him/her (albeit objects, languages, concepts, etc.) as an extended instrument of the body to interact with the world.[31] In the tacit structure, parts and whole relate in three basic relationships: functional, phenomenal and semantic. For our purpose I shall only focus on the last.

---

28   F. Niyi Akinnaso, "Bourdieu and the Diviner: Knowledge and Symbolic Power in Yoruba Divination," in *The Puisuit of Certainty: Religious and Cultural Formulation*, ed. Wendy James (London: Routledge, 1995), 235.

29   Zehner, "Orthodox Hybridities," 596.

30   Cf. Michael Polanyi, "Sense-Giving and Sense-Reading," in *Knowing and Being: Essays by Michael Polanyi,* ed. Marjorie Grene; (Chicago: University of Chicago Press, 1969), 182.

31   Polanyi, "Sense-Giving and Sense-Reading," 183.

In the semantic structure of tacit knowing, meaning is formed in the process of integration of the related things which we already tacitly know (*parts*).[32] In this integration, those things which we already tacitly know mean something only in the relation to the *whole* that they form.[33] Polanyi employs the word "meaning" in three distinct ways. First, it could refer to the meaning of a part in isolation (M1: the dictionary meaning of a word). Second, it could also be the meaning of a part in an integrated relation to the whole (M2: the meaning of the same word used in a discourse). Third, "meaning" is also used by Polanyi to refer to the meaning of the integrated whole (M3: the meaning of the discourse in which the word is used). In the tacit semantic integration of a discourse, one discovers that the dictionary meanings of words (M1) is relatively meaningless compared to the significance when their integrated meanings used in the discourse (M2) are accounted for within the whole discourse meaning (M3).[34] For Polanyi, it is not necessarily the word's dictionary meaning (M1) that adds to the joint meaning of discourse (M3), rather their integrated meanings (M2). As one seeks to comprehend the discourse meaning (M3), there is a transposition from words' dictionary meanings (M1) to their integrated meanings (M2). This semantic transposition is reflected in the fact that the dictionary meaning of words (M1) to varying degrees can be transformed when these words are examined in the context of integrated meaning of the discourse (M3). To look at this process differently, given the dictionary meanings of words (M1), their summation does not necessary guarantee the arrival of meaning of the discourse (M3). All in all, the knower cannot merely resort to the analysis of the isolated words in order to produce the integrative meaning of the discourse. In tacit knowing, the meaning of a discourse can come only through the integration of all of its interactive parts.[35]

In addition, Polanyi argues that sense-giving and sense-reading in communications are parts of the same process of tacit knowing governed by its structure and logic. In other words, tacit knowing concerns both discoveries (e.g., reading) and creation (e.g., writing) of meaningful communication. In sense-reading, one utilizes the cultural-linguistic elements (such as words, concepts, etc.) that he has seen, heard, touched, and experienced to help make sense of that which he intends to discover. While doing so, the meanings of these parts could be altered from their initial starting points.[36] Similarly in sense-giving, the knower imaginatively and intuitively gropes for cultural-linguistic elements from all that he has seen, heard, touched, and experienced to communicate that which he intends to say.[37] And in an instance of tacit integration, he endows these cultural-linguistic elements with meanings, which could likewise be

---

32   Polanyi and Prosch, *Meaning*, 52.

33   Polanyi expounds this semantic connection using the concept of indwelling. He puts forward that the act of comprehending is one of tacit integration, an ongoing absorption of external "reality" through indwelling of its parts. This process of indwelling helps to construct an ever-changing interpretive framework through which one comprehends other entities.

34   Cf. Polanyi, "Knowing and Being," 128.

35   See Polanyi, "Knowing and Being," 130. Even so, it seems clear that he does not dismiss the value of explicit analysis of the subsidiary parts. In fact, the process of discovery requires an appropriate weaving of integration and analysis. Polanyi, "Knowing and Being," 129. Also see Polanyi, "The Logic of Tacit Inference," 148.

36   Polanyi, "Sense-Giving and Sense-Reading," 184.

37   Polanyi, "Sense-Giving and Sense-Reading," 187, 191. Watson suggests that sense-giving is not just an act of communication, but is also one of tacit learning. Through writing, people learn. See Sam Watson, "The Tacit Victory and the Unfinished Agenda: Polanyi and Rhetorical Studies," *Tradition and Discovery* 18 (1991-1992): 19.

altered from their initial starting points. In the end then, both sense-giving and sense-reading operate on the same structures and process of tacit knowing.

Polanyi's proposal helps us to see that "meaning" is a function of *both* the cultural-linguistic system *and* its actual usages by people. For him, subsidiaries in tacit integrations are of course more than words in language systems, but they include everything in one's interpretive context. For our purpose, subsidiaries comprise elements of cultural-linguistic systems to which we belong: linguistic, cultural and religious words, concepts, practices, rituals, etc. These elements relate to Scripture in that theologizing involves on-going discoveries and holistic articulations of intricate reality of the Scriptures through the indwelling of both non-authoritative cultural-linguistic and normative canonical-linguistic elements. Polanyi exposes the limit of structural-ist approaches in their attempt to compare systems (M1), that is those of canonical-linguistic and of cultural-linguistic, rather than taking into account the agents and the actual discourses they produce (M2 and M3). Ingredients alone do not guarantee or dismiss authenticity. Granted that ingredients play a major part in any cooking process, a non-native but competent canonical cook can discourse his or her biblically authentic dishes with all kinds of cultural-linguistic elements. It would not be wise to accept or dismiss any cultural-linguistic elements prior to their actual usages in theological discourses.

## Fine Tuning the Evaluative Engine: A Cruising Metaphor

Thus far, we have uncovered two key limits of the current models evangelicals typically use to evaluate religious syncretism, but I have not yet proposed criteria of my own. To do so, our cooking metaphor does not prove to be sufficiently dynamic. For one thing, this metaphor leads to the appearance that the adjudicative process is highly subjective in two ways. First, a native or a competent non-native taster, who may or may not know how to cook or may or may not know anything about the ingredients of Thai cuisine, can typically tell if a dish is authentic by tasting it, even if he or she may not be able to give a reason why it is or is not so. Second, in cooking, a dish may be judged by one as authentic and by another as not, just as it is often accepted that one person's contextualization is another's syncretism.

There is always some subjectivity in this adjudicative process to be sure. However, I propose that a different metaphor may give us a more dynamic way of framing the issue and help move this complex problem forward by fine tuning the evaluative criteria. In particular, I suggest that in light of a direction metaphor, context-to-text movement provides better criteria to evaluate religious syncretism.[38] That is, a theological product is judged to be or not be syncretistic not so much by the presence of certain cultural/religious ingredients, but more so by whether or not that theological product "cruises" in the direction toward or away from Scripture.

The evangelical commitment to the Scripture principle necessitates a safeguard against religious syncretism. The context-to-text approach to contextual theology renders "thicker" evaluative criteria based on a proper construal of the Scripture principle without which there is no evalua-

---

38    This model does not solve all evaluative problems associated with religious syncretism. It only suggests a way forward for a new generation of evangelicals to consider. In fact, directional criteria might raise new and different questions and issues which we must address.

tive anchor to adjudicate religious syncretism. Without such an anchor, epistemic dependency ensues and all theology becomes trapped within its own categories.[39]

Context-to-text approach to contextual theologizing argues that the affirmations in the primacy of the Bible (i.e., the Scripture principle) and in the reality of a significant role for the interpretive context in all theological enterprise (i.e., the cultural-linguistic turn) can coexist only if there is a "movement"/transformation from context to the Text through the power of the language-in-use (i.e., discourse). This model requires the interpretive context and its cultural-linguistic elements to be dynamic, non-normative, and modifiable, the characteristics of which permit the discourse with its kinetic force to move from whence they begin toward the Text of Scripture. This movement is precisely that which structuralist approaches based on analyses of and between cultural-linguistic systems cannot provide.

Furthermore, the context-to-text model for contextual theology parallels the reality of sanctification process. In both, we have no choice but to begin from within our contexts. In sanctification, each of us progresses in our own distinctive ways and from within our unique contexts. We cannot be but who we are. Likewise, in our theological enterprises, we cannot but use subsidiaries we have embodied as tools to "sense-read" the meaning of Scripture and "sense-give" the meaning to our interpretive context and theological discourses. To be sure, our contexts are affected by sin and are in need of transformation. It is true that we *cannot be* who we are not, but because of the reality of sin, we also must *become* who we are not. This requires transformations through the work of dual agency (our human responsibility and the sovereign work of the Holy Spirit) in the discourses of our lives (Phil 2:12-13) toward the one destination of holy living marked out by Scripture.

The parallel between the context-to-text theologizing and the reality of sanctification helps to advance Zehner's work. The meaning of the conversion discourse is a dialogic interaction between language systems and their particular usages. A hermeneutics of such a testimony in the broader life context could unveil the direction of the "cognitive slippage" and thus inform the reader of the discourse of any underlying syncretism and help him/her to make a better evaluative judgment concerning the dynamic compositions of the transitional hybridities.

More importantly, the context-to-text model for contextual theology and its connection with sanctification process help to illuminate a set of new criteria to evaluate contextualization and syncretism. In both cases we ask similar evaluative questions. How do we know if our life or our theological product displays biblical authenticity? Which directions do our lives and theological products traverse? Are they moving toward or away from Scripture? With these similarities, I shall use two criteria for evaluating biblical authenticity in the process of sanctification and apply their counterpart to assess religious syncretism.

---

39    To be taken captive to a cultural-linguistic framework without canonical-linguistic primacy is syncretistic. In the end, Schreiter may do little more than "Constructing Local *Anthropologies*." While ethno/local-theologies focus on cultural contexts *per se* and overlook the possibility of discourse modifying the vernacular elements, evangelical contextual theologies must take an instrumental and transformative view of the interpretive contexts.

First, biblical authenticity of a Christian whose life remains unchanged and unaffected by the transforming power of the gospel must be questioned. In Romans 12:1-2, Paul urges Christians to be driven by God's mercy to holy (sanctified) living and to do so by *moving away from* the conformity of the pattern of this world and be transformed to (*moving toward*) God's good, pleasing and perfect will. Scripture, as the breath of God's will, is the destination of one's embodiment of holy and righteous living "thoroughly equipped for every good work" (2 Tim. 3:16-17). Hence, a sanctified living is one that is not held captive by one's context, but indeed moves and is transformed away from it. There is no sanctification and therefore biblical faith if lives remain unchanged and unaffected by the gospel.[40]

Likewise, syncretism seen in light of this criterion of epistemic dependency occurs when a particular theological product begins within and remains captive to a conceptual scheme. As such, there is no movement out from one's cultural-linguistic framework. Similar to the case of sanctification, we must ask if the Scripture is being allowed to transform one's interpretive context. This is precisely what Conn and Jennings are suggesting as a criterion for evaluating religious syncretism.[41] On the broader scale, a tell-tale sign of religious syncretism is when the church is identical with the society within which she is housed. On this side of glory, that should never happen. An authentic church, as it is with the lives of individual believers, is always reforming away from her sin-afflicted context. I want to suggest that in particular instances of contextual theologizing, if the semantics of the dominant cultural-linguistic subsidiaries (words, concepts, etc.) being used in a theological discourse (written and practiced) remain unchanged (i.e., M1s are identical to their respective M2s), we might suspect that some religious syncretism has occurred. For instance, if the concept of "karma" used in a particular theological discourse (e.g., to clarify the convenantal works of Adam and Christ in Romans 5) remains unchanged by the discourse, we may perhaps conclude that the theological discourse has been held captive by its conceptual framework, and thus syncretism has probably occurred in such an attempt at contextualization.[42]

The second criterion for examining biblical authenticity of a Christian has to do with the direction of the change in one's life. We have already seen that the first criterion examines whether or not there are changes in the believers. However, the presence of change alone does

---

40    This is precisely James' argument concerning authentic faith and works in James 2.

41    Jennings, "Suburban Evangelical Individualism: Syncretism or Contextualization?", 172. Similarly, Daniel Carrol warns against an underlying ideological captivity to capitalism in M. Daniel Carroll R., "The Challenge of Economic Globalization for Theology: From Latin America to a Hermeneutics of Responsibility," in *Globalizing Theology: Belief and Practice in an Era of World Christianity*, ed. Craig Ott and Herold Netland (Grand Rapids, MI: Baker, 2006). Both Ramachandra and Hiebert Meneses issue strong rebukes against syncretism of nationalism. Vinoth Ramachandra, "Globalization, Nationalism, and Religious Resurgence," in *Globalizing Theology: Belief and Practice in an Era of World Christianity*, ed. Craig Ott and Herold Netland (Grand Rapids, MI: Baker, 2006); Eloise Hiebert Meneses, "Bearing Witness in Rome with Theology from the Whole Church: Globalization, Theology, and Nationalism," in *Globalizing Theology: Belief and Practice in an Era of World Christianity*, ed. Craig Ott and Herold Netland (Grand Rapids, MI: Baker, 2006). Newbigin assesses the Western theology in his British context as syncretistic because her dominance prevents the larger ecclesial body from critiquing her Post-Enlightenment assumptions. Lesslie Newbigin, *The Open Secret: Sketches for a Missionary Theology* (London: SPCK, 1978), 172.

42    For a successful biblical example, see the uses of *logos* in John 1. Similarly in Chapter 3 of this volume, Dembele has convincingly showed that a number of indigenous divine names have been used and "pruned" by the biblical discourse to communicate her own distinct concept of God.

not guarantee biblical authenticity, for one could make changes toward something else other than the Bible. A biblical analogy to this is found with the case where Israel asks for a king (1 Samuel 8). It seems clear from Deuteronomy 17:14-20 that God has wanted to give his people a king under a broader theocratic rule. The king who was to rule Israel must be one of God's choosing. The act of asking for a king was not only an act of impatience (i.e., Israel could not wait for God to give them a king), but one of rebelliousness (i.e., they are rejecting the king God had planned for them). There is no question that Israel wanted change, but not the kind that God had wanted. The change that the people desired is characterized by a horizontal movement (i.e., "want a king over us … like all the other nations") rather than a vertical one.[43] Thus, a sanctifying Christian is one who continues to embody and move toward Scripture.

In a similar fashion, syncretism also takes place when the process of theologizing does not direct its product toward a proper anchor of Scripture.[44] If the first criterion inspects the movement away from the context of the reader, the second checks whether the movement is toward the Text. The semantic transformation of some cultural-linguistic elements does not guarantee the absence of syncretism. For example, a contextual theology that *only* moves toward a theology of another Christian community might be considered a form of religious syncretism. Even though semantic transformation of cultural-linguistic subsidiaries implies an alteration and therefore a movement of one's interpretive context, nevertheless, if such is not toward the canonical-linguistics, syncretism can develop. This calls for every ecclesial community to self-theologize.[45] We have already seen the risk of syncretism that stems from being taken captive by one's own interpretive context. Even so, the converse problem (the lack of self-theologizing) is equally risky albeit less apparent. If an indigenous church, whether by her own choice or by the pressure to conform to a set of contextual theologies from elsewhere, fails to self-theologize, we could suspect that some syncretism might be present.[46]

Contextualization and evangelical contextual theology must consist of a movement from one's interpretive context toward the canonically anchored text. However, this second criterion is more difficult to implement than the first.  How does a contextual theologian or a community of such know that they are traversing rightly from within their interpretive contexts toward the text of Scripture? In a postmodern milieu, this issue of epistemic justification is a part of a broader discussion concerning cultural-linguistic commensurability and intersubjective

---

43    The conformity to "the pattern of this world" in Romans 12:1-2 can also be considered a horizontal change. Cf. "Set your minds on things above, not on earthly things" of Col 3:1-2.

44    We can also frame this criterion a little differently by asking whether the meaning of Scripture is being transformed in the process of contextual theologizing. Jennings writes, "In so far as any of those religious myths might combine with the Christian faith so as to alter or even nullify biblical teaching, such a resulting belief or practice should be labeled 'syncretism.'" Jennings, "Suburban Evangelical Individualism: Syncretism or Contextualization?", 169.

45    The concept of indigenization has normally been associated with the Three-Selfs movement (self-supporting, self-governing and self-propagating) coined by Henry Venn (1796-1880) and Rufus Anderson (1796-1873). But in the late seventies, the shift from indigenization toward contextualization coincides with the discussion of the Fourth-Self (self-theologizing). Hiebert, *Anthropological Reflections*, 58.

46    By focusing on the movement toward the Text as a criterion to evaluate religious syncretism does not imply that we should dismiss an epistemic venture toward another context. In fact, learning another theological position is helpful and necessary in the "triangulation" of one's own context-to-text movement. See Tanchanpongs, "Discourse toward Scripture," 250-251, 292-306.

adjudication that must be addressed before moving to answer the primary question of how to verify or falsify a particular context-to-text movement.[47] In the end, just as discussions among competent non-native Thai cooks would tend to resolve the disagreements over the authenticity of a dish, the authenticity of context-to-text movement can be verified only in on-going catholic dialogues between non-native canonical cooks of theological discourse.

## Conclusion

In Matthew 7:13-14, Jesus commands us, "Enter through the narrow gate. For wide is the gate and broad is the road that leads to destruction, and many enter through it. But small is the gate and narrow the road that leads to life, and only a few find it." This portion of the text comes in the literary context of a warning to live (v. 12) and believe (vv. 15-20) Scripture. The imperative rings true with our proposal. A proper contextualization and contextual theologizing from an evangelical perspective must be seen as a discourse toward Scripture. Specifically, this act is a narrow road that moves from one's cultural-linguistic framework to that of the canonical-linguistic. Both streets which are only local within one's own interpretive context and highways directed toward other destinations run the risk of religious syncretism. From this perspective, the context-to-text approach provides more stringent criteria than those of the canon within a canon approach. Jennings is right to say, "Even though there are trustworthy signposts, the path down which such ongoing contextualization processes should go is not a straightforward, given matter. Nor is there any guarantee that syncretism, or contextualization gone awry, will not occur."[48] As such, contextual theologizing must be done with great care.

Granted that this narrow road approach is more daunting, it is also a more comprehensive one. Having a proper anchor is key to our context-to-text approach. The light anchor of a gospel minimalist approach has been found wanting, despite an admirable desire to affix evaluative criteria in the Scripture, for it too narrowly defines the scope of the canonic anchor. Here the context-to-text approach to contextual theologizing provides a measured dose of sociology of knowledge and a more holistic anchor of the canonical-linguistics as their respective remedies.

In addition, our proposal is an alternative to the structuralist anchor, whose sociology of knowledge focuses on the interaction between cultural-linguistic systems and is too static to evaluate the context-to-text movements (or lack thereof) in agents-driven processes of contextualization and contextual theologizing. The proposal here takes into consideration the reality that "meaning" is derived as a combination of cultural-linguistic systems and how these systems are used by agents when they create a theological discourse. The instrumental view of cultural-linguistics implies that meaning of a theological discourse is somewhat indeterminate prior to the communicative use. Hence, we cannot adjudicate a theological product for its biblical authenticity simply by analyzing its parts in isolation prior to its creation.

Contextual theologizing is not only a daunting, holistic and dynamic task, but it is also a necessary one, not only for the sake of local "relevancy," but also for that of catholic maturity. To live one's life biblically is a matter of wisdom and it has to do with faith seeking understanding

---

47    For a full discussion these topics, see the discussion under the heading of "Catholic Intersubjectivity," in Tanchanpongs, "Discourse toward Scripture," 277-304.

48    Jennings, "Suburban Evangelical Individualism: Syncretism or Contextualization?", 175.

to the glory of Christ Jesus. This is the meaning of theology. In the end, theology is about the formation of a Christian worldview and godly character needed for wise contextual living. This is one reason we must think theologically. Moreover, every Christian community should be an active theological contributor on the stage of the church catholic. This vision can be realized only if we all learn to think together theologically, without which, the universal Church would be poorer for it.

## Discussion Questions:

1. Summarize Polanyi's semantic structure and his understanding of meaning. Compare this with the pragmatic approaches to meaning.

2. Think of a way to apply the two context-to-text criteria to a particular attempt of contextualization in your own context. How well do they function as adjudicative tools? Make some suggestions for their improvement.

3. Why is the indigenous church that lacks any self-theologizing a fertile ground for syncretism?

# 8

# The Practice of Theology

## Osías Segura-Guzmán

*Osías Segura-Guzmán is Mission Professor at ESEPA in Costa Rica. He is Costa Rican, and married to Desiree Segura-April (Assistant Professor of Children-at-Risk at Fuller Theological Seminary). Osías has occupied pastoral and teaching positions in the United States and in Costa Rica. He travels between Pasadena, CA and San Jose, Costa Rica where he serves as an adjunct assistant professor at Fuller Theological Seminary and in his position as professor in the Grace Chapel Chair of Mission at Seminario ESEPA,. He has published in both English and Spanish, and his writing topics include church in mission, kingdom theology, folk-religion, evangelism, and contextualization of theology. Education: BA Sociology (Universidad of Costa Rica), MDiv (Asbury Theological Seminary), ThM (Asbury), DMiss ABD (Asbury).*

## Introduction

Good theology and its application, Christian praxis, has to begin with a community of believers bringing their experiences and struggles to the Scriptures, reflecting on them and putting that reflection into action, all with the purpose of spiritual growth and social transformation. This should be a local church's task, where a group of people talk to and about God, bringing God into their life struggles, listening to God and to one another, and bringing this reflection into the context in which they live. The result of this dynamic exercise is "theology" at a local or contextual level. Theology can be "taught and written, danced and sung, sculpted and painted, even dreamed and cried."[1] There is a problem, however. Some creative expressions of theology can be valued as "bad" by other Christian communities.

---

1    C. Sedmak, *Doing Local Theology: A Guide for Artisans of a New Humanity*, Faith and Culture Series (Maryknoll, NY: Orbis, 2002), 11.

Let me explain myself! Theology can be valued as bad when its source is not the Bible, if other sources besides the Bible are given equal value, when it is not guided by the Holy Spirit, when it is not centered on Christ, or when it is not done by and oriented to the people of God who seek to affect the world in which they live. Theology can be valued as bad if it does not bear the fruit of the Kingdom. What is good theology, then?

## Good Theology

Clemens Sedmak states, "the criterion of good theology is the kind of fruits it bears."[2] Sedmak suggests that four criteria are sketched by Jesus in Luke 10:1-12 that describe good theology. They are sustainability, appropriateness, empowerment, and challenge. The following figure illustrates these four criteria:

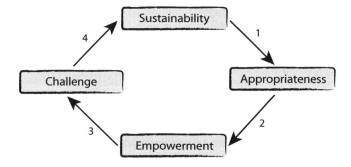

Figure 1: Four criteria for good theology

First, it is God's Kingdom narratives that *sustain* the mission of the church and aid in good theologizing. Second, *appropriateness* is demonstrated when Jesus told his disciples not to arrive "with ready-made tools and concepts; but instead, they should first assess the situation and accept the local quality of life."[3] Third, *empowerment* shows Jesus as one who "did not hold on to his powers… but shared them. The gospel passage … [Luke 10]… continues with reports of the disciples returning full of excitement and joy that their powers had worked."[4] Fourth, Jesus *challenged* the local cultures. "Jesus challenged people to take a different look at reality…. And indicated that there is a significant difference between knowledge of earthly things and knowledge of heavenly things (John 3:10-13)."[5]

This good theology also involves two sources: Scripture or Text[6] (including Christian tradition) and present human experience or the Context.[7] The Christian community cannot seek sus-

---

2    Ibid., 35.

3    Ibid., 37.

4    Ibid., 38.

5    Ibid., 39.

6    In this document I will use "Text" for Scripture and "Context" (intentionally capitalized) for sociocultural context. It is a way to play with the words, highlighting the importance of both elements for contextualization.

7    Stephen B. Bevans, *Models of Contextual Theology: Revised and Expanded Edition*, Faith and Biblical Series (Maryknoll, NY: ORBIS Books), 4.

tainability, appropriateness, empowerment, and be challenged if the Text does not engage the Context and vice versa. That is, good theology has to be practical for spiritual formation and social transformation.

Today, facing this new century, I believe it is time for the Latin American Christian heritage to remain firm in our love for the Text, but at the same time emphasize the praxis of the Text in the Context. We have to love the world as God has loved it. Imagine a church where the people of God study the Scriptures in order to put them into practice and where knowledge and practice feed one another in the everyday life issues of every Christian. If this obedient commitment would take place in our Bible study services, then we could discover ordinary Christians truly theologizing and the Spirit transforming their everyday life experiences.

## Theologizing: Context + Text

The task of theologizing involves bringing the Context and the Text into dialogue. By Context, I am referring to both the Christian Context from the past and the present Context of a particular community of faith. By Text, I mean the Christian Holy Scriptures.

We must always consider the unity and particularities of the Text. As well, we should have some understanding of the socio-cultural context of the time in which each book of the Holy Scriptures was written. In this way, we may know what that Text means for today because we have a sense of what it meant thousands of years ago. This way of approaching the Text helps us to learn to see it like a compilation of stories within one grand Story in which God and humans once interacted, and are still interacting today. Thus, the Text can shed light on current social and cultural problems.

Let's discuss more in depth what is meant by the term "Context." Latin American sociologist Tomas Austin defines the term as follows:

> (Con + text: *with* or *next to* text) comes from the Latin word *texere*, from which the word *textil* comes, meaning a woven fabric. This word may also mean the social and human environment (all that surrounds the human being) where the individual and their collective build a way to understand the world and to live in it. The context shows that those that share it notice likenesses of cultural identity as well as similarities in geography, climate, history, and the productive processes. The context is the maker of nets of meanings and relationships in which human beings participate daily.[8]

Therefore, a socio-cultural context is a very peculiar cultural expression of a human group that shares a territory, language, relationships and meanings. For that reason, culture is as much in the mind as it is in the atmosphere that surrounds the individual.

The identity that the Context creates depends on different levels of interaction, beginning with a family culture; extending to a neighborhood, a region, an organization, a nation, and ending

---

8    Thomas Austin, "Fundamentos Socioculturales de la Education," (access 15 September 2007), 40; available from www.geocities.com (translation mine).  http://www.geocities.com/tomaustin_cl/educa/libro1/introduccion.htm.

with a common global aspect among humans. Depending on the circumstances, people may identify culturally or socially with others on each of these different levels. Furthermore, to define a particular Context, it may be enough to ask a human group the following question: "Of those with whom you live near or with whom you share common elements, with whom do you identify most?"

It is the interaction of the Context with the Text and vice versa that creates theology. This reflection on the Text and the Context is an ongoing task. The Text remains the same through time, but the human Context and those reading the Text embody an extremely dynamic, changing, and complex society. The Text must respond to the Context, and from within the Context the community of theologians asks questions to the Text. This task of wondering and responding becomes one of dialogue. That is the reason theology is built in time and space. Theology is always in construction, and the professional theologian, along with all of the community of believers who share a Context, must engage in a process of contextualization. They are both actors and subjects who seek to affect the world in which they live but are also impacted by this world.

## Who Is the Theologian?

We need these social actors, the community of believers and their leaders, who engage in the process of doing good theology by contextualizing their reflections and actions. Among these social actors, there is a spectrum of theologians from "lay theologians" to "academic theologians."[9] They all have their place and their role in developing local theologies. A local theologian is a leader, a local pastor or a professional theologian, who belongs to a community and seeks to be a listener and observer, a pedagogist, a pastoral caregiver and an empowerer. "The role of the [leader or local theologian] in such a community is to midwife the birth of such theologizing, to order it, to provide it with the perspective of tradition, to organize the people's experience, and to assist them to articulate it more clearly."[10]

[T]he professional theologian serves as an important resource, helping the community to clarify its own experience and to relate it to the experience of other communities past and present. Thus, the professional theologian has an indispensable but limited role. The theologian cannot create a theology in isolation from the community's experience; but the community has need of the theologian's knowledge to ground its own experience within the Christian traditions of faith. In so doing, the theologian helps to create the bonds of mutual accountability between local and world church.[11]

To develop a good theology, we need good leaders to challenge the community to become the priesthood of all believers. This refers back to the need for appropriateness discussed at the beginning of this paper. In order to reach appropriateness, a leading theologian first must develop "not so much the ability to talk but the abilities to listen and to observe."[12] Second, producing

---

9    Stanley J. Grenz and Roger E. Olson, *Who Needs Theology? An Invitation to the Study of God* (Downers Grove, IL: InterVarsity Press, 1996), 26.

10    Bevans, *Models of Contextual Theology*, 75-6.

11    Robert J. Schreiter, *Constructing Local Theologies*, 10th Edition (Maryknoll, NY: Orbis, 2002).

12    Sedmak, *Doing Local Theology*, 14-15.

theology should not focus on authorship but rather on communal praxis. The local theologian, the leader, must become a director of the orchestra but not a player of all instruments. Third, the creation of theology, in addition to communal talking and listening, needs to become "also a pedagogical process liberating consciousness and inciting to action."[13] Fourth, the professional theologian needs to become a "local theologian" within the community of believers, guiding others to the King. Sedmak describes these points beautifully by saying,

> The local theologian can indeed be compared to a cook, and not to an employee in a pizza delivery where he or she delivers ready-made products. The theologian, however, is not free to cook anything he or she likes. A local theologian is not working in a "divine deli," where "anything goes." The local theologian is part of a community that provides ingredients and shares the food. The local theologian can be regarded as a cook in a kitchen that also has nonprofessional cooks (theologians) at work….. Good cooks, just like good theologians, do not always follow the recipes; they create recipes of their own, know how to cook without a book, know how to utilize locally available ingredients.[14]

Finally, the professional theologian, like any other leader, ought to become a pedagogist capable of listening more than talking, while guiding the community to reflective action. This is where appropriateness encounters empowerment, which happens when someone both discerns where the Holy Spirit is at work in the community and also on what the everyday-life questions are based. This local theologian should also provide pastoral care guiding the group in reflection, giving a voice to those with no voice, providing a face for the faceless, and lifting the marginalized and exploited. The idea is to help the community to own the reflection, process, product, and action of its theologizing.

## Who Makes Up the Community of Theologians?

The local theologian, a leader, must engage the local community in theologizing. The community must appropriate its Context. The Kingdom calls the church to become its agent in the world. Thus, the local theologian must create a community of theologians, a priesthood of all believers, rather than one theologian with a group of participants. Empowering the church for theologizing is not an easy task. Why? Scriptures have often been associated with philosophical presuppositions instead of being presented as the story of God and God's people interacting with one another in this world.

Theology is not constructed in a hole. "Theology is always done by people who are 'somewhere'—somewhere in a context, somewhere in a net of relationships, somewhere in their lives, somewhere in their intellectual and spiritual journeys."[15] It is essential that local theologians analyze how the biblical Text interacts with the sociocultural context of the readers and that they also consider the theological and cultural traditions, the history, and the need for social change. "The role of the whole community of faith is often one of raising the questions, of providing the experience of having lived with those questions and struggled with different

---

13   Schreiter, *Constructing Local Theologies*, 17.
14   Sedmak, *Doing Local Theology*, 19.
15   Ibid., 16.

answers, and of recognizing which solutions are indeed genuine, authentic, and commensurate with their experience."[16]

## Biblical Interpretations

The leader theologian (e.g., any church leader such as a lay, pastoral, or professional theologian) and her community must engage in biblical interpretation. This engagement is not a simple task, but it also is not as difficult as it is sometimes presented to be.

Because the understanding of the Word of God is always relative to the culture of the interpreter, theology in any culture always runs the risk of being, to some extent, a reduction of the gospel. No culture completely fulfills the purpose of God, in all cultures there are some elements unfavorable to the understanding of the gospel. For this reason, the gospel never becomes completely incarnate in any given culture. It always transcends cultures, even cultures that it has deeply affected.[17]

This is a twofold issue. First, the Text never incarnates completely in any particular culture because it needs to incarnate constantly through time and space. Second, no culture reigns supreme in biblical interpretation. All human contexts need constant transformation. God somehow reveals Godself to us in community. This is the mystery of the incarnation of the gospel. Facing these challenges, the community of believers must, nevertheless, engage the Text. A way to engage the Text is through reading it as a historical story. How does the local theologian engage her community to identify with some of the actors in the narrative? What role does God play in the story, and what is the role of the community of faith in it? We ask these questions because we are the people of God to whom the Text is addressed.

This leads us to the realization that the fundamental transformation that must take place is not the transformation of an ancient message into a contemporary meaning but rather the transformation of our lives by means of God's Word. This means that reading the Bible as Scripture has less to do with what tools we bring to the task, however important these may be, and more to do with our own dispositions as we come to our engagement with Scripture. Scripture does not present us with texts to be mastered but with a Word, God's Word, intent on mastering us, on shaping our lives.[18]

The Kingdom's Text intends to shape and master us. That is what sustains and makes good theology appropriate to the context. Our motivation should be to interpret that life changing experience with the Text in order to suit its meaning, which at the same time empowers us to challenge the church and the world. Biblical interpretation, however, has varied greatly throughout time and history.

There was a time during the premodern era (medieval times) where biblical interpretation was more imaginative and intuitive than analytic and systematic. The primary question was, "What

---

16    Schreiter, *Constructing Local Theologies*, 17.

17    C. Rene Padilla, *Mission between the Times: Essays on The Kingdom* (Grand Rapids, MI: Eerdmans Publishing Co, 1985), 88.

18    Joel B. Green, and Mike Pasquarello, *Narrative Reading, Narrative Preaching: Reuniting New Testament Interpretation and Proclamation* (Grand Rapids, MI: Baker Book House Co, 2003), 23.

does this story mean for us?" Another way of asking this question was, "How does studying [the Text]. . . in the company of other people enable me to see things that I would otherwise miss, or rescue me from misperceptions that arise from my personal agenda?" [19] From the premodern perspective it was acceptable not to be sure about the meaning of the text and to consider the text in the light of new life experiences. "The strength of premodern interpretation is its capacity to generate powerful application of Scripture that speaks directly to new contexts, addressing questions that arise there."[20]

Modern interpretations, on the other hand, began after the Renaissance, during the Reformation, and took shape during the Enlightenment, forming the idea that interpretation is a task of the mind. For that, it was necessary to create rational proof methods to attain the "real" interpretation of the text. It assumed that the biblical narrative was historical and "in principle the texts were always of univocal meaning."[21] So the Scriptures were read as historical documents that were in need of commentaries from experts who found the "real" meaning of the texts.

In absolutizing the importance of history, it brought its subjective priorities and aims to the text, and ignored other aspects of the text that it claimed to be seeking to interpret. The text was concerned with questions about God, truth and life, but modern study systematically bracketed out these questions. The nearest it would get was to consider matters such as faith, ethics, and spirituality, questions about what human beings believed or did rather than what was true or right. Indeed, modern study would rarely even reach these matters. Either way, modern interpretation failed to live up to its own professed concern to do justice to the text's own agenda.[22]

There are two principles for developing theology today that we can draw from these eras in theological history. First, good theologians must recapture the mystery in the Scriptures. For instance, Ignatius of Loyola believed that mysteries about the understanding of ourselves and of God are found in the Scriptures—from the beginning of creation, through the middle of the redemption, to its consummation, or Revelation. "The Holy Spirit uses Scripture to penetrate through our blindness to enable us to see ourselves before God. We can then think in linear fashion about such shafts of insight....But the insight comes more intuitively and imaginatively than linearly."[23]

Second, good theologians ought to remember that a biblical narrative must include historical story. While we enter into the lives of its characters and the unfolding scene, we must find our own place in the narrative. That is how we make appropriate the story that sustains, empowers, and challenges us. Ignatius of Loyola believed that God speaks to humans directly through the words of the Text. Ignatius' spiritual exercises were designed to encourage people to grow spiritually, reflecting and acting on what their lives were about. By reflecting on Scripture and

---

19  John Goldingay, *An Ignatian Approach to Reading the Old Testament* (Cambridge: Grove Biblical Series, Grove Books, 2002), 7.

20  Ibid., 4.

21  Ibid., 7.

22  Ibid., 6.

23  Ibid., 7.

personal life experiences, theologians discover from theology that which is practical and provides spiritual growth.

## Theological Praxis

We have discussed how the local theologian seeks to do theology with her community, guiding them to identify themselves as a community and individuals, as well as to identify with the characters of the stories in the Scriptures. The next element for good theology is that it needs to continue its good reflection for good practice. Among several models for doing contextual theology, Stephen Bevans presents the praxis model, which provides an example for doing good reflection and good practice.

As practitioners of the praxis model began to reread the Bible and Christian tradition, they began to discover many forgotten things about Christianity and its roots in Hebrew religion: that the Bible itself is a product of struggles for human freedom; that Jesus' message is a message not primarily of doctrines but of structure-shaking attitudes and behavior; that sin must be opposed not by compromise but by radical reordering of one's life. Social change—and the social location of the poor and the oppressed—began to be seen as a privileged source of theology. Commitment to social change in terms of Christian principles and from the perspective of the poor and marginalized led not only to social transformation but to a deeper and more challenging knowledge of God as such.[24]

Praxis theology reminds us that the Context conditions all theology or theologies. We should read other theologies and learn from them but must always remember that there is no theology that is universal. All theologies must be evaluated to analyze whether or not they are faithful to the Scriptures and faithfully relevant to a particular sociocultural context. For that reason, theologizing is an ongoing task for each generation, gender, subculture, social class, and political inclination. The church should always have a relevant message for the current needs that a changing world presents.

To begin thinking as theologians using the praxis model, we should first engage in the history of the culture in which the gospel must be communicated (appropriateness). That is to say, we must understand the historical thought forms and the paradigms of the local culture. The key is to achieve identification with the people who listen to the gospel of the Kingdom in their language and way of thinking, and then accept that narrative and reproduce the message for others within or outside their cultural network. In a few words, we need to understand that praxis does not just seek "practice" or "practical" theology, but a cycle of action-reflection-action-reflection.

Reflection and action are intertwined in a continuous action in praxis theology. "Theology cannot remain only with reflection; nor can it be reduced to practice. Good reflection leads to action, and action is not completed until it has been reflected upon."[25] The importance of praxis theology is that "we can move to know the competence of faith only through Christian performance. When that performance moves beyond an intellectual formulation into an

---

24    Bevans, *Models of Contextual Theology*, 73.
25    Schreiter, *Constructing Local Theologies*, 92.

engagement with its environment we discover its credibility or lack thereof."[26] In other words, action is based not only on orthodoxy but also on orthopraxis. Theology includes not only theory (knowledge), but also action (social transformation and spiritual formation) because good theological thinking considers both. Faith should look for understanding and for intelligent action, thus affecting the social context of the participants.

This takes us to a very important element for all theologians. Bible study must be closely related to the believer's ethical behavior and search for change in the social structures. Therefore, one of the best ways to begin to do theology is by creating a space of friendly conversation and good fellowship, recognizing our ethical responsibility for social transformation and spiritual growth. Social relationships within the community of believers is a primary ingredient for theologizing in a praxis way, which means that there must be a common-unity (community) among the believers. Along with this, there must be a commitment to seeking to obey the Scriptures and put them into practice. Our reflections may begin as conversations that can then become a process which takes us to interpreting the Scriptures that examine our religious ethics and motivate us to change social relationships.

Transcending the premodern and modern ways of interpretation, we should attempt to take theological reflection outside our academic and religious temples, and in this way arrive where common people face everyday life issues, even in the intimacy of our own homes. That is to say, building theology in our postmodern times should be an ethical and communal exercise seeking practical results. Finally, praxis theology has been identified with liberation theologies, which usually seek social transformation. Study of the Scriptures for just social transformation, however, without spiritual formation can get distorted into simply social activism. People's internal and external lives have to be transformed by Christ to produce true change. Ignatius of Loyola, father of the Jesuit missionary movement, thought about this almost four centuries ago and gives us an interesting model upon which to base our current understanding of "good" theology. Let us bring him back to life, although in a different setting, and stretch his model a little to fit our needs for theologizing.

## A Model for Doing Theological Praxis

As seen above, what characterizes praxis theology is the interaction between reflection on the Text and action to affect the Context. Ignatius of Loyola developed a pedagogy known today as "the Ignatian Pedagogical Paradigm" that he adapted from the methods he experienced at the University of Paris (*modus Parisiensis*). This Ignatian Paradigm includes three elements, which are experience, reflection, and action, within a process of five elements that also include Context and evaluation. Ignatius' purpose was to develop a pedagogy for teaching spiritual formation capable of engaging the Context of the participants with the Text and including spiritual exercises producing change in the inner person and change in the social Context. This pedagogy links very well with the process for praxis theology.

---

26   Schreiter, *Constructing Local Theologies*, 119.

Ignatius' process starts by locating reality in its context, experiencing vividly, reflecting over that experience, acting consequently, and evaluating the action to be taken.[27] For the learning process to be successful, however, we must consider the pre-learning (the context) and the post-learning (evaluation) phases of the process, as well as the other components. The following figure illustrates those concepts as a process.

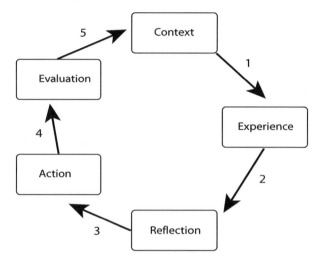

Figure 2. Ignatian pedagogical paradigm process

Let's explore the different components of this pedagogical process and how they connect with the process for doing praxis theology.

**Context** (Pre-learning): This paradigm is based on the idea of the professor (in our case the professional theologian) getting to know the student's spiritual development, while providing him or her a caring mentorship (*cura personalis*). To expound on this, the key is getting to know the student's world (in our case the socio-cultural context of the participants doing local theology). The student must also be ready to learn and grow. That is, the professional theologian is not doing simply an academic task, but also a pastoral task in getting to know the participants' perception of their reality.

**Experience**: The key of this system is to ensure that the participant will develop a learning experience of mind, heart, and hand. This will include motivating the participant to reflect on those elements that form his or her context. New knowledge presents a challenge to what is already known and will be added to what the participant already holds. The Context becomes a place on which to reflect for spiritual growth and to act for social change. This empowers the participant to act intelligently. In addition, experience means any affective activity added to knowledge that impacts the participants' life. According to Ignatius, affective feelings are mo-

---

27    Compañía de Jesús Apostolado Educativo Documentos Corporativos I, *La Pedagogía Ignaciana en América Latina- Aportes para su implementación 1993*, www.puj.edu.co, retrieved November 30th 2007, 377 [http://www.puj.edu.co/pedagogia/documentos/Documentos_Corporativos_Compania_Jesus.pdf.] (translation is mine).

tivational forces to engage understanding to action and commitment. In other words, feeling should be part of the process of theologizing.

**Reflection**: Knowing the Context and producing emotional and rational experience leads to reflection. Reflection works as a process where the student owns the learning experience through all of the senses, not only through reason. Reflection is twofold. One aspect involves understanding, which entails discovering the meaning of the experience by conceptualizing and elaborating possible interpretations. The second aspect is verifying, which has to do with judging the understood data with the experienced aspect of that data. In this phase of the exercises of Ignatius, one seeks "to ask what is it that one has lived in this experience, what is its meaning, [and] what relationship does it have with each of the dimensions of our life and of this particular situation."[28] Action: This paradigm teaches that through commitment and reflection one arrives at action. This is the challenge of any good theology. "Ignatian Pedagogy consists of challenging the person to go one more step: to assume a personal posture in light of the truth that has been discovered, revealed or constructed, and to act in coherence with it."[29] There are two components to this "action" stage. First, it involves a person facing the truth and being confronted with an ethical decision. Second, it involves operationalization, where the choice becomes concrete by "devising and securing the means and times that will allow them to effectively act; assuming values, attitudes and behaviors that are consistent with and follow from their choice, since 'love is demonstrated more by works than by words.'"[30]

**Evaluation**: After getting to know the Context, producing experiences, reflecting on those experiences and acting based on the reflection, the time for evaluation arrives. In order to assure that our actions are effective in reaching the previously established desired outcomes, the entire process must be evaluated. The point is to be sure that our actions are the results of our reflections, and vice versa. Evaluation helps us to know if we are really being obedient to the guidance of the Spirit while reflecting on the Scriptures.

The following chart integrates the Ignatian Pedagogical Paradigm with the four criteria for doing good theology:

---

28    Ibid., 381.
29    Ibid., 384.
30    Ibid., 385.

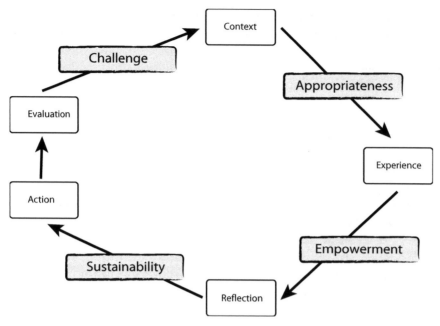

Figure 3: The four criteria for good theology intertwined
with the Ignatian pedagogical paradigm process

Moving from the context to the experience, the theologian needs to help the participant in assessing (appropriateness) his or her context. Once the participant has experienced the Text in Context, reflection makes it possible to move into action, and empowerment takes place. Then, between reflection and action lies sustainability. From reflection, the temptation is to resist moving into action due to fear of commitment. It is the gospel of God's Kingdom that sustains this commitment, not the church's proselytism. Finally, from action one moves to evaluation, and from there one finds challenge where local cultures and the local church are challenged by the gospel to transform the context. Once action has been taken and the evaluation of those actions completed, the challenge to produce change and keep producing it moves us to once again analyze the context of the participants. Social change is valid if it happens and if the lives of the participants are impacted and changed. The challenge is for the social actors and for those who are impacted by their actions. This process is complex and will develop differently in each context.

## How Can Praxis Biblical Study Take Place?

In order to help illustrate this complex process of praxis theology, let's look at a case study of a group of people working through the process in a particular context. Once upon a time in Costa Rica, a group of five couples, all busy professionals and second generation evangelical Christians, approached a seminary professor wanting a Bible study.[31] The professional theologian invited them to his house for coffee and to listen to their proposal. This community

---

31    This story is for illustration purposes, and it is in part true and in part hypothetical.

of Christians wanted more depth than what the local church was providing. They had been talking for a long time about a common need for a deeper study and worship, a challenging process to penetrate the Scripture. The theologian listened, took notes of their requests and their repeated excuses about limited time for meetings, and then asked them to pray during the week for the next meeting. They all agreed to meet at the theologian's home each Wednesday night from 7:30-9:30 p.m. This meeting included child care, coffee and bread.

The second meeting was designed to explain the rules of the activity. The theologian presented himself as the leader of the study, not the professional who would explain to them "the secrets of heaven" (*empowerment*). The community had to be willing to participate in a study that would involve prayer and reading the Scriptures. The goal of the study was to put the Scriptures into action (to seek *appropriateness* in the context). They all would be expected to allow the place and time to be relaxed and enjoyable, to arrive on time, and to call if they could not come. They were to bring a Bible, a journal, and a pencil as key elements for their work together. Meeting around the table, the participants would stimulate one other to share, while the leader of the study became a facilitator and discerner (not a preacher) through the biblical narratives. The group sought to emphasize that God was present with them and must enable them to see and feel things and to respond to what they experience.[32]

During the week, they would read the passage and take notes of their feelings and thoughts, or lack of them. The leader explained that feelings are important as a window to discern our spiritual walk, and therefore they should take note of their feelings, or the lack of them, and the verses that stimulated their reaction. "Stop as soon as something strikes you—as soon as you feel something. You may sense something encouraging or some puzzlement, a frustration or an anxiety.... Shut your eyes and explore the feeling. Ask what is going on in you."[33] The leader exhorted them that Bible study is not just for analytical, rational thinking (*challenge*). The biblical passage should become a story that calls the participants to put one another in the scene and to identify themselves with the actors. The passage also should call us to do worship in creative ways. They all agreed to the rules and the challenges of the study.

After the participants left that night, the seminary professor, facilitator of the study, reminded himself that he was there to provide pastoral care by getting to know the participants' needs and spiritual development (*context*) as well as to help them to discern actions. He reflected on the idea that this was necessary for the participants to appropriate the Text. The participants were there not only to expand their knowledge of the Text, but also to experience it, to reflect on it, to put it into action, and to evaluate the whole process (criteria for good theologizing).

The following Sunday, one of the participants of the previously mentioned group invited all of the group members and the leader for lunch after church, and they spent the afternoon at her house, a beautiful home up in the mountains with a view of the city. The road to her place was narrow at times, and the contrast between rich homes with high walls and poor homes was noteworthy. The leader brought up that observation during the conversation. All those professional people began commenting how much they would love to do something to help those

---

32    Goldingay, *An Ignatian Approach to Reading the Old Testament*, 13.
33    Ibid., 13.

poor families. The group included lawyers, medical doctors, dentists, and journalists. They all shared a series of frustrations and a burning desire to do something. They knew that everything they had was by God's grace, but how to do something was a key question for them. They themselves were folks in deep need of pastoral care. Their busy lifestyles were damaging their marriages and also their health. They were not content with their lives and wanted more direction from God on how to manage their lives as upper middle class Christians. The leader asked them if these concerns might become the topic of the study, and they all emphatically agreed.

Based on this reflection, the homework for the study on Wednesday took shape. They were all to bring concerns and questions from their daily life (*experience*). This was the best way to empower the participants to develop good theology. They began taking note of those deep questions and concerns in their personal, family, and work life. They were all advised that not all of those questions and worries would be addressed at once in one study. They discussed the importance of listening to the experiences of the participants and take them to the story of the Text.

During the third meeting, the method was to begin focusing on reading a biblical passage as a part of history, opening all the senses and with an attitude of listening. After much prayer and discernment and an evaluation of the Context (by a discussion on the analysis of government's socioeconomic data of the area) of the participants, the leader suggested the passage for the next weeks of study. The text selected was Luke 16:19-31. The leader of the study explained that this chapter could be called the "economy of the Kingdom." Concepts like help, possessions, hospitality, the poor, and friendship, illustrate the ethical behavior that those focusing on the Kingdom should demonstrate in the world. The story of Lazarus and the rich man serves as a conclusion and a summary of the two other topics in Luke 16: (1) the riches and the Law, and (2) how to use possessions to show hospitality in the Kingdom.[34]

The leader discussed with the group that this biblical story presents three characters, and the participants will likely identify with one (or more) of these characters. First, the story presents an authority figure, which is God, illustrated as Abraham. Second, we see the rich nameless man, and, finally, the story includes the poor man who only has his name, Lazarus. The passage presents a set of contrasts between Lazarus and the rich man. The leader asked the participants to compare those contrasts, and they spent time listing their different ideas. The following chart [35] is a hypothetical listing of what the group might have discussed:

|  | In this life | In the other life |
|---|---|---|
| **Lazarus** | • Wished for bread crumbs<br>• Is outside the door of the rich man<br>• Received illnesses<br>• Is hungry | • Has abundance of fresh water<br>• Is Near Abraham<br>• Receives consolation<br>• Is satisfied |

---

34 Joel Green, *The Gospel of Luke: New International Commentary on the New Testament*, (Grand Rapids, MI: Eerdmans Publishing Co., 1997), 588.

35 Chart adapted from Oscar Campos, *Teologia Evangelica para el Contexto Latinoamericano: Ensayos en honor al Dr. Emilio A Nuñez* (Buenos Aires: Kairos Ediciones, 2004), 226 (translation is mine).

| **The rich man** | • Banquets every day<br>• Lives in a mansion<br>• Receives goods<br>• Is satisfied | • Wished for a drop of water<br>• Is in Hades<br>• Is tormented<br>• Is in need |
|---|---|---|

The study for that week was over. Before prayer, they listened to the Scriptures with the intention of opening up to the direction of the Holy Spirit. God was challenging them to act before and after the reading, allowing the Scriptures to challenge the ethical behavior of everyone. The homework for the next week was to read the passage every day taking notes on their feelings and thoughts, or the lack of them, and bring them to the next meeting.

When they gathered for the fourth meeting, their observations and questions were around *Sheol* as heaven or hell and if those in hell and in heaven could talk to each other. The leader emphasized that it is a parable, not an exact doctrine about those issues, and that the author is transmitting something deeper than that, which is that there is a place for the just and another for the unjust. Their observations continued, now focusing on how each one of the two characters received certain treatments in the after life according to their ethical behavior in this life. They all shared their struggle in identifying themselves with the characters. Only one expressed himself as identifying with the rich man. The others were fighting with the idea of wealth because they did not consider themselves as rich as the rich man of the Text. The leader mentioned to them that this is a point of prayer and discernment. Their feelings were steered by the story to the point of confusing their thoughts. The study ended. The homework was to take note of those feelings regarding their identification with any character in the story.

Before their fifth meeting the leader of the group began receiving calls on Tuesday. The meeting that week had to be cancelled because more than half of the couples were not able to make it. They presented a series of excuses like having other commitments or simply having a headache. The leader decided to have the group meet again in two weeks. In the meantime, he told them he would visit each of the five couples. The leader was able to visit all of them and chat with them about the study. It was obvious that God was speaking to them, and they did not want to hear God's voice and decided to run away from the Scriptures. The fifth meeting took place, but only with three of the five couples.

Finally, the participants as theologians were able to own the story (*reflection*). The learning experience took the participants into discovering the meaning of the experience, thus leading to possible interpretations of themselves in the Text. They came to the conclusion that the theme of the whole chapter of Luke 16 was about the use of possessions. They realized that the two characters in the story represented two kinds of people in society but not necessarily rich and poor. They determined that the term "rich" referred to an attitude represented by circumstances full of injustice, a lack of hospitality, hedonism, and egocentrism. The spiritual lesson is ethical and goes beyond the personal life into macrosocial ethical issues. The final destination of the rich was a place of suffering, contrary to the comforts they experienced while on earth, while the destination of Lazarus was a place where he experienced the comforts that were not shared with him while on earth.

The story, however, did not end there. The rich man appealed to his religious inheritance, calling Abraham "father." Then he recognized Lazarus by name, which indicated that he knew Lazarus when they were both on earth, and he was indifferent to his situation. Now he was appealing to Abraham to be treated like Lazarus and asking for mercy. Despite the rich man's appeals to Abraham, his situation in the afterlife did not change. This impacted our community of theologians because they realized that not all of the sons and daughters of God will be in paradise. They concluded that our indifferences toward those in need are indifferences toward God, and that this attitude and ethical behavior carries divine judgment.

The passage called everyone to repentance and a change of conduct. With these ideas, the meeting was over. Homework continued, and the last section of the story was to be discussed at the next meeting. During the week, the community of theologians began raising questions such as, "What should I, and we, do in our communities (i.e., church, neighborhood, and family) with what we are learning in our study?" In other words, we not only wondered what a particular story meant, but also how practical we could become with what we learned in this passage. The professional theologian reflected on how the participants were moving through the process of reading on to reflection and challenge that would lead to an action and social transformation. In this way, the community of believers would obey what they were reading and take part in building the Kingdom of God on earth.

As the next week approached, the facilitator knew that a commitment to act beyond one's inward spirituality was necessary (*action*). Facing the revealed truth, the participants would be confronted with an ethical decision. Each one would need to decide and, as a small community, act. In the midst of fellowship and the poeisis where different expressions of worship bloom, action was required. This motivated the discussion of the sixth meeting. The participants looked at how the passage ends with the rich man begging Abraham to send a message to his family so they may repent. This implies that the rich man recognized that his family lived the same ethical behavior of injustice and knew that at death they would join him. Abraham, however, responded that if they knew the law and did not respond to it, no message from the other world would change their hearts. With this response, the Scriptures are presented as the only source necessary for teaching right living. The Bible study participants recognized that their wealth, even though it may not seem like much, must be used to benefit the Kingdom that exalts those in need. They decided to motivate the professionals at church to organize one Saturday morning a month to serve poor communities. They agreed that costs would be covered by the participants and by donations. The activities were a success, and other churches even joined in their efforts.

After they had been serving in poor communities for awhile, the participants evaluated the experience of inner and communal change and the impact of their action through which they sought true social transformation (*evaluation*). They noticed that Bible studies that challenged them to act and to grow spiritually were good ways to change their religiosity into a strong spiritual life. Many more Bible studies would be necessary to challenge them further, but they were responding faithfully to God, according to what was revealed to them.

# Conclusion

This case study illustrates several things. First, reading a biblical story with implications for personal and social transformation may sound radical for some Christians! However, what is the value of reading the Bible with the purpose of only studying it cognitively? We must come near to the biblical stories with the purpose of knowing God in an intelligent way, using all of our senses, while also transforming our spirituality and our environment. This is a very contemplative approach to the study of the Scriptures. We meditate and listen to our partners in ministry, our Christian community, and in prayer seek to allow the Holy Spirit to direct and transform us and our social context. This contemplative-active reflection involves a biblical study and an exegesis of the realities of our context.

Second, the case study illustrates the criteria for good theology, which are sustainability, appropriateness, empowerment, and challenge. It also shows how the sources for good theological reflection are the analysis of our context, the Scriptures, and our theological background. This process must begin with a commitment to action before reading the Scriptures and approaching the context. The Kingdom that seeks to affect all things created sustains our reflections that become actions. The community of faith is challenged to become an alternative community and often even a counter-cultural community. Then, we reflect on our learning experiences mainly in those areas that need transformation, not only personal but also social. Good theological reflection includes a commitment to intelligent action, directing the action toward the purpose of personal (inner) and social transformation. The process does not stop here, however. Every time after our study of the Bible finishes, we return to our communities with a commitment to prophetic action. Inspired by the reading of the biblical stories, we commit actively with our communities to appropriate the Text and to see our communities transformed. In this way, theological work could become something common for our churches.

Let us remember, however, that without spiritual experience and reflection, our committed action can become social activism, lacking a commitment to the Kingdom. The priesthood and the prophetic work of all believers are a necessary combination to achieve a holistic change in our personal, social, and cultural context. This change is guided by the Holy Spirit, while we read, pray, and act. We pray, read and meditate; and then read, pray, act, and meditate once again. Then, after that process, the committed action, through deep discernment, may arrive. This reflection goes beyond a simple evaluation, moving into a communal discernment that accompanies a rereading of the biblical stories. The idea is to discern the Holy Spirit's direction as we evaluate our actions. In this way, we read the Scriptures before, during, and after our action.

This theological approach requires learning our context, making our experience appropriate to the context, considering our reflection, and evaluating our action. This way of constructing theology is a task of building community and also a pastoral function of sharing our wounds and our visions for a society that needs transformation. We must be willing to face the hard questions about the human situation, consider the values of the Kingdom, and confront those excluded from the possibility of meditating on the Scriptures. Thus, we understand that theology is not simply expressed through academic writing, but it can also be expressed through a process of praxis theology that includes spiritual formation and social transformation. This is good Christian praxis and good evangelical theology!

## Discussion Questions

1. I am sure that you have had the same experience with Bible studies at church: The pastor *preaches,* rather than teaches, for forty-five minutes and then provides a fifteen minute question/answer time at the end of his presentation. Sometimes it gets worse when the pastor is not very engaging at presenting his exegetical findings, if any, to a crowd waiting to be fed. Consequently, the study becomes a boring intellectual activity, and at times with no practical applications. Why do some Bible studies have to be like that? They become a purely intellectual exercise where information, instead of formation, is supreme. The result is that you see people heading home commenting about all that interesting information the pastor found in the Bible. If that has been your experience, discuss among yourselves: Where is the spiritual formation, the theological reflection as a community of believers, the responsive action from being obedient to the Scriptures, while participating in Bible studies?

2. What do you understand by the word "theology"? Have you ever thought that theology can be danced and sung, sculpted and painted, even dreamed and cried? Have you found "theology" in poems, songs, novels, movies, paintings, and in the gestures we express at church or at home such as kneeling, embracing, singing, and keeping silent?

3. The author quotes Clemens Sedmak, who illustrates very well what contextualization of theology is. Read the following quote and discuss: Do we seek to deliver pizza or cook our own creative recipes when we gather together in our bible studies?

   > *The local theologian can indeed be compared to a cook, and not to an employee in a pizza delivery where he or she delivers ready-made products. The theologian, however, is not free to cook anything he or she likes. A local theologian is not working in a "divine deli," where "anything goes." The local theologian is part of a community that provides ingredients and shares the food. The local theologian can be regarded as a cook in a kitchen that also has nonprofessional cooks (theologians) at work. . . . Good cooks just like good theologians, do not always follow the recipes; they create recipes of their own, know how to cook without a book, and know how to utilize locally available ingredients (2002, p. 19).*

4. The author of this article highlights several times the importance of bringing the Scriptures into a reflective action. One good example could be evangelism. How does your church engage in evangelism? How do Christians, in your Bible studies, achieve identification with non-believers who need to listen to the gospel in their own language and cultural forms? In other words, how can believers present the Good News in a language and within a secular culture that they perhaps cannot speak or understand?

# 9

# Theologizing Locally

## Paul Siu

**Paul Siu** *is Professor of Theology at Alliance Theological Seminary, New York. He received his Ph.D. from Trinity Evangelical Divinity School of Trinity International University, Deerfield, Illinois. He has contributed articles to Alliance Academic Review and book reviews to Journal of Evangelical Theological Society. He frequently travels to China and Taiwan to teach. Currently, he is engaged in a writing project of a four-volume systematic theology in the Chinese language, intended to be used as textbooks in the Chinese church community. The first volume, titled The Horizon of Theology, deals with the prolegomenous issues of systematic theology and was published in 2007 in Taiwan. He is now working on the second volume, which deals with humanity and the problem of evil and suffering. Education: BTh (Alliance Bible Seminary, Hong Kong), MDiv (Canadian Theological Seminary); MTh (Bethel), PhD (Trinity Evangelical Divinity School).*

Globalization is not only a hot topic for academicians to discuss and debate in their own areas of expertise; it is also a worldwide phenomenon affecting people and nations in a subtle way. It is, therefore, of no surprise that in the last decade or so, the topic of globalization has generated much interest and discussion in theological circles. This paper intends to add one more voice to the discussion by providing a theological reading of globalization from the standpoint of constructing local theologies. I will first delineate briefly the realities of globalization that people and nations are now experiencing. I will also examine globalization's relation to a contemporary condition called postmodernity. In the midst of the challenges of globalization and postmodernity, how then should we undertake the task of contextualization? In answering this crucial question, I will explore two goals for globalizing theology. I will finally set forth a proposal for globalizing a local systematic theology from the East Asian perspective, which I believe will address some of the issues and needs within this age of globalization and postmodernity.

# The Realities of Globalization

No one would deny that we are now living in an increasingly compact world, as though we are interacting in a global village on this planet. We find ourselves in an age of globalization. It is, however, difficult to come up with a one-line statement that can succinctly define the complexity of globalization. As Robert Schreiter candidly writes, "There is no one accepted definition of globalization, nor is there consensus on its exact description. Nearly all would agree, however, that it is about the increasingly interconnected character of the political, economic, and social life of the peoples of this planet."[1]

Thomas Friedman describes this significant worldwide change in terms of three great historical eras, which he calls globalization 1.0, 2.0, and 3.0. The first era—globalization 1.0—lasted from 1492 to around 1800. It began when Columbus set sail to the New Continent, opening trade between the Old World and the New World. The driving force in this globalization era was "countries globalizing." The second era—globalization 2.0—lasted from 1800 to 2000, interrupted by the Great Depression and World Wars I and II. The dynamic force driving this global integration was "multinational companies." The third era—globalization 3.0—began around the year 2000 and extends into present day. The dynamic driving force of this global economy has become the individual. It is the power of individuals, particularly non-white, non-Western groups of individuals, to collaborate and compete in the global context.[2] It is now possible for more people to collaborate and compete with other people on different kinds of work from different corners of the planet and on more equal footing than ever. The competitive global playing field is being leveled. "The world is flat"—as Friedman so titled his best-selling book.[3]

Indisputably, the world economy is a dominating force of current globalization. It is the flow of capital and commerce across national borders. It is the international financial markets and multinational corporations, represented by transnational agencies and organizations such as the World Economic Forum (WEF), the World Bank, the World Trade Organization (WTO), and the International Monetary Fund (IMF).[4]

The spectrum of globalization, however, far exceeds the economic sphere. It is a *de facto* multidimensional phenomenon, which involves politics, arts and sciences, technology, culture, spirituality, theology, religion, and so on. Globalization is best understood from a comprehensive,

---

1    Robert Schreiter, *The New Catholicity: Theology between the Global and the Local* (Maryknoll, NY: Orbis Books, 1997), 4-5.

2    Thomas Friedman, *The World Is Flat: A Brief History of the Twenty-First Century*, Updated and Expanded Edition (New York: Farrar, Straus and Giroux, 2006), 9-11.

3    Ibid.

4    Robert Schreiter observes that since the collapse of the Soviet socialist system in 1989, there has been the worldwide spread of market capitalism, which can be characterized by "its ignoring of national boundaries, its ability to move capital quickly, and its engagement in short-term projects that maximize the profit margin." Robert Schreiter, *The New Catholicity*, 7. See also Ira Rifkin, *Spiritual Perspective on Globalization: Making Sense of the Economic and Cultural Upheaval* (Woodstock, VT: Skylight Paths Publishing, 2003).

multidisciplinary perspective. I agree with what Muqtedar Khan, professor at the University of Delaware, says in an article titled *Teaching Globalization*:[5]

> While all discipline-specific studies of globalization do advance a rich and nuanced understanding, each discipline merely explains a part of the phenomenon—just like the proverbial description of an elephant by six blind men. That is why globalization is best understood as a concept that transcends individual disciplines—and also unites them. Globalization must therefore be approached from a multidisciplinary perspective.

Therefore, in the pages that follow I will attempt to participate in the multidisciplinary exploration of globalization by providing a theological reading of globalization from the standpoint of constructing local theologies. In order to better understand this theological view on globalization, we need to first examine the intriguing relationship between globalization and the postmodern condition.

## The Postmodern Critique

Many scholars point out that globalization is closely tied up with the process of modernization. It is, in many ways, an extension of modernity to all parts of the world.[6] The characteristics of this global modernization include the development of the personal computer and the internet, the World Wide Web, the profound interconnectedness between individuals and nations, market-driven capitalism, the promotion of the democratic form of government, job outsourcing and cheap labor, increased productivity and availability of goods, and so on. Many would consider these the benefits of globalization and call these benefits "good global." There are, however, negative by-products of globalization that cause grave concerns and they are labeled "bad global." These destructive by-products have inflicted the people of the Third World most severely. They include:[7]

- Hegemony of the technocrats of the Information Age.
- An ever-growing gap between the rich and the poor.
- An ever-growing gap between the wealthy nations and impoverished ones.
- Mounting injustice and political oppression.
- Neo-imperialism and neo-colonialism.
- Consumerism.
- Ecological destruction.
- The loss of cultural heritage.

---

5 Muqtedar Khan, "Teaching Globalization," The Globalist.http://www.theglobalist.com, accessed February 5, 2008.

6 See Ulrich Beck, *Risk Society: Towards a New Modernity* (London: SAGE Publications, 1992, 2004). Beck argues that industrial society has now become an agent producing both wealth and risks. Science has changed from a study in the service of truth to a study without truth. Modernization contains a tendency toward globalization that ignores the boundaries of nation states, which results in continuous global endangerment. See also Anthony Giddens, *The Consequences of Modernity* (Stanford, CT: Stanford University Press, 1990). See also Robert J. Schreiter "Globalization, Postmodernity, and the New Catholicity" in *For All People: Global Theologies in Contexts* (Grand Rapids, MI: Eerdmans, 2002), 19.

7 Daniel G. Groody, *Globalization, Spirituality, and Justice* (Maryknoll, NY: Orbis Books, 2007), xv.

- The clash of civilizations.
- The danger of nationalism.

In view of these deleterious by-products, Robert Schreiter criticizes that "much of modernity flaunted by globalization has led to a fundamental rejection of globalization in its cultural and social dimensions. There are more and more calls to develop a more humane form of globalization that restores local autonomy."[8] The call for a more humane form of globalization is coming from many quarters, one of which is the postmodernist's. We are now in the phase of globalization "where we experience a conjunction of two phenomena: globalization and the postmodern condition."[9] The postmodern critique of modernity, which in many ways is the critique of globalization, is not to be taken lightly by evangelical contextualizers. Postmodernism, despite all its flaws and fallacies, may become a platform on which we stand to analyze and evaluate more fairly the process of globalization. I wish to point out two areas of concern in which the postmodern critique may shed some light on our undertaking of contextualization in the global context. In both areas I will present my observations from the Third World perspective, particularly from the Asian reality.

## The Postmodern Asian Society

The rapid expansion of Western modernity to all parts of the world also means that postmodernism—as a critique of modernity—follows its path around the globe. Asia, in many ways, sees itself transitioning from modernity to postmodernity. Postmodern thinking and lifestyle, for better or for worse, seem to pervade many metropolitan cities in East Asia.

In Asian Chinese communities, for instance, there has been a surge of publications on the subject of postmodern thought and its impact on society.[10] But I must hasten to point out that the form of postmodernism found most influential and popular in Asia is not the literary deconstructionism advocated by Derrida, Foucault, Baudrillard, and Lyotard. Rather, it is the socio-political postmodern critique popularized by Daniel Bell, Fredric Jameson and Richard Rorty. This socio-political form of postmodern thought reacts against existing social economic structures and critiques the postindustrial society. In 1985, for instance, Fredric Jameson was invited to Beijing University to deliver a lectureship on the topic of "Postmodernism and the Theory of Civilization" in which he explored the validity of the critical theory and neo-Marxism in the context of the postmodern critique of the postindustrial phenomenon in society. The manuscript of the lectureship was translated and published in China, Hong Kong, and Taiwan.[11]

---

8    Robert J. Schreiter "Globalization, Postmodernity, and the New Catholicity" in *For All People: Global Theologies in Contexts* (Grand Rapids, MI: Eerdmans, 2002), 19.

9    Ibid, 16-17.

10    In addition to the writings on modernity and postmodernity authored by national Chinese, many foreign titles have also been translated into Chinese, including works by Foucault, Derrida, Daniel Bell and many others. Postmodern scholars Richard Rorty and Fredric Jameson have made trips to Hong Kong, Taiwan, and Beijing to deliver lectureships on postmodern society.

11    The Chinese version of Jameson's work was published in 1989. Jameson personally wrote a foreword to this Chinese edition. Moreover, Daniel Bell's works, such as *The Cultural Contradictions of Capitalism* and *The Coming of Postindustrial Society,* are frequently discussed in the academic communities in both China and Taiwan.

This socio-political form of postmodernism is creating quite an impact in the intellectual community. This is not difficult to understand, since economic development over the past few decades has become almost the sole concern in Asian countries.[12] More than a decade ago John Naisbitt, a well-known scholar of futurology, described the Asian economic trends in *Megatrends Asia* saying, "We are witnessing a dramatic shift from labor-intensive agriculture and manufacturing to the state-of-the-art technology in manufacturing and services, most pronounced in the rush to computers and telecommunications."[13]

Nevertheless, such rapid social and economic changes under the banner of modernization and globalization are not all positive and beneficial. They severely undermine the social values and the traditional and personal virtues that have given Asian countries identity and stability. Asian countries are facing the challenges of post-industrialization in the process of globalization. Economic and technological developments have created urban and environmental problems that Asian cities have never encountered before. Pollution is so perilous that some cities are heading toward ecological destruction. The ever-widening gap between the rich and the poor, and between wealthy nations and impoverished countries, is disheartening. Furthermore, there have been serious doubts about whether the Western-style of democracy would work in Asian countries, which have never had strong democratic traditions in their cultures. Many scholars agree that forced imposition of Western democracy on non-Western countries will only lead to a "clash of civilizations"—as Samuel Huntington so forewarns in his book.[14]

Disillusionment sets in when Asian countries begin to realize that economic growth—a catalyst of globalization—may one day be hampered. In fact, since 1995, for the first time in a long while, Japan has lost its leading role in the global economy.[15] Many Asian countries find themselves struggling with economic crises. Economic development, promised by modernization and globalization, has driven Asian countries and their people into a plight. Disillusionment cannot simply be addressed on economic terms, for its cause may well be something profoundly spiritual.

It is here that the postmodern critique sheds light on our undertaking of contextualization, reinforcing the need for us to proffer a theological hermeneutic of globalization by addressing those waxing issues of spirituality, justice, poverty, hopes and fears in a *local context*.[16] In

---

12    As early as in 1992, *Time Magazine* made a prediction of the rapid Asian economic growth in the 21st century, saying, "On the other side of the world, the astonishing Asians will continue their success story, but with more diversity and less coordination than Europeans. Japan will not have things so much its own way in the next century… Communism will collapse in China, clearing the way of the powerhouse of Taiwan to join Hong Kong as a special economic zone of the Chinese motherland" (See *Time*, 140, no. 27 (Fall, 1992): 36-38. See also Peter L. Berger and Hsin-Huang Michael Hsiao, eds., *In Search of an Asian Development Model* (New Brunswick, CT: Transaction Books, 1988); Gustav Reins, John Fei, and S.Y. Kuo, *Growth with Equity: The Taiwan Case* (London: Oxford University Press, 1979).

13    John Naisbitt, *Megatrends Asia: Eight Asian Megatrends That Are Reshaping Our World* (New York: Simon and Schuster, 1996), 15.

14    Samuel Huntington, *The Clash of Civilizations and the Remaking of World Order* (New York: Simon & Schuster, 1996).

15    John Naisbitt, *Megatrends Asia*, 41.

16    See, for example, Daniel G. Groody, *Globalization, Spirituality, and Justice: Navigating the Path to Peace* (Maryknoll, NY: Orbis Books, 2007).

so doing we may be able to render a more humane form of globalization that will restore and preserve *local* integrity and identity. For most non-Westerners in the twenty-first century, the burning issues are not metaphysics and rationality but relationality, reconciliation, poverty, and injustice. There is a dire need for evangelical contextualizers to remain vigilant and resilient by addressing the issues that come out of the heart cry of the people in the *local context*. We are determined to grapple with the dark side of modernization and globalization with the true light of the Gospel of the glory of Christ (2 Cor. 4: 4-6).

## The Western Theological Hegemony

Ever since the official launching of the task of contextualization in 1972,[17] there has been growing discontent among Third World theologians, asking why theologians from other parts of the world must play by Western rules when they construct their theology. Western theologians have given the impression that they have a monopoly on God, the gospel, and the way of constructing theology. Ironically, contextualization carries the idea that theology is to be worked out based on critical assessment of the particulars in any given local context. Kwame Bediako, the African theologian, complains, "Western theology was for so long presented in all its particulars as *the* theology of the church, when, in fact, it was geographically localized and culturally limited, European and Western, and not universal."[18]

As early as 1968, Gustavo Gutiérrez, regarded by many as the father of Liberation Theology, in a pivotal conference of Latin American theologians held in Chimbote, Peru, presented a paper titled, *Toward a Theology of Liberation*. He challenged the long accepted philosophical basis of rationality as well as the rules of constructing theology in the West. He viewed the function of theology as a reflection on action—action propelled by a commitment of love and charity toward the poor. Ortho-praxis is to be substituted for the Western orthodoxy.[19]

Choan-Seng Song, the Asian theologian, likewise complains about Western theology's enslavement to an either-or rationalist logic and argues that theology "deals with the concrete issues that affect life in its totality and not just with abstract concepts that engage theological brains.… Theology has to wrestle with the earth, not with heaven."[20] In one of his controversial works, Song espouses that theology should begin with the heart, a "third eye" that enables us to apprehend the deeper level of reality. Hence, the task of Christian theology is a spiritual quest, integrating Christian spirituality with Asian spirituality that will lead one "to see the power of God's love at work in the world as well as the convergence of history of God and history of humanity."[21] Jung Young Lee, the Korean theologian, is similarly critical of Western

---

17    In 1972 the Theological Education Fund of the World Council of Churches (WCC) launched its mandate *Ministry in Context* for which it coined the term contextualization.

18    Kwame Bediako, *Jesus and the Gospel in Africa: History and Experience* (Maryknoll, NY: Orbis Books, 2004), 115.

19    See Gustavo Gutiérrez, *A Theology of Liberation: History, Politics, and Salvation*, rev. ed. (Maryknoll, NY: Orbis Books, 1988). See also Gustavo Gutiérrez, *The Truth Shall Make You Free: Confrontations* (Maryknoll, NY: Orbis Books, 1990); *Las Casas: In Search of the Poor of Jesus Christ* (Maryknoll, NY: Orbis Books, 1993).

20    C.S. Song, *Tell Us Our Names: Story Theology from an Asian Perspective* (Maryknoll, NY: Orbis Books, 1984), 6-24. In the book, Song has advanced ten positions that he thinks are helpful in breaking from the Western ways of constructing theology and to ultimately formulate a unique Asian theology.

21    C. S. Song, *Third Eye Theology*, revised edition. (Maryknoll, NY: Orbis Books, 1991), 48, 93.

theology's captivity to Aristotelian logic because it is contrary to the both-and, yin-yang think-ing of Asia.[22]

Amusingly, Third World theologians are not the only ones who are disgruntled by Western theological hegemony; the Christian postmodernists in the United States are as well—par-ticularly those who find themselves in the evangelical camp. The Third World theologians and evangelical postmodernists have become strange comrades on this front. Carl Raschke attempts to "dehellenize" evangelical theology claiming that it is overtly dependent on concep-tual categories taken from secular philosophy.[23] Stanley Grenz and John Franke leveled strong criticisms against propositionalism and foundationalism upon which, they have claimed, Western evangelical theology has so erroneously chosen to anchor.[24] Grenz has sought to take the idea of "relational ontology", couple it with the doctrine of the Trinity, and show that the characteristic of relationality is right there within the Triune Godhead.[25] Human beings are created in the *imago Dei* of which the capacity for relationality, and not rationality (the empha-sis of modernity), is to be accentuated. Human beings are created in a dependent relationship to their Maker and to one another. Carl Raschke sums up this approach by saying,[26]

> The modernist principle of social and political organization was encapsulated in He-gel's epigram that the 'real is rational and the rational is real.' Perhaps a postmodern, post-Hegelian, post-rationalist rule of Christian corporate life could be summed up as follows: the real is relational and the relational is real. On this institution the post-modern Christians take their stand.

Let me hasten to say, with no intention to take sides with the evangelical postmodernists, that such accentuation on relationality in theological construction and social ethics is highly conge-nial with Asian social and cultural values, which are inextricably intertwined with Confucian imperatives of relationships. The idea of relationality, I must say, is a welcome theological mo-tif in Asian context. I will revisit relationality as a theological theme later in this paper when I present my proposal for constructing contextual systematic theology.

Meanwhile, we must say the sooner Western theology renounces hegemony the better. There are, at least, two compelling reasons for doing so. First, hegemony must be renounced because of the shifting of the center of Christianity from the Western to the Southern hemisphere. World Christianity today looks dramatically different than it did in the last few decades in the twentieth century. Philip Jenkins, in his landmark work *The Next Christendom*—first pub-lished in 2002 expanded and revised in 2007, meticulously documented that Christianity's center of gravity has now moved southward to Africa, Latin America and Asia.[27]

---

22    Jung Young Lee, *The Theology of Change: A Christian Concept of God from an Eastern Perspective* (Maryknoll, NY: Orbis Books, 1979). See also *The Trinity in Asian Perspective* (Nashville, TN: Abingdon, 1999).

23    Carl Raschke, *The Next Reformation: Why Evangelicals Must Embrace Postmodernity* (Grand Rapids, MI: Baker Academic, 2004), 207-215.

24    Stanley J. Grenz and John R. Franke, *Beyond Foundationalism: Shaping Theology in a Postmodern Context* (Louisville, KY: Westminster John Knox Press, 2001).

25    Ibid., 195.

26    Carl Raschke, *The Next Reformation*, 158, italics his.

27    Philip Jenkins, *The Next Christendom: The Coming of Global Christianity*, expanded and revised. (New York: Oxford University Press, 2002, 2007), 1.

The numbers are staggering. According to the center for the Study of Global Christianity, there were 2.1 billion Christians in the world in 2005. By location there are 531 million Christians in Europe, 226 million in North America, 511 million in Latin America, 389 million in Africa, 344 million in Asia.[28] In total, Christians in the Southern hemisphere far outnumber Christians in the West—1.24 billion to 757 million. Jenkins projects that this comparative gap will continue to increase in the future. Christianity will continue to flourish in countries in the Southern hemisphere, while Christianity in Europe will continue to decline.[29]

I think Justo Gonzalez puts this momentous shift in proper perspective when he says that we must still recognize "the vast majority of the financial resources of the church are still in the North Atlantic... The same is true of the number of magazines and books published, resources invested in media, and so on."[30] He thinks that the map of present day Christianity is "polycentric." Although there are more Christians in the Southern hemisphere, there really is no single place that can be called *the* center of Christianity. It is because many different countries are contributing to the new face of world Christianity today. Exciting new theological insights are coming from the North Atlantic as well as from Africa and Latin America and Asia. This new polycentric reality is a positive manifestation of globalization.[31]

Second, hegemony must be renounced for the sake of Christian humility and unity. When writing the postscript of *Evangelical Truth: A Personal Plea for Unity, Integrity and Faithfulness*, John Stott poured his heart out by imploring, "I make so bold as to claim [sic], in this postscript, that the supreme quality which the evangelical faith engenders (or should do) is humility."[32] Similarly, Andrew Walls, Tite Tienou, and others have emphatically called upon the West to abandon the "rule of the palefaces" and *listen* to genuine insights from various viewpoints of the Third World so that there will not be a "dialogue of the deaf" between the two worlds.[33] I must say we ignore their pleas only to our peril!

---

28    Ibid., 2.

29    Ibid., 95-96.

30    Justo L. Gonzalez, *The Changing Shape of Church History* (St. Louis, MO: Chalice Press, 2002), 14.

31    Ibid., 15.

32    John Stott, *Evangelical Truth: A Personal Plea for Unity, Integrity and Faithfulness,* revised edition. (Downers Grove, IL: InterVarsity Press, 2003), 122, parenthesis his.

33    In his *Cultural Forces in World Politics*, Ali Mazrui observes that America and the Third World are engaged in a dialogue of the deaf. He contends that in this dialogue of the deaf, "Americans are brilliant communicators but bad listeners." (London: James Currey, 1990), 116. Lamenting the fact that quality theological scholarship from Africa, Latin America and Asia has been marginalized, Andrew Walls writes, "... the impact on scholarship of this core of highly qualified people, taken as a whole, does not seem to commensurate with their talents and training ... But the rule of the palefaces over the academic world is untroubled. The expected publications do not materialize; or they have little international effect" ("Structural Problems in Mission Studies," *International Bulletin of Missionary Research* 15, no. 4 (October 1991): 152. Voicing the same concern, Tite Tienou chides, "Today, America's bad listening skills prevent it from hearing the Third World. Are Western Christian scholars better listeners than Mazrui's America? If they were, they would not continue the practice of marginalizing third world theologies and Christian scholarship. I see bad listening from Western Christians and theologians when, for them, the rubric 'third world theologies' mean that 'the contextuality and historical process of their development are neglected and/or homogenized.'" See "Christian Theology in an Era of World Christianity" in *Globalizing Theology: Belief and Practice in an Era of World Christianity*, ed. Craig Ott and Harold A. Netland (Grand Rapids, MI: Baker Academic, 2006), 48.

But humility works both ways. It requires the change of attitude from both parties in order for it to do the public good. The Western theologians, on the one hand, need to renounce hegemony, while the theologians in the Third World, on the other, need to resist the temptation of taking advantage of the situation to make the Western church a whipping boy. Genuine dialogue is essential for the success of global partnership and collaboration. Genuine communication involves both criticisms and self-criticisms in the spirit of reconciliation, with mutual respect, acceptance and forgiveness between two parties. We must do our utmost to guard against cultural imperialism on the one hand, and arrogant provincialism on the other. Our basic premise of genuine dialogue is that each culture of the world should have a place at the table and should have a right to speak. As David Clark fairly states, "Globalization is a relativizing ethos that celebrates the individuality of cultural perspectives even as it refuses to assign ultimacy to any of them."[34] We believe this healthy and positive form of globalization provides a context in which the task of contextualization will facilitate the reality of "globalizing theology." What then is globalizing theology? What are the goals of globalizing theology?

## The Goals of Globalizing Theology

Prior to the discussion on the goals of globalizing theology, we need to ask what globalizing theology is.

### What Is Globalizing Theology?

I will begin with the negation—what it is *not*. Globalizing theology is not the attempt to homogenize all local theologies into a universal church dogma for the sake of an all-embracing sameness, utilizing "one rule to rule them all."[35] Such an attempt is what we call "bad global." This is theological imperialism in its crudest form. Globalizing theology is not to be conceived as "world theology," to which all Christian communities throughout the world should comply invariably. Rather, globalizing theology is to be seen as an ongoing process of *glocalization* (i.e., globalization of the local) in theological reflection. It is the process of taking seriously our own local theology and uploading it to the world in hopes of gaining a listening ear that there will not be a "dialogue of the deaf" between the East and the West. It is the perennial interchange of theological acumen in the global arena between varied local theologies, of which Western theology is one.

Since globalizing theology is the dialectical process of theological reflection and dialogue in the global arena, it is not to be regarded as a finished product. It is a global journey toward God, toward a fuller understanding of his truths revealed in Scripture, and toward an effective application of those truths in the global community. Globalizing theology means that Christian theologians of many interconnecting cultures are prepared to give their prophetic voice as they, based on their understanding of the teaching of Scripture, grapple with the pressing issues

---

34    David Clark, *To Know and Love God* (Wheaton, IL: Crossway Books, 2003), 101. See also Stanley Grenz, "Community as a Theological Motif for the Western Church in an Era of Globalization," *Crux* 28, no. 3. (September 1992): 10

35    Kevin J. Vanhoozer candidly uses the famous line in *The Lord of the Rings* by J. R. R. Tolkien to depict the "monological rule of reason in the modern era of scientific method" in his essay "One Rule to Rule Them All?" *Globalizing Theology*, 85. I use the phrase here to signify simply the attempt to dominate.

that concern not only the local but also the global. And they are also prepared to listen to proper peer review, in whatever forms this may take—direct forms of critique or indirect forms of communication—with humility and trust, realizing that our views need to be put under the scrutiny of Scripture.

## What Are the Goals of Globalizing Theology?

### First, Striking a Healthy Balance between the Global and the Local

While globalization has the potential to homogenize cultures, it has also the potential to nour-ish cultural diversity.[36] The term "glocalization" refers to the way in which people in a certain locale react to globalization, marking out the way the local goes global. Healthy globalization encourages glocalization, which means global issues are to be handled simultaneously in par-ticular, local, cultural ways.[37]

Hence, the goal of globalizing theology is to strike a healthy balance between the poles—the global and the local. For that to happen, Paul Hiebert suggests that local theology must be in constant dialogue with other Christian communities worldwide. This ongoing process of dialogue may then lead to "a growing consensus on theological absolutes."[38] He explains,

> Just as believers in a local church must test their interpretations of Scriptures with their community of believers, so the churches in different cultural and historical con-texts must test their theologies with the international community of churches and the church down through the ages. The priesthood of believers must be exercised within a hermeneutical community. [39]

Wilbert Shenk, in a similar vein, aims right for the center when he asserts,

> To engage in 'globalizing theology' today means that we must guard the commit-ment to the particular and the local while taking account of the fact that we live with an intensified awareness of the global. If theology is to serve the church throughout the world, it must reflect this bifocal way of seeing; this becomes the vantage point from which we must rethink and revise theology conceptually, methodologically, and programmatically. [40]

### Second, Promoting Reconciliation of Relationships with Justice to the World

As Friedman reminded us earlier, we are now in the third stage of globalization, which is the age of post-colonialism. The majority of Third World countries have experienced colonial oc-

---

36    Thomas L. Friedman, *The World Is Flat,* Updated and Expanded Edition, (New York: Farrar, Straus & Giroux, 2006) 506-7.

37    Charles Van Engen in "The Glocal Church: Locality and Catholicity in a Globalizing World" defines glocalization as the attempt to "perceive the world through the lens of the simultaneous interaction, the interweaving influences, the dynamic, always-changing, multicultural interrelatedness of the global and the local." See Craig Ott and Harold Netland, eds., *Globalizing Theology,* 159.

38    Paul Hiebert, *Anthropological Reflections on Missiological Issues* (Grand Rapids, MI: Baker Books, 1994), 103.

39    Ibid.

40    Craig Ott and Harold Netland, eds., *Globalizing Theology,* 11.

cupation at one time or another. For example, the year 1492 marked the beginning of European colonization in Latin America; 1498 for Asia, especially for India when the Portuguese landed on the South West coast of India; and 1625 marked the European occupation of South Africa. The Philippines was colonized from 1521-1898 by Europeans and later by Americans. It is no exaggeration to say that the aftermath of European imperialism and colonialism is far-reaching. The souls of the people in Third World countries bear deep scars inflicted by their colonial past.

In the beginning of 1800, there were the European missionary endeavors to the Third World. Unfortunately, in the eyes of the nationals, Christianity came with swords or paper treaties in one hand and the Bible or a case of gin in the other.[41] The Bible, in the eyes of numerous nationals, was a "Colonial Book," used by the colonialists to justify their imperialistic conquest and unjust governance. As the South African Black theologian Mofokeng bemoans: "When the white man came to our country he had the Bible and we had the land. The white man said to us 'let us pray'. After the prayer, the white man had the land and we had the Bible."[42]

The Indian scholar R. S. Sugirtharajah highlights some of the marks and legacies of 'colonial hermeneutics' in his book *The Bible and the Third World: Pre-colonial, Colonial and Post-Colonial Encounters.* He then reports a heartbreaking event in 1985 when the Andean Indians wrote a letter to Pope John Paul II, asking him to take back the Bible:[43]

> We, the Indians of the Andes and America have decided to give you back your Bible, since for the past five hundred centuries [sic] it has brought us neither love, peace, or justice. We beg you take your Bible and give it back to our oppressors, whose hearts and minds are in greater need of its moral teachings. As part of the colonial exchange we received the Bible, which is an ideological weapon of attack. The Spanish sword used in the daytime to attack and kill the Indians, turned at night into a cross which attacked the Indian soul.

In addition to the deep scars of the colonial past, most of the Third World countries are battling with severe problems of political oppression, poverty, environmental issues, widespread malnutrition, the high rate of infant mortality, child labor, child prostitution, diseases, HIV epidemics and so on. Listen to the heart cry of an African theologian, Musa Dube, on the plight of HIV victims in Africa:[44]

> Some of us remember the struggle for political liberation. Indeed, only yesterday we were fighting for our liberation from colonialism… Only yesterday did we leave the

---

41   R. S. Sugirtharajah, *The Bible and the Third World: Pre-Colonial, Colonial, and Post-Colonial Encounters* (Cambridge, UK: Cambridge University Press, 2001), 45.

42   T.A. Mofokeng, "Black Christians, the Bible and Liberation," *Journal of Black Theology in South Africa.* 2, no. 1 (November 1988): 34.

43   R. S. Sugirtharajah, *The Bible and the Third World*, 222. See also Pablo Richard, "1492: The Violence of God and Future of Christianity," in *Concilium: International Journal for Theology* (1990, accessed 5 February 2008), 66; available from http://www.concillium.org/english/ct906.htm; internet.

44   Musa Duba, Associate Professor of Theology and Religious Studies at the University of Botswana, says in HIV/AIDS and the Curriculum: Methods of Integrating HIV/AIDS in Theological Programmes. See also John Parratt, *An Introduction to Third World Theologies* (Cambridge, UK: Cambridge University Press, 2004), 158.

delivery room, smiling, with the new born baby: a free and independent Africa…
And just as we begin to smile, watching this child lift its foot to take its first step as an
independent being… bang! Another oppressor struck Africa: HIV/AIDS!…

Our worst enemy is among us. It is everywhere—between men and women, boys and
girls, husbands and wives. It is in the beds of our intimacy—in the best moments of
our lives. When we kiss and make love, the enemy is there. It is now in our veins, in
our blood, in our cells, in our fluids, in our minds. HIV/AIDS makes love drag us to
death.

It is, therefore, of little wonder to see Shenk and other evangelical theologians agree on the
premise that valid globalizing theology must "motivate and sustain the church in witness and
service to the world."[45] Globalizing theology cannot be merely an intellectual exercise; it must
include growth in practical wisdom of life that generates Christ-like compassion and social engagement.[46] Christian practical wisdom is "the ability to see the world as God would have us
see it."[47] The fabric of globalizing theology in all its practicality is globalizing theological ethics. Theology and ethics (both personal and social) work hand in hand. Robert Schreiter sees
four global theological flows that are of universal concerns, all of which are ethical in nature.
They are liberation, feminism, ecology, and human rights.[48] More recently, he adds one more
to the list—reconciliation. He explains, "The cry for reconciliation grows out of an acute sense
of the brokenness experienced on such a broad scale in the world today… It is a calling out for
a new set of relationships so that the terrible deeds done in the past cannot happen again."[49]

Daniel Groody, in his recent book *Globalization, Spirituality, and Justice,* provides his theological insight for globalization. He believes spirituality and justice are the central aspects of
globalizing theology. In internal justice, Christians are put in a right relationship with God.
Through external justice, Christians are led to respond to God's grace through good deeds.
"God's justice, in other words, is not principally about vengeance or retribution but about
restoring people to right relationship with God, themselves, others, and the environment."[50]

---

45    Wilbert Shenk, "Recasting Theology of Mission: Impulses from the Non-Western World," *International Bulletin of Missionary Research* 25, no. 3 (July 2001): 105.

46    Kevin J. Vanhoozer says it well, "Theology must therefore be more than a *scientia* of the text; it must aim for *sapientia* in the present context. The goal is practical wisdom, not a theoretical system." *The Drama of Doctrine: A Canonical-Linguistic Approach to Christian Theology* (Louisville, KY: WJK Press, 2005), 307. See also David Clark's "Theology as Sapientia" in *To Know and Love God,* 208-212. He says, "…a major purpose of theology as *sapientia* is to shape and guide the faith, experience, and character of Christians. And this is surely central to the life and mission of the church," 209.

47    Richard S. Briggs, *Reading the Bible Wisely* (Grand Rapids, MI: Baker Book House, 2003), 111.

48    Robert Schreiter, *The New Catholicity: Theology between the Global and the Local* (Maryknoll, NY: Orbis Books, 1997), 16.

49    Robert Schreiter, "Globalization and Reconciliation: Challenges to Mission" in *Mission in the Third Millennium,* ed. Robert Schreiter (Maryknoll, NY: Orbis Books, 2001), 140.

50    Daniel Groody, *Globalization, Spirituality, and Justice* (Maryknoll, NY: Orbis Books, 2007), 27.

# Glocalizing Theology in an East Asian Perspective: A Proposal

In this section I attempt to present a way of constructing local theology from the East Asian perspective, which seeks to address some of the issues and challenges brought about in the process of globalization. My intention is to upload this local theology to the world arena for peer review in order to expand my theological horizons and clarify my theological direction. This is why I call it "glocalizing theology." Thus, this constructive task of glocalizing theology in an East Asian perspective is to be seen as a participation in the ongoing process of the worldwide theological dialogue. What follows is a proposal that I have initially presented in other places,[51] and have modified slightly for our present purposes. This proposal has served as a guide for my writing project of a four-volume systematic theology in the Chinese language, which attempts to break with the traditional Evangelical Theology done in North America. The first volume, titled *The Horizon of Theology*, deals with the prolegomenous issues of systematic theology and was published in May 2007 in Taiwan.[52]

## The Prelude to Theological Construction

I have observed four theological and cultural factors in the process of constructing theology in the East Asian context:

### First, Moving toward Doctrinal Exploration

It is noteworthy that, at the outset, dealing with biblical doctrines does not require us to explore them through a Western framework. Western theology does not have a monopoly on biblical doctrines. For some reason, the tendency in today's Asian contextual theology is to overlook the content of biblical doctrines. Some contextual theologies have become so issue-oriented that they either neglect or trivialize the doctrinal content of Christian theology. Examples include C. S. Song's *Third-Eye Theology* and *Tell Us Our Name: Story Theology from an Asian Perspective*, and Kosuke Koyama's *Waterbuffalo Theology*.[53] Their primary concern is to deal with preliminary issues, such as the relation of theology and culture, theory and praxis, social change and religious faiths. While these prolegomenous issues are important and worthy of our attention, they should not replace the exploration of doctrinal content, which is the substance of God's revelation. I am afraid if we deal with prolegomenous issues at the expense of doctrinal content, we may inadvertently distort the gospel of Christ. Daniel J. Adams, a seasoned contextualizer who has been a missionary-teacher in Taiwan, Korea, and Japan for a long period of time, made the following observation:[54]

---

51     The paper was first presented at the Evangelical Theological Society Annual Meeting in Orlando, FL on November 19-21, 1998, titled "Constructing Contextual Theology in a Postmodern Asian Society." Later, it was published in the *Alliance Academic Review* (May 2000): 87-99

52     Paul Siu, *The Horizon of Theology: Constructing a Method for Evangelical Theology* (Taipei, Taiwan: Campus Evangelical Fellowship, 2007).

53     C.S. Song, *Third-Eye Theology*. rev. ed. (Maryknoll, NY: Orbis Book, 1990); Song, *Tell Us Our Names: Story Theology from an Asian Perspective* (Maryknoll, NY: Orbis Books, 1984); Kosuke Koyama, *Waterbuffalo Theology* (Maryknoll, NY: Orbis Books, 1974).

54     Daniel J. Adams, *Cross-Cultural Theology: Western Reflections in Asia* (Atlanta, GA: John Knox Press, 1987), 83-84, italics mine.

Contextual theologies may become so issue-oriented and localized that they lose sight of comprehensive Christian theology or forget that contextualization assumes *there is something there to be contextualized.* A firm grasp of systematic theology provides a balanced perspective that includes the totality of theology and serves as a safeguard against the ever-present dangers of syncretism and reductionism.

True contextualization, I believe, is primarily concerned with the translation of the *whole* gospel of Jesus Christ into the thought forms and the daily lives of the people with whom we communicate in any given culture. Wisely, Lesslie Newbigin wrote, "The gospel is not an empty form into which everyone is free to pour his or her own content."[55] The *content* of the gospel of Christ is to be understood in the context of biblical history of God's revelation to humanity—the words and works of God—recorded in both the Old and New Testaments. The whole Bible *is* the gospel of Jesus Christ. As John Stott wrote, "The Bible does not just contain the gospel; it *is* the gospel. Through the Bible God himself is actually evangelizing, that is, communicating the good news to the world."[56] Evidently, the Bible was written in particular cultures and bears the marks of these cultures. Yet the Bible is applicable and translatable to any culture in today's world.[57] Systematic theology, through its concentration in doctrinal studies of the whole Bible, seeks to provide direction for the church to know and love the God of the Gospel, and to live for him by participating in his mission to the world. I, therefore, concur with Daniel Adams' assertion that a firm grasp of systematic theology, based on the total teachings of Scripture, provides an encompassing approach to communicating the whole gospel of Christ, and thereby may avoid some of the dangers of syncretism and reductionism.

## Second, Venerating the Written Text

When one engages contextualization in the East Asian context, one must come to terms with the reality that the people are deeply ingrained with the heritage of three major religions: Confucianism, Daoism, and Buddhism, each of which has profoundly influenced Asian's outlook on life, their apprehension of spirituality, and their ways of conduct.

Because of the Confucius heritage, the East Asian cultures in general, and the Chinese culture in particular, up to present day still have a peculiar veneration for the written word—the text. Such veneration has produced tremendous interest in the writings of earlier times. For over two thousand years, Chinese scholars have reinterpreted the ancient writings, which are known as the "Five Classics" and the "Four Books," so as to glean from them ideas and wisdom for each new generation.[58] This mentality of respect for the written word may partially explain why the socio-political form of postmodernism has greater impact on Asian countries than the

---

55    Lesslie Newbigin, *The Gospel in a Pluralist Society* (Grand Rapids, MI: Eerdmans, 1989, 1994), 152-53.

56    John R. W. Stott, "The Bible in World Evangelization," in *Perspectives on the World Christian Movement*, revised edition, ed. Ralph D. Winter and Steven C. Hawthorne (Pasadena, CA: William Carey Library, 1992), A6.

57    Kevin J. Vanhoozer, *The Drama of Doctrine*, 323. Vanhoozer writes, "Better, the truth of Jesus Christ is that of a *catholic universal:* not a universal truth that exists apart from specific cultural forms but, on the contrary, a universal that is infinitely translatable into all cultural forms." (Italics his).

58    The Five Classics are Confucian classics: Shih Ching (Classic of Songs or the Book of Poetry), Shu Ching (Classic of Documents or the Book of History), I Ching (Classic of Changes or the Book of Changes), Ch'un Ch'iu (Spring and Autumn Annals), and Li Chi (Record of Rituals or the Book of Rites). The Four Books are shorter texts of Confucian teachings. They are: Analects (or Conversations of Confucius), Mencius (or Meng-tzu), Ta Hsueh (or the Great Learning), and Chung Yung (or the Doctrine of the Mean).

deconstructionist, which I have alluded to in a previous section. I think John K. Fairbank and Edwin O. Reischauer are on target when they write,

> In East Asian civilization the written word has always taken precedent over the spoken; Chinese history is full of famous documents—memorials, essays and poems—but lacks the great speeches of the West. The magic quality of writing is perhaps one of the reasons why the peoples of East Asia have tended to place a higher premium on book learning and on formal education than have the peoples of any other civilization.[59]

Generally speaking, the people in East Asia have high regard for the authority of the Bible. The Bible in the Chinese language is transliterated as the "Sacred Classic." A recent poll among Chinese scholars shows that the Bible tops the list of 60 "must read" books.[60] Even in the tumultuous time of China's "Anti-Christian Movement" in the 1920s, in spite of severe opposition and criticism directed toward Christians and the church, the Bible itself was not the center of controversy. Wing-Hung Lam correctly observes "the dominant problem of the Chinese church in the twenties was not the infallibility of Scripture but the salvation of the nation."[61] It is because Asian people are basically pragmatic and down to earth. They are more concerned with how the Bible is relevant to life situations than with debating the inerrancy of the Bible.[62] I think their veneration for the written word gives a huge advantage to theologians in East Asia who attempt to construct contextual theology in ways that uphold the Bible as the authority of our faith and practices.

### Third, Examining the Religious Heritage

All East Asian countries share a common Confucian heritage in core social values.[63] Confucianism has formed the bedrock of East Asia civilization. Throughout China's five thousand years of civilization, the quest of Chinese philosophy has primarily centered on a person's relationships to oneself, to others, to nature, and to Heaven (*Tien*). Julia Ching, the world-renowned scholar of Chinese thought, writes "Confucius was a religious man, a believer in Heaven as a personal God, a man who sought to understand and follow Heaven's will."[64] To the people of East Asia, an individual's relationship to social order and to the supernatural is

---

59    John K. Fairbank and Edwin O. Reischauer, *East Asia – The Great Tradition* (Boston, MA: Houghton Mifflin, 1960), 43. See also John K. Fairbank, *China: A New History* (Cambridge, MA: Harvard University Press, 1992).

60    Philemon Choi, *Not One Less: Rethinking the Youth and the Ministry*, Chinese Edition (Hong Kong: Breakthrough Ltd., 2005), 19.

61    Wing-Hung Lam, *Chinese Theology in Construction* (Pasadena, CA: William Carey Library, 1983), 92-93, esp. 53.

62    I think Ralph Covell is correct in his description of the Chinese mind; he writes, "Many observers have noted that the Chinese are characterized by common sense, a reasonable, pragmatic spirit, a tendency to choose the middle path rather than go to extremes… They think in synthetic, concrete terms…" I tend to think this description can be applied to Asians at large. See Ralph R. Covell, *Confucius, the Buddha, and Christ: A History of the Gospel in Chinese* (Eugene, OR: Wipf & Stock, 2004), 11. See also the background and his analysis of the Anti-Christian Movement in the 1920s, 182-205.

63    Edmond Tang "East Asia" in John Parratt, *An Introduction to Third World Theologies*, 76.

64    Hans Küng and Julia Ching, *Christianity and Chinese Religions* (New York: Doubleday, 1989), 67.

essential to one's own meaningful existence. The harmony in relationships, it is taught and believed, will give the individual ultimate fulfillment.

Thus, the East Asian mind is exceedingly humanistic. It is person-oriented, focusing on harmonious relationships. Nevertheless, this form of humanism is not to be confused with the humanism of Renaissance Europe characterized mainly by autonomy, individualism, and anti-authority. The Chinese philosopher Wing-Tsit Chan sums it up well,[65]

> If one word could characterize the entire history of Chinese philosophy, that word would be humanism—not the humanism that denies or slights a Supreme Power, but one that professes the unity of man and Heaven. In this sense, humanism has dominated Chinese thought from the dawn of its history... Human was the outgrowth of historical and social change. It began in Shang (1766-1122 B.C.) period and gradually reached its climax in Confucius.

The Chinese humanistic spirit has always had a high ethical ideal. According to the *Analects*, humaneness (*ren*) is a supreme and all-embracing virtue. It refers to the practical manifestations of being humane. This term has had a variety of translations: kindness, goodness, human-heartedness, and benevolence. The Chinese pictogram for *ren* is made up of two symbols, one for person and the other for number two. So *ren* means an attitude of harmony and goodness that is prevalent between two persons. It denotes not only the personal virtue, but it ideally embraces all social virtues.[66] To be authentically human (*ren*) is to be able to love others according to one's proper relationship toward them. These horizontal relationships will lead toward the unity between Heaven and humanity (*tian ren heyi*)—the ultimate harmony. This concept of the unity of Heaven and humanity underscores the essentiality of reconciliation between the individual life and the Heavenly Way. From an evangelical standpoint, we can be sure that all these humanistic elements in East Asian civilization are God's general revelation, which is non-redemptive, given to the peoples in Asia that they may be prepared for the Gospel of Christ.

### Fourth, Taking Suffering as Transcendental Experience

East Asia has seen a mosaic of affluence and poverty. Many peoples in East Asia have their share of pain and suffering. But we must be aware that people in East Asia have a unique concept of suffering that is different from people in most parts of the world. People in Latin America, for example, view suffering as a socio-political problem that must be resolved. The entire Liberation Theology in Latin America is built on this premise. Nevertheless, people in East Asia tend to take suffering as a reality to be transcended to the level where they experience the connectedness with the deity. They treat suffering not as a problem to resolve but as an opportunity for spiritual (religious) experience. Such conceptualization of pain and suffering is the result of the long-standing influence of Buddhism and Daoism, and the combination of which is called Zen Buddhism in Japan, popularized by D. T. Suzuki and Allan Watts.

---

65   Wing-Tsit Chan, *A Source Book in Chinese Philosophy*, (Princeton, NJ: Princeton University Press, 1973), 3. See also Hans Kung and Julia Ching, *Christianity and Chinese Religions*, 59-127.

66   Confucius, *The Analects*, translated by Raymond Dawson (Oxford, UK: Oxford University Press, 1993, 2000), xxi. See also Deborah Sommer, ed. *Chinese Religion: An Anthology of Sources* (Oxford, UK: Oxford University Press, 1995), 41-48.

Buddhism claims that the origin of pain and suffering is desire and the way to eliminate desire is through the Noble Eightfold Path, that is, the rules for right living. The objective of right living is Nirvana where all desires will be eliminated. Nirvana is the "enlightened existence" where one will transcends all pain and suffering, because one will then be connected to the ultimate reality.[67] More practical than Buddhism in some ways, Daoism's primary concern is for the individual person to fit into the pattern of nature, which is described as the *Dao,* literally meaning the "Way" in a metaphysical sense. According to the Tao Te Ching of Lao-tzu, the mythical sage meaning "Old Master," the *Dao* is founded on a nameless and formless "non-being." It cannot be heard and cannot be seen and cannot be spoken to. But it is, in essence, the totality of the natural processes to which humans must conform. Humans who can transcend the mundane and become one with the *Dao* are "beyond all harm" and achieve "tranquility in the midst of strife." Merging with the *Dao* is then the goal of eliminating pain and suffering. The key to merging with the *Dao* of nature is *wu-wei,* or "doing nothing." The 48th verse in the Tao Te Ching says, "Decreasing and decreasing, until doing nothing. When nothing is done, nothing is left undone." By this the Taoists did not mean complete inaction, but rather doing what is natural.[68]

## Toward a Systematic Theology in an East Asian Perspective

My proposal of constructing systematic theology in the East Asian perspective has the following five distinctive features:

### First, Beginning with the Human Person Made in the Image of God

It diverges from the traditional Western order of systematic theology, which begins with the doctrine of Scripture and then discusses God, man, sin, Christ, salvation, Holy Spirit, the church, and the last things. My proposal begins with the human person made in the image of God (*imago Dei*). This starting point, I believe, goes well with the East Asian cultures, which are basically person-oriented, relational, and humanistic, as I have already pointed out earlier. This proposal seeks to address the Asian context that can be characterized by the postmodern dictum: *the real is relational and the relational is real.* It addresses the "relational ontology" that fares well with the ancient Confucian emphasis on harmonious relationships at multiple levels—relationship with heaven, with oneself, with others, with nature, and the ultimate harmony between heaven and humanity. At the center of these multiple relationships is the image of God (*imago Dei*) at work binding them together.

### Second, Engaging the Ancient-Current Cultural Context

This proposal takes seriously the ancient-current cultural context of East Asia. On the one hand, it is keenly aware of the profound influences of the three major religions, Confucianism, Daoism, and Buddhism that have shaped the hearts and minds of Asians in ages past. On the other hand, it addresses the current social and economic conditions in which the East Asian people are adjusting to the process of globalization. Therefore, this proposal intends to make

---

67  See Deborah Sommer, ed. *Chinese Religion: An Anthology of Sources,* 119-151.

68  For a contemporary interpretation and popular application of the Tao Te Ching, see Wayne W. Dyer, *Change Your Thoughts, Change Your Life: Living the Wisdom of the Tao* (Carlsbad, CA: Hay House, Inc., 2007), esp. 234 for the interpretation of the 48th verse.

theology relevant and practical, believing that theology finds its fulfillment not only in "right thinking" (*ortho-doxy*), but also in "right acting" (*ortho-praxy*).

However, my approach to engaging the cultural praxis is one of critical analysis and transformation based on the teaching of Scripture. I believe that the Gospel of Christ calls into question all cultures because there are both good and bad elements found in every culture. The Bible not only answers the concerns and questions coming from culture but also transforms them. The light of the gospel has the innate power to recast the issues that culture raises.[69] I am, therefore, in alignment with Newbigin when he comments on the relation of gospel and culture, saying, "True contextualization accords the gospel its rightful primacy, its power to penetrate every culture and to speak within each culture, in its own speech and symbol, the word which is both No and Yes, both judgment and grace."[70] This position is also in line with the declaration of *The Lausanne Covenant* stating, "Culture must always be tested and judged by Scripture… The gospel does not presuppose the superiority of any culture to another, but evaluates all cultures according to its own criteria of truth and righteousness and insists on moral absolutes in every culture."[71]

### *Third, Rendering Fidelity to Scripture*
This integrative model determines to render fidelity to Scripture and takes the Bible as the primary source for constructing local theology in the East Asian context. Although Scripture is not the starting point in this model, it is used *presuppositionally* to formulate a biblical anthropology that addresses the experiences of the "knowing subject" in the image of God. My way to *presuppose* the authority of the Bible fares well with the general culture of East Asia that already has a respect for ancient text. It is true that Asia itself is replete with resource materials relevant to constructing local theologies. Samuel Rayan has pointed out four areas of resources, one of which is Asian writings and folklore. There are numerous folk religions, legends, myths, and poems that will help us better understand the religiosity of the people.[72] While

---

69    What I have said about the relation between culture and theology goes way beyond Paul Tillich's method of correlation. For Tillich, the culture asks the questions and theology provides the answers. David Clark rightly pointed out that Tillich's error lies in the fact that he overlooks the corrective function of the Bible and the necessity of challenging the form of the questions raised by culture, for culture tends to shape people's concerns and questions. For a fuller discussion on the relation and interaction between culture and Scripture, see David Clark's, "A Dialogical Model for Evangelical Contextualization" in *To Know and Love God*, 113-122.

70    Lesslie Newbigin, *The Gospel in a Pluralist Society*, 152; see also 195.

71    *The Lausanne Covenant*, 10, in Gerald H. Anderson and Thomas F. Stransky, eds., *Mission Trends No.2: Evangelization* (New York: Paulist Press, and Grand Rapids, MI: Eerdmans, 1975), 245. "We must understand the context in order to address it, but the context must not be allowed to distort the Gospel." *Manila Manifesto*, 10, in *Proclaim Christ until He Comes* (Lausanne Conference on World Evangelism, 1989), 35.

72    Samuel Rayan, "Reconceiving Theology in the Asian Context" in *Doing Theology in a Divided World*, eds. Virginia Fabella and Sergio Torres (Maryknoll, NY: Orbis Books, 1985), 131-141. The four areas of resources are: (1) The People—Asians themselves, their experience of life and their rich humanness. The courage and the strength that have enabled Asians to survive, despite great adversities and sufferings. (2) Asian Writings and Folklore—in addition to the three major religions mentioned in this paper, there are numerous folk religions, legends, myths, poems, and others that will help us better understand the religiosity of the people. (3) The Spiritual History—the spiritual history of Asians is a history of a relentless quest for truth, meaning, and freedom to be applied to the whole of life. (4) The Liberative Potential—Asian people are poor and oppressed.

Rayan's observations may have some merits, we must insist that all these sources for theology must be put under the scrutiny of the Bible. However relevant they may appear to be, they must be considered secondary to the Bible.

### Fourth, Referencing Church Traditions in the East and West

This proposal takes into consideration the long-standing traditions of the Western church in its formulation of doctrinal beliefs. Admittedly, church tradition is regarded as a secondary source of constructing theology and must be submitted to the authority of the Scriptures. What is important in this approach is the attempt to incorporate theological insights of Western theology. There is much to be learned between the East and the West. There are rich resources in the church history of the West as there are in the spiritual history of the East. In formulating an adequate local theology in the East Asian perspective, it would be imprudent not to consult the insights of those theological giants in the West and learn from them. We ignore their theological acumen to our own impoverishment. This approach chooses to cover the spectrum of Western theology, but presents it in a fashion that addresses the real need of the people in East Asia. It seeks to interact with the theological ideas of Western scholars and to cultivate a genuine dialogue between the two worlds.

### Fifth, Using Hope as the Central Motif

This approach uses "hope" as the integrative motif for constructing this local theology. People in East Asia need to find a new life, a new meaning for existence, and a new hope for their future. Such a living hope is promised to all humanity based on faith in Jesus Christ (1 Pet. 1: 3-5). This hope motif is illustrated in the following section.

## The Framework of a Systematic Theology in the East Asian Perspective

1. **Human Person in Religious and Social Context**

   With increased globalization and modernization in East Asia and with the transition to postmodernity, the influences of the three major religions, Confucianism, Daoism and Buddhism remain strong. East Asians are experiencing the dark side of globalization and modernization characterized by dehumanization, alienation, and despair. A spiritual vacuum pervades society in spite of the flourishing of religious faiths. A genuine quest for meaning of life resonates in the hearts of the people in East Asia. They realize they are in a predicament. The heart cry of the people is, "Is there any hope?" The Christian answer is, "Yes!" There is hope for humanity and for the people in East Asia. As a matter of fact, humans are valuable and significant because they are created in the image of God (*imago Dei*).

2. **The Predicament of Humanity**

   Humanity is in a predicament because we are alienated from God, the creator of the universe and humankind. This alienation was brought about by sin. We see sin residing in the human heart as well as in the structure of society. Consequently, the dark side of globalization has gripped society. There is a widening gap between the rich and the poor. There is massive corruption in the bureaucratic government. Growing unemployment, the unstable economy, and increasing inflation weigh heavily on people. All these mishaps contribute to people's spiritual emptiness and uncertainty about the future. They are longing for hope.

3. **The Gospel of Grace**

The Christian answer is the Gospel of Christ—the Good News. Jesus Christ, who is fully God and fully man, came to die for our sins. The Just died on behalf of the unjust that people may be reconciled to God and be justified. Through his death on the cross, Jesus has provided humanity with new life and real freedom. There is genuine hope for humanity.

4. **The Spiritual Family Established**

In this life on earth, God has prepared for his children a spiritual family, which is also called the church. This familial metaphor will find favor in East Asian cultures. We worship God and fellowship with one another in this spiritual family, acknowledging Jesus Christ as the Head of the family. We also encourage one another to be involved within society in the hope of making a positive impact with our transformed lives and renewed minds. In doing so, we are spreading genuine hope for humanity.

5. **The God-Man Jesus**

The glorious and living hope mentioned above is actualized in the person of Jesus Christ. Who is Jesus Christ? He is the God-Man. He is fully God and fully man. Jesus' resurrection from the dead is the grandest evidence for what He claims to be—God.

6. **The Triune God**

Jesus is God incarnate. The Christian God is a triune God, who is infinite and personal and who is the Sustainer and Governor of all things. God in holy love has taken the initiative to reveal himself to us in the person of Jesus Christ. The Holy Spirit is the third person of the Trinity. God the Spirit is one who enables beings and things to become what they are created to be, fulfilling their created purpose of giving glory to God.

7. **The New Humanity**

The hope for postmodern society will fully be realized when Jesus returns to earth, ushering in the millennium and the new world order, which Marxist ideology has promised but failed to deliver. Marxism and socialism may deserve a place of respect for their emphasis on the need for the creation of a new man and a new society, but they have proven to fall short of attaining such a noble goal. When Christ comes, humanity's perfect society of peace and justice will fully materialize. The tension between "things as they are" and "things as they ought to be" will be resolved, because the new world order with God's righteousness as the center will be brought in.

Thus, the genuine hope for mankind is realized.

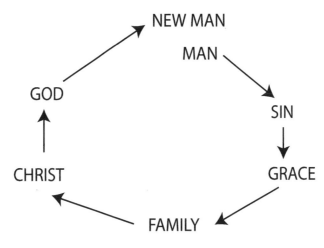

Figure 1: New Man

## Conclusion

In this paper, I have attempted to provide a theological reading of globalization from the standpoint of constructing local theologies. I have delineated the realities of globalization and its relation to the postmodern condition. I have explained what globalizing theology is and explored some of its goals. Finally, I have glocalized a theology from the East Asian perspective.

As mentioned earlier, the objective of this contextual theology in the East Asian perspective is meant to be missional. The situation of globalization and postmodernity, now as ever, demands a rebirth of the human person made in the image of God. Without God's gracious act of regeneration in the lives of people, humanity is still dead in sin and remains hopeless. I believe that this construction of Christian theology will serve evangelistic purposes and thus participate in the completion of the Great Commission. The theological content of this construction is less confessional, but comparatively more dynamic and interactive than traditional Western theology. I believe this is more relevant to the contemporary cultural setting of the East Asian context.

## Discussion Questions:

1. What is your understanding of globalization? In your opinion, what are the benefits of globalization and the problems that it has created?

2. What is your take on the Western theological hegemony? Do you agree with the author's analysis of the situation?

3. What is your understanding of postmodernism? According to the author, why have the Third World theologians and the evangelical postmodernists become strange comrades?

4. What is globalizing theology? What are its goals?

5. What is your evaluation of the four theological and cultural factors that the author discussed in his prelude to constructing theology in the East Asian perspective?

6. What is your evaluation of the author's theological framework of a systemic theology in the East Asian perspective?

# 10

## Evangelical Models of Contextualization

### A. Scott Moreau

*Scott Moreau is Professor of Intercultural Studies and Missions at Wheaton College, editor of Evangelical Missions Quarterly, managing editor of Strategic Network KnowledgeBase (www.strategicnetwork.org) and series editor of Encountering Mission (Baker Books). Prior to teaching at Wheaton, he served for a decade in Africa while on staff with Campus Crusade for Christ. He has written or edited more than ten books and hundreds of articles in journals, magazines, and dictionaries. He earned degrees from Wheaton College and Trinity Evangelical Divinity School.*

The literature on contextualization has exploded over the past two decades. In the midst of this explosion, evangelicals are playing significant roles such as exploring boundaries, keeping important issues in the forefront, challenging and critiquing each other as well as non-evangelicals, proposing new ways of thinking about and implementing uncounted contextualized ministry methods.

Because our focus is on evangelical approaches, it was important to confine the research done for this essay to the evangelical spectrum. To do that, we drew from two important sources that operationalize what it means to be "evangelical." The first was British church historian David Bebbington's widely-accepted four-fold characterization of evangelicals as those who emphasize 1) conversion (the belief that lives need to be changed), 2) activism (the expression of the gospel in effort, especially evangelism and missionary work), 3) biblicism (giving special importance to the Bible), and 4) crucicentrism (Christ's atoning sacrifice on the cross is central).[1] The second operationalizing source was John Stott's identification of key doctrinal issues that are of importance to all evangelicals, namely that 1) the gospel comes from God and not human ingenuity; 2) that the gospel is Christological, biblical, historical, theological, apostolic

---

1    David W. Bebbington, *Evangelicalism in Modern Britain: A History from the 1730s to the 1980s* (London: Unwin Hyman, 1989).

and personal; and 3) that it is effective because it is revealed by God himself.[2] Together these criteria offer a broad-based and yet appropriately constrained set of markers for determining contextual models and practices that can be identified as distinctively evangelical.

At the same time, they do not impose uniformity or ensure agreement among evangelicals. For example, there is currently a vigorous debate within evangelical circles whether so-called C5 churches (communities of Muslims who follow Jesus yet remain culturally and officially Muslim[3]) should be seen as a permanent goal,[4] a transitional point,[5] or as an illegitimate reality[6] of contextualized witness in Muslim settings. While advocates of each position clearly meet Bebbington's and Stott's criteria, the vigor of the debate indicates a healthy variety among evangelicals as they seek to contextualize.

The accessibility of online databases made it possible to examine a "universe" of roughly five thousand English contextualization resources (articles,[7] chapters, and monographs) from which those that met the above criteria[8] could be identified and examined more closely. While the resulting literature review was not exhaustive, it can be argued that it was comprehensive enough to give an accurate picture of contemporary evangelical contextualization approaches and ministry practices.

## Models and Maps of Models

In the broadest sense, by "models" we mean artificially developed *categories* or *approaches* intended to describe in broad brush strokes a frame that fits real-life examples. They are simplified and representative rather than detailed and specific. They are not intended to be literally accurate in detail, therefore the examples within each model category will often be more multifaceted and differentiated[9] than the model they exemplify.

---

2    John W. Stott, *Evangelical Truth,* revised edition (Downers Grove, IL: InterVarsity Press, 2003), 25-30.

3    John Travis, "The C1 to C6 Spectrum," *Evangelical Missions Quarterly* 34, no. 4 (October 1998): 407-408.

4    See John Travis, "Must All Muslims Leave 'Islam' to Follow Jesus?" *Evangelical Missions Quarterly* 34, no. 4 (October 1998): 401-415; Kevin Higgins, "Identity, Integrity and Insider Movements: A Brief Paper Inspired by Timothy C. Tennent's Critique of C-5 Thinking," *International Journal of Frontier Missions* 23, no. 3 (Fall 2006): 117-23; Rick Brown, "Biblical Muslims," *International Journal of Frontier Missions* 24, no. 2 (Summer 2007): 65-74.

5    See Phil Parshall, "Danger! New Directions in Contextualization," *Evangelical Missions Quarterly* 34, no. 4 (October 1998): 404-406, 409-10; Gary Corwin, "A Humble Appeal to C5/Insider Movement Muslim Ministry Advocated to Consider Ten Questions," *International Journal of Frontier Missions* 24, no. 1 (Spring 2007): 5-20; Timothy Tennent, "Followers of Jesus (Isa) in Islamic Mosques: A Closer Examination of C-5 "High Spectrum" Contextualization," *International Journal of Frontier Missions* 23, no. 3 (Fall 2006): 101-15.

6    See Larry Poston, "'You Must Not Worship in Their Way . . .' When Contextualization Becomes Syncretism (Syncretism among Messianic Jews)," in *Contextualization and Syncretism: Navigating Cultural Currents,* ed. Gailyn Van Rheenen (Pasadena, CA: William Carey Library, 2006), 243-63; Samuel Schlorff, *Missiological Models in Ministry to Muslims* (Upper Darby, PA: Middle East Resources, 2006).

7    This included the complete indices of numerous journals.

8    In some cases, the source (e.g., *Evangelical Missions Quarterly, International Journal of Frontier Missiology*) or the publisher (e.g., William Carey Library, Baker Books, InterVarsity Press) ensured that the model/method was at least being presented from an evangelical perspective.

9    Avery Robert Dulles, *Models of Revelation* (Garden City, NY: Doubleday, 1983), 30.

More specifically, a "model" of contextualization is a *prototype or an idealization under which a variety of real-life examples will conform in a broad sense.* Thus, under each model we will group together examples that are not identical but are still close enough to be categorized together under adherence to a chosen rubric, such as a common philosophical orientation, a goal, or a method being followed.[10]

From the late 1970s on, people have developed multiple maps or schema intended to help categorize the ever-growing diversity of contextualization models. These schema have ranged from more simple bi-polar approaches (e.g., "dogmatic" versus "existential"[11]) to those with numerous options along a spectrum.[12] Each was developed with differing purposes. Missiologist David Hesselgrave intends that his schema be *prescriptive* in helping us distinguish viable evangelical models from non-evangelical ones,[13] while missiological anthropologist Dean Gilliland is more *descriptive*, explaining the models and how they are used rather than evaluating them.[14] Roman Catholic missiologists Stephen Bevans and Robert Schreiter explore what they perceive of as strengths and weaknesses for each model;[15] while missiological theologian Charles Van Engen notes the ways each perspective in his schema is viable for its intended purposes.[16]

---

10    This is in contrast to the way Charles Kraft uses the term in *Christianity in Culture*, in which "models" are more particular proposals or propositions than prototypes; see *Christianity in Culture: A Study in Dynamic Biblical Theologizing in Cross-Cultural Perspective* (Maryknoll: Orbis, 1979), 31-33; idem, *Christianity in Culture: A Study in Dynamic Biblical Theologizing in Cross-Cultural Perspective*, 25th Anniversary Edition (Maryknoll, NY: Orbis, 2005), 25-26.

11    Bruce J. Nicholls, *Contextualization: A Theology of Gospel and Culture* (Downers Grove, IL: InterVarsity, 1979).

12    Dean Gilliland, "Appendix: Contextualization Models," in *The Word Among Us: Contextualizing Theology for Mission Today*, ed. Dean S. Gilliland (Dallas: Word Publishing, 1989), 313-317; idem, "Contextualization," in *Evangelical Dictionary of World Missions*.

13    David J. Hesselgrave, "The Contextualization Continuum," *Gospel in Context*. 2, no. 3 (July 1979): 4-11.

14    Gilliland, "Contextualization Models."

15    Robert J. Schreiter, *Constructing Local Theologies* (London: SCM Press, 1985); Stephen J. Bevans, "Models of Contextual Theology" *Missiology* 13, no. 2 (April, 1985): 185-202; idem, *Models of Contextual Theology* (Maryknoll, NY: Orbis, 1992); idem, *Models of Contextual Theology: Revised and Expanded Edition* (Maryknoll, NY: Orbis, 2002).

16    Charles H. Van Engen, "Five Perspectives of Contextually Appropriate Missional Theology," in *Appropriate Christianity*, ed. Charles Kraft (Pasadena: William Carey Library, 2005), 183-202.

| Nicholls | Hesselgrave | Bevans | Schreiter | Gilliland | Van Engen |
|---|---|---|---|---|---|
| Dogmatic | Apostolic Accommodation | Translation | Adaptation | Adaptation | Indigenization |
| | | | Translation | Translation | Communication |
| | | | | Critical (critical realism) | |
| | | | | | Translatability |
| | Prophetic Accommodation | Countercultural (GOCN) | | | Epistemological |
| | | Praxis | Liberationist | Praxis | Local Theologizing |
| Existential | Syncretistic Accommodation | Anthropological | Ethnographic | Anthropological | |
| | | | Enculturation | Semiotic (Schreiter) | |
| | | Synthetic | | Synthetic | |
| | | Transcendental | | Transcendental | |

Table 1: Schema of Contextualization Models[17]

The various schemas are arranged left to right in Table 1 in the chronological order in which they first appeared in print. The models that have been seen as being more viable by evangelicals, and which we will briefly introduce, are in the shaded boxes across from the top to the middle rows. Those considered less viable by evangelicals are arranged from the middle to the bottom rows. Of the six schemas listed, Bevan's is the most frequently cited by other missiologists as a viable way to map the entire field.

## Terms Used for Models Favored by Evangelicals

Evangelical missiologists and theologians have proposed literally dozens of terms or labels for "contextualization," ranging alphabetically from "appropriate Christianity"[18] to "vernacular theology"[19]—often without reference to the growing list of alternate terms.

---

17   Nicholls, *Contextualization*; Hesselgrave, "The Contextualization Continuum;" Bevans, *Models of Contextualization*; Schreiter, Constructing Local Theologies; the fifth column blends non-identical schema described by Gilliland in "Appendix: Contextualization Models," and "Contextualization" in EDWM; Van Engen, "Five Perspectives"—his is not a schema per se, but an outline of "perspectives of contextualization that have developed over the past several centuries of missionary activity," Ibid., 183 (emphasis mine).

18   Charles Kraft, ed., *Appropriate Christianity* (Pasadena, CA: William Carey Library, 2005).

19   William A. Dyrness, *Invitation to Cross-Cultural Theology: Case Studies in Vernacular Theologies* (Grand Rapids, MI: Zondervan, 1992).

Drawing from Table 1, in this section of the chapter we briefly introduce seven terms (and their variations) that have been used to describe the type of contextualization models utilized by evangelicals. The first two terms historically preceded the coining of contextualization in 1972, while the remaining five were introduced after it. It will help to bear in mind that our ultimate goal is not on identifying or categorizing the *terms*, but on identifying the underlying *types of contextualized models and ministry methods* evangelicals use.

## Adaptation

Though preceding contextualization, adaptation as a viable means of contextualization is still used by many evangelicals and conservative Catholics. Those who do so seek to develop an explicit philosophical map of the worldview of the culture, which forms a basis for developing a Christian theology for the local context.[20] The principle behind adaptation is "to make, as much as possible, the historical foci of systematic theology fit into particular cultural situations."[21] While still used today, it was in part the limitations of adaptation that led to the need to find new ways to contextualize.

## Indigenization

Indigenization is another historical term that "has to do with the fit between the forms and life of a church and its surrounding context."[22] The understanding and practices of indigenization were initially developed and employed in the nineteenth century. They are most commonly seen in the development of what is called the indigenous church, which is a church that is 1) self-governing, 2) self-financing, and 3) self-propagating. With some modifications and the more recent addition of "self-theologizing,"[23] indigenizing is still valued by many evangelicals today as one of the guiding ideals for contextualization.

## Translation

The most common designation for the contextualization model followed by evangelicals is "translation." It was first used in 1983 by Krikor Haleblian to distinguish two major approaches to contextualization, the "translation" approach of anthropologist Charles Kraft and "semiotic" approach of Robert Schreiter.[24] The essential idea of the translation model is that there is a core message of universal truth which must be translated into each new cultural setting in a way that remains faithful to the core.[25] Because the content of that message is absolute and authoritative, the contextualizer's task is to change the *form* of the message so that its content may be *understood*[26] or *may have the same impact*[27] on the contemporary audience that it did

---

20   Robert Schreiter, *Constructing Local Theologies*, 9-10.

21   Gilliland, "Appendix: Contextualization Models," 315.

22   Van Engen, "Five Perspectives," 187. See more extensive discussion below on the indigenous church model.

23   Paul G. Hiebert, *Anthropological Insight for Missionaries* (Grand Rapids, MI: Baker, 1985), 195-196; 216-219.

24   Krikor Haleblian, "The Problem of Contextualization," *Missiology* 11, no. 1 (January 1983): 104-106.

25   Bevans, *Models Revised*, 37.

26   Hesselgrave's approach, as seen in "The Contextualization Continuum."

27   Kraft's approach, as seen in *Christianity in Culture*.

on the original hearers through accommodating it to the receptor culture.[28] Those who use this model seek to "*translate* and *communicate* the biblical message with understanding to each particular culture."[29] Alternate labels for this model include *dogmatic contextualization*[30] and *apostolic accommodation*.[31]

It should be noted that Charles Van Engen prefers to call this approach *communication* (or accommodation or adaptation)[32] because 1) that is the primary emphasis of the variety of approaches which use this model and 2) *translation* is too easily confused with the idea of the infinite cultural "translatability" of the gospel as discussed by Andrew Walls, Kwame Bediako and others.[33] Van Engen advocates that *translatability* be used as a separate label for this latter model (see below).[34]

## Critical Contextualization

Dean Gilliland names Paul Hiebert's critical contextualization as a separate model. By "critical," Hiebert refers to the epistemological approach of critical realism, which "sees all human knowledge as a combination of objective and subjective elements, and as partial but increasingly closer approximations of truth."[35] Critical contextualization involves exegeting both Scripture and culture followed by developing a culturally authentic and biblically appropriate response. The goal of the critical method is to arrive at contextualized practices which have the consensus of the redeemed community.[36] We expand on this in the presentation of linear approaches below.

## Counter-cultural

Another contemporary term used of evangelical models is the counter-cultural (or epistemological)[37] model. The goal of this model is to "truly *encounter* and *engage* the context" and the method to do this is "respectful yet critical analysis and authentic gospel proclamation in word and deed."[38] In the process we learn new things about God as "Christian knowledge about God is seen as cumulative, enhanced, deepened broadened and expanded as the gospel takes new shape in each new culture."[39]

---

28    Hesselgrave, "The Contextualization Continuum."

29    Bruce J. Nicholls, "Towards a Theology of Gospel and Culture," in *Gospel & Culture. The Papers of a Consultation on the Gospel and Culture, Convened by the Lausanne Committee's Theology and Education Group*, ed. John R. W. Stott and Robert T. Coote (Pasadena, CA: William Carey Library, 1979), 70 (emphasis mine).

30    Ibid.

31    Hesselgrave, "The Contextualization Continuum."

32    Van Engen, "Five Perspectives," 185.

33    See, for example, Andrew Walls, "The Translation Principle in Christian History," in *Bible Translation and the Spread of the Church: The Last 200 Years*, ed. Philip C. Stine (Leiden: E. J. Brill, 1990), 24-39.

34    Van Engen, "Five Perspectives," 184.

35    Paul G. Hiebert, "Critical Contextualization," *International Bulletin of Missionary Research* 11, no. 3 (1987): 111.

36    Gilliland, "Appendix: Contextualization Models," 317.

37    Charles Van Engen, "Five Perspectives," 196-201. Note that he places Hiebert's critical contextualization in this category due to its epistemological slant (201).

38    Bevans, *Models Revised*, 119.

39    Van Engen, "Five Perspectives," 197.

## Translatability

As explained previously, Van Engen proposes the *translatability* of the gospel, based in its incarnational nature (and expressed by Catholics as inculturation), be identified as another perspective. The essential thrust is oriented around the

> . . . incarnational nature of the gospel as being infinitely translatable into any and all human cultures—a faith-relationship with God that can be woven into the fabric of any and all worldviews. The gospel of Jesus Christ can be incarnated, given shape, lived out, in any cultural context—it is infinitely universalizable.[40]

Translatability is "broader, deeper and more pervasive than mere communication of a message."[41] As the gospel is planted in new soil, it takes on characteristics of the soil in ways that allow it to flourish as an indigenous plant. However the process is started (e.g., Bible translation, evangelism, church planting), it is the gospel and the church that are translated so that they have what Lamin Sanneh called "vernacular credibility."[42] Because this is interpreted as God's agenda as seen in the Incarnation, it is not amenable to human control, and the role of the contextualizer is to participate in the process rather than try to direct it.

## Praxis

Praxis (or local theologizing[43]), from the Greek word for "acts," has tended to refer to contextualization efforts to engage in social change in a local setting, and is typically framed in terms of humanization or justice. It focuses on "the impact of socio-political, economic, cultural and other forces in a context on the task of doing theology in that context"[44] and the need for "social change on behalf of (or in cooperation with) marginalized populations."[45] The most well-known praxis approaches are the varieties of liberation theologies found around the world.

Evangelicals have had mixed reactions to praxis approaches, in large measure because of concerns over 1) the way the Bible is handled by proponents; 2) context taking priority over the biblical text, and 3) the uncritical application of social scientific tools in hermeneutical methods (especially Marxist economic analysis). This model has tended to be less widely accepted as an appropriate evangelical approach than the other models by Western evangelicals,[46] though insights from advocates have been more widely accepted by evangelicals coming from or ministering in marginalized settings in the Global South.[47]

---

40 Ibid., 187

41 Ibid., 188.

42 Cited in Ibid.

43 In Ibid. Van Engen uses the term "local theologizing," more typically used by Roman Catholics; 192-196. This would fit Hesselgrave's category of Prophetic Accommodation.

44 Ibid., 192.

45 A. Scott Moreau, "Contextualization that Is Comprehensive," *Missiology* 34, no. 3 (July 2006): 328.

46 For example, David J. Hesselgrave and Edward Rommen, *Contextualization: Meanings, Methods, and Models* (Grand Rapids, MI: Baker, 1989), 150 -154.

47 See, for example, Osias Segura's chapter in this volume; Samuel Escobar's discussion on holistic mission in *The New Global Mission: The Gospel from Everywhere to Everywhere* (Downers Grove, IL: InterVarsity Press, 2004), 142-54; and many of the essays in Vinay Samuel and Chris Sugden, eds., *Sharing Jesus in the Two Thirds World* (Grand Rapids, MI: Eerdmans, 1983).

# A Schema of Evangelical Models of Contextualization

At this stage we have introduced seven labels for the variety of contextual models that are used by evangelicals: adaptation, indigenization, translation, critical contextualization, counter-cultural, translatability, and praxis. However, being drawn from a variety of authors, there is no consistent rubric to help us distinguish one label from another or place the huge variety of contextual practices used by evangelicals within this set.

In the rest of this chapter, we will outline a rubric for categorizing the models and practices, present our schema of categories of evangelical models based on the rubric, explain one model and describe ministry methods and practices that exemplify each category, and offer preliminary evaluations of the particular strengths and weaknesses of each category.

The first challenge is choosing what type of rubric to use in arranging the evangelical models into a consistent map. Given the operationalization of "evangelical" around Bebbington's and Stott's parameters, it is not surprising that the boundaries among evangelical models tend to be fuzzy rather than sharp and distinct. For example, they are largely in agreement on the norma-tive role of Scripture played in contextualization, so that will not be a helpful rubric. Further, there was no clear indication among the models that denominational or doctrinal orientation was a consistent or even a primary factor in driving the development or advocacy of particular approaches.[48]

From our review of the literature and exposure to literally hundreds of examples, it was decided that arranging them by their *flow* enabled the development of coherent and well-defined categories and avoided both the artificiality of other rubrics and the framing of the models in ways that inappropriately biases or favors their evaluation. In all, four directions of flow were identified: 1) a one-way flow, 2) a two-way flow, 3) a cyclical flow, and 4) an organic flow (or a systems approach), which can also be characterized as being simultaneous flow in multiple-directions.

Following this rubric, then, a schema of evangelical models of contextualization was developed that has four primary categories: 1) linear models, 2) dialogical models, 3) cyclical/spiral/helix models, and 4) organic models. While evangelical ministry methods and practices can often be easily placed within one of the various categories, it should be borne in mind that they are rarely specifically linked to a particular model by the practitioners themselves. Thus there is a certain fuzziness of how well the contextualized methods are connected in the minds of the practitioners to the categories in which they are placed in Tables 2 to 5. Additionally, ministry approaches may blend different types of flow in different phases, so one phase may fit the lin-ear model while a different phase may be more cyclical. Finally, the flow of the model does not limit or determine the extent of contextualization that is possible using that model. Starting from a radical set of presuppositions, for example, a linear model may go far deeper in contex-tualization than an organic model which starts from a very conservative set of presuppositions.

---

48    Because so many models were not based on and did not determine church polity or doctrine, for example, Pentecostals could just as easily use the same or similar models as dispensationalists.

In the remainder of this chapter we explain the orientation of each category, describe one substantive model and two contextual evangelical ministry practices/methods that fit the category, and offer preliminary evaluation of the strengths and weaknesses of models that fit the category.

Because of the importance evangelicals place on activism, from the many examples we could use to illustrate each category we have chosen those that concentrate on the ways evangelicals engage in evangelism, discipling, and church planting.

## Category 1: Linear Models and Methods

Linear models are characterized as following a single-direction path through a set number of steps as the process of contextualization.[49] While those who have developed linear models often recognize that the task of contextualization is never-ending, they usually either do not expand on the recursive nature of the process or—if they do—they envision each use of the process as discrete.

While the examples in Table 2 use a linear flow, the points from which they start, the steps they outline or follow, and the goals for which they aim can all differ significantly. For example, starting points have been identified as: 1) when issues arise in the culture;[50] 2) when the interpretation of Scripture is applied in the local culture;[51] 3) or when one finds an eternal truth that needs to be fitted into local cultural forms.[52] Goals can range from more effective evangelistic methods[53] to helping local churches develop better contextualized theological understandings of their particular settings.[54]

| Model | Practices and Methods |
|---|---|
| • Critical contextualization | • Guidelines for determining whether dreams are from God<br>• Camel method of evangelism and church planting |

Table 2: Linear Models, Practices and Methods[55]

---

49    See, for example, Paul Siu's chapter in this volume, which outlines a five-step process of developing a systematic theology in Asia.

50    Hiebert, "Critical Contextualization," 287-96.

51    David J. Hesselgrave and Edward Rommen, *Contextualization: Meanings, Methods, and Models* (Grand Rapids, MI: Baker, 1989); Larkin, *Culture and Biblical Hermeneutics.*

52    Wing-luk Seto, "An Asian Looks at Contextualization and Developing Ethnotheologies," *Evangelical Missions Quarterly* 23, no. 2 (April 1987): 138-141; Jason Borges, "A Muslim Theology of Jesus' Virgin Birth and His Death," *Evangelical Missions Quarterly* 41, no. 4 (October 2005): 458-463.

53    Kevin Greeson, *Camel Training Manual* (Bangalore, India: WIGTake, 2004).

54    John H. Gration, "Willowbank to Zaire: The Doing of Theology," *Missiology* 12, no. 1 (January 1984): 95-112.

55    Paul G. Hiebert, "Critical Contextualization," *Missiology* 12, no. 3 (July 1984): 287-96; Scott Breslin and Mike Jones, *Understanding Dreams from God* (Pasadena, CA: William Carey Library, 2007); Greeson, *Camel Training Manual.*

## *Linear Model: Critical Contextualization*

Paul Hiebert's *critical contextualization* is perhaps the most widely used evangelical model in academic research.[56] As noted above, "critical" refers to Hiebert's epistemological approach of critical realism. Critical contextualization involves a four-step linear process.[57]

The first step is the *exegesis of the culture* (or particular presenting issue). This may come through a crisis in the church over a particular practice or belief in the culture. Or it may come simply as a question addressed to or by the local church. It is important in this step that analysis of the cultural issue or question is done phenomenologically. A phenomenological approach has as it central ideology the suspending of any evaluation (whether the issue is right or wrong or the belief is true or false) until the issue or belief is truly understood on its own terms. It involves gathering and analyzing any and all traditional beliefs and customs associated with the question at hand without making prior judgments about their truth or their value.

In the second step, a leader or group of leaders guides the community in *exegesis of the Scriptures* related to the issue being examined. These leaders—whether indigenous or expatriate—must have a "metacultural framework that enables them to translate the biblical message into the cognitive, affective, and evaluative dimensions of another culture."[58] There are times when the Scriptures are quite clear even on particular practices found in other cultures (e.g., infanticide). More likely, however, a variety of types of scriptural evidence will be needed since the question at hand is not one directly addressed in the Bible or one in which the Bible is not as clear as some might prefer (e.g., what a polygamous convert should do). The goal in this step is not to find a single passage or teaching as a type of "magic bullet," that completely answers the question, though that may occur. Rather, it is to look at the whole of biblical evidence to uncover God's attitude towards the practice or question at hand.

The third step is a *community-wide critical evaluation of cultural practice in light of Scripture* together with a decision on how to respond. In this step, Hiebert identifies three possible responses: the community may 1) keep old ways which are not unbiblical, 2) reject old ways which are unbiblical, or 3) modify the old ways to make them biblically acceptable. He further identifies at least four options if they choose to modify the old ways: they may a) keep the form of the old ways but give new meanings to them (e.g., the Christmas tree),  b) substitute new symbols/rites to replace the old ones (e.g., building a church where an idol was worshipped), c) adopt new rites drawn from Christian heritage (e.g., worshipping together on Sundays), or d)

---

56    Darrell L. Whiteman, "Anthropological Reflections on Contextualizing Theology in a Globalizing World," in *Globalizing Theology: Belief and Practice in an Era of World Christianity*, eds. Craig Ott and Harold Netland (Grand Rapids, MI: Baker, 2006), 57.

57    Hiebert, "Critical Contextualization," (1987); see also R. Daniel Shaw, "Contextualizing the Power and the Glory," *International Journal of Frontier Missions* 12, no. 3 (July-September 1999): 155-60; and Paul G. Hiebert, "Cultural Differences and the Communication of the Gospel," in *Perspectives on the World Christian Movement*, eds. Ralph D. Winter and Steven C. Hawthorne (Pasadena, CA: William Carey Library, 1999), 381-82.

58    Hiebert, "Critical Contextualization," (1987): 109.

develop new symbols or rituals that still feel and look indigenous to their culture (e.g., developing something like a Christian ashram[59] or a messianic synagogue[60]).

The fourth and final step is for *the community to arrange any new practices into a contextualized ritual* that expresses the Christian meaning of the event, thus (when appropriate) enabling a transformation through attaching new meanings to indigenous forms. While a linear process, Hiebert notes that these four steps are to be repeated as necessary; critical contextualization is "an ongoing process in which the church must constantly engage itself."[61]

## Linear Ministry Methods

Of the many contextualized methods we could have used to illustrate linear approaches, we have chosen two contextualized evangelistic methods developed in Muslim settings. The first was developed as a response to a continual stream of questions from Muslims on how to understand dreams they had. The second was developed indigenously by Muslims who had come to faith in Christ and wanted to reach their own people with the good news. Neither has an explicit connection to Hiebert or any other theoretical model, a reminder that many of the methods for contextualization practiced by evangelical are not tethered to approaches developed by other evangelicals.

### Guidelines for Determining Whether Dreams Are from God

Scott Breslin and Mike Jones originally developed the method explained in *Understanding Dreams from God* as an evangelism tool for use among Muslims in the Middle Eastern country where they serve. Over the course of more than a decade, Muslims approached them on a regular basis asking for help in understanding the dreams they had. Recognizing that theirs was not an isolated experience, they decided one way to help their Muslim inquirers sort through the issues was to write a book that would respond to their questions and could be used in leading people to a relationship with Christ.[62] Originally written in a local language, throughout the English version they use Islamic vocabulary for parts of the Old and New Testaments so that the English reader can bear in mind the originally intended audience of a Muslim questioner who would be confused by unfamiliar Christian terms.

Starting with the assertion that God speaks to people through dreams today, Breslin and Jones offer four possible reasons for such dreams based on Job 33:14-18: God gives us dreams to keep the dreamer 1) from doing wrong; 2) from pride; 3) from the pit; and 4) from perishing. They chose the Job passage as their starting point because it is less controversial to a Muslim audience than other passages. However, they use biblical case studies for each of these reasons to connect the dreamer to Old and New Testament events.

---

59    Helen Ralston, *Christian Ashrams: A New Religious Movement in Contemporary India* (Lewiston, NY: Edwin Mellen, 1987).

60    Phil Goble, *Everything You Need to Grow a Messianic Synagogue* (Pasadena, CA: William Carey Library, 1974); idem, "Reaching Jews through Messianic Synagogues;" Faña Spielberg and Stuart Dauermann, "Contextualization: Witness and Reflection Messianic Jews as a Case," *Missiology* 25, no. 1 (January 1997): 15-35.

61    Ibid., 111.

62    Breslin and Jones, Understanding Dreams from God, 5-6.

Having explained the possible reasons that God gives dreams to people today, they turn to advise the Muslim dreamer how he or she can know if a dream is from God. To do this, they establish a set of guidelines followed by a four-step process the dreamer can follow to determine the source of their dream.

The primary focus of the guidelines is to establish possible sources for the dream, since not all dreams are from God. They explain—with illustrations and discussion—that dreams can also result from anxiety, chemical imbalances, and from evil spirits. While the last point would need far more explanation in a Western setting, it fits well within the Muslim worldview.

With the possible sources of dreams established, the dreamer is offered four steps to follow that will help them understand their dream. First, he or she needs to confirm that the dream does not conflict with the teachings of the Scriptures. Second, the Muslim dreamer should consult with those who love and follow Jesus about the dream to see how they understand it. The third step, assuming the dream is from God, is to discern the reason for the dream, using the four options from Job 33:14-18 outlined above. The final step is to resolve to obey the leading of God as seen in the dream. In their concluding chapter, they challenge the dreamer to make a commitment to Christ based on what they have learned.

### *The Camel Method of Evangelism and Church Planting*

The Camel method, originally developed by Muslims who had come to Christ, integrates evangelism and church planting. Kevin Greeson was invited to observe the resulting movement of churches that had been planted. Prior to this, Greeson's team of missionaries had gathered twenty-three Muslims to make baskets for export, but with no conversions. Drawing on his observations of the methods of the indigenous movement, he and a team of others put the method into practice, inviting the husbands of the basket-makers to a meeting and using the evangelism component of the Camel method (see below). During the next four and one-half years they saw over 15,000 Muslims baptized and the planting of more than 800 churches.[63] According to David Garrison, altogether the Camel method has been used to lead more than a quarter of a million Muslims to a living relationship with Christ.[64]

The *evangelism* component of the Camel method uses three steps with a focus of finding a person of peace. It is framed to start with the Koran, which Muslims know, and lead them to the Bible, which they do not know. The first step is to arouse curiosity. This can be done through a question such as "I have discovered an amazing truth in the Koran that gives hope of eternal life in heaven. Would you like to read Surah Al-Imram 3:42-55 so we can talk about it?"[65] Alternately, this may be accomplished by introducing the old Muslim cultural tradition that there are actually one-hundred names of God, not just the ninety-nine that all Muslims know. According to the tradition, only the camel knows the one-hundredth, and the camel is not talking![66]

---

63  Kevin Greeson, *Camel Training Manual* (Bangalore: WIGTake Resourses, 2004), 3.
64  David Garrison, "Preface," in *Camel Training Manual* (Bangalore: WIGTake Resources, 2004), i-ii.
65  Greeson, *Camel Training Manual*, 56-57.
66  Thus, while the evangelist is free to choose among methods, this is still the first step in the process.

For those who want to learn about hope of eternal life or who are curious about the one-hundredth name of God, the second step is to use Surah Al-Imram 3:42-55 to demonstrate that Jesus is more than a "Prophet"—he is in reality 'Isa Masi (Jesus the Messiah). CAMEL is now used as an acronym for the key points from the passage: Mary was Chosen to give birth to 'Isa (Jesus); Angels announced the good news to her; 'Isa would do Miracles; he is the way to Eternal Life. The main focus in evangelism is to enable the Muslim to see that the Koran teaches that 'Isa is holy; has power over death, and knows the way to heaven.[67]

The purpose of the second step is to identify whether the listener is a "person of peace" who is interested in further exploring the implications of the ideas presented. If he or she is, then the third step is to bridge to the Bible for an explanation of Christ and give the person of peace an opportunity to respond. This step can take weeks to months to complete.

Once a person comes to Christ, the next stage involves training the new believers in evangelism and sending them to witness to family members and incorporating them into a fellowship of like-minded believers. In the original movement which developed the method, the believers referred to themselves as Isahi Muslims ("followers of Jesus" Muslims), which was seen as appropriate within their culture and aroused further curiosity among their families, leading to opportunities for witness.[68] As the new believers now begin to look for other persons of peace (starting with their own family members) and the gospel spreads along extended family lines, a church planting movement that is separate from the known local "Christian" community— and from their stigma as "Christians"[69]—is developed. While almost all of the new believers still initially experience persecution, the gospel has spread so fast that severe persecution is not seen as frequently.[70]

## Strengths and Weaknesses of Linear Models and Methods

In evaluating linear methods, it should be kept in mind that it is the type of flow that is consistent within the models and methods, not the starting point, the actual steps, or the goal.

One of the greatest strengths of a linear flow in contextualized models and methods is that it is the easiest for practitioners to implement. Through the step-by-step approach, implementers are encouraged by seeing progress being made. Linear approaches also make it easier to keep the larger picture in mind as the issues are worked through, and easier to keep on track towards the final goals.

Perhaps the greatest weakness is that linear models can give the illusion that contextualization for a particular problem or issue is done once and the task is then complete. If that illusion is allowed to control the process, the decisions made can become static and calcified. More problematic, however, is that linear models are not as useful in handling multi-cultural environments, keeping up in times of social change, or working out contextual solutions to complex

---

67  Ibid., 58-60.

68  Ibid., 11.

69  Bear in mind that in many Muslim settings, "Christians" are equivalent to "Westerners" and seen as immoral and secular. Even where there are known Christian communities, they do not always have a good reputation among local Muslims.

70  Ibid., 15.

issues such as systemic social injustice. Perhaps most problematic for the linear approach is that it is too easy for one voice or perspective to dominate. All too frequently this is the outsider or "expert" voice, who then controls the process, stifling local initiative.

# Category 2: Dialogical Models and Methods

Dialogical models emphasize the nature of contextualization as a dialogue or conversation among culture, Bible, and contextualizer.[71] While not all use the term "dialogue,"[72] it is still the most popular descriptor. Among evangelicals it is not used to imply an equal partnership, nor a dialectical process. Rather, for evangelical dialogical models, the Bible is the normative pole[73] in the dialogue and the term refers to the process of each bringing questions to the other.

| Model | Practices and Methods |
| --- | --- |
| • Relational center contextualization | • Nurturing Insider Movements <br> • New Song Workshops |

Table 3: Dialogical Models, Practices and Methods[74]

## Dialogical Model: Relational Center Contextualization

One of the early examples of dialogical contextualization is Bruce Nicholls' relational center approach. As illustrated in Figure 1, Nicholls proposes four sets of simultaneous two-way dialogue anchored around an orienting center of the Christ of the Scriptures. While the dialogue process is that of the interpreter simultaneously engaging in dialogue with God, the Bible (text), the church and the local context, it is Christ that serves as the anchor for the dialogue. Thus, in Figure 1 Nicholls places "Christ of Scriptures" at the center rather than the interpreter.

---

71    See, e.g., Rodrigo D. Tano, "Towards an Evangelical Asian Theology," in *The Bible and Theology in Asian Contexts: An Evangelical Perspective on Asian Theology*, eds. Bong Rin Ro and Ruth Eshenaur (Taiching, Taiwan: Asia Theological Association 1984), 94; Darrell L. Whiteman, "Contextualization: The Theory, the Gap, the Challenge," *International Bulletin of Missionary Research* 21, no. 1 (January 1997): 2-7.

72    For example, see Kirsteen Kim, "Missiology as Global Conversation of (Contextual) Theologies," *Mission Studies* 21, no. 1 (2004): 48-49.

73    For example, see Paul D. Feinberg, "An Evangelical Approach to Contextualization of Theology," *Trinity World Forum* 7, no.3 (Spring 1982): 7; Grenz, *Revisioning Evangelical Theology*, 90.

74    Nicholls, *Contextualization*; and idem., "Hermeneutics, Theology, and Culture with Special Reference to Hindu Culture," in *The Bible and Theology in Asian Contexts: An Evangelical Perspective on Asian Theology*, eds. Bong Rin Ro and Ruth Eshenaur (Taiching, Taiwan: Asia Theological Association, 1984), 256-61; See, for example, John Travis, "Messianic Muslim Followers of Isa: A Closer Look at C5 Believers and Congregations," *International Journal of Frontier Missions* 19, no. 1 (Spring 2000): 53-59; Roberta A. King, "Singing the Lord's Song in a Global World: The Dynamics of Doing Critical Contextualization Through Music," *Evangelical Missions Quarterly* 42, no. 1 (January 2006): 68-74.

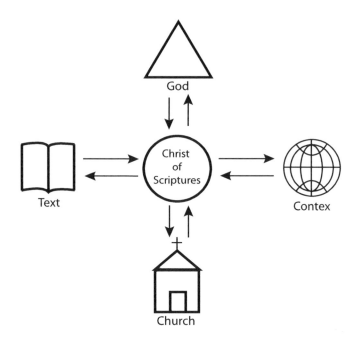

Figure 1: Relational Center Contextualization[75]

The first area of dialogue is the interpreter with God. This involves having a right relationship with him and in which God is the initiator and the interpreter is the respondent. In terms of dialogue, it involves both the interpreter bringing petitions to God and God speaking to the interpreter (primarily through his Word).

The second area is a dialogue of the interpreter with the text of the Bible, which involves uncovering the interpreter's own pre-understandings and how they influence her or his approach to the text, the skilled use of biblical scholarship, and letting the text speak to the interpreter through meditation.

The third area of dialogue is that of the interpreter with the people of God—the church. This includes the historical church traditions (what have previous interpreters said about this concern?), contemporary traditions in other cultures (what do my sisters and brothers around the world today say about this concern?), and the understanding of the local people of God (what does my pastor and the ordinary family in the congregation say about this concern?).

The final area of dialogue is the interpreter with the world. "The meaning of the text has to be translated for today in the context of our commitment to God's mission in the world. . . . Such a dialogue involves withdrawal through critical study and identification with the sufferings of the world."[76]

---

75    Nicholls, "Hermeneutics, Theology, and Culture," 257.

76    Ibid., 259.

## Dialogical Ministry Methods

To illustrate dialogical ministry methods we have chosen two examples that focus on how to form a community of Christ-followers with as little dislocation as possible. One method focuses on the socio-cultural side, while the other focuses on using local music. Both have been developed with an incarnational principle in mind that will enable those who come to Christ to remain "at home" in their cultural settings as they gather together into fellowships.

### Nurturing Insider Movements

In 1973, Charles Kraft wrote about "the possibility of 'Muslim Christians' or 'Christian Muslims' to signify those who, while committing themselves to God through Christ simply remain culturally Muslim (as an American remains culturally American)."[77] Over the past several decades this has developed into the idea of insider movements, which has been defined[78] as:

"... any movement to faith in Christ where (a) the gospel flows through pre-existing communities and social networks and where (b) believing families, as valid expressions of the Body of Christ, remain inside their socio-religious communities, retaining their identity as members of that community while living under the Lordship of Jesus Christ and the authority of the Bible."[79]

Insiders in Muslim settings often choose to avoid referring to themselves as "Christians" because of the highly negative connotations of the term in their societies.[80] Instead, a variety of alternate terms have been coined. In addition to the most commonly used "Muslim Background Believers" (MBB), alternate terms include "Muslim Culture Believers," "new creation Muslims,"[81] "Messianic Muslims,"[82] "Messianic Cultural Muslims,"[83] and "Biblical Muslims."[84]

---

77    Charles H. Kraft, "Toward a Christian Ethnotheology," in *God, Man and Church Growth: A Festschrift in Honor of Donald Anderson McGavran*, ed. Alan R. Tippett (Grand Rapids, MI: Eerdmans, 1973), 119.

78    See the discussions from various people in "An Extended Discussion about 'Insider Movements:' Responses to the September-October 2005 *Mission Frontiers*," *Mission Frontiers* (January-February 2006): 16-23; Rick Brown, "Brother Jacob and Master Isaac: How One Insider Movement Began," *International Journal of Frontier Missions* 24, no. 1 (Spring 2007): 41-42.

79    Rebecca Lewis, "Insider Movement: The Conversation Continues: Promoting Movement to Christ within Natural Communities," *International Journal of Frontier Missions* 24, no. 2 (Summer 2007): 75-76.

80    See discussion in Rick Brown, "Biblical Muslims," *International Journal of Frontier Missiology* 24, no. 2 (Summer 2007): 68. For similar concerns in Hindu settings, see Herb Hoefer, "What's in a Name? The Baggage of Terminology in Contemporary Mission," *International Journal of Frontier Missiology* 25, no. 1 (Spring 2008): 25-29.

81    Mike Brislen, "A Model for a Muslim-Culture Church," *Missiology* 24, no. 3 (October 1996): 355-367.

82    John Travis, "Messianic Muslim Followers of Isa: A Closer Look at C5 Believers and Congregations," *International Journal of Frontier Missions* 19, no. 1 (Spring 2000): 53-59.

83    Rick Brown, "Contextualization without Syncretism," *International Journal of Frontier Missiology* 23, no. 3 (Fall 2006): 127-33.

84    Brown, "Biblical Muslims," 65-74; other terms found "Believers of Muslim Background," "Christians of Muslim Background" and a more controversial "Muslim Believers."

The biblical orientation for this method of ministry is typically established on case studies from the Jerusalem Council (Acts 15)[85] and most notably Paul's teaching for those who come to Christ to remain as they are (1 Cor. 7:17-24).[86]

Fewer ministry models are drawing more attention—including controversy[87]—among evangelicals than that of nurturing insider movements,[88] and perhaps the biggest challenge leveled at advocates is the extent to which followers of Christ remaining in their former *religious* contexts is biblically viable.[89] To cultural outsiders, insiders look like Muslims in dress, language, and even religious rituals. Those who seek to facilitate insider movements point out that their goal is to ensure that the insiders' allegiance is to Christ within the context of their cultural constraints.[90]

While there is no single method of nurturing an insider movement, the general approach follows a dialogical flow of at least four partners: 1) *practitioners* empower 2) *insiders* to make wise decisions about how to build viable fellowships of believers from within their socio-cultural contexts as they study 3) *the Word of God* and follow the leading of 4) *the Holy Spirit*.

*New Song Workshops*

While the idea of utilizing indigenous hymnody for Christian nurture can be seen as early as 1964, [91] contextualizing music and worship did not gain traction among evangelical missionaries until the 1990s.[92] Since then the establishment of formal positions in ethnomusicology in agencies like Wycliffe as well as the founding of groups such as the International Council of Ethnodoxologists (www.worldofworship.org) have given even greater visibility to the urgent need of missionaries to facilitate the development of indigenous music and worship forms.

---

85    John Ridgway, "Insider Movements in the Gospels and Acts," *International Journal of Frontier Missiology* 24, no. 2 (Fall 2007): 77-86.

86    Whether this is an appropriate use of Paul's statements is strongly debated; see, for example, Basil Grafas, "Insider Movements: An Evangelical Assessment," *InVision* (August 2006) [article on-line] accessed 19 January 2009; available from http://www.mtw.org/home/site/templates/mtw_invision.asp?_resolutionfile=templatespath. mtw.itw_invision.asp&area_2=public/Resources/Invision/2006/08/InsiderMovements.

87    For example, Parshall, "Danger! New Directions in Contextualization;" Schlorff, "The Translational Model for Mission," idem, *Missiological Models in Ministry to Muslims* (Upper Darby, PA: Middle East Resources, 2006); Mark S. Williams, "Aspects of High-Spectrum Contextualization in Ministries to Muslims," *Journal of Asian Mission* 5, no. 1 (2003): 75-91; Corwin, "A Second Look: Insider Movements and Outsider Missiology," idem, "A Humble Appeal," idem, "A Response to My Respondents," *International Journal of Frontier Missions* 24, no. 2 (Summer 2997): 53-55; Tennent, "Followers of Jesus (Isa) in Islamic Mosques."

88    See the array of thinking and practice in J. Dudley Woodberry, ed., *From Seed to Fruit: Global Trends, Fruitful Practices, and Emerging Issues among Muslims* (Pasadena, CA: William Carey Library, 2008).

89    Note especially Corwin's comments in "An Extended Discussion," 17-20.

90    Higgins, "Identity, Integrity and Insider Movements;" idem, "Acts 15 and Insider Movements among Muslims: Questions, Process and Conclusions," *International Journal of Frontier Missions* 24, no. 1 (Spring 2007): 29-40.

91    For example, Elaine T. Lewis, James M. Riccitelli, and William A. Smalley, "Practical Problems: More about Developing Non-Western Hymnody," *Practical Anthropology* 11, no. 1 (January 1964): 35-46.

92    See, e.g., K. Gordon Molyneux, "The Place and Function of Hymns in the EJCSK (Eglise de Jésus-Christ sur terre par le Prophète Simon Kimbangu)," *Journal of Religion in Africa* 20, no. 2 (June 1990): 153-187; idem, *African Christian Theology: The Quest for Selfhood* (San Francisco: Mellen Research University Press, 1993); Mary Anne Isaak, "Zairian Theology in Four-Part Harmony," *Direction* 22, no. 2 (Fall 2003): 39-50. (accessed 12 November 2008); available from http://www.directionjournal.org/article/?802.

Our ministry method comes from WorldVenture missionary Roberta King, who enables the development of ethnomusicology and ethnodoxology through New Song workshops.[93] In the workshops, Christians are shown how to develop their own Christian music so as to transform scriptural truths into distinctly indigenous songs that enable those who sing them to develop a deep connection with God's word.[94]

While built with reference to Hiebert's linear critical contextualization, the workshops are themselves dialogical. The participants are taught to weave the traditional scales and indigenous tunes together with the Word of God to create new songs. It is easy to see the dialogical process from King's description of a workshop among the Senufo:

> Group discussions and compositions in each vernacular soon occurred. The groups then sang their new songs for one another. The songs would often come slowly and tentatively at first and then accelerate in a fashion reminiscent of popcorn! As we "harvested" the songs each day, people responded spontaneously to the textually and musically-authentic Senufo pieces. Many would rise up and dance with joyful abandon. They began to understand the significance of God's word within their own setting and further developed the songs by reflecting on the Scripture passages.[95]

A significant goal of these workshops is to empower indigenous song-writers to develop musically indigenous hymns that honor God in ways that make sense to the local people. The development, acceptance and dissemination of such hymns involve dialogical processes that include the artist, the local Christian community, and their understanding of the Bible in a three-way conversation that allows them to express who they are in ways that glorify their Creator.

## Strengths and Weaknesses of Dialogical Models

As with the evaluation of the linear models, we remind the reader that our focus is on the strengths and weaknesses of the dialogical flow rather than the actual content of models that use this flow.

An important strength of the dialogical methods is that they—more readily than linear ones—can ensure that everyone in the process is given a voice and that everyone else is actually listening. When carried out properly, each component (or representative) has a role to play in the contextualization process. With more people having a voice, a dialogical flow to contextualizing makes it more likely that issues of concern to everyone can be given due consideration.

One area of concern for this flow is that in multi-cultural settings—where there will be multiple voices rather than just two or three—the voices of minorities within the church may be stifled. Further, the dialogical process is more likely to generate conflict than a linear process. Finding ways to handle such conflict or (even worse) church splits will be a necessary part of the process. Finally, it is not always clear to the outsider just how the underlying cultural values (such as individualism and collectivism, use of social power, gender role separation and so

---

93 King, "Singing the Lord's Song in a Global World," 68-74.
94 Ibid., 70.
95 Ibid., 70-71.

on) will or even should shape the process of dialogue in the local Christian community. If the interpreter has one set of values about how dialogue should proceed, but the local community has a differing set of values, the dialogue "medium" can become the "message" that is conveyed, however unintentionally.

# Category 3: Cyclical Models and Methods

Cyclical approaches are a natural extension of dialogue approaches. Those who utilize them recognize that contextualization is not a one-time process, and that it will never really be complete. Building on insights of the hermeneutical circle (or spiral) developed by liberation theologian Juan Luis Segundo,[96] models built on a cyclical flow[97] envision that the process results in an ever-tightening spiral that intertwines our experience of life, the text of Scripture, new ways to see Scripture in light of life experiences, and new approaches to experiencing life.

| Model | Practices and Methods |
|---|---|
| • Hermeneutical circle | • Dynamic-equivalence "churchness" <br> • Pauline church planting cycle |

Table 4: Cyclical (Spiral/Helix) Models, Practices and Methods[98]

## *Cyclical Model: The Hermeneutical Spiral*

Rene Padilla was among the first evangelicals to formally propose using the hermeneutical spiral as a means of contextualizing. He posits four interrelated elements that are part of the interpretive process: 1) the world and life views of the interpreter, 2) historical settings, 3) theology, and 4) Scripture. All of these work together in a mutual feedback system such that a change in any one area affects all four of them (see Figure 2).[99] Interpretation is not a static, once-for-all delivered process, but a dynamic one that is ever-spiraling closer to Scripture. Our understanding of Scripture and our context is never adequate unless they are both feeding into each other and thereby mutually correcting each other. As Padilla notes,

> Hermeneutics may thus be conceived as having a spiral structure in which a richer and deeper understanding of the Bible leads to a greater understanding of the historical context, and a deeper and richer understanding of the historical context leads to

96    Juan Luis Segundo, *Liberation of Theology* (Maryknoll, NY: Orbis, 1976).

97    See, for example, Segura's chapter in this volume, which frames theological development as an ongoing dialogue between text and context. It is his explicit acknowledgement that theology is always in construction as an ongoing process that makes his model cyclical.

98    C. Rene Padilla, "The Contextualization of the Gospel," in *Readings in Dynamic Indigeneity*, eds. Charles H. Kraft and Tom N. Wisely (Pasadena, CA: William Carey Library, 1979), 286-312; Kraft, *Christianity in Culture*, 247-56; David J. Hesselgrave, *Planting Churches Cross-Culturally: North America and Beyond*, Second Edition (Grand Rapids, MI: Baker, 2000).

99    C. Rene Padilla, "Hermeneutics and Culture: A Theological Perspective," in *Gospel & Culture: The Papers of a Consultation on the Gospel and Culture*, convened by the Lausanne Committee's Theology and Education Group, eds. John R. W. Stott and Robert T. Coote (Pasadena, CA: William Carey Library, 1979), 98.

a greater comprehension of the biblical message from within the concrete situation, through the work of the Holy Spirit.[100]

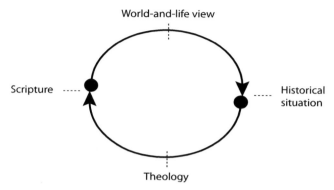

Figure 2: Padilla's Hermeneutical Spiral[101]

## Cyclical Ministry Practices

For our ministry methods we have chosen two approaches to contextualized church planting and development. One is framed in light of the idea that the *impact* of church forms and structures of today should be equivalent to the impact of the church forms and structures in the New Testament. The other takes Paul as an archetype of church planting and builds a cycle of the process based on observations of Paul's ministry as seen in Acts. Both have been widely used in evangelical circles as appropriate models of contextualized church planting.

### Dynamic Equivalence "Churchness"

The term "dynamic equivalence" was initially developed in linguistic theory for use in translation by missionary linguist Eugene Nida.[102] Kraft utilized the basic concept and developed it into a contextualization approach having as its goal "to see expressed in the lives of the receptors the meanings taught in Scripture."[103]

The *dynamic* component of dynamic equivalence frames Kraft's approach to contextualization as an ever-changing process.[104] The *equivalence* component of dynamic equivalence is focused on *receptor impact* rather than information transfer, and thus on methods that will enable people to be impacted with the significance of Christ the way people were in New Testament times.[105] Kraft proposes that all cultures are "adequate and equal in potential usefulness as vehicles of God's interaction with humanity,"[106] so that we focus on methods that will en-

---

100   Ibid., 102.

101   Ibid., 99.

102   Eric M. North, "Eugene A. Nida: An Appreciation," in *On Language, Culture and Religion: In Honor of Eugene A. Nida*, eds. Matthew Black and William A. Smalley (The Hague: Mouton, 1974), xii.

103   Charles H. Kraft, "Meaning Equivalence Contextualization," in *Appropriate Christianity*, ed. Charles Kraft (Pasadena, CA: William Carey Library, 2005), 168.

104   Adapted from Charles H. Kraft, *Christianity in Culture: A Study in Dynamic Biblical Theologizing in Cross-Cultural Perspective*. 25th Anniversary Edition (Maryknoll, NY: Orbis, 2005).

105   Adapted from ibid.

106   Ibid., 43.

able people to be impacted with the significance of Christ and align their allegiance with God through a minimum of worldview shift. While widely utilized, the value and hazards of Kraft's dynamic equivalence approach to contextualization have been debated strongly in evangelical circles.[107]

Kraft proposed that we plant dynamic equivalent churches. As he envisions it, a dynamic equivalent church

> . . . (1) conveys to its members truly Christian meanings, (2) functions within its own society in the name of Christ, meeting the felt needs of that society and producing within it the same Christian impact as the first century Church in its day, and (3) is couched in cultural forms that are as nearly indigenous as possible.[108]

The process of developing dynamic equivalence churchness is a five-step process, with the last three steps being repeated cyclically. As Figure 3 illustrates, the process involves two phases. In the first phase, we 1) decode those functions of the church which are 2) essential through proper study of the Bible, ensuring we bring all of the tools we have to the task, including those of the social sciences as well as those of theology. Only then are we ready to move into the second phase, in which we 3) analyze the forms in the new culture which can be 4) utilized and transformed to serve similar functions that will 5) have the same impact in the new culture as the church did on its culture in New Testament times. Steps 3 through 5 are then cyclically repeated, especially as the culture in which the dynamic-equivalent church is planted is undergoes change.

---

107   See, for example, Donald A. Carson, "The Limits of Dynamic Equivalency in Bible Translation," *Evangelical Review of Theology* 9, no. 3 (1985): 202-205; David Hesselgrave, *Paradigms in Conflict: 10 Key Questions in Christian Missions Today* (Grand Rapids, MI: Kregel, 2005), 243-77; idem, "Syncretism: Mission and Missionary Induced?" in *Contextualization and Syncretism: Navigating Cultural Currents* ed. Gailyn Van Rheenen (Pasadena, CA: William Carey Library, 2006), 82-83; and Grant Osborne, *The Hermeneutical Spiral: A Comprehensive Introduction to Biblical Interpretation* (Downers Grove, IL: InterVarsity, 1991), 319-23.

108   Charles H. Kraft, "Dynamic Equivalence Churches," *Missiology* 1, no. 1 (January 1973): 40; see also idem, "The Church in Culture: A Dynamic Equivalence Model," in *Gospel & Culture. The Papers of a Consultation on the Gospel and Culture, Convened by the Lausanne Committee's Theology and Education Group*, eds. John R. W. Stott and Robert T. Coote (Pasadena, CA: William Carey Library, 1979), 295-97.

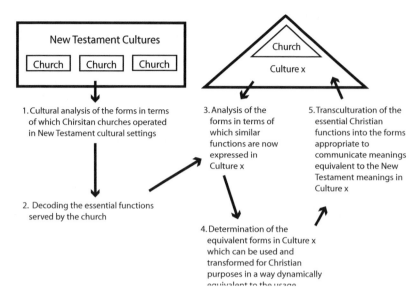

Figure 3: The Process of Developing a Dynamic -Equivalent Church[109]

*Pauline Church Planting Cycle*
David Hesselgrave examined Paul's church planting cycle as seen in Acts and developed a ten-step process for church planting (Figure 4). As he traces the process throughout Acts, he starts with the commissioning of missionaries, cycles through the ten steps outlined in Figure 4, and the cycle restarts with the commissioning of new missionaries from the churches that had been planted in the first cycle.

According to Hesselgrave, while this church planting method has a beginning and an end, it is cyclical, and so will continue until the Lord returns. It is a process in which the planter can proceed through step-by-step as well as work on all steps simultaneously. It is intended to apply to a church in any stage of its existence as well as to pioneer situations.[110]

---

109  Kraft, *Christianity in Culture*, 255.
110  Ibid., 49-51.

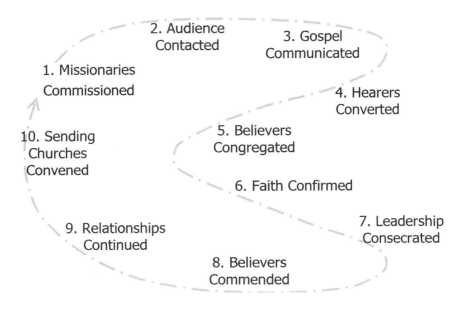

Figure 4: Pauline Church Planting Cycle[111]

## Strengths and Weaknesses of Cyclical Models

We can identify several strengths and weakness of contextualization built on a cyclical approach. The first strength is their emphasis on the never-ending nature of the contextualization process. Peoples and cultures are ever changing, and cyclical models account for that reality. Second, they also help to ensure that all sides are given appropriate consideration. The intertwining of context and text (and interpreter and receptor) ensures that each is given due attention in turn. Finally, cyclical models are more able to provide space for issues of social justice (even though this can still be ignored[112]).

On the other hand, a potential weakness of cyclical models is that those engaged in the cycle may not always be able to distinguish whether in reality they are spiraling *in* or *out* (closer to appropriate contextualization or further away). In addition, the complexity of some models hinders practitioners from keeping the big picture in mind.[113] Finally, enabling the necessary transition from the first generation to the next generation—and giving the next generation freedom to make the process their own or even start the process anew—can give rise to friction between generations.

# Category 4: Organic Models and Methods

Proponents of the most elastic evangelical contextual models do not focus on outlining sets of steps to follow as much as they build flexible orientations for approaching contextualization

---

111    Adapted from Hesselgrave, *Planting Churches Cross-Culturally*, 47.

112    For example, Hesselgrave's *Pauline church planting cycle* does not address issues of social justice at all.

113    See, for example, Charles Van Engen, "Toward a Contextually Appropriate Methodology in Mission Theology," in *Appropriate Christianity*, ed. Charles Kraft (Pasadena, CA: William Carey Library, 2005), 203-226.

in a variety of contexts. From narrative[114] and case study[115] approaches to metaphors[116] and comprehensive[117] models, organic approaches establish principles of map reading rather than charting out directions from one point to the next. For example, metaphoric approaches propose a root metaphor to guide us in understanding contextualization without constraining us to a particular method: contextualization is a *river* that we navigate,[118] a *living tree* to which we can emotionally connect,[119] *wisdom* in which we grow,[120] or a *theodrama* in which we improvise through life by being faithful to the divine drama of the Bible.[121]

| Models | Practices and Methods |
|---|---|
| • Theodrama | • Narrative evangelism: the travel guide<br>• Church planting movements |

Table 5: Organic Models, Practices and Methods[122]

## Organic Models

We have chosen as our example a metaphoric frame that focuses on the living nature of theological reflection and development.

### *Theodrama*

Kevin Vanhoozer is the primary architect of the "theodramatic" approach to contextualizing theology in the midst of everyday life. A theodramatic orientation "views the gospel as essentially dramatic, the Bible as a script, doctrine as theatrical direction, and the church as part of

---

114 Karl Franklin, "Re-Thinking Stories," *International Journal of Frontier Missions* 22, no. 1 (Spring 2005): 6-12.

115 Paul Fritz, "Contextualizing the Message Through Use of Case Studies," *International Journal of Frontier Missions* 12, no. 3 (July-September 1995): 147-52.

116 Daniel A. Rodriguez, "No Longer Foreigners and Aliens: Toward a Missiological Christology for Hispanics in the United States," *Missiology* 31, no. 1 (January 2003): 51-67; Natee Tanchanpong's approach to understanding syncretism in this book is an organic model using the metaphors of cuisine and cruising.

117 Moreau, "Contextualization: From an Adapted Message to an Adapted Life."

118 Bruce J. Nicholls, "Contextualisation in Chinese Culture," *Evangelical Review of Theology* 19, no. 4 (1995): 368-380.

119 Sunil H. Stephens, "Doing Theology in a Hindu Context," *Journal of Asian Mission* 1, no. 2 (September 1999): 181-203.

120 Harley Talman, "Comprehensive Contextualization," *International Journal of Frontier Missions* 21, no. 1 (Spring 2004): 10; Adeney, *Strange Virtues*, 54-78.

121 Kevin J. Vanhoozer, *The Drama of Doctrine: A Canonical-Linguistic Approach to Christian Theology* (Louisville: John Knox, 2005); idem, "'One Rule to Rule Them All?' Theological Method in an Era of World Christianity," in *Globalizing Theology: Belief and Practice in an Era of World Christianity*, eds. Craig Ott and Harold Netland (Grand Rapids, MI: Baker, 2006), 85-126.

122 Ibid.; Rick Richardson, *Reimagining Evangelism: Inviting Friends on a Spiritual Journey* (Downers Grove, IL: InterVarsity Press, 2006); see also Tom A. Steffen, "Reaching 'Resistant' People through Intentional Narrative," *Missiology* 28, no. 4 (October 2000): 471-486; Jeff Morton, "Narratives and Questions: Exploring the Scriptures with Muslims," *Evangelical Missions Quarterly* 40, no. 2 (April, 2004): 172-176; Garrison, *Church Planting Movements*, idem, "Church Planting Movements vs Insider Movements: Missiological Realities vs Mythological Speculations," *International Journal of Frontier Missions* 21, no. 4 (October-December 2004): 151-154; idem, "Church Planting Movements: The Next Wave?" *International Journal of Frontier Missions* 21, no. 3 (July-September 2004): 118-121.

the ongoing performance of salvation."[123] Because God is a missionary God, "the whole theo-drama is essentially missional, consisting in a series of historical entrances and exoduses (e.g., incarnation, crucifixion, resurrection, ascension, Pentecost)."[124] In this orientation, theology is "faith seeking theodramatic understanding,"[125] and "all other truths must be engrafted into and encompassed by the drama of Jesus Christ."[126]

Theodrama is founded on what Vanhoozer calls the *canonic principle*: "the Spirit speaking *in Scripture* about what God was/is doing is the supreme rule for Christian faith, life and understanding."[127] While the canonic principle is the overarching frame, three other principles are also integrated in the theodramatic approach:

- The *contextual* principle, which recognizes that the people of God engage Scripture in and from their particular locations.
- The *critical* principle, namely that the Bible can be interpreted in ways that address situational injustice.
- The *cultural* principle, which recognizes that we can forge theology out of indigenous materials.[128]

Life is seen not just as drama, but as a *theo*drama in which Christians are to improvise ways of living and acting that are congruent with God's character as revealed in the Bible and centered on God's work for the world through Jesus Christ. We are not to slavishly or literalistically follow some divinely ordained script, but to improvise as led by the Spirit in ways that conform to God's revealed will. Thus, the actual drama will change from setting to setting following the principles noted above. The ultimate goal of doctrinal framing and living is not developing universal statements of truth but rather faithful improvisation of the script in every local setting. The principles guide the process, but do not determine a specific set of steps or a static method for faithful improvisation.

## Organic Ministry Practices

The very flexibility of organic ministry methods makes them the hardest to describe. Even when they have an orienting method—such as narrative—how that method is implemented is fluid and ever-changing. The two practices we have chosen to describe focus on evangelism and church planting.

---

123 Vanhoozer, "'One Rule to Rule Them All?'" 109.
124 Ibid., 110.
125 Ibid., 109.
126 Ibid., 110.
127 Ibid., emphasis mine.
128 Ibid., 108-109.

## Narrative Evangelism: The Travel Guide

The significance of a narrative approach to evangelism has been seen across a broad array of ministry settings,[129] from work among Muslims[130] and Hindus[131] to work among oral learners[132] and post-moderns.[133] The organic nature of narrative approaches is particularly appealing to those who are not satisfied with traditional linear evangelistic presentations that focus on "closing the deal," especially in Western contexts.[134]

Rick Richardson's *Reimagining Evangelism* follows a narrative approach in which Christians think of themselves as travel guides who facilitate the journeys of those who do not know Christ in compelling rather than coercive ways. This orientation releases would-be evangelists from canned approaches that ignore the personal histories of those who want to learn about Christ but do not yet know him.

A good travel guide recognizes that people are on journeys in life and that multiple guides can each play significant roles in that journey. Some guides give the traveler sage advice at important junctures along the road, others warn him or her of impending dangers on the path, and still others share their own doubts and travails of the journey. The particular role of each travel guide (or evangelist) will vary depending on where the traveler is on his or her journey. Additionally, since each person's journey is unique, how to play the role of the travel guide is dependent on the particular circumstances of the traveler and the promptings of the Holy Spirit in the life of the travel guide.

Richardson points out several advantages of being a travel guide rather than a traditional evangelist:[135] The guide can collaborate with the Holy Spirit rather than be burdened with forcing conversations; he or she is part of a community of travel guides rather then one person who must provide all the answers; there is freedom to pursue friendship rather than an agenda in the life of the traveler; the guide participates in a story rather than delivering dogma. Ultimately, evangelism is no longer confined to an event—it is a journey in which friendships are formed, opportunities for help are given and taken, and the ultimate destination is a healthy love relationship with Jesus rather than a means of reaching heaven.

---

129  Tom A. Steffen, *Reconnecting God's Story to Ministry: Cross-cultural Storytelling at Home and Abroad* (La Habra, CA: Center for Organizational & Ministry Development, 1996); Franklin, "Re-Thinking Stories."

130  Morton, "Narratives and Questions."

131  Hoefer, "Proclaiming a 'Theologyless' Christ."

132  John D. Wilson, "What it Takes to Reach People in Oral Cultures," *Evangelical Missions Quarterly* 27, no. 2 (April 1991): 154-158; *Making Disciples of Oral Learners* (N.P.: International Orality Network; Lausanne Committee for World Evangelization, 2005).

133  Wong Tok Kim, "Discovering God's Prior Work in Bringing People to Himself," *Evangelical Missions Quarterly* 41, no. 1 (January 2005): 78-85; Richardson, *Reimagining Evangelism*.

134  Richardson, *Reimagining Evangelism*, 17.

135  Ibid., 28-29.

## Church Planting Movements

Initially church planting movements, defined as "indigenous, rapid reproducing of new believers and new fellowships that sweeps through a people group,"[136] were *discovered* rather than intentionally developed.[137]

Church planting movements are typically comprised of house or cell churches that grow along natural social webs. To qualify for the label, the growth of the movement has to be so rapid that there is not enough time for building church structures. This reality ensures that the movements are decentralized, requires the rapid development of local leadership, and, in sensitive locations, makes it easier to stay under the public radar when a public presence would result in persecution.

Since the discovery of such movements in multiple locations around the world, practitioners have been strategizing on how to develop such movements[138]—as well as how not to hinder them.[139]

The flow of developing a church planting movement is organic in that there is no set of steps to follow that will produce a church planting movement. Instead, a cluster of five inter-dependent, reproducing elements have been found to be part of every successful church planting movement: [140]

1. *Effective ways of initiating a gospel witness*: while the means by which a gospel witness can be initiated vary from location to location, at least one or more such means have been identified and are being regularly used;

2. *An effective gospel witness*: the actual method of witness (such as the Camel method explained above) is effective in that those who hear it clearly understand the gospel and can respond to it meaningfully;

3. *Immediate, basic discipleship*: components of discipleship that are seen in church planting movements include introduction to fundamentals of the faith, enabling daily communion with God through prayer and reading or hearing of the Word, and equipping the new believer to share his or her new faith with family and friends;

4. *Effective fellowship formation*: new believers are gathered into fellowships which focus on multiplication of smaller groups rather than aggregation into a large group, and the

---

136 David Garrison and Seneca Garrison, "Factors that Facilitate Fellowships becoming Movements," in *From Seed to Fruit: Global Trends, Fruitful Practices, and Emerging Issues among Muslims*, ed. Dudley Woodberry (Pasadena, CA: William Carey Library, 2008), 208.

137 David Garrison, *Church Planting Movements* (Richmond, VA: International Mission Board of the Southern Baptist Convention, 1999).

138 Ray G. Register, Jr., *Back to Jerusalem: Church Planting Movements in the Holy Land* (Enumclaw, WA: WinePress, 2000); S. Devasahayam Ponraj and Chandon K. Sah, "Communication Bridges to Oral Cultures: A Method that Caused a Breakthrough in Starting Several Church Planting Movements in North India," *International Journal of Frontier Missions* 20, no. 1 (January-March 2003): 28-31; Garrison and Garrison, "Factors that Facilitate."

139 David Garrison, "How to Kill a Church-Planting Movement" *Mission Frontiers* 26, no. 6 (November 2004): 14-17.

140 Garrison and Garrison, "Factors that Facilitate," 212-213.

people in the fellowships that form are effective in nurturing and encouraging each other;

5. *Ongoing leadership development*: the explosion of new fellowships requires a corresponding growth in leaders whose development blends doctrinal growth with leadership skills growth through immersing them in the daily, practical work of a fellowship leader. These leaders are lay leaders, since paying them (even with purely indigenous funding) motivates them to grow their own fellowships rather than continually splitting off new ones.[141]

## Strengths and Weaknesses of Organic Models

We can identify five strengths and four potential weaknesses in organic approaches. An obvious strength is that they are the most flexible of the models, with enough cognitive space for addressing both social justice and social change. Second, they help practitioners avoid the trap of a more mechanical approach to what is in reality a living process—without losing perspective. Third, they offer the richest variety of approaches since they are not tied to any particular set of steps. Fourth, organic models can be more holistic than other models. Finally, organic models tend to be closer to the real-life of the church—including its messiness—than are abstract, artificial models.

On the negative side, while the most flexible, organic models are also the hardest to utilize. Second, their very flexibility also makes it harder to train followers for the unexpected contingencies that inevitably will come. Third, they tend to be the most open to aberrations (e.g., being faithful to a metaphor still allows for doctrinal unfaithfulness or syncretism). Finally, while closer to real-life, their very closeness can make it easier to forget the process because life gets in the way.

# Conclusion

It is clear that evangelicals are passionate about contextualization, and about developing and implementing methods of contextualizing that make a difference in the lives of others. The richness of evangelical resources, together with the healthy diversity in approaches bodes well for the future of evangelical contextualization.

Areas that we can anticipate will be of ongoing concern to evangelicals in contextualization include the development of even more organic models and comprehensive approaches—especially methods based on orality. We can hope for greater synthesis on the questions being asked in relation to insider movements. Finally, we can expect in the future to see the addition of significant Pentecostal contributions to all of these issues plus new ones, and—hopefully—greater international collaboration in contextualization. At Tim Tennent notes, "It takes a whole world to understand a whole Christ"[142]—may it be so!

---

141 Ibid., 216.
142 Timothy C. Tennent, "The Challenge of Churchless Christianity: An Evangelical Assessment," *International Bulletin of Missionary Research* 29, no. 4 (October 2005): 176.

## Discussion Questions

1.  In what ways is it both healthy and unhealthy to have so many differing approaches to contextualization?

2.  If you were asked to defend one approach as the best among the models discussed in this chapter, which one would you choose and why?

3.  Based on what you have read in this chapter, what criteria would you propose to use to analyze new models of contextualization that will be developed in the future?

4.  Which of the models presented in the discussion is the most troublesome to you? What is it about that model that is troublesome?

# 11

## Bridging Theory and Training

### *Patricia Harrison*

*Patricia Harrison has been head of the Department of Intercultural Studies at Tabor College NSW, Australia, since 1992. She teaches missiology and theology and is involved each year for one quarter in overseas theological education both as education consultant and as adjunct professor. Patricia has also worked with African-American, US Hispanic and Australian Aborigine populations, and served as a resource and consultant for numerous organizations and theological education projects. Education: PhD in cross-cultural theological education, (University of Queensland). MA in Christian Political Ethics (Oxford), MA, MDiv and ThM (Fuller), TESOL University of South Australia, BA Honours in Modern Languages (U of New England, Australia), Graduate Diplomas in Education, Multicultural Education and Aboriginal Education.*

## The Pressing Need for Deep Contextualization of the Gospel

"The 20th Century was the bloodiest century in human history…. We came to accept, with truly astonishing alacrity, the deaths of hundreds of thousands of non-combatant civilians…as a tolerable price to pay for uncertain political incomes."[1]

Despite a Christian heritage of 2000 years, the previous century saw war, bloodshed and atrocities almost beyond comprehension in Europe—in particular two World Wars, the Holocaust, Communist brutality, and the horrors of the Balkan wars. It is therefore appropriate for those of us from the Western world to remind ourselves of recent European history before addressing problems in "younger" churches.

However, profoundly disturbing developments continue in many parts of the world known for their apparently strong Christian churches. We cannot dodge the issue by blaming atrocities

---

1    Eric Hobsbawm, quoted in Inga Clendinnen, "The History Question: Who Owns the Past?" (Sydney, Australia: *Quarterly Essay* No 23, 2006).

and corruption wholly on non-Christians or "liberals." Many barbarities of the Rwandan genocide were perpetrated by "Christians" in a region once famous for continuous revival. Some African countries with substantial evangelical populations are plagued with endemic corruption, and white South African Christians defended apartheid from a supposedly biblical base.

Papua New Guinea, with a higher proportion of evangelicals than most Western countries, has fallen prey to serious, widespread corruption, and its Highlands provinces often suffer from tribal warfare. Christians fight Christians and burn one another's villages when tribal loyalties and "payback" are valued above Christian principles. A vicious civil war was waged for years on the PNG island of Bougainville and another in the Solomon Islands, both areas where nearly everyone claims a Christian affiliation, many villagers attend church daily, and "liberalism" is almost unknown.

Ethical issues are not confined to war. We all know about the spread of AIDS, often (not always) through promiscuity, about sexual abuse by clergy, and about the corruption and hypocrisy of certain televangelists. The International Bulletin of Missionary Research reports that "ecclesiastical crime" worldwide has reached an all-time high of US $27 billion in 2009, an especially disturbing figure in comparison with the total income of $25 billion for global missions in the same year. Corruption in Christian circles is increasing every year by 5.77%, and is expected to reach US $65 billion in 2025![2] Clearly evangelicals, with Christians of other traditions, must confront the serious dissonance that often exists between biblical principles and the situation in their churches and spheres of influence.

But what has this to do with contextualization? —A good deal. True, there are many factors involved in such wholesale jettisoning of basic Christian values, and many reasons that Christians fail to resist temptation, and clearly, the fundamental problem is original sin, and the systemic evil to which it gives rise.

But is it not likely that a contributing factor could be the failure of some churches to help members contextualize Christian values and apply these to all aspects of life? Is it not also possible that contextually weak Bible teaching at the congregational level is related to weak contextualization in pastoral education? This writer's personal experience with Bible colleges in many countries, both "North" and "South," for over thirty years, suggests that much evangelical theological education, while emphasizing personal morality, gives less attention to Christian social ethics. This could mean students are inadequately prepared to apply biblical teaching to the full range of local and national issues.[3]

---

2    Statistics from "Christian World Communions: Five Overviews of Global Christianity, AD 1800-2025." *International Bulletin of Missionary Research,* January 1, 2009 (Column 63). No definition of "ecclesiastical crime," is provided, but it evidently covers a wide range of fraud and corruption in Churches and Christian organizations. The term has been used for some years by the statisticians who publish these figures each January, and who also compile *World Christian Encyclopaedia.* Their work is internationally recognized, and is almost certainly the most comprehensive and reliable source of statistics relating to the worldwide church.

3    I have served as Secretary for Theological Education with the World Evangelical Alliance Theological Commission for a number of years, and in a consultant capacity, conducted many seminars for theological educators and visited numerous Bible colleges and TEE programs around the world. I continue similar work in a private capacity and conducted doctoral research dealing with some persistent problems in Protestant theological education in the Majority World.

Of course, this is not to say that believers will necessarily do what they know to be right. Teaching on sexual morality, for instance, often fails to prevent immoral behavior. But it seems likely that a movement in our colleges and churches towards what I call "Deep Contextualization" [4] might have some positive impact on the grave ethical situation in much of the global church.

# Responses

So how can we help our students better contextualize the Christian message? This paper will suggest a few practical strategies that may help us achieve this.

## Clarify the Task of Contextualization

As various papers in this volume have indicated,[5] our task is not to contextualize any particular theology. The aim is not to find the best ways of packaging Western theology for export, though we may see this as part of our task, given the importance of that tradition. Our task here is rather to suggest ways of exploring and interpreting Scripture that will help us construct a biblically-based theology in the context of a particular cultural and historical milieu.[6]

In one sense, Christian theology is contextualization, given that it is incarnational rather than supra-cultural in essence. True, historically speaking, Western contextual formulations have dominated the theology and pastoral training that have been exported to much of the world. The North Atlantic tradition has become a vital component of our collective patrimony, and cannot be omitted from our curricula or from our theological deliberations. The problem is that the dominance of this tradition can make it difficult to "do theology" in other contexts.

## Recognize the Need for Deep Contextualization

If we accept the need to practice and teach deep, comprehensive contextualization, our mission statements, educational objectives, policies, curriculum, and actual practice should all reflect that choice. However, defining and implementing contextualization can be a demanding exercise, as evidenced by other chapters in the present volume.

## Recruit as Students Actual and Potential Leaders

Some years ago in Papua New Guinea, SIL anthropologist, Dr. Wayne Dye, was invited to address a Theological Commission seminar for theological educators. He made a statement that startled a number of participants. Many Bible school teachers, he claimed, were *training the wrong people in the wrong place and in the wrong way.*

---

4    My concern here is that contextualization be both broad in the areas it covers (as in Response No. 7 below) and deep in the degree to which it addresses real local issues. Cf. Moreau's "contextualization that is comprehensive." (A counter-example of more superficial contextualization might be changing personal and place names in an anecdote or simplifying some theological vocabulary. Such changes are probably necessary, but insufficient of themselves.)

5    E.g., Natee Tanchanpongs' interesting "cruising metaphor," (chapter 7, this volume). And for a perspective on how to build a local theology with emphases appropriate to a particular culture, see Paul Siu's chapter in this volume (chapter 9).

6    I am indebted to Rob Haskell (private correspondence) for some helpful suggestions in this section.

What did he mean?

- That it could be a poor strategy to devote most of our pastoral training resources to untried youth in societies where only older, experienced people are respected as leaders.

- That we may be training them in locations too far removed from the contexts in which they will serve, and

- That too often we were using unsatisfactory methods to teach inadequately contextualized curricula.

To quote Dr. Michael Griffiths, a past president of London Bible College,

> There is sometimes a danger of training young people who carry little or no status in their own communities. At one time in Thailand, missionaries...were encouraging teenagers to come for training—some even sent their bad boys to the college to reform them! We ought not to think they will be recognized as spiritual leaders when they have no voice in a society ruled by elders twenty to thirty years older than themselves! In some cultures the young and unmarried carry little credibility as pastors.[7]

Many whom we train for the ministry never become pastors, as alumni records often testify, while numerous very worthy "functional pastors" [8] have little or no access to training.

In some countries, youth who enroll in Bible College are often those who failed to gain entry to University or Teachers' College. Their real, perfectly reasonable goal is to earn a diploma and get a good job. Even a Bible school diploma is perceived as being better than nothing! Such students usually have no calling to ministry and would be better served by a Christian vocational training program. It is not that their training is wasted, but if the main goal of an institution is to produce pastors, this is hardly a cost-effective way to achieve that goal.[9]

There are good reasons to structure training programs to provide more opportunities for mature students. That generally means offering part-time courses in regions where most churches are located. This strategy still caters for keen young people, but also opens the door to mature, dedicated Christian leaders with families, many who are already functioning as pastors.

---

7    "The Contextualization of Overseas Theological Education," in Roger Kemp (ed.) *Text and Context in Theological Education* (Springwood, Australia: ICAA, 1994).

8    I believe this is Dr. Ralph Winter's term. It denotes dedicated, unordained people performing the functions of a pastor, often voluntarily and usually without training.

9    Dr. Jim Plueddemann commented on this problem in an African context some years ago in an influential article entitled *The Diploma Disease* (in J. Plueddemann, ed. *ECWA News* (Jos, Nigeria: Challenge Publications, 1978, and earlier editions). We note here that the success or otherwise of a training program must be measured in terms of its objectives. If the aim is simply to provide theological training for all who come, or for young people in particular, there is no problem if few graduates become pastors. (But a full-time residential college is probably not the best way to provide broad-based lay training, since few working people with families can afford years away from paid employment.) However, most theological schools have as a major objective the provision of pastors for their Churches, in which case it will be important to know what proportion of graduates become pastors, and how many are serving where most churches are located.

It was in response to the need to produce pastors for growing churches that the TEE movement (Theological Education by Extension) was born in Guatemala in the early 1960s.[10]

Along with TEE, other ways of targeting the right people include offering evening classes, short-term intensive courses, and various types of distance education.[11] Many residential colleges add extension or evening courses to their schedules, thus catering for a much wider range of students, and also adding to their income.[12]

If we seek successful contextualization in the churches, it is important to provide training for those who are, or will become leaders, and who will have maximum influence in their churches and communities.

## Prioritize Training in Contextually Relevant Settings

Wayne Dye, as noted above, questioned the wisdom not only of training "the wrong people," but also of extracting students from their own contexts for several years. This raises complex issues concerning the comparative merits of training by extraction from the environment in which graduates will work, versus training by extension in the work environment – issues that have been central to the discussion surrounding TEE from its beginnings, and which are also much discussed in other types of vocational education.[13]

Generally speaking, field-based training allows for better contextualization, while institution-based training has greater potential to enlarge students' horizons and provide access to new ideas and a wider range of contacts with teachers and peers. The particular mix of components in some part-time training models, including TEE, may provide benefits of both kinds, while prioritizing contextual education.

We should note, however, that the relative merits of extension and extraction training are themselves related to context. In many countries, most churches are in rural areas while Bible

---

10    For a comprehensive discussion of the theology, philosophy and practice of the TEE movement, see F. Ross Kinsler, *The Extension Movement in Theological Education: A Call to the Renewal of Ministry* (Pasadena, CA: Wm Carey Library, 1978). For case studies in TEE from a number of countries, see also F. Ross Kinsler, ed., *Ministry by the People: Theological Education by Extension* (Geneva: World Council of Churches, 1983).

11    Distance education with no personal contact is unlikely to succeed in societies where personal relationships are paramount, or where students are not used to studying alone. It can fulfill a role when there is no alternative, and works best with short courses, or for advanced learners. When I used to attend conferences of the International Council for Distance Education (a UNESCO subsidiary), a dropout rate of around 80% was considered normal for correspondence courses. TEE largely overcame this problem by ensuring regular face-to-face contact with tutors and peers, while retaining many of the advantages of distance education. (The dropout rate is probably lower in online courses, as modern technology provides increasing opportunity for contact with teachers and peers, but this delivery mode would be impractical in many of the contexts we are addressing.)

12    A good example is the Christian Leaders' Training College in Papua New Guinea, which has a TEE program reaching several thousand students across the nation and beyond, in addition to a strong residential program.

13    Related questions regularly arise in other types of vocational training as educators debate the benefits of institution-based versus field-based training. Assuming students need some of each, is it better to train nurses primarily in a university, or primarily in a hospital; teachers primarily in schools, or primarily in teachers' colleges?

colleges are located in cities. Students extracted from rural areas to study for years in the city can easily become decontextualized, and lose the incentive to serve in regions they now regard as backward.

For advanced students destined to serve as denominational leaders, seminary teachers, or pastors in sophisticated city churches, however, there are important benefits in extractive education, which then becomes more relevant to the contexts in which they will minister.

## Recruit Teachers Who Understand the Relevant Contexts

To teach students to contextualize effectively, we must first model this in our teaching. Sometimes we teach more by example than by explicit instruction.

This can be difficult in situations where expatriate teachers come and go on a short-term basis, with little opportunity to learn the language and culture. Even long-serving expatriate faculty may fail to adequately understand the culture if their work largely confines them to an institution.

To again quote Michael Griffiths,

> Expatriates who have not served their apprenticeship within the indigenous churches may be ignorant of the context for which they are training workers. It is folly to think we can teach because we have theological qualifications in the West, without first studying the target audience in cultural context. [14]

To improve contextualization and reduce dependence on foreign personnel, boards of Majority World seminaries seek to minimize the number of missionary teachers and appoint local faculty. National teachers who have studied abroad can bring fresh and valuable insights to colleges in their homelands, especially when they combine these effectively with a deep understanding and appreciation of their own culture. These teachers fulfil a vital role in helping students interpret theology contextually in an increasingly global environment.

However, perhaps surprisingly, appointing national teachers is of itself no guarantee of contextualization. Some who have studied for long periods abroad, especially in their formative years, can lose touch with, or even empathy for their own cultures, or may live in hope of emigration to a wealthier nation. A teacher's aspirations for a better life abroad are understandable, but these do little to help students develop pride in their own culture and enthusiasm for ministry among their own people. Hence there are potent arguments, some contextual, for training younger faculty in their own areas, while providing overseas study opportunities for more mature leaders with a proven commitment to their own people. [15]

---

14  Op cit.

15  I have studied abroad myself, mixed with scores of overseas students, and taught many of them in Australia. This experience alerts me to the fact that most of those who study in countries more affluent than their homelands aspire to permanent residence in the richer country upon graduation, and many achieve that goal. This applies as much to theological students as to others. Of course there are numerous cases where the Lord has led individuals to emigrate for His purposes, and with excellent results. But overall, the sheer scale of this brain drain constitutes a serious loss to many nations and their Churches, even allowing for the many remittances sent home to families. Yet again, wealthy nations benefit at the expense of poorer ones.

It is worth noting that in Western colleges it is not generally considered a particular advantage to appoint only national faculty. Teachers from different nations and traditions are welcomed to help expand students' horizons.[16]

## Recognize and Address Multiple Contexts and Target Groups

When as theological educators we seek to contextualize our teaching, we must be aware that we are often dealing with multiple contexts, and with two or more levels of "target population." Our primary target group consists of our students, in the immediate context of our particular college or training program, the denomination/s it represents, and the nation and region in which it is situated.

But our job is not complete when we have tailored our program to the immediate context. We are training students to minister to others, both Christians and unbelievers. Our students may come from different ethnic, tribal and linguistic backgrounds, from diverse socio-economic contexts, and perhaps from different countries. To help them meet their future ministry needs we must endeavour to teach to the contexts in which they will serve after graduation. So the people among whom our students will minister constitute our *secondary target groups*. These secondary target groups should always be kept in mind. They should be carefully studied and their needs addressed. Suppose, for example, that our students will serve in a region where folk Buddhism is the predominant belief system. We cannot assume that because our students are Christians, our curriculum can largely ignore the folk religion of the general population. Nor should we assume we can adequately address their context with a course on classical, philosophical Buddhism. This may be useful, but it is not the real religion of the secondary target group. As Ruth Julian notes in chapter 5 of this volume, folk religion should not be ignored, but should rather become the focus of contextualization.

It is also important to train students at levels appropriate to their contexts.[17] A student with a weak educational background and a Bible school certificate, for example, can rarely minister satisfactorily to a city congregation of professionals, though he may be very effective in another situation.

## Recognize and Address the Multiple and Evolving Dimensions of "Context"

Every context has multiple components—a complex, more-or-less integrated range of traditions, activities, values and beliefs. There are both traditional and modern aspects to culture and worldview, and since cultures and contexts are always changing, contextual education means preparing students to relate creatively and biblically to the evolving environment in which they are called to serve.[18]

---

16     See below, under recommendations for avoiding parochialism.

17     For further discussion of the contextual importance of this, and the need to prepare students for the actual tasks they must perform, see Michael Griffiths, op. cit., pp 4-5. Note also the recommendation in the present paper that we undertake a survey of our target populations prior to designing or updating a curriculum.

18     Ruth Julian's chapter in this volume issues a timely reminder that as well as ongoing interaction with the changing context, there should ideally be dialogue with other theologies, and opportunities for Christians from different cultures to learn from, and lovingly critique one another's theologies. If this is to occur in the churches, we

When we think about contextualization, what usually first comes to mind is the overall *cultural and religious context*. Closely connected is *worldview*, the complex nature of which is discussed elsewhere in this book by Ruth Julian. However, there are other dimensions and subdivisions of context, and it is helpful to identify some of these.

A denominational college, for example, is normally located in the *ecclesial and theological contexts* of local and national churches, including regional and diocesan ecclesial bodies, while an interdenominational college has greater independence but must relate to a wider Christian constituency. The broad religious context may be nominally Christian, or the church may be a small, possibly persecuted minority. The community may be pluralist, with several main religious groups, either living in harmony or with some degree of tension.

Each community also has its *geographical setting*, and importantly, *a historical context* that helps the people define who they are, who their heroes are, and what they value as a people. Closely related to their history and identity is language. The *linguistic context* often includes several language groups, and significant sociolinguistic issues.

*Political and socio-economic issues* form a critical part of the context, and may be quite complex. We often focus on traditional culture, but in some situations the policies of a multi-national corporation, the world price of coffee, the drug trade, or political upheaval may have more bearing on people's daily lives.

## Make Serious Efforts to Contextualize the Curriculum

When we think of contextualization in theological education, we often think first about curriculum. This merits at least a chapter in its own right, but for present purposes, we offer a few practical suggestions for teaching our students to contextualize in their own ministries:

### Help Students Understand the Parameters of Contextualization

As we noted in the first of these "responses" above, the dominance of Western theology can make it difficult to develop a theology that is both biblically-based and contextual in a non-Western environment. Teachers as well as students may well find this challenging.

The first challenge is often to help students to even *conceive of* alternative approaches to theology which could be both biblical and contextual. This is especially difficult for those raised in a denomination which, at least in a given region, effectively represents its particular doctrinal position as the final depository of truth.

I find it helps more advanced students to contextualize to their own environments if I first introduce them to other Christian traditions, both historic and contemporary, and encourage them to evaluate these critically from a biblical perspective. They must search not only for points to criticize, but also for valuable insights. Students should know they will forego great

---

will need to begin the process in our seminaries. This also relates to points below about helping students understand the parameters of contextualization when we plan our curriculum, and about helping our students grow as "World Christians."

learning opportunities if they dismiss entire Christian traditions because they disagree with parts of them!

Sometimes we ask students to role play discussions or debates between adherents of different traditions, or to take the roles of famous theologians. Starting from positions closest to our own, we look at various Protestant and Roman Catholic theologies, and then proceed to the less familiar Eastern and Oriental Orthodox traditions, and to some modern contextual theologies. Sometimes we visit other churches or invite a representative to speak to us.

A number of seminaries offer similar courses, which can be a valuable in opening fresh avenues of thinking.[19] However, for students with minimal education, many such comparisons would just be confusing. Nonetheless, we should inform all students, at whatever academic level, that there are other ways of viewing some aspects of theology, and that Christians may interpret the Bible in different ways.

*Design a Curriculum to Meet Real Needs in the Areas Where Graduates Will Minister*
To contextualize, we must resist the temptation to simply base the curriculum on that of our own *alma mater*, unless it was designed well, and for the same target population. I highly recommend undertaking a survey of felt needs in the areas where our students will minister, and incorporating the results into our curriculum. We often assume we know these needs, but a well-designed survey of pastors, elders and ordinary church members usually turns up issues we had not thought about. We need to include some questions on topics like these, adapted to the situation:

*What are the most important practical and spiritual issues in your church and community?* Syncretism is likely to be a spiritual issue, and if it is not raised, further questioning may bring this up. Practical issues might include such things as AIDS, drought, lack of clean water, inadequate health care, frequent absences of the village school teacher, lack of employment or a myriad of other needs. The Bible school may help meet some needs by including practical skills in pastoral training.

Issues important in Western churches are often included in the curricula of Bible schools where they are largely irrelevant. These may include, for example, debates about certain interpretations of prophecy. Yet issues vital to local churches may be omitted.[20] This, of course, is not to

---

19     An example of a different theological orientation is the emphasis the Eastern Churches place on worship in the context of doing theology. For the Orthodox, worship rather than analysis is the first and most appropriate response to the Triune God, and human theologizing is always limited by the sacred mysteries that are ultimately beyond our understanding. A little of this approach may fit better into some contexts than does the Western tradition of academic theology with its emphasis on philosophical propositions. But this is a matter of relative emphases, not of one approach versus the other.

20     In much of Africa and the Pacific, for instance, vital themes that need to be addressed include polygamy, sorcery, the causes of sickness and death, dreams, bride price, taboos, omens, charms and fetishes, the role of ancestors, nationalism and independence. In Papua New Guinea, the relationship between payback, modern law and Christian forgiveness is a critical subject. In East Asia, ancestor veneration is an issue, and in India, questions of arranged marriages and dowry, as well as a Hindu worldview cannot be ignored. Interesting examples of survey results collected in the Pacific Islands of Kiribati and Tonga by Dr. Clifford Wright appear in his unpublished papers, *Christ and Kiribati Culture* (Melbourne, 1981), and *Seeds of the Word: Tongan Culture and Christian Faith* (Melbourne, 1979). I have encountered many similar issues in Africa.

deny the value of the inherited theological traditions which Christians share, or to argue for a purely pragmatic curriculum that addresses only issues of immediately cultural relevance.[21] There are fundamental truths that belong in every theological curriculum, though these may be addressed in different ways. The point is rather to ensure that ample time is devoted to those issues that are most pressing in the local community, while still covering all doctrinal essentials. From a deeper consideration of issues raised in other cultures may come fresh insights into biblical truth for us all.

Context will determine the extent to which we attempt to teach the full range of the theological tradition. A graduate seminary in a sophisticated city is one context. A village Bible school for new literates is quite another. In the former, it may well be necessary for students to study the differences between Calvinism and Arminianism, for example. In the latter, such distinctions will probably be fairly meaningless to the students unless specific circumstances warrant it.

*What types of leaders do you think your church needs most? Can you estimate how many of each group you may need in the next five to ten years?* You might suggest various types of voluntary ministries, such as elders, deacons, youth workers, musicians, Sunday School teachers, lay preachers, etc., as appropriate. Estimates of future requirements will depend on how much churches are growing.

*What do pastors and elders do? Are there other things you would like them to be able to do?* The idea here is to explore the *actual* and potential roles of pastors, elders, Sunday school teachers, and other leaders in their communities. These may not always be what we expect, e.g., in an illiterate community, the pastor may serve as village scribe, interpreter, liaison officer with government officials, or as a de facto teacher or nurse.

It is worth noting that a genuinely contextual curriculum for lay people will be different from one designed for training pastors. Good arguments may also be advanced for specialized curricula for Christians in some of the professions, to help them work out their faith in some of the most influential positions in society. [22]

## Contextualize Strategies for Teaching and Learning

Although we may use modern teaching aids, pedagogical contextualization requires that much of the content and method of our teaching be *reproducible*, with circumstantial adjustments, by our students. Otherwise they may assume they can not reteach what they have learned because it is too difficult, or because they lack DVD players, data projectors, etc.[23]

---

21    See, for example, Paul Siu's comments in this volume on the value of our inherited Christian tradition for the whole Church.

22    Some years ago, I worked with a group in Papua New Guinea to design a curriculum for lay people. This curriculum was developed in concentric circles around the themes of personal life, family life, church life, vocation, community life, Christian and cultural identity, citizenship of the nation, and becoming a "World Christian." Unfortunately, the curriculum was never implemented due to staffing changes.

23    One is reminded of Joseph Bayly's humorous warnings about relying on modern technology for evangelism. This is reprinted in his *Gospel Blimp and Other Modern Parables* (Colorado Springs, CO: David C. Cook, 2002).

Craig Blomberg encourages us in another chapter to be a bit adventurous in developing contextual language and imagery. This may lead us to explore traditional means of teaching practical skills and passing on knowledge, values, stories and songs to the next generation. Indigenous cultural forms such as ballads, songs, stories, drama or *wayang* shadow puppetry often communicate more effectively than lectures, and help affirm the value of traditional culture.

As an example of a different way of learning, we might note that in tribal societies, people often learn by observing a complete process several times with little commentary, and then trying it themselves. Westerners more often learn by listening to a step-by-step explanation, with or without a demonstration. Another traditional way of learning is by repetition with increment. In oral cultures, memorization is vital to the preservation of culture, and is strengthened by songs, dances, or rhythmic repetition. We can make good use of memorization so long as the material is understood. Visual teaching, drama and demonstration can also be very effective.

Storytelling is central to many cultures, and suits much of our Bible teaching. Where appropriate, stories usually communicate better than lectures and are better remembered. [24]

We should also note the kind of education our students have experienced in the local school system. This may help or hinder our Bible teaching. It can be helpful to visit local schools, and chat with lecturers in a local teachers' college. Many schools in developing countries still reproduce the rote memorization teaching styles imported in colonial times, and long superseded in their countries of origin. Although methods are generally being updated in teachers' colleges nowadays, change may be slow in filtering down to the schools, especially in rural areas. Students may not have been encouraged to think for themselves, or to question what they read or hear. Sometimes Christian leaders have unwittingly exacerbated this problem. We emphasize the trustworthiness of Scripture, but sometimes, dangerously, people accord similar trust to anything in print.

In some Asian countries, teachers are greatly honoured and placed high on a pedestal. It is fine to respect one's teachers, but problems arise if students believe their teachers are virtually infallible and their own views are worthless. Plagiarism needs careful explanation if this is an issue in our school. After all, what could be better than to repeat exactly what the experts have said? And of course, under totalitarian regimes a docile, unquestioning attitude is often deliberately cultivated in the schools.

Sometimes implicit assumptions hinder learning and hence contextualization. Asking the questions may help us evaluate such assumptions. For example:

### Is Lecturing Really the Best Contextual Way to Teach Theology?
The Danish theologian Kierkegaard is said to have believed it was heretical to try to impart Christianity by lecturing. Perhaps that is rather extreme, but research over many years[25] suggests that while lectures are useful for conveying information, they are generally less useful than discussion in shaping attitudes and values. It is important to note that preaching is not

---

24    Cf. Scott Moreau's discussion of narrative evangelism in this volume.
25    E.g. Donald Bligh, *What's the Use of Lectures?* (New York: Penguin Books, 1972), passim, and many studies before and since.

the same as lecturing. Preaching may be inspirational and life changing, but few of us could maintain that level of inspiration through ten or fifteen hours of lecturing every week! The lecture is a basic mode of discourse in the Western theological tradition, and it is natural that we should use it, especially where students are accustomed to it. But this will not be the case in all cultures or at all educational levels. To contextualize effectively, we must first ensure that what we teach is understood. We cannot ignore insights into how people learn. To model good teaching methods, some of which are reproducible by our students, we will often need to develop interactive, interesting and imaginative methods of teaching, and use lectures, or shorter lecture segments, more sparingly. Simply mentioning something in a lecture does not mean it is learned, as we soon realize when we set tests or spot check the notes students take in class!

A good motto for teachers might be *"Nothing is taught until it is learned."*

Often students and/or teachers must communicate in a second or third language. Experience suggests that in such situations, more information may be lost in lecturing than many teachers realize. It is vital to adjust our communication to the linguistic and educational context. [26]

### Can I Assume that Students Will Transfer Knowledge and Skills to New Situations More or Less Automatically?

There are several dimensions to the concept of transfer in education. We may expect students to transfer what they learn in the national language to the vernacular in which they will minister. We may assume they will transfer general principles to particular situations, and specific examples to other specific situations. But in fact, even the brightest University students studying in their native language often have difficulty with transfer. Training students to take what we have taught them and contextualize it for a different target group is a complex undertaking. First, they must really understand the material—something too often assumed rather than systematically checked. Then they need to be able to apply, adapt and transfer their knowledge and skills to other contexts, all without syncretism and without loss or distortion of biblical truth.

Hence, training students to contextualize requires that we assist them in transferring knowledge and skills to new situations. *As a general principle, the less formal education students have had, the more our teaching needs to be situation-specific, and the more we must help them with various types of transfer.*

---

26    This usually means speaking slowly, repeating and illustrating key ideas, explaining new terms, and avoiding unfamiliar jargon and idioms. We also need to help students take lecture notes. Effective note-taking demands complex skills and requires considerable practice. Students must listen, comprehend, select key points, summarize these, and write them down quickly, probably using their own abbreviations, all while listening to the next part of the lecture. In a second language this is almost impossible for many, making incomplete, inaccurate notes inevitable. So students often request a complete set of printed notes. However, full notes can render lectures almost redundant, and may lead to inattention or absence from class. Some students may try to memorize notes by heart. To avoid these problems I often use "Swiss Cheese Notes." These provide the main framework of a lecture, include proper nouns and explain new terms. Spaces (holes in the cheese!) are left in the notes for students to fill in details as they listen. Where appropriate, the notes include maps, diagrams and pictures to aid comprehension and add interest. Preparing "Swiss Cheese Notes" takes time, but generally results in greater attention, and certainly in more accurate notes. A simpler method is to put the outline and all new words on the board.

Let us consider some practical ways we can help the transfer process.

When students must minister in different languages from the language of instruction, it is vital that we help them understand and translate theological concepts. Otherwise, serious distortion of the Christian message is possible, and Christianity may be viewed as a foreign religion that can only be understood and communicated in a foreign language. When the target language lacks equivalents for Western theological terms, vernacular Scriptures may help us find suitable vocabulary. Also, it is often worthwhile to consult missionary linguists and well-educated locals.

A wise teacher will pause regularly for comprehension checks, particularly in a Theology or Biblical Studies class.[27] It is also useful to divide students into small discussion groups according to language background and provide questions to help them tease out the meaning of key Christian concepts and consider the best ways to convey these in their own languages.

In helping students with little formal education to develop transferable, contextually-relevant skills it is essential to make our training as specific to their contexts as possible. For example, when training a group of Australian Aboriginal Christians to teach Sunday School, some of us found there was little point in giving lectures on child development and teaching methods. It was too difficult for them to transfer such general principles to classroom situations. So we made our training situation-specific. The trainees worked with children in a real Sunday School, first taking small parts of the lesson in a team teaching situation, then gradually teaching more. General principles were learned inductively in real-life situations. [28] A similar method may be used for teaching preaching, evangelism, and other skills.

## Contextualize the Learning Situation

Actions often speak louder than words, so we must note the power of the "hidden curriculum" or the unintended "para-message" of our training structures. A few questions may help us unpack this concept and implement structural contextualization. (A couple of prompts are provided with the first question to help you get the idea....)

- What messages are conveyed when lectures and sermons are long and dull, perhaps delivered in language half understood by students? (Is Christianity boring, and does God give Brownie points for "sitting it out"?!)

- What para-message is conveyed when a Bible college provides its expatriate faculty with the best housing on campus, and gives second-rate accommodation to national faculty?

---

27    For example, when teaching the concept of repentance, we might relate several brief anecdotes and ask students to identify those that illustrate genuine repentance, and to explain why (a valuable exercise in "shame cultures" where it is important to differentiate repentance from shame at being found out.)

28    Each week we met to plan the next Sunday's lesson. We prayed for our classes and planned the lesson. We practiced telling the Bible story and chose choruses to fit the theme. Then we prepared simple teaching aids and activities for the children. And each week we discussed the previous week's lesson and possible solutions to any problems that had arisen. This method was thoroughly contextual and much more successful. It generated enthusiasm and the trainees developed the motivation and confidence to continue teaching once the course was over. True, situation-specific training is intensive, and demands more teacher time. But better outcomes often justify the effort.

- What messages may be conveyed by the structure of the college whose principal once told me, "We have so many rules the students complain they can't remember them"?

- What messages are conveyed by a library full of books most students can not read, either because they are in a foreign language, or because the language and concepts are too difficult for the target group? [29]

- What messages may be conveyed by a very small library of tattered old books in a foreign language, obviously donated by people of good will, but never checked for their value in a theological school?

- What messages are conveyed by a college that teaches only its own theological position, denigrates others, and represents its sponsoring denomination as, in effect, the sole arbiter of truth?

We need our training programs to convey strong, positive para-messages consonant with what we teach verbally. A well-run Bible college can serve as a positive model for the churches its graduates may pastor—an honest, caring Christian community seeking under God's guidance to foster mutual respect and affirm the priesthood of all believers. Students as well as staff will have a say in how the college is run, and will be encouraged to contribute ideas and suggestions. A Student Council can provide valuable practice in communal planning and decision making. Such a model may be especially valuable in areas where churches tend to be legalistic, and dominated by the pastor, with few opportunities for believers to develop their own gifts.

Many Bible colleges, however, are run on quite authoritarian lines, following earlier practice in mission-sending countries. Such training models risk reinforcing in their graduates legalism, authoritarian forms of leadership, and a lack of trust in other Christians.[30] Of course every college needs rules; the question is how many, and of what kind. One reason for the numerous rules in many residential schools is the preponderance of young students, who still require monitoring by an authority figure in *loco parentis*.

It is worth noting that interdenominational seminaries often provide more fertile ground for fruitful contextual thinking than do denominational institutions, though this is by no means always the case. Some denominational colleges teach only their own, often imported, theological tradition and in effect present this as the whole, infallible truth. Students seeking ordination know they must be able to sign the Church's doctrinal basis. If the institutional context is also authoritarian, students will be further discouraged from "thinking outside the box."

It is natural for a denomination to maintain its distinctives, and many good denominational colleges manage to do this while still exposing students to different points of view and encouraging contextual thinking. On the other hand, there are colleges which, while formally interdenominational, in reality represent just one evangelical tradition.

---

29    Cf. the following section.

30    Many cultures tend towards legalism, so the question is raised as to how far the church should go in adapting to the culture. While there is room for some variation here, I believe Galatians and the New Testament as a whole support responsible freedom in Christ, the development of people's gifts, and the priesthood of all believers.

Any position that dismisses the concept of *semper reformanda* and disallows fresh insights from Scripture and from other believers is a position inimical to serious contextualization. At the same time of course, it is essential students learn where to draw the lines to maintain a biblical perspective.

## Promote the Provision of Resource Materials in the Target Language/s

I teach regularly in a Bible school in Latvia. I can never set essays or research projects because there are virtually no theological resources in the Latvian language. My colleague and I must create all our own notes and materials. This situation will be familiar to many readers teaching in languages with relatively few speakers, or in areas with more widely-spoken languages, but few Christians.

It is extremely difficult for a pastor to provide solid, contextual Bible teaching when few resources are available in his language. Since realistically, only those with substantial education can benefit from theological books in foreign languages, translations of key theological works and reference books are sorely needed in many countries, along with more contextual material written by nationals. International Christian bodies often do make an invaluable contribution to the churches by funding the translation and writing of theological material in minority languages. Sales will never generate a profit, but in the computer age, desktop publishing means basic resource materials need no longer be so expensive to produce, and those with computer access will also be able to read them on disk or online. The main cost is in the time needed for writing or translation.

Could we all work towards more coordinated international efforts to provide theological literature in a number of "smaller" languages? We add daily to the abundant Christian literature available in English and other world languages. Could we not dispense with some of these books and free up funds to provide minority groups with essential resources?[31]

# Limitations

Our discussion would be incomplete if we failed to note that although contextualization is essential in theological education, it has its limitations and potential pitfalls. Several of these are addressed below.

## Syncretism

This is the most obvious pitfall, but it is no reason to fear contextualization. The present volume addresses this issue in various ways. For example, Matthew Cook reminds us that while

---

31    Funds in this case would not be directed towards general Christian literature, (though this is also needed) but towards provision of indispensable reference books such as concordances, commentaries and Bible Dictionaries, and towards basic Bible college textbooks. Since many theological students and pastors in the Majority World have had limited education, we need compact books that avoid arcane language. Examples might be Justo Gonzalez' concise *Church History: An Essential Guide* (Nashville, TN: Abingdon, 1996), supplemented by some local church history. Or, given the widespread problems of fanciful interpretations of Scripture, an excellent investment could be a translation of Fee and Stuart's *How to Read the Bible for all its Worth*. 3rd ed. (Grand Rapids, MI: Zondervan, 2003).

evangelical theology, like other theologies, is socially located, this need not preclude objectivity, despite the elusive nature of what Benno van den Toren calls a "humanly accessible supracultural core." Osias Segura-Guzmán identifies some sources for sound theological reflection that can help keep us on track, while Natee Tanchanpongs suggests criteria for determining the biblical authenticity of our attempts at contextualization.

## Idealization or Demonization of Cultures

Human beings are created in God's image, a great positive. They are also affected by sin and the fall, a major negative. And many human customs and practices are ethically neutral. Since cultures are created by human beings, they also have positive, negative and morally neutral aspects. This means we must never idealize any society. There will always be culture traits at variance with the Christian message, and in these instances contextualization means taking account of and addressing the problems, not succumbing to them.[32]

At the same time, we must take care, in comparing a society with biblical ideals, that we do not fall into the opposite trap of effectively demonizing the local culture by highlighting only what is wrong with it! Teachers from abroad need to indicate awareness of unbiblical aspects of their own cultures, to avoid unwittingly communicating neo-colonial attitudes. [33]

## Parochialism

Excessive concentration on the local context may inadvertently promote parochialism and limit students' horizons. There are theological as well as practical reasons for addressing the full range of contexts from which our students come, but also for balancing contextualization with a broader, global perspective.[34] An essential mark of the church is its universality. Hence it is important for theological students to see themselves as part of the worldwide church in all its variety. If we want students to become "World Christians," well informed about the world and the wider church, we must systematically build into our courses an informed global perspective, along with respect for other Christians, although we will inevitably disagree with them on some issues. An emphasis on mission is also vital, and students living in traditional "mission

---

32    One example is the low status of women in many cultures. At times churches have inadvertently reinforced this by marginalizing women, and promulgating oppressive interpretations of male headship.

33    One problem with sending youth abroad for training is that some have serious difficulty coming to terms with major economic and cultural differences. Although overseas study is obviously a great learning experience, I have often seen young students develop a tendency to idealize the new culture at the expense of their own, or the reverse. This can happen when youth from a wealthy country go to a poorer country or vice versa, and can distort the worldview they communicate if they return home to teach. Older students can generally evaluate differences in a more balanced way (cf. Paul Hiebert's concept of "critical contextualization," which resists uncritical acceptance or rejection of culture traits). If we wish to train youth overseas and have them return and contribute to their home churches, the desired outcomes are more likely if we provide them with adequate preparation before departure, spiritual and psychological support while abroad, and debriefing on return. The best help will be given by mature Christians who understand both cultures, and preferably have some training in counseling.

34    The term "globalization" is sometimes used in contrast to contextualization, but that term has acquired new meanings and connotations in recent years, some negative enough to inspire riots! Hence my preference is to employ terms like "global perspective" or "World Christians" in the present discussion, and to use "globalization" more in reference to international economic and similar trends, as Paul Siu does in this volume. But of course such trends also form part of the global context for which we must prepare our students.

fields" should know that the days are long past when mission was a unidirectional movement from the West to other countries.

In denominational colleges we naturally emphasize the teachings and work of own church, but to shape a training program exclusively to a limited denominational context is to distort Christian reality, raising ethical as well as educational issues.[35]

There follow a few suggestions that may help our students avoid parochialism and become "World Christians":

- Engage some permanent and visiting faculty from other countries and other denominations. As noted above, it is good to have a majority of local faculty, but especially in degree-level institutions, it will be an advantage to include several teachers from other places and traditions. In particular, we should try to avoid a situation where almost all teachers are graduates of the college where they are teaching, or of a single overseas institution—usually the main college of the relevant denomination in the US or elsewhere.

- Invite Christian workers from other places and denominations as guest lecturers or chapel speakers.

- Include in the curriculum a core overview course in Mission, perhaps similar to the internationally popular *Perspectives* course, initiated by Dr. Ralph Winter and the William Carey International University in Pasadena, CA, and based on a well-known reader.[36]

- Add international and cross-cultural dimensions to various subjects in the curriculum. This can be done without minimizing contextualization.

- Provide regular news and prayer requests from churches around the world. Prayer meetings should focus not only on local needs, but also on current events and the worldwide church.

---

35    The more isolated the Bible school and the less educated the students, the greater our responsibility to interpret the wider world accurately to them. Our school may be the students' main source of information about the outside world. In such situations it would be a reprehensible distortion of the facts to exaggerate the international significance of a small denomination. It would likewise be unethical to misrepresent the doctrinal positions of other churches or to stress only points of disagreement. The author has encountered theological students in some countries who have come to see their own small denomination as the only true Church, and to view all other churches, even closely related evangelical denominations, with suspicion. This does nothing to promote fellowship and understanding among believers.

36    Cf. R. Winter and S, Hawthorne eds., *Perspectives on the World Christian Movement,* 3rd ed. (Pasadena, CA: Wm Carey Library, 1999). Variants of this valuable course are taught in many countries, including a short version. *Perspectives* addresses biblical, historical, cultural and strategic aspects of mission. Previous editions of the reader deliberately and commendably emphasize world evangelization, but give scant attention to the enormous amount of practical, loving service provided by missions and para-church organizations in such areas as medicine, education, agriculture, community development and the promotion of justice and peace. They also confine their attention almost entirely to evangelical organizations. For these reasons I believe that despite the daunting size of the reader, this course needs some pruning and supplementing to provide a more comprehensive and balanced coverage of world mission. (At the time of writing I have not seen the 4th edition, due in 2009, which may possibly address some of these concerns.) A similar introductory course on mission could be put together where this book is unavailable, or where more local content is needed.

- Organize an annual mission conference in conjunction with local churches, to help broaden students' horizons.

- Remember that World Christians are well informed, not only about the church, but about current events and human need. If a college subscribes to a quality newspaper and students are encouraged to follow world events by TV or radio it is easier for them to pray intelligently for others.

## Discussion Questions

The following questions are suggested as discussion starters for teachers interested in developing contextual theological education. As indicated above, we need to apply principles of contextualization not only to the content of what we teach, but also to other components of the program, so some questions address these aspects of contextualization.

1. *"For evangelicals, the curriculum is a given."* Discuss this statement with reference to evangelical theological education.
   a.   Identify some important theological issues for the churches in your region. Are these issues adequately addressed in courses in your seminary, Bible school or TEE program?
   b.   Identify some important pastoral and ethical issues for the churches in your area. Are these issues adequately addressed in the Ethics and Pastoral Theology course/s in your seminary, Bible school or TEE program?

2. In your own training program:
   a.   How do you contextualize your teaching methods?
   b.   How do you take account of the educational backgrounds of your students?

3. What specific policies and procedures has your training program developed:
   a.   To promote contextualization in all aspects of training?
   b.   To help students contextualize their own ministries?

4. Consider the structures of your college or training program, and try to identify some of the para-messages these convey. Are you satisfied that these implicit messages match the principles and values you teach explicitly in the classroom?

5. How does your training program help students develop a global perspective? Is there more you could do to promote such a perspective?

# Suggested Reading

Adams, Daniel J. *Cross-Cultural Theology: Western Reflections in Asia*. Atlanta, GA: John Knox Press, 1987.

Ahn, Kyo Seong. "Christian Mission and Mongolian Identity: the Religious, Cultural, and Political Context." *Studies in World Christianity* 9, no. 1 (2003): 103-124.

Akinnaso, F. Niyi. "Bourdieu and the Diviner: Knowledge and Symbolic Power in Yoruba Divination." In *The Pursuit of Certainty: Religious and Cultural Formulation,* 234-258. Edited by Wendy James. London: Routledge, 1995.

Amirtham, Sam, and S. Wesley Ariarajah, eds. *Ministerial Formation in a Multifaith Milieu.* Geneva: WCC, [1986?].

Ariaraja, S. Wesley. "Do Christians and Muslims Worship the Same God? Part Four." *The Christian Century*, June 1 2004, 28-29.

Arnold, Clinton E. *The Colossian Syncretism: The Interface between Christianity and Folk Belief at Colossae*. Grand Rapids, MI.: Baker, 1996.

Bediako, Kwame. *Christianity in Africa: The Renewal of a Non-Western Religion*. Maryknoll, NY: Orbis, 1995.

--------. *Theology and Identity: The Impact of Culture upon Christian Thought in the Second Century and Modern Africa*. Oxford: Regnum Books, 1992.

--------. *Jesus and the Gospel in Africa: History and Experience*. Maryknoll, NY: Orbis Books, 2004.

--------. "The Doctrine of Christ and the Significance of Vernacular Terminology." *International Bulletin of Missionary Research* 22 (1998): 110-111.

Beekman, John, and John Callow. *Translating the Word of God*. Grand Rapids, MI: Zondervan, 1974.

Bevans, Stephen. *Models of Contextual Theology*. Revised and expanded ed. Maryknoll, NY: Orbis, 2006.

Black, Matthew, and William A. Smalley, eds. *On Language, Culture and Religion: In Honor of Eugene A. Nida.* The Hague: Mouton, 1974.

Bligh, Donald. *What's the Use of Lectures?* New York: Penguin Books, 1972,

Bosch, David J. *Transforming Mission: Paradigm Shifts in Theology of Mission.* Maryknoll, NY: Orbis, 1991.

Briggs, Richard. "Gender and God-talk: Can We Call God 'Mother'?" *Themelios* 29, no. 2 (Spring 2004):15-25.

--------. *Reading the Bible Wisely.* Grand Rapids, MI: Baker Book House, 2003.

Brown, Rick. "Contextualization without Syncretism." *International Journal of Frontier Missions* 23, no. 2 (2006): 127-133.

--------. "Delicate Issues in Mission: Part I: Explaining the Biblical Term 'Son(s) of God' in Muslim Contexts." *International Journal of Frontier Missions* 22 (2005): 91-96.

--------. "The 'Son of God': Understanding the Messianic Titles of Jesus." *International Journal of Frontier Missions* 17, no. 1 (2000): 41-52.

Campos, Oscar. *Teología Evangélica para el Contexto Latinoamericano: Ensayos en Honor al Dr Emilio A. Nuñez.* Buenos Aires: Kairos Ediciones, 2004.

Carroll, Robert. "Between Lying and Blasphemy or On Translating a Four-Letter Word in the Hebrew Bible: Critical Reflections on Bible Translation." In *Bible Translation on the Threshold of the Twenty-First Century, Authority, Reception, Culture and Religion*, eds. A. Brenner and J. W.van Henten, 53-64. Sheffield, UK: Sheffield Academic Press, 2002.

Carson, D. A., ed. *Biblical Interpretation and the Church: The Problem of Contextualization.* Nashville, TN: Tomas Nelson Publishers, 1984.

--------. "Church and Mission: Reflections on Contextualization and the Third Horizon." In *The Church in the Bible and the World: An International Study*, ed. D. A. Carson, 213-257. Grand Rapids: Baker, 1987.

--------. *The Gagging of God: Christianity Confronts Pluralism.* Grand Rapids, MI: Zondervan, 1996.

--------. "The Limits of Dynamic Equivalence in Bible Translation." *Evangelical Review of Theology* 9 (1985): 200-13,

--------. "A Sketch of the Factors Determining Current Hermeneutical Debate in Cross-Cultural Contexts." In *Biblical Interpretation and the Church: The Problem of Contextualization*, ed. D. A Carson, 11-29. Nashville, TN: Tomas Nelson Publishers, 1984.

Carson, D. A., and John D. Woodbridge, eds. *Hermeneutics, Authority, and Canon*. Grand Rapids, MI: Zondervan, 1986.

--------. *Scripture and Truth*. Grand Rapids: MI: Zondervan, 1983.

Childs, Brevard S. *Biblical Theology of the Old and New Testaments: Theological Reflection on the Christian Bible*. Minneapolis, MN: Fortress Press, 1993.

Choi, Philemon. *Not One Less: Rethinking the Youth and the Ministry*. Chinese edition. Hong Kong: Breakthrough, 2005.

Clark, David. *To Know and Love God*. Wheaton, IL: Crossway Books, 2003.

Clark, Kelly James. *Return to Reason: A Critique of Enlightenment Evidentialism and a Defense of Reason and Belief in God*. Grand Rapids, MI: Eerdmans, 1990.

Clendinnen, Inga. "The History Question: Who Owns the Past?" *Quarterly Essay* No. 23 (2006).

Conn, Harvie. "Contextualization: A New Dimension for Cross-Cultural Hermeneutics." *Evangelical Missions Quarterly*, January 1978, pp. 39 ff.

--------. "Contextual Theologies: The Problem of Agendas." In *Constructive Christian Theology in the Worldwide Church*, ed. William R. Barr, 91-104. Grand Rapids, MI: Eerdmans, 1997.

--------. *Eternal Word and Changing Worlds: Theology, Anthropology and Mission in Trialogue*. Grand Rapids, MI: Zondervan, 1984.

Corley, Bruce, Steve W. Lemke, and Grant I. Lovejoy, eds. *Biblical Hermeneutics: A Comprehensive Introduction to Interpreting Scripture*. Nashville, TN: Broadman and Holman Publishers, 2002.

Corwin, Gary. "Telling the Difference." *Evangelical Missions Quarterly* 40 (2004): 282-83.

Covell, Ralph R. *Confucius, the Buddha, and Christ: A History of the Gospel in Chinese*. Eugene, OR: Wipf & Stock, 2004.

Davis, John J. "Contextualization and the Nature of Theology." In *The Necessity of Systematic Theology*, ed. John J. Davis, 169-85. Washington: University Press of America, 1978.

Demarest, Bruce A., and Richard J. Harpel. "Don Richardson's 'Redemptive Analogies' and the Biblical Idea of Revelation." *Bibliotheca Sacra* 146 (1989): 330-340.

Droogers, A. F. "Syncretism: The Problem of Definition, the Definition of the Problem." In *Dialogue and Syncretism: An Interdisciplinary Approach,* ed. Jerald D. Gort, 7-25. Grand Rapids, MI: Eerdmans, 1989.

Dulles, Avery Robert. *Models of Revelation.* Garden City, NY: Doubleday, 1983.

Dyer, Wayne W. *Change Your Thoughts, Change Your Life: Living the Wisdom of the Tao.* Carlsbad, CA: Hay House, Inc., 2007.

Dyrness, William A. *Emerging Voices in Global Christian Theology.* Grand Rapids, MI: Zondervan, 1994.

---------. *Invitation to Cross-Cultural Theology: Case Studies in Vernacular Theologies.* Grand Rapids, MI: Zondervan, 1992.

---------. *How Does America Hear the Gospel?* Grand Rapids, MI.: Eerdmans, 1996.

---------. *Learning about Theology from the Third World.* Grand Rapids, MI: Zondervan, 1990.

Escobar, Samuel. *Changing Tides: Latin America and World Mission Today.* American Society of Missiology Series, no. 31. Maryknoll, NY: Orbis, 2002.

--------. "The Search for Missiological Christology in Latin America." In *Emerging Voices in Global Christian Theology,* ed. William A, Dyrness, 199-228. Grand Rapids, MI: Zondervan, 1994.

Farley, Edward. *Theologia: The Fragmentation and Unity of Theological Education.* Philadelphia, PA: Fortress Press, 1983.

Fee, Gordon D., and Douglas Stuart. *How to Read the Bible for All It's Worth.* Grand Rapids, MI: Zondervan, 2003.

Flemming, Dean. *Contextualization in the New Testament: Patterns for Theology and Mission.* Downers Grove, IL: InterVarsity Press; Leicester: Apollos, 2005.

--------. "The Third Horizon: A Wesleyan Contribution to the Contextualization Debate." *Wesleyan Theological Journal* 30 (Fall 1995): 139-163.

Gadamer, Hans-Georg. *Truth and Method*, 2nd ed. Translated by Joel Weinsheimer and Donald G. Marshall. New York: Crossroad, 1989.

Gehman, Richard J. *Doing African Christian Theology: An Evangelical Perspective.* Nairobi, Kenya: Evangel Publishing House, 1987.

Gilliland, Dean S., ed. *The Word Among Us: Contextualizing Theology for Today*. Dallas, TX: Word, 1989.

Goble, Phillip, and Salim Munayer. *New Creation Book for Muslims*. Pasadena, CA: Mandate Press, 1989.

Goldingay, John. *An Ignatian Approach to Reading the Old Testament*. Cambridge: Grove Books, 2002.

--------. *Models for Scripture*. Grand Rapids, MI: Eerdmans; Carlisle: Paternoster, 1994.

González, Justo, and Catherine Gunsalus González. *Liberation Preaching*. Abingdon Preacher's Library. Nashville: Abingdon, 1981.

Greeson, Kevin. *Camel Training Manual*. Bangalore, India: WIGTake, 2004.

Grenz, Stanley J. "Community as a Theological Motif for the Western Church in an Era of Globalization," *Crux* 28, no 3 (September 1992), 10.

--------. *Revisioning Evangelical Theology: A Fresh Agenda for the 21$^{st}$ Century*. Downers Grove, IL: InterVarsity, 1993.

Grenz, Stanley J., and John R. Franke. *Beyond Foundationalism: Shaping Theology in a Postmodern Context*. Louisville, KY: Westminster John Knox Press, 2001.

Grenz, Stanley J., and Roger E. Olson. *Who Needs Theology? An Invitation to the Study of God*. Downers Grove, IL: InterVarsity Press, 1996.

Groody, Daniel G. *Globalization, Spirituality, and Justice: Navigating the Path to Peace*. Maryknoll, NY: Orbis Books, 2007.

Gutiérrez, Gustavo. *Las Casas: In Search of the Poor of Jesus Christ*. Maryknoll, NY: Orbis Books, 1993.

--------. *A Theology of Liberation: History, Politics, and Salvation*. Revised edition. Maryknoll, NY: Orbis Books, 1988.

--------. *The Truth Shall Make You Free: Confrontations*. Maryknoll, NY: Orbis Books, 1990.

Haleblian, Krikor. "The Problem of Contextualization." *Missiology: An International Review* 6, no. 1 (January 1983): 95-111.

Harlan, Mark. "De-Westernizing Doctrine and Developing Appropriate Theology in Mission." *International Journal of Frontier Missions* 22, no. 4 (2005): 159-166.

Harrison, Patricia J. "Contextualization" and "Globalization." In Kinsler, F Ross, and James H. Emery, eds. *Opting for Change: A Handbook on Evaluation and Planning for Theological Education by Extension.* Geneva: WCC Programme on Theological Education; Pasadena, CA: William Carey Library, 1991.

--------. "Education for Liberation? An Analysis of Some Recurrent Problems in Third World Protestant Ministerial Formation." Ph.D. diss., University of Queensland, Australia, 1992.

Hesselgrave, David J. *Paradigms in Conflict: 10 Key Questions in Christian Missions Today.* Grand Rapids, MI: Kregel, 2005.

Hesselgrave, David J., and Edward Rommen. *Contextualization: Meanings, Methods, and Models.* Grand Rapids, MI: Baker, 1989.

Hiebert, Paul G. *Anthropological Reflections on Missiological Issues.* Grand Rapids, MI: Baker, 1994.

--------. "Beyond Anti-Colonialism to Globalism." *Missiology* 19 (1991): 263-281.

--------. "Critical Contextualization." *International Bulletin of Missionary Research* 11, no. 3 (July 1987): 104-111.

--------. "The Flaw of the Excluded Middle." *Missiology* 10, no. 1 (January 1982): 35-48.

--------. *Missiological Implications of Epistemological Shifts: Affirming Truth in a Modern/Postmodern World.* Harrisburg, PA: Trinity Press International, 1999.

--------. *Transforming Worldviews: An Anthropological Understanding of How People Change.* Grand Rapids, MI: Baker Academic, 2008.

Hiebert, Paul G., R. Daniel Shaw, and Tite Tiénou. *Understanding Folk Religion: A Christian Response to Popular Beliefs and Practices.* Grand Rapids, MI: Baker Books, 1999.

Higgins, Kevin. "Identity, Integrity, and Insider Movements." *International Journal of Frontier Missions* 23:2 (2006): 117-23.

Hoefer, Herbert E. *Churchless Christianity.* Pasadena, CA: William Carey Library, 2001.

Howell, Brian M. "Globalization, Ethnicity, and Cultural Authenticity: Implications for Theological Education." *Christian Scholar's Review* 36, no. 1 (Fall 2006).

Huntington, Samuel. *The Clash of Civilizations and the Remaking of World Order.* New York: Simon & Schuster, 1996.

Hyatt, Irwin T. Jr. *Our Ordered Lives Confess: Three Nineteenth-Century American Missionaries in East Shantung.* Cambridge, MA: Harvard University Press. 1976.

International Orality Network. *Making Disciples of Oral Learners.* Richmond, VA: International Mission Board SBC, 2007.

Jenkins, Philip. *The Next Christendom: The Coming of Global Christianity.* Expanded and revised. New York: Oxford University Press, 2002, 2007.

Johnston, David L. "Are God and Allah the Same?" *Mission Frontiers* January–February 2002.

Johnston, Robert K., ed. *The Use of the Bible in Theology: Evangelical Options.* Atlanta, GA: John Knox, 1985.

Karkkainen, Veli-Matti. *Christology: a Global Introduction.* Grand Rapids, MI: Baker Academic, 2003.

--------. *The Doctrine of God: A Global Introduction.* Grand Rapids, MI: Baker Academic, 2004.

--------. *An Introduction to Ecclesiology: Ecumenical, Historical & Global Perspectives.* Downers Grove, IL: InterVarsity Press, 2002.

--------. *An Introduction to the Theology of Religions: Biblical, Historical, and Contemporary Perspectives.* Downers Grove, IL: InterVarsity Press, 2003.

--------. *Trinity and Religious Pluralism: the Doctrine of the Trinity in Christian Theology of Religions.* Burlington, VT: Ashgate, 2004.

Kemp, Roger, ed. *Text and Context in Theological Education.* Springwood, NSW Australia: ICAA, 1994.

Khan, Muqtedar. "Teaching Globalization." *The Globalist.* http://www.theglobalist.com, accessed February 5, 2008; Internet.

Kim, Kirsteen. "Missiology as Global Conversation of (Contextual) Theologies." *Mission Studies* 21, no. 1 (2004): 39-53.

Kimpalu, Justin. *Language and Culture: Learning Lesson.* Brazzaville, Congo: APROLAF (Association pour la Promotion des Langues Africaines), 2002.

Kinzer, Mark. *Postmissionary Messianic Judaism: Redefining Christian Engagement with the Jewish People.* Grand Rapids, MI: Brazos Press, 2005.

Kinsler, F. Ross. *The Extension Movement in Theological Education: A Call to the Renewal of Ministry.* Pasadena, CA: William Carey Library, 1978.

Koyama, Kosuke. *Waterbuffalo Theology*. Maryknoll, NY: Orbis Books, 1974.

Kraft, Charles, ed. *Appropriate Christianity*. Pasadena, CA: William Carey Library, 2005.

--------. *Christianity in Culture: A Study in Dynamic Biblical Theologizing in Cross-Cultural Perspective*. Maryknoll, NY: Orbis, 1979.

--------. "Contextualization and Time: Generational Appropriateness." In *Appropriate Christianity*, ed. Charles H. Kraft and Dean S. Gilliland, 255-73. Pasadena, CA: William Carey Library, 2005.

--------. "Contextualization in Three Crucial Dimensions." In *Appropriate Christianity*, eds. Charles H. Kraft and Dean S. Gilliland, 99-115. Pasadena, CA: William Carey Library, 2005.

--------. *Communication Theory for Christian Witness*. Revised edition. Maryknoll, NY: Orbis, 1991.

Kraft, Siv Ellen. "'To Mix or Not to Mix': Syncretism/Anti-Syncretism in the History of Theosophy." *Numen* 49 (2002): 142-177.

Küng, Hans, and Julia Ching. *Christianity and Chinese Religion*. New York: Doubleday, 1989.

Lam, Wing-Hung. *Chinese Theology in Construction*. Pasadena, CA: William Carey Library, 1983.

Larkin, William J. *Culture and Biblical Hermeneutics: Interpreting and Applying the Authoritative Word in a Relativistic Age*. Grand Rapid, MI: Baker, 1988.

Lee, Archie C. C. "Naming God in Asia: Cross-Textual Reading in Multi-Cultural Context." *Quest: An Interdisciplinary Journal for Asian Christian Scholars* 3, no. 1: 21-42.

Lee, Jung Young. *The Theology of Change: A Christian Concept of God from an Eastern Perspective*. Maryknoll, NY: Orbis Books, 1979.

--------. *The Trinity in Asian Perspective*. Nashville, TN: Abingdon, 1999.

Levenson, Jon D. "Do Christians and Muslims Worship the Same God? Part One." *The Christian Century*, 20 April 2004, 32-33.

Lindbeck, George A. *The Nature of Doctrine: Religion and Theology in a Postliberal Age*. Philadelphia, PA: Westminster Press, 1984.

Lingenfelter, Sherwood G. *Transforming Culture: A Challenge for Christian Mission*, 2nd ed. Grand Rapids, MI: Baker, 1988.

Loewen, Jacob A. "Translating the Names of God: How European Languages have Translated Them." *The Bible Translator* 36 no. 4 (1985): 401-09.

Lovejoy, Grant, James B. Slack, and J. O. Terry, eds. *Chronological Bible Storying Manual: A Methodology for Presenting the Gospel to Oral Communicators* [book on-line]. Ft. Worth, Texas: Southwestern Baptist Theological Seminary, 2001. Accessed September 12, 2008. Available from: http://chronologicalbiblestorying.com/Portals/1/downloads/ Methodology/InstructionManuals/SWsem_ed/CBSManualSWBTS2001.zip; Internet.

Luzbetak, Louis. *The Church and Cultures*. Maryknoll, NY: Orbis Books, 1988.

MacIntyre, Alasdair. *Whose Justice? Which Rationality?* London: Duckworth, 1988.

Mackay, John. *The Other Spanish Christ*. London: Student Christian Movement Press, 1932.

Massey, Joshua. "His Ways Are Not Our Ways." *Evangelical Missions Quarterly* 35 (1999): 188-197.

--------. "Misunderstanding C5: His Ways Are Not Our Orthodoxy." *Evangelical Missions Quarterly* 40 (2004): 296-304.

--------. "Should Christians Use 'Allah' in Bible Translation?" *Evangelical Missions Quarterly* 40 (2004): 284-85.

Mayers, Marvin K. *Christianity Confronts Culture: A Strategy for Cross-Cultural Evangelism*. Grand Rapids, MI: Zondervan, 1987 [1974].

McCurry, Don M., ed. *The Gospel and Islam: A 1978 Compendium*. Monrovia, CA: MARC, 1979.

McGrath, Alister E. "The Importance of Tradition for Modern Evangelicalism." In *Doing Theology for the People of God: Studies in Honour of J.I. Packer,* eds. Donald Lewis & Alister McGrath, 159-173. Leicester: Apollos, 1996.

Mettinger, Tryggve N.D. *In Search of God: the Meaning and Message of the Everlasting Names*. Translated by Frederick H. Cryer. Philadelphia, PA: Fortress Press.

Mofokeng, T.A. "Black Christians, the Bible and Liberation." *Journal of Black Theology in South Africa*. 2 no. 1 (November, 1988), 34.

Molyneux, K. Gordon. *African Christian Theology: The Quest for Selfhood*. San Francisco, CA: Mellen Research University Press, 1993.

Moreau, A. Scott. "Contextualization that is Comprehensive." *Missiology* 34, no. 3 (2006): 325-335.

--------. "The Human Universals of Culture: Implications for Contextualization." *International Journal of Frontier Missions* 12 (1995): 121-125.

Moreau, A. Scott, and others, eds. *Evangelical Dictionary of World Missions.* Grand Rapids, MI: Baker, 2000.

Moreau, A. Scott, and others, eds. *Deliver Us from Evil: An Uneasy Frontier in Christian Mission.* Monrovia, CA: MARC and World Vision, 2002.

Morton, Jeff. "Narratives and Questions: Exploring the Scriptures with Muslims." *Evangelical Missions Quarterly* 40 (2004): 172-176.

Mushete, Ngindu. "Modernity in Africa." In *Trends in Mission: Toward the 3rd Millennium,* eds. William Jenkinson and Helene O'Sullivan, 143-154. Maryknoll, NY: Orbis Books, 1991.

Naja, Ben. *Releasing the Workers of the Eleventh Hour: The Global South and the Task Remaining.* Pasadena, CA: William Carey Library, 2007.

Nebeker, Gary. "'Who Packed Your Bags?': Factors that Influence Our Preunderstandings." 2002. Accessed February 6, 2008. Available from http://www.bible.org/assets/worddocs/herrick_preunderstanding.zip; Internet.

Netland, Harold A. *Dissonant Voices: Religions Pluralism and the Question of Truth.* Grand Rapids, MI: Eerdmans, 1991.

Newbigin, Lesslie. *The Gospel in a Pluralist Society.* Grand Rapids, MI: Eerdmans, 1989.

Nicholls, Bruce J. *Contextualization: A Theology of Gospel and Culture.* Downers Grove, IL: InterVarsity Press, 1979.

O'Rear, Mike. "Missions on the Web: A World Tour of Contextual Theologies." *Evangelical Missions Quarterly* 40, no. 3 (July 2004): 374-379.

Osborne, Grant R. *The Hermeneutical Spiral: A Comprehensive Introduction to Biblical Interpretation.* Downers Grove, IL: InterVarsity Press, 1991.

Ott, Craig, and Harold A. Netland, eds. *Globalizing Theology: Belief and Practice in an Era of World Christianity.* Grand Rapids, MI: Baker Academic, 2006.

Padilla, C. Rene. "Christology and Mission in the Two Thirds World." In *Sharing Jesus in the Two Thirds World,* eds. Vinay Samuel and Chris Sugden, 12-32. Grand Rapids, MI: Eerdmans, 1984.

--------. *Mission Between The Times: Essays On The Kingdom.* Grand Rapids, MI: Eerdmans, 1985.

Palmer, Alison J. "Learning Styles of Pacific Islanders and the Relevance of Theological Education by Extension." Unpublished Paper. Auckland: Bible College of New Zealand, 1986.

Palmer, Richard E. *Hermeneutics: Interpretation Theory in Schleiermacher, Dilthey, Heidegger, and Gadamer*. Evanston, IL: Northwestern University Press, 1969.

Parratt, John. *An introduction to Third World theologies*. Cambridge; New York: Cambridge University Press, 2004.

Parshall, Phil. "Lifting the *Fatwa*." *Evangelical Missions Quarterly* 40 (2004): 288-93.

--------. "Danger! New Directions in Contextualization." *Evangelical Missions Quarterly* 34 (1998): 404-10.

Pocock, Michael, Gailyn Van Rheenen, and Douglas McConnell. *The Changing Face of World Missions*. Grand Rapids, MI: Baker, 2005.

Polanyi, Michael, and Harry Prosch. *Meaning*. Chicago: University of Chicago Press, 1975.

Poythress, Vern. *Symphonic Theology: The Validity of Multiple Perspectives in Theology*. Grand Rapids, MI: Zondervan, 1987.

Ralston, Helen. *Christian Ashrams: A New Religious Movement in Contemporary India*. Lewiston, NY: Edwin Mellen, 1987.

Raschke, Carl. *The Next Reformation: Why Evangelicals Must Embrace Postmodernity*. Grand Rapids, MI: Baker Academic, 2004.

Rausch, David A. *Messianic Judaism, its History, Theology, and Polity*. New York: Mellen Press, 1982.

Rayan, Samuel. "Reconceiving Theology in the Asian Context." In *Doing Theology in a Divided World*, eds. Virginia Fabella and Sergio Torres, 124-142. Maryknoll, NY: Orbis Books, 1985.

Richardson, Don. *Peace Child*. Glendale, CA: Regal Books, 1974.

Richardson, Rick. *Reimagining Evangelism: Inviting Friends on a Spiritual Journey*. Downers Grove, IL: InterVarsity, 2006.

Rifkin, Ira. *Spiritual Perspective on Globalization: Making Sense of the Economic and Cultural Upheaval*. Woodstock, VT: Skylight Paths Publishing, 2004.

Ritchie, Mark A. *Spirit of the Rainforest: a Yanomamo Shaman's Story*. Chicago, IL: Island Lake Press, 1996.

Ro, Bong Rin. "Communicating the Biblical Concept of God to Koreans." In *The Global God: Multicultural Evangelical Views of God*, ed. Aída B. Spencer and William D. Spencer, 207-230. Grand Rapids, MI: Baker, 1998.

Ro, Bong Rin, and Ruth Eshenaur, eds. *The Bible and Theology in Asian Contexts: An Evangelical Perspective on Asian Theology*. Taiching, Taiwan: Asia Theological Association, 1984.

Rode, Daniel J. "La adaptación de San Pablo y San Pedro." In *Misión y contextualización: Llevar el mensaje bíblico a un mundo multicultural,* ed. Gerald A. Klingbeil, 189-209. Libertado San Martín, Entre Ríos, Argentina: Editorial Universidad Adventista del Plata, 2005.

Rommen, Edward, ed. *Spiritual Power and Missions: Raising the Issues*. Pasadena, CA: William Carey Library, 1995.

Sanneh, Lamin. *Translating the Message: The Missionary Impact on Culture*. New York: Orbis, 1989.

--------. "Domesticating the Transcendent. The African Transformation of Christianity: Comparative Reflections of Ethnicity and Religious Mobilization in Africa." In *Bible Translation on the Threshold of the Twenty-First Century, Authority, Reception, Culture and Religion*, ed. A. Brenner and J W.van Henten, 71- 85. Sheffield, UK: Sheffield Academic Press, 2002.

--------. "Do Christians and Muslims Worship the Same God? Part Two." *The Christian Century*, 4 May 2004, 35-37.

Schineller, Peter. "Inculturation and Syncretism: What Is the Real Issue?" *International Bulletin of Missionary Research* 16 (1992): 50-53.

Schlorff, Sam. *Missiological Models in Ministry to Muslims*. Upper Darby, PA: Middle East Resources, 2006.

Schreiter, Robert. "Globalization and Reconciliation: Challenges to Mission." In *Mission in the Third Millennium*, ed. Robert Schreiter. Maryknoll, NY: Orbis Books, 2001.

--------. *The New Catholicity: Theology between the Global and the Local*. Maryknoll, NY: Orbis Books, 1997.

--------. "Defining Syncretism: An Interim Report." *International Bulletin of Missionary Research* 17 (1993): 50-53.

--------. "Globalization, Postmodernity, and the New Catholicity." In *For All People: Global Theologies in Contexts,* ed. Pederson and others. Grand Rapids, MI: Eerdmans, 2002.

--------. *Constructing Local Theologies*, 10th ed. Maryknoll, NY: Orbis Books, 2002.

Sedmak, Clemens. *Doing Local Theology: A Guide for Artisans of a New Humanity*. Faith and Culture Series. Maryknoll, NY: Orbis Books, 2002.

Segundo, Juan Luis. *Liberation of Theology*. Maryknoll, NY: Orbis, 1976.

Shaw, R. Daniel. "Contextualizing the Power and the Glory." *International Journal of Frontier Mission* 12, no. 3 (July 1995): 155-160.

Shaw, R. Daniel, and Charles E. Van Engen. *Communicating God's Word in a Complex World: God's Truth or Hocus Pocus?* Lanham, MD: Rowman and Littlefield, 2003.

Siu, Paul. *The Horizon of Theology: Constructing a Method for Evangelical Theology*. Taipei, Taiwan: Campus Evangelical Fellowship, 2007.

Smart, Ninian. *Dimensions of the Sacred: An Anatomy of the World's Beliefs*. Berkeley, CA: University of California Press, 1996.

Sommer, Deborah, ed. *Chinese Religion: An Anthology of Sources*. Oxford, UK: Oxford University Press, 1995.

Song, C.S. *Tell Us Our Names: Story Theology from an Asian Perspective*. Maryknoll, NY: Orbis Books, 1984.

-------. *Third Eye Theology*. Revised edition. Maryknoll, NY: Orbis Books, 1991.

Spencer, Aída B., and William D. Spencer, eds. *The Global God: Multicultural Evangelical Views of God*. Grand Rapids, MI: Baker Books, 1998.

Steffen, Tom A. *Reconnecting God's Story to Ministry: Cross-cultural Storytelling at Home and Abroad*. La Habra, CA: Center for Organizational & Ministry Development, 1996.

Stewart, Charles, and Rosalind Shaw. "Introduction: Problematizing Syncretism." In *Syncretism/Anti-Syncretism: The Politics of Religious Syncretism*, ed. Charles Stewart and Rosalind Shaw, 1-26. New York: Routledge, 1994.

Stine, Philip C., ed. *Bible Translation and the Spread of the Church: The Last 200 Years*. Leiden: E. J. Brill, 1990.

Stott, John, and Robert T. Coote, eds. *Gospel and Culture: The Papers of a Consultation on the Gospel and Culture, Convened by the Lausanne Committee's Theology and Education Group*. Pasadena, CA: William Carey Library, 1979.

Sugirtharajah, R. S. *The Bible and the Third World: Pre-Colonial, Colonial, and Post-Colonial Encounters*. Cambridge, UK: Cambridge University Press, 2001.

Suk, John, ed. *Doing Theology in the Philippines.* Quezon City, Philippines: Asian Theological Seminary, 2005.

Sundermeier, Theo. "Inculturation and Syncretism." *Scriptura* 10 (1992): 32-48.

Taber, Charles. "Is There More Than One Way to Do Theology?" *Gospel in Context* 1, no. 1 (January 1978): 4-10.

Tanchanpongs, Natee. "Discourse toward Scripture: A Methodological Proposal for Evangelical Contextual Theology." Ph.D. diss., Trinity Evangelical Divinity School, 2007

Tanner, Kathryn. *Theories of Culture: A New Agenda for Theology.* Minneapolis, MN: Augsburg Fortress, 1997.

Taylor, William D., ed. *Global Missiology for the 21st Century: The Iguassu Dialogue.* Grand Rapids, MI: Baker, 2000.

Tennent, Timothy. "Followers of Jesus (Isa) in Islamic Mosques: A Closer Examination of C-5 'High Spectrum' Contextualization." *International Journal of Frontier Missions* 23, no. 2 (2006): 101-123.

Thiselton, Anthony C. *The Two Horizons: New Testament Hermeneutics and Philosophical Description with Special Reference to Heidegger, Bultmann, Gadamer, and Wittgenstein.* Grand Rapids, MI: Eerdmans, 1980.

Tippett, Alan R. *Introduction to Missiology.* Pasadena, CA: William Carey Library, 1987.

Torrance, Thomas F. *God and Rationality.* London: Oxford University Press, 1971.

--------. *Reality and Evangelical Theology: The Realism of Christian Theology.* Downers Grove, IL: InterVarsity Press, 1999.

Travis, John, and Anna Travis. "Appropriate Approaches in Muslim Contexts." In *Appropriate Christianity*, eds. Charles H. Kraft and Dean S. Gilliland, 397-414. Pasadena, CA: William Carey Library, 2005.

Travis, John. "The C1 to C6 Spectrum." *Evangelical Missions Quarterly* 34 (1998): 407-8.

Van Engen, Charles. *Mission on the Way: Issues in Mission Theology.* Grand Rapids, MI: Baker, 1996.

Van Huyssteen, J. Wentzel. *The Shaping of Rationality: Toward Interdisciplinarity in Theology and Science.* Grand Rapids, MI: Eerdmans, 1999.

Van Rheenen, Gailyn, ed. *Contextualization and Syncretism: Navigating Cultural Currents.* Pasadena, CA: William Carey, 2006.

Vanhoozer, Kevin. *The Drama of Doctrine: A Canonical-Linguistic Approach to Christian Theology.* Louisville, KY: Westminster John Knox, 2005.

--------. "'One Rule to Rule them All?' Theological Method in an Era of World Christianity." In *Globalizing Theology: Belief and Practice in an Era of World Christianity,* eds. Craig Ott & Harold A. Netland, 85-126. Leicester: Apollos (IVP), 2007.

--------. *To Stake a Claim: Mission and the Western Crisis of Knowledge.* Maryknoll, NY: Orbis Books, 1999.

Visser 't Hooft, Willem Adolph. *No Other Name: The Choice between Syncretism and Christian Universalism.* Philadelphia, PA: Westminster, 1963.

Wagner, C. Peter, ed. *Breaking Strongholds in Your City: How to Use Spiritual Mapping to Make Your Prayers More Strategic, Effective and Targeted.* Ventura, CA: Regal Books, 1993.

Walls, Andrew. *The Missionary Movement in Christian History.* Edinburgh: T. & T. Clark, 1996.

Wheeler, Ray. "The Legacy of Shoki Coe." *International Bulletin of Missionary Research* 26, no. 2 (April 2002): 77-80.

Whiteman, Darrell L. "Contextualization: The Theory, the Gap, the Challenge." *International Bulletin of Missionary Research* 21 (1997): 2-7.

--------. "The Function of Appropriate Contextualization in Mission." In *Appropriate Christianity,* eds. Charles H. Kraft and Dean S. Gilliland, 49-65. Pasadena, CA: William Carey Library, 2005.

Winter, Ralph, and Steve Hawthorne. *Perspectives on the World Christian Movement, 3rd ed.* Pasadena, CA: William Carey Library, 1999.

Woodberry, J. Dudley. "Contextualization among Muslims: Reusing Common Pillars." *International Journal of Frontier Missions* 13 (1996): 171-186.

--------. "Do Christians and Muslims Worship the Same God? Part Three." *The Christian Century,* 18 May 18 2004, 36-37.

Woodbridge, John D., and Thomas Edward McComiskey eds. *Doing Theology in Today's World.* Grand Rapids, MI: Zondervan, 1991.

Woods, Scott. "A Biblical Look at C5 Muslim evangelism." *Evangelical Missions Quarterly* 39 (2003): 188-195.

Wright, Clifford. *Christ and Kiribati Culture.* Unpublished manuscript. Melbourne: Ivanhoe, 1981.

--------. *Seeds of the Word: Tongan Culture and Christian Faith*. Unpublished manuscript. Melbourne: Ivanhoe , 1979.

Yamamori, Tetsunao, and Charles R. Taber, eds. *Christopaganism or Indigenous Christianity?* Pasadena, CA: William Carey Library, 1975.

Yamamori, Tetsunao, Bryant Myers, and David Conner, eds. *Serving with the Poor in Asia*. Pasadena, CA: MARC, 1995.

Yego, Josphat K. "Appreciation For and Warnings About Contextualization." *Evangelical Missions Quarterly* 16 (1980): 153-157.

Yung, Hwa. *Mangoes or Bananas? The Quest for an Authentic Asian Christian Theology*. Oxford, UK: Regnum Books International, 1997.

Zahniser, Matthias. *Symbol and Ceremony: Making Disciples Across Cultures*. Monrovia, CA: MARC, 1997.

Zdero, Rad. *The Global House Church Movement*. Pasadena, CA: William Carey Library, 2004.

Zehner, Edwin R. "Orthodox Hybridities: Anti-Syncretism and Localization in the Evangelical Christianity of Thailand." *Anthropological Quarterly* 78 (2005): 585-617.

--------. "Unavoidable Hybrid: Thai Buddhist Conversions to Evangelical Christianity." PhD diss., Cornell University, 2003.